PLAN COLOMBIA

Antioquia Department

APARTADÓ
COUNTY

Caribbean Sea

PANAMA

VENEZUELA

Pacific
Ocean

Magdalena
Atlántico
Guajira

Cesar

Sucre

Córdoba
Bolívar

Norte
de
Sant-
ander

Antioquia
• Barrancabermeja

• Medellín
Santander
Arauca

Chocó
Boyacá

Caldas
Cundina-
marca
Casanare

Risaralda

Quindío
Vichada

Tolima
★ Bogotá

Valle del
Cauca
Meta

Guainía

Cauca

Huila
Guaviare

Nariño

Putumayo
Caquetá
Vaupés

ECUADOR

Amazonas
BRAZIL

PERU

Colombia. MAP BY DOUGLAS MACKEY.

PLAN COLOMBIA

U.S. Ally Atrocities and
Community Activism

John Lindsay-Poland

DUKE UNIVERSITY PRESS   DURHAM AND LONDON   2018

Library of Congress Cataloging-in-Publication Data
Names: Lindsay-Poland, John, author.
Title: Plan Colombia : U.S. ally atrocities and community activism /
John Lindsay-Poland.
Description: Durham : Duke University Press, 2018. |
Includes bibliographical references and index.
Identifiers: LCCN 2018014914 (print)
LCCN 2018016182 (ebook)
ISBN 9781478002611 (ebook)
ISBN 9781478001188 (hardcover : alk. paper)
ISBN 9781478001539 (pbk. : alk. paper)
Subjects: LCSH: Military assistance, American—Colombia. |
Atrocities—Colombia. | Economic assistance, American—
Colombia. | Drug control—Colombia. | Comunidad
de Paz (San Jose de Apartado, Colombia) | Peace movements—
Colombia. | Colombia—Relations—United States. |
United States—Relations—Colombia.
Classification: LCC F2271.52.U6 (ebook) | LCC F2271.52.U6 L56
2018 (print) | DDC 986.1—dc 3
LC record available at https://lccn.loc.gov/2018014914

Cover: Artwork by James Groleau

For all the members of the
PEACE COMMUNITY OF
SAN JOSÉ DE APARTADÓ
and
FOR HELEN LINDSAY

CONTENTS

ABBREVIATIONS

ACCU   Autodefensas Campesinas de Córdoba y Urabá (Peasant
              Self-Defense Forces of Córdoba and Urabá)

ACIN   Asociación de Cabildos Indígenas del Norte del Cauca
              (Northern Cauca Indigenous Councils Association)

ACOOC   Acción Colectiva de Objetores y Objetoras de Conciencia
              (Colombian Collective Action of Conscientious Objectors)

AFL-CIO   American Federation of Labor and Congress of Industrial
              Organizations

ANUC   Asociación Nacional de Usuarios Campesinos (National
              Peasant Association)

ASFADDES   Asociación de Familiares de Detenidos y Desaparecidos
              (Association of Family Members of Detained and
              Disappeared in Colombia)

ATCC   Asociación de Trabajadores Campesinos del Carare
              (Peasant Workers Association of Carare River)

AUC   Autodefensas Unidas de Colombia (Self-Defense Forces of
              Colombia)

CCEEU   Coordinación Colombia–Europa–Estados Unidos
              (Colombia-Europe-U.S. Human Rights Observatory)

CIA   Central Intelligence Agency

CINEP	Centro de Investigación y Educación Popular (Center for Research and Grassroots Education)
CNP	Policía Nacional de Colombia (Colombian National Police)
CSN	Colombia Support Network
DAS	Departamento Administrativo de Seguridad (Administrative Department of Security)
DEA	Drug Enforcement Administration
DH	Derechos Humanos (human rights)
DIH	Derecho Internacional Humanitario (international humanitarian law)
ELN	Ejército de Liberación Nacional (National Liberation Army)
EPL	Ejército Popular de Liberación (Popular Liberation Army)
FARC	Fuerzas Armadas Revolucionarias de Colombia (Revolutionary Armed Forces of Colombia)
FBI	Federal Bureau of Investigation
FEDEGAN	Federación Colombiana de Ganaderos (Colombian Federation of Cattle Ranchers)
FOR	Fellowship of Reconciliation
GAULA	Grupos de Acción Unificada por la Libertad Personal (Unified Action Groups for Personnel Rescue)
INSITOP	Informe de Situación de Tropas (Troop Location Report)
ISS	Infrastructure Security Strategy
JPM	Justicia Penal Militar (Military Justice System)
JSOU	Joint Special Operations University
JTF	Joint Task Force
NGO	nongovernmental organization
NSA	National Security Agency
OAS	Organization of American States
ONIC	Organización Nacional Indígena de Colombia (National Indigenous Organization of Colombia)
PBI	Peace Brigades International

Pepes	Personas Perseguidas por Pablo Escobar
PGN	Procuraduría General de la Nación (Inspector General's Office)
RECORRE	Red de Comunidades en Ruptura y Resistencia (Network of Communities in Resistance)
REDEPAZ	Red Nacional de Iniciativas Ciudadanas por la Paz y contra la Guerra (National Network of Initiatives Against War and for Peace)
RIME	Regional de Inteligencia Militar del Ejército (Army Regional Military Intelligence Unit)
SINTRAINAGRO	Sindicato Nacional de Trabajadores de la Industria Agropecuaria (National Union of Agricultural Workers)
SOA	U.S. Army School of the Americas
SouthCom	U.S. Southern Command
UN	United Nations
UP	Unión Patriótica (Patriotic Union)
WHINSEC	Western Hemisphere Institute for Security Cooperation

ACKNOWLEDGMENTS

There is no way I can possibly name all those who, knowingly or unknowingly, aided my research and the development of this book. I am nevertheless deeply thankful to each of them.

Colombia is still experiencing violent conflict, and information is used in that conflict to punish and hurt those who speak, or those who are spoken of. Many human rights workers, retired and active duty military officers, civilian officials, and victims of human rights violations spoke with me off the record or on the condition their names not be used, while others imposed no conditions.

By name, I first thank San José Peace Community leaders and members, including those who visited the United States through the Fellowship of Reconciliation (FOR): Gildardo Tuberquia, Javier Sánchez, Brigida González, Renato Areiza, Jesús Emilio Tuberquia. I am grateful to Cecilia Zarate-Laun of Colombia Support Network and to Eduar Lancheros for introducing me to the Peace Community. Their subsequent deaths are a deep loss.

I could not have written this book without collaboration on previous projects with Alberto Yepes, Adriana Pestana, and other staff of the Coordinación Colombia–Europa–Estados Unidos. Many other human rights defenders in Bogotá, Medellín, Apartadó, Huila, and Arauca organized interviews, provided contact information, and offered insights. These included Father Javier Giraldo, Liliana Uribe of Corporación Justicia Libertad, Rosa Liliana Ortiz of Observatorio Surcolombiano de Derechos Humanos, and others too numerous or at risk to name here. Gabriel Arias, Camilo Bernal, and Michael Reed Hurtado at the United Nations Office of the High Commissioner for Human Rights in Colombia were always helpful.

Colombian and U.S. military officers, soldiers, and diplomatic officials generously agreed to interviews that, though frequently off the record or on background, were fundamental to helping me understand both their institutions and U.S. military assistance to Colombia. Maiah Jaskoski at the Naval Postgraduate School and Kara Oryan and Jose Torres of National Defense University helped me meet and interview faculty and Colombian graduates from their institutions. Congressional staff who were helpful in informing my analysis or provided information include Tim Rieser, Sascha Foertsch, Michael Kuiken, Asher Smith, Cindy Buhl, Teddy Miller, Emily Mendrala, and Jonathan Stivers.

Many people generously shared documents and other key information with me, including Moira Birss, Gwen Burnyeat, Leah Carroll, Michael Evans, David Feller, Janice Gallagher, Lisa Haugaard, Adam Isacson, Oliver Kaplan, Sarah Kinosian, Maria Milena Mendez, Jorge Molano, Diana Murcia, Paul Paz y Mino, Peace Brigades International (PBI) Colombia staff, Renata Rendon, Francesc Riera, William Rozo, Christian Salazar, Matt Schroeder, Arlene Tickner, Paola Torres, Gustavo Trejos, Alirio Uribe, Sarah Weintraub, and Paul Wolf. Karen Mejía and Liliana Ávila García helped me with official information requests in Colombia.

I have learned much from other fellow thinkers and chroniclers, including Sandra Alvarez, Enrique Daza, Nadja Drost, Jenny Escobar, Chris Kraul, Francisco Leal Buitrago, Alex Sierra, Winifred Tate, Curt Wands, and Michael Weintraub.

Tomas Monarrez, Emiliano Huet-Vaughn, Lucia Chiappara, and Gitanjali Shukla generously helped me understand statistical relationships in human rights and assistance data, while Camice Revier, Emily Schmitz, Isabel Moris, Daniel Horgan, Seth Kershner, and Leah Vincent aided in data management. David Figueroa and Jamie Connatser transcribed interviews.

I am deeply grateful to both Jesús Abad Colorado and Jutta Meier Wiedenbach for their generous permission to use the powerful photographs they took in San José de Apartadó. Douglas Mackey very graciously produced the maps used in this book. Thank you to James Groleau for the beautiful artwork on the book cover.

I am always thankful to Cristina Espinel and Charlie Roberts for their hospitality over many years. The PBI and FOR teams and Sara Koopman and Alberto Yepes graciously hosted me in Colombia.

FOR and the American Friends Service Committee have been supportive homes for research and writing. FOR's support for work on Colombia was critical to my learning process over many years. I am thankful to FOR staff, especially Jutta Meier Wiedenbach, Susana Pimiento, Liza Smith, Candice Camargo, Pat Clark, and Mark Johnson, and FOR Colombia team members who served during the period described in this book, including Patricia Abbott, Isaac Beachy, Moira Birss, Kevin Coulombe, Chris Courtheyn, Joe DeRaymond, Mireille Evans, Denise Fraga, Janice Gallagher, Brad Grabs, Marion Hiptmair, Amanda Jack, Paul Kozak, Aimee Krouskop, Marcie Ley, Dan Malakoff, Chris Moore-Backman, Mayra Moreno, Camila Nieves, Jon Patberg, Lily Ray, Renata Rendon, Nico Udu-gama, Gilberto Villaseñor, and Sarah Weintraub.

Duke University Press has been supportive and tolerant, and I especially thank Gisela Fosado, Lydia Rose Rappoport-Hankins, Stephanie Gomez Menzies, and Liz Smith. My deep thanks also to the four anonymous readers who commented on the manuscript.

I am grateful for funding for research that has contributed to this book, from Open Society Foundations, Appleton Foundation, Fund for Nonviolence, Latin America Working Group, and Nonviolent Peaceforce. Global Exchange, Pacifistas sin Fronteras, and the Colectivo de Abogados José Alvear Restrepo provided additional resources for travel to Colombia.

I am especially thankful to a number of people for their extra encouragement and friendship. I have been extremely fortunate to be accompanied in writing this book by Chris Courtheyn, Peter Cousins, Cristina Espinel, Dana Frank, Charlie Roberts, Janey Skinner, Jenine Spotnitz, and Winifred Tate, who read and commented on part or all of the manuscript. To Dana Frank I owe a special debt for the close reading she gave the manuscript when it was truly needed. Leah Carroll, Jenny Escobar, Patrick Sullivan, and David Vine provided key encouragement. Thank you to Lora Lumpe for your questions, editing, and institutional support, and Janice Gallagher for your research and accompaniment.

As always, I am profoundly grateful to my mother, Helen Lindsay, who showed me how to be an activist, and James Groleau, the love of my life.

0   5   10
                         Miles

LAS FLORES

SABALETA

RODOXALLI

PLAYA LARGA

LA HOZ

Mulatos River

ARENAS BAJAS

EL PORVENIR

EL SALTO

ARENAS ALTAS

LA UNION

LA ESPERANZA

EL GAS

GUINEO ALTO

EL GUINEO

EL CUCHILLO

LAS NIEVES

LA BALSA

BUENOS AIRES

San José Town Center

LA RESBALOZA

MULATOS

Apartadó City Center

BELLAVISTA

LA VICTORIA

LAS PLAYAS

LA LINDA

MULATOS CABECERA

LA CRISTALINA

MIRAMAR

LA MIRANDA

LA PEDROZA

LA DANTA

APARTADO COUNTY

San José de Apartadó District

San José de Apartadó. MAP BY DOUGLAS MACKEY.

PROLOGUE

> Force does not work the way its advocates seem to
> think it does. It does not, for example, reveal to the
> victim the strength of his adversary. On the contrary,
> it reveals the weakness, even the panic of his adversary,
> and this revelation invests the victim with patience.
> Furthermore, it is ultimately fatal to create too many
> victims. The victor can do nothing with these victims,
> for they do not belong to him, but—to the victims.
>
> —James Baldwin, *No Name in the Street*

On the morning of the day he was murdered, Monday, February 21, 2005, Luis Eduardo Guerra awoke in the house of his stepmother, Miryam Tuberquia, in a small settlement of Colombia's Abibe Mountains, called Mulatos. For the previous three days, in the dense foliage and steep trails near the house, intense combat had raged between government forces, paramilitary troops allied with them, and guerrilla fighters.

Luis Eduardo had hiked to Mulatos on Saturday afternoon from his home in the town center of San José de Apartadó, together with his son Diener, eleven years old, and his girlfriend, Beyanira Areiza. He visited Miryam every month or so, and he planned to harvest cocoa beans on land he had near her house, where he also grew corn and beans, and return to San José the following day. On Sunday, however, the combat nearby was intense, and they stayed in the house in Mulatos out of caution. The military had killed a guerrilla known as Macho Rusio in a nearby settlement.

Luis Eduardo did not take lunch with him when he left the house on Monday morning at about 7:00 a.m., telling Miryam that he would be back by 3:00 p.m. He left with Diener, Beyanira, and his half brother, Dario, known as El Gurre.[1]

The Abibe range, located in northwestern Colombia, is composed of very rugged but fabulously fertile, tropical land. Paths connect settlements in the range, over which people move on foot, mule, or horseback, often through rocky mud that receives more than one hundred inches of rain annually. (The area of Miryam's house was called El Barro, "the mud.") The district of San José spreads over more than three hundred square kilometers on the western side of the range. The rugged terrain and its location have made it a refuge of choice for civilians fleeing political violence, as well as for insurgents and other armed groups—first Liberals fighting with Conservatives from 1948 to 1956, and beginning in the late 1960s, leftist guerrillas of the Revolutionary Armed Forces of Colombia (Fuerzas Armadas Revolucionarias de Colombia, FARC).[2] In the 1990s, the army and allied right-wing paramilitary groups contested the guerrillas' control, leading to frequent combat in and around peasant settlements and farmland. In response, Luis Eduardo Guerra and other peasants in San José de Apartadó declared themselves a peace community in 1997. They would not support any armed group, would not join them, sell food, give information, or carry arms. It was a strategy for survival—since armed groups retaliated against civilians who collaborated with their enemies—and for staying and continuing to work the land.

The landscape that Luis Eduardo and his family traversed that day was intensely beautiful, with richly diverse flora and fauna: hardwood trees (ceiba, Colombian mahogany), many palm species, flowering trees that produced spiny husks with an almond-like nut, a rich understory with dozens of kinds of orchids, creeping vines, bromeliads, and bright flowers like the birds of paradise that dangled near the path. The Abibe Mountains are also home to many bird species, and residents sometimes find monkeys and ocelots roaming there. If not for the war, it would be like a national park.[3]

But that morning, as Luis Eduardo and the others walked through the shallow waters of the Mulatos River, soldiers and paramilitaries spied them from upstream, then hid in order to ambush them.[4] When they saw the soldiers, El Gurre said they should run, but Luis Eduardo said no, that he had nothing to hide. His son Diener, with a severe leg injury, could not run in any case. El Gurre then fled, and the armed men attacked Luis Eduardo, Beyanira, and Diener with machetes, beheading Diener in the process. They left their bodies on the side of the river, exposed to the tropical heat and animals.

Farther up the mountain, less than an hour's walk away in a settlement called La Resbalosa, another army-paramilitary troop exchanged gunfire that day with a guerrilla militia member named Alejandro Pérez, killing him, and fired a mortar at a house nearby. The mortar crashed through the kitchen roof and hit Sandra Tuberquia in the head, killing her; the explosion was heard from hills around the area.

Her husband, Alfonso Bolívar Tuberquia, was hiding nearby with other local men, but after he heard the gunfire and explosion, he returned to the house. By that time, the armed men already had gotten his two young children, Natalia and Santiago, ages six years and eighteen months, out from under the bed where they had hidden. Santiago was still breast-feeding.[5] Alfonso begged the men not to kill the children, to take him instead. But they killed all three of them with machetes and covered them with a mound of cocoa leaves.

Two days later, Renata Rendon, Trish Abbott, and Joe DeRaymond were sitting on the back porch of a small wooden house in the village of La Unión, about six hours on foot from Mulatos, when they received the startling news.

Rendon, then twenty-six, grew up in New York City, the daughter of a Medellín native. Abbott, twenty-four, was from Newcastle, England, and had arrived in Colombia only the month before, while DeRaymond was considerably older—fifty-four—a taciturn paralegal from the steel mill region of eastern Pennsylvania. They worked for a U.S. peace organization called the Fellowship of Reconciliation (FOR), which had established a team of two to three volunteers in San José three years before in order to strengthen security for residents of the community.

The day before, in the early afternoon of February 22, they heard an army helicopter launch three rockets and fire machine guns for twenty minutes. The helicopter circled around La Unión, passing in front of a large cross on a hill on the edge of the village, shortly before the combat ended. Then it was calm.

Wilson David, a cherubic-faced community leader who spoke quickly, arrived at the house ashen-faced and shaken, to say that Luis Eduardo Guerra, his family, and five others had been massacred in a settlement farther up in the mountains. Eight people had been killed, including three children. Wilson asked the foreigners if they would accompany him and other leaders to the town center, from where a larger group would go up to the massacre site. They said they would.

Early Friday, a group of about a hundred from the community, as well as Rendon and Abbott, two international health volunteers, and human rights activists departed from the San José town center to hike the steep trails to Resbalosa.

After they arrived at the farm where a witness had discovered the fresh shallow grave in the settlement of Resbalosa, they watched as investigators disinterred the cut-up bodies of Alfonso Tuberquia's family. But the bodies of Luis Eduardo, Beyanira, and Diener were not there. "For a moment we thought maybe Luis Eduardo had survived," another community leader, Gildardo Tuberquia (no relation), said later.[6]

It was then they heard that the other bodies had been found on the banks of the Mulatos River, an hour hike down the mountain. A delegation separated from the group and made its way there; this group found the remains of Luis Eduardo, Beyanira, and Diener. The boy's skull lay apart from the rest. The community group and international accompaniers held vigil by the bodies to keep the vultures from eating them. They waited that night and all the next day, and again the following night, as the international volunteers' satellite phone battery died and they considered carrying away the bodies themselves. But a legal investigative unit finally arrived Sunday morning to gather the bodies and other evidence.

By the time the massacre occurred, more than 115 members of the Peace Community had been killed since it declared itself in 1997, while others had been forcibly disappeared, bombed, injured, threatened, displaced, tortured, or illegally detained. Paramilitary gunmen who operated with the blessing of the army's Seventeenth Brigade, or army soldiers themselves, had killed 97 members, while guerrillas of the FARC had murdered another 19.[7]

Why did the armed groups, especially the army-paramilitary alliance, single out for such relentless and brutal violence a community that openly committed itself to nonviolence and refused support for any armed group? What threat did they represent? Why did they target Luis Eduardo Guerra and Alfonso Bolívar and the women and children in their families? And why did the military participate so brazenly, not even hiding their uniforms or culpability?

The community represented a thorn in the side of adversaries who could not accept nonaffiliation of communities where they operated. The paramilitaries took over Colombia's northwestern Urabá region by blood and bullet in 1995–98, pushing the organized Left and armed guerrillas out of labor unions, towns, and most of the rural communities where peasants and Afro-Colombians lived. Even villages that during that period also called themselves peace communities with accompaniment by the Catholic Church subsequently lowered their profiles, accommodated guerrillas or paramilitaries, or displaced to larger towns, where their projects of peace and neutrality dissipated. Except for some Afro-Colombian and indigenous communities, the Peace Community of San José de Apartadó proved to be the sole exception to the army-paramilitary monopoly of force over the region's population.

Yet these responses lead to further questions. What was the role of the United States, both official government policy—represented most prominently by the multibillion-dollar military aid program known as Plan Colombia—and private U.S. citizens who sought to support the community and other initiatives like it? What might have prevented these crimes? And what are the implications of the United States' history in the war in Colombia for its role in the rest of the world?

Answering these questions requires understanding the context of the armed conflict in Colombia and U.S. involvement in it.

INTRODUCTION

CHALLENGING AMERICAN EXCEPTIONALISM

> Colombia . . . taught us that the battle for the narrative is
> perhaps the most important fight of all.
>
> —General John F. Kelly, "Colombia's Resolve Merits Support"

What is the future of the United States' military engagement around the world? Washington policy makers have increasingly since the Cold War committed the United States to strengthening the military capacity of allies through assistance and arms sales, made explicit in the 2015 U.S. military strategy, which emphasizes "building partner capacity" and "interoperability." Military leaders stated in the strategy that success "will increasingly depend on how well our military instrument can support the other instruments of power and enable our network of allies and partners."[1] The first revision of the strategy issued by President Trump in 2017 continued the emphasis on "a strong commitment and close cooperation with allies and partners because allies and partners magnify U.S. power and extend U.S. influence."[2]

The model most often cited for such foreign military assistance, proclaimed by a broad spectrum of establishment thinkers, is Colombia. Deploying from above a narrative of the miraculous protégé, U.S. officials point to Colombia as a model to emulate in other conflicts. For the foreseeable future, U.S. military cooperation with Colombia from the late 1990s to 2017, especially the series of aid packages known as Plan Colombia, serves as a principal template for U.S. military strategy and reference for success in the rest of the world.

Unpacking the context of decisions about U.S. intervention—and how policy debates that interpret Plan Colombia inform those decisions—is thus essential to understanding the criteria and values shaping U.S. military engagement. It is also crucial to understand the outcomes of U.S. policy in Colombia and the reasons why the lessons learned by most Washington policy makers, on the one hand, and by human rights advocates, on the other, are so diametrically opposed to each other.

The United States has increased its reliance on training and equipping foreign armed forces, especially since 2001, and is likely to continue doing so. "Across the globe," a 2012 version of U.S. military strategy says, "we will seek to be the security partner of choice, pursuing new partnerships with a growing number of nations—including those in Africa and Latin America . . . relying on exercises, rotational presence, and advisory capabilities."[3] This reliance on partners was embodied in U.S. assistance to armed forces and police in at least 152 countries in 2016. From 2010 through 2014, the United States spent more than $96 billion on international military and police assistance, a nearly three-fold increase from a decade before.[4]

Even so, as *Congressional Quarterly* reported in 2013, "the military brass and its backers often note [that] it's far cheaper and generally more effective to train others to fight local battles than to send in American forces."[5] The massive American troop deployments to Iraq and Afghanistan from 2001 to 2009 were debacles on several scores, and the lessons from and backlash to those failures established a much higher bar for large deployments of U.S. troops overseas. The enormous legacy costs to the federal budget of those wars will constrain spending further, deepening the incentives to operate more through client states, which bear more of the costs.

Plan Colombia as Model

At the height of U.S. war operations in Iraq and Afghanistan, between 2002 and 2008, Colombia had more military and police personnel trained by the United States than either country where the U.S. was waging war using its own troops. A massive counterdrug military and economic aid package approved in 2000, known as Plan Colombia, was transformed after the September 11, 2001, attacks into an openly counterinsurgent program with high-level U.S. commitment to the Colombian military and state.

Twenty-five years after President George H. W. Bush declared a war on drugs in Latin America in 1989, military monographs and Congressional testimony on Colombia employed phrases like "the Colombian miracle," "road to recovery," and "back from the brink."[6] Colombia is "the model for winning the fight against violent insurgencies" and "one place where we got it right," claimed the top military commander for the region.[7] Such accolades come routinely from Democrats and Republicans, military and civilian leaders. Colombia is "one of the great stories of Latin America," said John Kerry in his 2013 confirmation hearing as secretary of state, or "a model for hope," according to former Central Intelligence Agency (CIA) director David Petraeus.[8] U.S. officials also lavished praise on Colombia's ex-president Álvaro Uribe Vélez (2002–10) and his ministers, who one Pentagon official told me in 2010 were "the right men at the right time—the great man theory in plural."[9]

Moreover, the United States now funds Colombian personnel to train military and police forces in Central America, Mexico, and other countries not yet certified as "successes." Colombia has become, in effect, a superclient of the United States, and its use to train other nations' armed forces is cited as evidence that U.S. training was a success. The practice of using Colombia to train other nations' militaries was pioneered at the former U.S. Army School of the Americas (SOA) in Fort Benning, Georgia, where the number of Colombian instructors nearly doubled between 2001 and 2011, despite the risks that Colombian instruction is replicating the flawed ethics embodied in Colombian police and military collaboration with paramilitary death squads or killings of civilians.[10]

Washington reiterated this discourse when President Juan Manuel Santos—Uribe's defense minister in 2006–9—committed to a negotiated end to the war with the leftist FARC guerrillas in 2012. By 2016, when the accords were signed, the argument was that U.S. commitment to Colombia's armed forces had brought peace, to be rewarded by Washington. But even in peacetime, that reward included increased military assistance to expand the military's presence, purportedly in order to prevent "the vacuum" generated by the FARC's demobilization from being filled by existing criminal organizations.[11] The allied state that the United States is rescuing, building, or supporting in its foreign assistance is nearly always military first—followed closely by the state that promotes commerce and the privatization of its own functions.

Plan Colombia came out of a history of U.S. interventions in Colombia and elsewhere and elite premises for those interventions, as we will see. But it also confronted grassroots actors who contested elite premises. This book will demonstrate that the U.S. military assistance carried out during Plan Colombia, while serving as a template for future interventions, had a mostly negative impact on respect for human rights and social equality.

"Boots on the Ground" versus Client Forces

When President Barack Obama's administration announced the "surge" of U.S. troops in Afghanistan in 2009, the projected annual cost for deployment of each U.S. soldier was a million dollars, not including postdeployment costs such as veterans' medical, disability, and other benefits, equipment replacement, interest on borrowed funds, and opportunity costs.[12] The soldiers themselves, of course, were not seeing the vast majority of that money. But costs for long-term health care for veterans of the Iraq and Afghanistan conflicts—itself an area contested between cost-cutters and veterans in need—will peak in thirty to forty years after deployment, and add another $300,000 or more in current dollars per soldier. These costs are greater than in previous conflicts, as more veterans survive with injuries or are diagnosed with disorders resulting from trauma, and health care costs have soared.[13] In all, the contract costs to transport these soldiers, create new bases and facilities, deliver fuel and other supplies, provide "force protection," and arm them with the full technological panoply of the twenty-first century were vastly greater than the costs of training, arming, and paying Afghan soldiers on their own soil.[14]

It is no wonder, then, that even as Obama sent thirty-three thousand additional U.S. troops for the "surge" in 2010, the United States was rushing to expand the Afghan army and police, funneling large amounts of funds into training and equipping them. Obama made the political calculation that the surge would last only a limited period; then the additional soldiers would be withdrawn, leaving Afghans to fight Washington's enemies. That is why Afghanistan was during this period the largest recipient of U.S. military and police assistance, by far: from 2010 through 2012, the three years of the surge, it amounted to more than $30 billion, nearly *half of all* U.S. military and police aid globally for those years.[15] This cost was, nevertheless, only a fraction of that required for the direct deployment of U.S. soldiers in Iraq and Afghanistan, which consistently topped $100 billion annually between 2006 and 2012.[16]

The emphasis on building up allied militaries continued after Obama's presidency. In 2017 the U.S. Army established six brigades, with five hundred officers and soldiers each, just to train and advise other nations' militaries, and even set up an academy to train trainers of foreign forces.[17] One of Donald Trump's first military policy moves was to signal to North Atlantic Treaty Organization (NATO) countries that they must shoulder more costs of the alliance.[18] Such a shift in payment for international military bills might replicate the arrangement Washington has with Japan, which pays the United States for the costs of having U.S. military bases on its soil. But it could also lead to reduced U.S. troop levels in Europe and a concurrent reliance on NATO troops to deploy to conflicts where Washington expresses an interest, as they did in Afghanistan.

Compared with U.S. troop deployment, foreign military assistance is frequently financially advantageous for the United States in another way that is not often observed: what begins as grant aid, especially in the form of equipment, graduates to high levels of purchases by the client state of the same equipment from U.S. corporate suppliers. This progression from assistance to sales is consistent with other trades as well: A company gives away a product, the client trains with it and grows accustomed to using it, then needs to replace, repair, or expand it. The client is likely to return to his or her donor to buy additional models.

The five-year periods from 1999 through 2013 for Colombia illustrate the phenomenon (see figure I.1). In the initial years of Plan Colombia and those just preceding it, from 1999 through 2003, U.S. military and police aid totaled $2.3 billion, more than four times the amount of military sales for the five-year period. Aid peaked from 2003 to 2007, after which it began a steady decline. At the same time, U.S. arms sales to Colombia multiplied, more than quintupling from $326 million in the 1997–1999 period to over $1.7 billion in 2012–2014. The growth in sales was not an accident: U.S. officials repeatedly pressed Colombians to change specifications for aircraft purchases that Lockheed Martin desired to supply and that the United States regarded as "skewed" to Brazil's Embraer, for example.[19] The net result was that the United States supplied even more military equipment to Colombia, through sales, even as grant assistance declined.

The same pattern of large military aid packages followed by vastly increased sales was repeated in Mexico and Iraq. While U.S. assistance to Mexican military and police through the Merida Initiative peaked in 2009 at $682 million and declined to $79 million in 2015, arms sales agreements grew to an average of $1 billion dollars annually for 2012 through 2014. In Iraq, after authorizing no arms sales in the early part of the war, the United States green-lighted more than $3.9 billion worth of sales in 2008, and another $17 billion over the following six years.[20]

The Trump administration gave early indications in 2017 that its arms sales would prioritize wealthy clients such as Saudi Arabia, Bahrain, and the United Arab Emirates, while proposing steep cuts in overt assistance to militaries in Africa, Latin America, and Asia. And despite Trump's promises

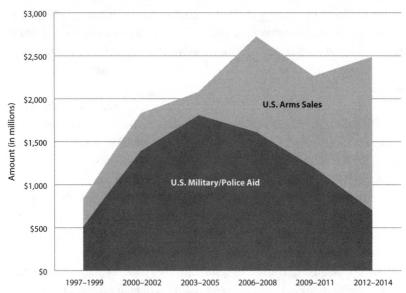

Fig. I.1. U.S. military and police aid and arms sales to Colombia, 1997–2014.
SOURCE: SECURITY ASSISTANCE MONITOR, HTTPS://SECURITYASSISTANCE.ORG.

to build up the U.S. military force, his initial budget for 2018 called for an increase in active-duty military personnel of less than one-half of a percent, still more than 100,000 troops *below* the levels of 2010, when Obama deployed U.S. forces for the "surge" in Afghanistan.[21] If the Pentagon under Trump wanted to deploy a large number of new U.S. troops, it was not in a hurry to do so.

Whether the United States focuses on assistance to allied forces or deploying its own forces is also a function of the extent to which the countries share a strategic vision and the level of trust between their militaries. If the leaders of respective nations share a worldview and objectives, and U.S. planners trust them—though such trust and congruity is often partial and fragile—the U.S. partners can be counted on to carry out the objectives for which assistance is intended. Otherwise, imperial policy makers are more likely to turn to direct U.S. troop deployments, either on bases and naval ships or in warfare itself.

Political Costs of Intervention

The antipathy to deploying large numbers of U.S. soldiers in armed conflicts in other countries is not only a preoccupation of the Pentagon or those seeking to balance the federal budget. The human and political costs of harm and death for U.S. personnel also make the commitment of large numbers of U.S. boots on the ground much more difficult for political leaders. Such deployments typically last several years, and public opinion turned against every U.S. war since the Korean War as they dragged on.[22] This opposition from both above and below to massive U.S. involvement in overseas wars has broad implications for the activities of U.S. empire.

In addition, U.S. troops that intervene directly in Muslim countries are likely to be perceived as occupiers and to generate religious and nationalist backlash that strengthens their opponents. A University of Chicago study found that 95 percent of all suicide attacks globally between 1980 and 2010 were in response to foreign occupation.[23] The drawdown of U.S. forces in Iraq that began in 2009 was largely the outcome of broad Iraqi antipathy to the large U.S. military presence.[24]

Frequently, military action that falls short of large-scale U.S. troop deployments also provokes opposition. When President Obama floated the prospect of a Congressional authorization for U.S. war in Syria in 2013, in response to chemical attacks that killed hundreds of civilians there, overwhelming popular opposition across a broad political spectrum forced Obama and Congress to drop the plan. A central reason for opposition was the belief that bombing strikes could lead to a long-term commitment in Syria—especially when Secretary of State John Kerry refused to rule out the commitment of U.S. troops and expensive deployments.[25]

Obama asked the public and Congress to weigh in on a direct military attack, but the public is rarely asked about foreign military assistance. After the administration backed off from direct military intervention in Syria, it undertook assistance to Syrian rebels without seeking a public response. When the public is consulted about training and equipping other nations' militaries, the results are mixed and vary depending on the country receiving aid, news events at the time of polling, and the framing of the question.[26] As early as 1989, when President George H. W. Bush launched a highly visible drug war push in Latin America, substantially more U.S. residents who were polled favored giving military aid and sending advisors for Colombians to fight drug traffickers than favored sending U.S. troops. This framed the low level of U.S. troops deployed in Colombia, which was capped at eight hundred from 2004 onward.[27]

A reckless leader operating without substantial restraints may still undertake major interventions involving ground troops, but the costs—economic, political, diplomatic, and moral—will be prohibitive in an increasing number of cases. Indeed, the report that Trump had, in his first week in office, casually threatened (or offered) Mexican president Enrique Peña Nieto with sending U.S. troops to go after "bad hombres" generated widespread opposition, especially in Mexico.[28]

Shifting Rationales for Engagement

Supporters of military assistance normally envision its goals as strengthening order, stability, and democratic state authority against illegal, disorderly, violent actors. These goals may be articulated as reduction of overall violence, prevailing over a destabilizing enemy, stemming human rights violations by state forces, or a combination of these aims. A second set of stated goals includes policing the production of narcotics and the movement of both drugs and people, especially across borders. A third set of goals for military engagement is economic in nature. These goals, less often stated openly, include establishing conditions for investment, extraction of resources, and trade.

Plan Colombia encompassed all these goals in varying measures, but the emphasis that U.S. officials placed on each goal changed over time. In the late 1990s, in the countryside where multiple armed and unarmed actors disputed territory for most of the twentieth century, Washington and Bogotá collaborated on the war, an escalation of military intervention that sought to prevail over the insurgency. In addition to counterinsurgency goals and a radical reduction in cocaine production, Plan Colombia also explicitly aimed to strengthen respect for human rights in Colombia through training and other aid for the military, police, prosecutors, judicial investigators, the United Nations High Commissioner for Human Rights, and the protection of witnesses and human rights groups.[29] *Plan Colombia* will focus especially on evaluating outcomes for this policy goal.

After 2010 the drug war, which was the principal driver for the initial U.S. commitment to Plan Colombia, was no longer the main mission by which the plan's success was measured in official circles, since the drug war was also widely discredited, with even the Colombian president calling it a "stationary bike."[30] "The basic premise of our war against drugs has proved to have serious shortcomings," former Guatemalan president Otto Pérez Molina told the United Nations (UN) in 2012.[31] As more U.S. states legalized marijuana for medical and recreational uses, a trend with national and even international momentum, the logic and coherence of global prohibition became increasingly broken. As a result, the human costs for enforcing it on the supply side in Latin America were progressively less acceptable to Latin

American governments, including very militarized ones, leading to a reform-oriented UN General Assembly Special Session on Drugs in April 2016.

Even some U.S. military analysts involved in nominally U.S. counter-narcotics programs in Latin America have expressed reservations about the drug mission. A RAND analyst noted, "In Colombia, strategic cooperation and large amounts of U.S. aid failed to stem the production of narcotics."[32] An otherwise glowing evaluation by the conservative Center for Strategic and International Studies recognized by 2007 that "the original eradication goal established in Plan Colombia has not been met."[33]

The centerpiece of Plan Colombia's counterdrug operations was aerial fumigation—defoliation, essentially, of coca crops, which had begun in the mid-1990s. (The coca leaf is an essential ingredient in the production of cocaine, and grows only in the Andean region.) In these operations, pilots of DynCorp contracted by the U.S. State Department sprayed glyphosate, produced by Monsanto Corporation, paired with U.S.-trained Colombian counterinsurgency troops in U.S.-produced Blackhawk helicopters. Peasant communities and environmentalists from the beginning asserted that the fumigation was generating health, environmental, and agricultural damage. The World Health Organization eventually ratified the claim that glyphosate is "probably carcinogenic to humans" in a study published in 2015.[34] The Colombian government suspended aerial spraying of the defoliant shortly thereafter.

Coca growers adapted to fumigation by moving to new areas of Colombia and other countries, by planting coca in smaller plots that were harder for pilots to detect, and by techniques such as washing leaves, rotating plots, and isolating leaves from the effect of glyphosate.[35] As a result, after an initial decline in coca production, aerial fumigation failed, and by 2007 Colombia produced nearly as much coca as when Plan Colombia kicked in. But as the Colombian state won control over more territory, it was able to deploy manual eradicators who cut down plants on the ground, a method that had greater success in destroying coca fields. Nevertheless, by 2014, while reduced from peak levels of 2001, by all measurements Colombia was still growing a lot more coca leaf than it was in the mid-1990s, when U.S. fumigation operations began.[36]

Instead of counternarcotics results, military aid supporters cite other metrics: reduced numbers of massacres and kidnappings, demobilized paramilitaries, economic growth, and weakened guerrilla forces. In effect, if the state is able to weaken armed opposition enough to claim a monopoly on the use of violence, military proponents assert, this is a victory for legitimacy and for the strategy used in Colombia.

Deconstructing the Stated Goals for Assistance

The increased U.S. support for the Colombian Army in 1999–2002 occurred at precisely the time when paramilitary forces committed the largest number of atrocities of any actor or any period of the war. These forces were organized in the Self-Defense Forces of Colombia (Autodefensas Unidas de Colombia, AUC), which had grown out of earlier generations of private armed groups in the 1950s and 1960s that the armed forces used against Liberal Party, peasant, and insurgent groups. The paramilitaries were allied with regional political elites and broad sectors of the army, prompting Human Rights Watch in 2001 to call the AUC an additional division of the army.[37] Paramilitaries were responsible for nearly three of every four political killings for which an author was identified in 1998.[38] Paramilitary as well as guerrilla and army violence led to the displacement of between 200,000 and 400,000 Colombians every year from 1997 through 2011.[39] The proponents of U.S. assistance to the armed forces in Colombia thus supported state actors that were allied with disorderly, violent paramilitary organizations acting illegally.

Since U.S. aid to "security" forces benefited groups that sowed disorder in Colombia, what other criterion explained or rationalized military support? Washington's economic agenda was central: economic development can take place only *after* security is established by the state, the thinking went. "If you don't have security, you don't have anything," one U.S. military advisor told me in 2010. This premise has dominated U.S. aid policy since the late 1950s, when U.S. military assistance in the hemisphere began its long, steady growth. "Without internal security, and the general feeling of confidence engendered by adequate military forces, there is little hope for any economic progress," concluded a commission appointed by President Dwight D. Eisenhower.[40] Indeed, six years into Plan Colombia, Washington and Bogotá signed a trade agreement that would ratify a neoliberal model of economic development.

Many scholars concur in this economic analysis and assert that the conflict in Colombia is fundamentally about control of the country's rich natural resources, and therefore territorial in nature.[41] Colombia is a large and biologically diverse country, with tropical lowlands both coastal and inland, lush valleys, snowy peaks, flat savannah, and desert regions. Its subsurface holds extensive coal, oil, gold, and emeralds, while above ground it has rich agricultural land and extensive water resources. According to critics' analysis, that is why nonviolent and unarmed communities in areas of exploitable resources are targeted for violence: some are actively organizing for community control, and whether or not they resist, communities' displacement by terror benefits those with economic interests in the lands of those who flee.[42]

Plan Colombia proponents' claims that it fulfilled human rights goals strained credulity. From 2004 through 2008, in the wake of the peak of U.S. assistance to the Colombian military, the army committed widespread killings of unarmed persons, known as "false positives." In these crimes, army units announced combat killings that were actually executions of civilians, carried out in order to claim larger numbers of "positive" kills, which were the military's primary measure of battlefield success. Though the murders initially received little attention, Colombian prosecutors and human rights groups have documented more than 5,700 alleged executions by Colombian armed forces between 2000 and 2010.[43]

In the San José massacre of 2005 recounted in this book, the military could not claim that the child victims were killed in combat, so its leaders used a different technique: they attributed the murders to guerrillas, although this narrative collapsed in 2007, when an army captain confessed his participation in the killings. The massacre was one of several cases that eroded the Colombian military's claims to legitimacy, ultimately impacting U.S. assistance.

Supporters of U.S. military involvement claim that the "false positive" killings were an anomaly in an otherwise progressive arc toward greater respect by the Colombian military for human rights. From this perspective, the Colombian military in the 1970s and 1980s was both brutal and ineffective (these two being related to each other), leading it to become known internationally for its poor human rights record. In the 1990s, the military began adopting human rights training and standards and then, with accelerated training, support, and disincentives from the United States,[44] substantially improved its human rights record over the following decade, reducing both ties to paramilitaries and the direct commission of serious abuses.

Indeed, this argument continues, the number of reported army killings of civilians from 2008 to 2015 was just a fraction of those reported from 2002 to 2008 and an even smaller fraction of those committed in the 1990s by paramilitaries allied with the army. Supporters of the decade of escalated U.S. involvement insist that the reduced army violence against civilians was the result of its greater commitment to human rights. "Every place that we've given aid and sustained aid, human rights abuses have gone down. And that's a fact. El Salvador and Colombia are pretty good cases," said a man who worked as a U.S. military trainer in Colombia and Pentagon coordinator of Colombia policy.[45]

An unstated but implicit assumption in this narrative is that U.S. human rights doctrine also improved after the Cold War and Vietnam War. Most serious military observers recognize that U.S. bombing and the ground war in Southeast Asia led to many thousands of civilians killed. Many also accept that the doctrine taught to Latin American officers at the SOA during the 1970s and 1980s did not distinguish between civilian activists and armed insurgents. Since most Colombian Army leaders in the 1980s were trained in U.S. doctrine at the SOA and other U.S. military schools, it would be hard to argue that U.S. influence on Colombian human rights practices only came into play in the twenty-first century.

Instead, the premise appears to be that the U.S. post–Cold War embrace of human rights laws and training, as well as technology designed to minimize civilian casualties, were reflected in its influence on Colombia. In other words, the idea is that the *nature* of U.S. influence changed and incorporated greater respect for human rights than was reflected in the Cold War doctrines promoted in the hemisphere.

American exceptionalism—the belief that the United States has a uniquely positive influence in the world—implies that U.S. military doctrine is the most professional and respectful of human rights in the world, which can only be a good thing for human rights in nations whose militaries it assists. Such an imagined standard is often referenced indirectly: "not even the United States has such a standard." As one Pentagon official said in 2004: "American Army personnel don't need to go into the same depth of human rights and democracy training [as Latin Americans] because US personnel have a pre-existing cultural understanding of this before they get anywhere near training."[46]

Conversations with both Colombian and U.S. military officers, however, suggest that it was not U.S. material assistance or training that had the most impact, even though helicopters facilitated the Colombian military's mobility. Instead, it was Washington's high-level and sustained political and moral support, confirmed by the substantial aid packages, when Colombia was increasingly isolated on human rights issues. Colombian leaders experienced this support as a vote of confidence in their war against insurgents. General Mario Montoya, who was army commander from 2006 to 2008, told me that the most important support from the United States was moral and political: "They have been our number 1 ally. The United States is the only country that has supported us openly. They have been our unconditional allies."[47]

Equally important to evaluating human rights claims is an analysis of the causes for decreases in state violations. Human rights conditions on U.S. assistance and other U.S. actions may have played a part in the decline in "false positive" killings, but the United States acted after other actors, both Colombian and international, documented and denounced the pattern of killings. When the United States did speak, its message was mixed with continued military support.

A closer reading of events strongly suggests that other actors played a more important role than the U.S. government in the initial steep decline in killings. First, many family members of those killed decided to publicly denounce the killing of their children, husbands, and other family members. Beyond the fact of killing, many times it was the lie that the military told about their loved ones—that they had been guerrillas—that especially made families indignant, similar to the fury generated by lies and disrespect for the dead in cases of police killings of black men in the United States and the forty-three students from Ayotzinapa, Mexico, killed in September 2014.[48] Army participants in civilian killings in Colombia testified that the practice there targeted individuals who were marginalized, and whom the army believed no one would miss.[49] In this respect, the military miscalculated the political cost of these killings.

Moreover, there were strategic military reasons to reduce the number of civilian killings. In late 2008, when the military cut off the widespread practice of "false positives," the guerrillas operated at a substantially reduced level, compared to 2002–6, when the practice was growing. The government had established a permanent police presence in nearly every county, and the FARC launched the smallest number of combat actions in the previous twelve years.[50] By 2012, when the decline in army killings could be seen as sustained over time, the FARC was at the negotiating table and corporate gold and coal mining of Colombian territories was in the ascendant. In that context, the reduced state violations may be more a consequence of mostly undisputed state territorial control than of either supposed changes in the military's organizational culture or influence by the United States.

Debating the Effects of U.S. Assistance

So what impact has the United States—its government and people—had on state violence against civilians in Colombia, and what impact could it have? Does U.S. military involvement increase or worsen such violence, or have no effect at all? What did the United States have to do with the massacre that occurred in San José de Apartadó? Can and did the responses of nongovernmental citizens from a superpower positively affect such a community confronting political violence? How would we know the answers to these questions? What assumptions guide our responses? Addressing these questions requires inquiring deeply into the history of the relationship of the United States with Colombia, which is one of the main goals of this book.

The debates on these issues are frequently infused with a kind of magical thinking. Neither elites nor opponents present systemic empirical evidence for their claims about the effects of military aid. Proponents often cite inputs (the number of soldiers trained, the amount of money provided) or the ascendance of protégés as their metrics of success, while discarding evidence of wrongdoing as aberrations, a "bad apple" or two.[51]

Very few people or agencies have collected relevant data on the operational outcomes of U.S. military and police assistance—either positive or negative. Even fewer have sought to credibly examine the impacts of this aid on armed forces' respect for the basic human rights of the local population. As a consequence, both critics and supporters of the U.S. role generally rely on anecdotal data. Many observers conflate correlation of U.S. assistance and positive or negative changes in human rights violations with causality.

Critics of security assistance start from an assumption of skepticism. "Instead of helping secure just democratic institutions, U.S. aid left countries with a legacy of repression and violence," one critic concluded.[52] Bolivian president Evo Morales said that U.S. military schools were training militaries to "destabilize democratic governments and defend imperialist and capitalist interests."[53]

The very vocabulary of the debate has embedded bias. The Pentagon refers to military aid as "building partner capacity," an adept use of three words with positive connotations. The even more common phrase "security assistance" strongly implies that the assistance will increase the security of people in the country whose armed forces receive assistance, but this is obviously not always the case. Instead, where possible, I use the descriptive phrases "military assistance" or "police assistance."

Above and Below

Above and *below* are types of vantage points from which people experience and understand the conflict in Colombia and U.S. policy, and they are also attitudes and approaches to conflict and policy. Some people move between these perspectives and attitudes, literally through travel, and over time through changes in their approach and ideas. Others stay firmly within their chosen or given vantage points. The helicopters that represented the largest U.S. investment in drug war and counterinsurgent strategy in Colombia, and were used to give tours for visiting U.S. officials, operated always from above, as did the satellites that guided bombs to guerrilla camps. Those who are "above" have important knowledge, which may be cold, detached from its consequences on the ground; so too do those who are "below," whose visceral experience may contribute to deep understanding, limit cognitive capacity through trauma, or both. Perspectives from below are typically tangible, particular, vivid; they are concerned with immediate threats, with individuals and parcels of land, and with the *practice* of policy. Perspectives from above are more abstract and macro, and use words like "democracy" and "judicial reform"; acronyms for bureaucratic agencies, funding streams, or organizations; and in the academic world, words such as "problematize" and "sites."

Such abstraction is a source and frequently an indicator of power—institutional power over others, but also the intellectual power to extrapolate, to move between situations, to generalize. Generalization can be an analytical weakness as well, which is why the material particulars of perspectives from below are so valuable, even to those looking from above. For those on the ground, there is also a temptation to generalize from a lived situation that may be much less than universal or even characteristic. Nevertheless, we can never understand the human dynamics of a conflict or a policy unless we witness how it is lived by people—and this living is specific and personal as much as it is linked to larger social, political, and economic forces and processes. It has names, places, and history, emotions and uncertainties, commitments and responsibilities. That is why in this book I discuss my own experiences with policy makers, military officers, and communities that have experienced political violence: in such direct encounters we can begin to understand how power, which is personal as well as structural, is exercised in practice.

What is a model for most of Washington has been a humanitarian and policy disaster for many communities and U.S. critics who experience Colombia from outside these dominant assumptions, especially those who live and work *below* the policy rhetoric, in conflict zones. Many are also critical of guerrilla practices in these regions. They point to army-paramilitary collaboration, civilian killings made to look like combat operations, more than five million Colombians forcibly displaced from their homes, failed counterdrug fumigation that damaged legal crops and human health, and trade agreements with the United States, Canada, and Europe that favor multinational corporate interests over economic sustainability by the majority, especially rural producers.

The responses to violence in Colombia from below, of grassroots activists, churches, and unions in the United States and Colombia, were built on a narrative that was different from those constructed from above, and led to many actions of solidarity in war zones and persistent advocacy in the United States throughout the early twenty-first century. In the boldest of these, international observers physically accompanied Colombian human rights defenders, communities, and organizations threatened with political violence, as a measure to strengthen their security and the prospects for continuing their work inside the country. Some groups organized dozens of delegations to regions in Colombia impacted by the war and the U.S. military role in it.

These groups often focused on Colombian communities and organizations whose vision and work opposed the dominant paradigm of war, corporate control, and patriarchy. Because of that opposition, the Colombian state harbored a special hatred for some of these communities and organizations. Crimes committed against prominent Colombian communities, like the Peace Community of San José de Apartadó, invoked especially strong activism for justice but also encountered persistent resistance to criminal prosecution by forces with influence over the Colombian state. For policy makers in Washington, it was typically easier to express support for justice in cases of specific human rights abuses than to reexamine the overall policy. Sometimes, however, activists were able to leverage this support to chip away at policy approaches that focused U.S. commitments on the Colombian military.

Advocacy organizations in Washington working with Colombian human rights groups developed a strong voice against the overwhelmingly militarized policy. As Latin Americans elected more leftist governments in the first decade of the twenty-first century, the counternarrative had powerful allies that isolated Colombia in the region and were decisive in turning back an agreement to host U.S. troops on military bases in Colombia over the long term.

This Book's Method

In these pages, I will explore the dynamics of U.S. military assistance in Colombia: its aims, history, and changes; its financial beneficiaries and material implementations; its geography and the conflicts in Colombia into which it was inserted; the military units and leaders who received U.S. aid; and their human rights records and attitudes. I measure human rights outcomes primarily by extrajudicial executions, which are more reliably documented than other gross rights violations; the Colombian Army allegedly committed over 5,700 such executions between 2000 and 2010. I will examine what U.S. citizens and nongovernmental groups did in relation to the conflict in Colombia; their acts of solidarity, advocacy, and accompaniment; and the impacts of these actions. I will also explore in detail the lived example of one community's trials: the Peace Community of San José de Apartadó. The book proceeds chronologically, alternating between the micro-dynamics of events in San José and the macro-dynamics of the U.S.-Colombian military relationship. Like most things, the war in San José and the U.S. relationship to the war in Colombia as a whole become more complex as you get more intimate with them, if no less tragic and compelling.

My method is driven by experience, qualitative research, and quantitative data. I spoke with victims of human rights violations, military officers, human rights workers, legislators, and journalists. Working to change U.S. policy has not required me to suspend my curiosity in order to pursue an objective. On the contrary, I want to understand policy better, and the experience of activism offers insights through encounters with people who design, execute, report on, and are impacted by policy. I have sought out ways to meaningfully measure U.S. involvement and respect for human rights in Colombia, and to compare and map these between different times and places. Conversations informed my research on data, and findings from quantitative research helped me formulate questions in interviews.

I come to this topic as a U.S. citizen, a descendant of *Mayflower* passengers and of a naval captain who led the first U.S. foreign military intervention, authorized by the Continental Congress, in 1775. And I live and work in the tradition of generations of U.S. citizens who have opposed U.S. military intervention, especially in the Americas. In the 1980s, I was immersed in the mass protest movement for human rights and against the Ronald Reagan administration's interventions in Central America. In 1986 and 1988 I participated in international unarmed teams that accompanied relatives of the disappeared and other activists threatened with political violence in Guatemala and El Salvador, as a way to strengthen their security.[54] In the 1990s, I worked on campaigns to close U.S. military bases in Panama and Vieques, Puerto Rico.

These experiences taught me some important lessons. I learned from reading, through testimonies of Central Americans and Puerto Ricans, and in interviews with active and former U.S. officials themselves about the destructive role the United States has often played in Latin America. I joined others to witness the environmental and health legacies of bombs dropped by the U.S. Navy on the populated island of Vieques. I documented U.S. military experiments with mustard gas in Panama to determine whether Puerto Rican and white soldiers would respond differently. I met and read the work of Jesuit priests who were murdered by Salvadoran troops recently trained by the United States, and interviewed U.S. military officers who were haunted by what they had done in Latin America. I spoke with U.S. engineers of Gatling guns used in the war in El Salvador, and with activists getting in the way of the guns' production in Vermont. Many U.S. officials and arms producers believed they were doing positive things that benefited Latin Americans, but the outcomes, as measured in violence or social indicators, were at best ambiguous. More often they were setbacks, and often devastating to populations in the region—a lesson about how those of us raised to believe we are good can self-deceive, and about how good intentions are not enough, including for activists who oppose intervention.

I learned about the complicated and persistent resistance—both unarmed and armed—of Latin Americans to U.S. intervention. Such resistance normally focused on local economic and political elites and their military or police enforcers, perceived to be in close alliance with—or at the bidding of—U.S. institutions and capital. Because people governing both the United States and countries in the region never valued Latin American lives as much as U.S. lives (or often, even, U.S. property), this resistance was carried out at great risk. Most media attention focused on armed resistance, on guerrilla movements from those of Emiliano Zapata in Mexico and Agosto César Sandino in Nicaragua in the early twentieth century to those of the 1960s, 1970s, and 1980s throughout Latin America inspired by Cuba's revolutionary success, liberation theology, and global anticolonial movements. But the many nonviolent movements, campaigns, and actions in Latin America for human rights and an end to war were arguably at least as pervasive and important for change as armed insurgents.[55] It was these movements whose people I met while traveling and working in the region.

I also learned that grassroots movements inside and outside the United States (and especially in combination) can have a substantial impact on limiting or stopping U.S. military intervention. International human rights advocacy led the dictatorships in Chile, Argentina, and Brazil to end several policies of abuse or release political prisoners in the 1970s.[56] While Central America experienced massive suffering from the wars supported by the United States in the 1980s, the Central America movement in the United

States made a direct U.S. invasion of Nicaragua (of the kinds in Grenada, Panama, or Iraq) impossible, and limited the resources of the United States in El Salvador. Grassroots movements had even more success in movements to close U.S. military bases: in the San Francisco Bay Area in the 1980s; in Kahoʻolawe, Hawaiʻi, where the navy operated a bombing range; in Panama, despite an attempt to negotiate continued U.S. bases after 1999; in Vieques, where nonviolent civil disobedience combined with legal protest, media work, and legislative advocacy to stop naval bombing; and eventually in Manta, Ecuador, site of a U.S. military facility that was moved from Panama when bases there closed.

Finally, I learned that I have a passion for detailed and deep research about U.S. intervention. I found that such research can be useful to activists, to Latin American officials, and to U.S. policy makers, in work to make the U.S. military less expansive and more accountable for the effects of its activities.

Thus, when it came to working for human rights and affecting U.S. policy in Colombia, I brought both some insight into how bad war is for people and a sense of agency, that collective and sustained commitment to making things better could do something meaningful. Colombia is a large country, whose history of internal conflict and of military alliance with the United States is long, and its war is endlessly complex. As one friend involved in human rights work in Guatemala said to me before joining a human rights project in Colombia, "I'm afraid I'll fall in love with another country." That could mean a long commitment.

Still, I was ready to enter the stream of U.S. relations with Colombia when I visited the Urabá region in northwestern Colombia in 2000. I knew that as a U.S. citizen, I already had a relationship with Colombia; I just needed to be more aware and informed about it. Any attempt to understand that relationship requires knowing more of the history of the country, the Urabá region, and how the United States has impacted them. We turn now to that history and region.

CHAPTER 1
THE LONGEST WAR

U.S. MILITARY INFLUENCE
IN COLOMBIA, 1952–1995

The U.S.-Colombian military relationship is deep-rooted, beginning in the early 1940s with agreements for the presence of U.S. military missions in Bogotá, and continuing to deepen throughout the Cold War, the war against the Medellín drug cartel in the 1990s, and the counterinsurgency surge represented in Plan Colombia from 2000 to 2016. Each chapter of U.S. military involvement produced consequences that shaped and facilitated subsequent interventions.

The United States initiated its military interventions in Colombia in the 1850s, in support of the U.S. owners and users of the Panama Railroad, located in what was then still part of Colombia. After the United States "took Panama" from Colombia, in the words of Theodore Roosevelt, in 1903, relations with Washington were cool, though improved after the U.S. formally compensated Colombia for Panama in 1914.

From the Thousand Days' War of 1899–1902 until World War II, Colombia's army had been historically allied with the conservative, land-owning class and trained by German officers, with a Prussian military doctrine for conventional warfare. Throughout the 1940s and 1950s, the Colombian Army's doctrine—like that of other Latin American militaries—focused principally on fighting external enemies through hemispheric defense, enshrined in the Rio Pact of Reciprocal Assistance in 1947. In the late 1940s, on the advice of the U.S. Army mission, Colombia reorganized its military command structure on the U.S. model, with sections for personnel, intelligence, operations and training, and services and support.[1] U.S. influence was consolidated during the Korean War, when a battalion of Colombian Army troops fought alongside U.S. soldiers in Korea; Colombia was the only Latin American country to do so. The Colombia Battalion fought in Korea from May 1951 to July 1953, and Colombia also sent a naval frigate that was refitted in the United States before steaming to Korea.[2]

After it returned home, the Colombia Battalion, using methods learned in Korea, was deployed in La Violencia, the decade-long, cataclysmic political violence from the mid-1940s to the late 1950s, in which some 200,000 people died in fratricidal violence between Liberal and Conservative Party members. Both sides committed atrocities, but the violence of armed Conservatives, known as *pájaros* (birds), prefigured the limitless violence of paramilitaries four decades later. Between 1953 and 1956, while Colombia was under military rule, Washington rewarded Colombia for its Korean service with weapons and military aircraft that the army used against Liberal guerrillas, despite a prohibition on internal use of the weapons. The Pentagon ensured that there was no protest against the misuse.[3]

The Korea experience established a precedent for participation in a number of multinational missions by the Colombian military, first on the Sinai Peninsula, later in Yugoslavia and Haiti, and subsequently as trainers and advisors in dozens of countries from Central America to the Arab world. At least as important, it cemented relationships between Colombian and U.S. officers.

After the Korean armistice in 1953, the Colombian military assumed control of the government at home, largely under the rule of Gustavo Rojas Pinilla. Rojas seized power through a coup in June 1953, shortly after a stint in the United States and amid increased interparty violence and governmental crisis.[4] The exclusion of civilians from the government was "an extraordinary opportunity for closer bilateral military relations," according to a U.S. Southern Command historian, and Rojas requested and received more U.S. military advisors.[5]

U.S.-Colombian military relations flourished during Rojas's term. In 1955 Colombia established a training center for counterinsurgency operations by elite troops on the model of U.S. Army Rangers, part of the sprawling Tolemaida base established in response to a U.S. Army colonel's recommendation. Four Colombian officers who themselves had been sent to be trained in Fort Benning, Georgia, ran the training at Tolemaida, with a U.S. captain serving as a special advisor. These Colombian special forces were increasingly used in the internal conflict in Colombia.[6] A military junta threw out Rojas in 1957, before convening elections the following year.

During the same period, the Colombian military began to acquire and use more U.S. equipment. From 1949 to 1959 U.S. military assistance to Colombia totaled $40.7 million.[7] In 1950 the Colombian Army adapted its small arms and munitions to calibers used by the United States. As Colombia developed its own government-run military production industry, it did so according to specifications required for U.S. equipment.[8] The use of the U.S. Army mission as a platform for arms sales to Colombia would repeat itself in the early twenty-first century.

La Violencia was settled in a pact in 1958, called the National Front, which alternated the presidency and divided state and local governments between the two parties but excluded large segments of peasant, indigenous, and Afro-Colombian people, leading ultimately to insurgency. Colombia's civilian leaders also struck an explicit deal with the military in 1960: the military would not interfere with civilian governance, and the civilian state would allow the military free rein in public security. Because there have not been formal military coups in Colombia since the 1950s, it is easy to forget that the agreement to grant the military autonomy occurred while the military dictatorship of 1953–57 was still fresh in the minds of civilian leaders. "Its bipartisan de-politicization allowed the military to acquire relative political autonomy, which was reflected in its independence in the management of public order and the acquisition of institutional prerogatives," writes sociologist Francisco Leal Buitrago. "The civilian directives for military policy were supposed to be revised and updated, as circumstances changed. But that didn't happen." Civilian governments did not involve themselves in military policy again until the 1990s.[9]

The military had long been separate from civilian life. "In Colombia there has been a very pronounced divorce between civilians and the military since the Spanish colony," according to historian Armando Barrero.[10] The effect of this, especially as the internal armed conflict emerged and developed, was to deepen the isolation from the rest of society of an army that—more than in most other countries—developed its own culture, rules, ethos, and expectations. Once the insurgency began, the army would be on its own in war against the guerrillas.

The decision by Colombian civilian leaders to stay out of military affairs coincided with the increased involvement of the U.S. military in Colombia. In the wake of the Cuban Revolution in 1959, the United States shifted its military focus for Latin America from continental defense to suppressing internal subversion, in the form of National Security doctrine. This doctrine rationalized domestic repression in defense not only of the state and its representatives but of capitalist economic activities, perceived as under threat from organizing for economic and political reforms as well as revolutionary change. Colombia adopted the doctrine despite the absence of an insurgency at the time.

In June 1959 President Alberto Lleras Camargo met with U.S. military chiefs in Colombia to request their aid in forming a counterguerrilla force in the Colombian Army.[11] That October, a CIA-led team traveled to Colombia to evaluate security and the prospects for U.S. assistance. The team included a CIA operative who had just been in Guatemala to train Cuban exiles for what became the Bay of Pigs invasion; all but one member of the team had never been to Colombia before.[12] They recommended expanding Colombia's military intelligence and psychological warfare capacity, implemented through courses in Colombia and Panama by both U.S. instructors and non-U.S. nationals to covertly bring "skills and experience acquired in their own country which might be difficult to find in the United States."[13]

President John F. Kennedy visited Colombia in December 1961, not long after he witnessed a glittering military display of Special Forces commandos and weaponry in Fort Bragg, North Carolina, which deeply impressed him.[14] A high-level U.S. military team visited Colombia two months after President Kennedy, in February 1962, following up on the 1959 CIA survey. Led by General William Yarborough, commander of the Special Warfare Center in Fort Bragg, North Carolina, the team extended the 1959 CIA mission's proposals.[15]

The team focused its recommendations primarily on the Colombian Army, because it was "the most important and plays the most active role" of the five armed forces branches in counterinsurgency operations. Its report said the army's lack of technical communications capacity was its most serious deficiency, while also calling for propaganda campaigns and psychological operations among civilian communities where government opponents were active. As would U.S. military advisors four decades later, the Yarborough team urged the army to become more mobile, through "imagination and initiative" by commanders, less reliance on fixed outposts, and specific resources for air mobility, which would be provided by the United States.[16]

The light aircraft that Yarborough recommended for the Colombian Air Force were "Helio Couriers," a lightweight plane used extensively by the CIA in operations at that time in Africa and Indochina. The U.S. State Department had already recommended in 1960 that the Colombian government purchase Helio Couriers, as U.S. law still barred grants of equipment to Latin America police or militaries for use in internal operations.[17]

In a secret annex to his report, Yarborough recommended "development of a civil and military structure" that "should be used to pressure toward reforms known to be needed, perform counter-agent and counter-propaganda functions and as necessary execute paramilitary, sabotage and/or terrorist activities against known communist proponents. It should be backed by the United States."[18]

To counter the absence of state entities, Yarborough promoted an extensive police presence in conflict zones. He urged "an intensive civilian registration program . . . so that [everyone] is eventually registered in government files together with fingerprints and photographs."[19] (Such censuses later were conducted in San José de Apartadó in advance of killings.)[20]

The Colombian Army developed and implemented the Yarborough commission's military recommendations in the summer of 1962 through deployment of troops against rural communist enclaves in an operation dubbed Plan Lazo.[21] In September 1962 the Colombian Army adopted translations of U.S. training manuals and incorporated national security doctrine into its own training, putting the civilian population and the entire country into the field of military battle. U.S. forces did not participate in direct combat, but Plan Lazo became a template for subsequent U.S. military involvement in Colombia: intensive assistance in doctrine, design of training programs, aircraft and other equipment, psychological operations, engineering, communications, intelligence, and supply guided and often directed the Colombian military's counterinsurgent war.[22]

The National Front pact of 1958 had ended most interparty violence, but it excluded large swaths of rural producers, unionized labor, and the legal communist party, who could not participate in the pact's alternating patronage, which in any case did not address structural inequalities. In response, some peasant communities in southern Colombia drew on the remnants of Liberal guerrillas to form self-defense forces against pájaros and government troops in 1960–62.[23] With the new U.S. support, the military attacked these areas during the Plan Lazo offensive, which was expanded in 1964, led by Colonel Hernando Currea Cubides, who had been trained at Fort Sill, Oklahoma, and Fort Leavenworth in 1952 and 1956.[24] The offensive prompted the armed groups to establish the Revolutionary Armed Forces of Colombia (FARC) in 1964.[25] Inspired by the Cuban Revolution, groups of university students and Catholics grounded in liberation theology formed the National Liberation Army (Ejército de Liberación Nacional, ELN) the same year.

During the 1960s, the U.S. military supervised an expanded counterinsurgency, sending more military training teams to Colombia than to any other country in Latin America. Colombia in 1965 formally authorized the arming of private paramilitary groups that supplemented military and police counterinsurgency operations, and the United States provided radio communication equipment to link these groups to state forces in more than half a dozen regions.[26] From the end of that decade until the late 1980s, U.S. military involvement in Colombia continued, but it took a back seat to U.S. involvement, first in Indochina and then, in the 1980s, in Central America. State Department officials calculated in 1972 that eliminating the Colombian insurgency would require "vast amounts of resources which are better utilized elsewhere."[27]

In keeping with the Lleras Doctrine, by which Colombian civilian and military leaders left each other alone, the country's military was also notoriously insular, limiting the involvement of civilian actors. One U.S. advisor said that, in the 1980s, the Colombian military was "just mean. They were mean, they were closed; everything was a secret."[28]

While anti-Communism and National Security doctrine promoted by the United States defined the Colombian military's ideology, national forces also oriented the military during different periods of the Cold War. In the 1950s, a new generation of officers emerged from the experience in Korea, supported by the Kennedy administration's turn toward irregular, counterinsurgency warfare and the battle for "hearts and minds." When this group of officers, led by General Alberto Ruiz Novoa, failed to obtain support from Colombia's economic and political elites for agrarian reform, another group came to the fore in the late 1970s and 1980s that sought to destroy the guerrillas' civilian support and expanded the army's support for paramilitary groups.[29] The paramilitary expansion in the 1980s and 1990s also required private economic support, which came from traditional landowners, such as cattle ranchers, as well as Colombia's new wealthy entrepreneurs, drug traffickers.

Nevertheless, the U.S. military was the principal external compass for the Colombian Army, especially on issues of doctrine. A critical step for the generation of trust by Pentagon leaders in an allied military force is the incorporation of doctrine, or guide to military action, with the same goals, concepts, and organization used by the United States. Once that occurs, the allied force is much more likely to pursue the same objectives as U.S. forces would if they were intervening directly on foreign soil. And "the Colombian Army's doctrine is completely U.S." in origin, several Colombian officers told me in 2013. "The armed forces," said a U.S. diplomat in 1975, "of all the key groups in the nation, are the most pro-U.S. in outlook."[30]

In the 1960s and 1970s, Colombia also sent nearly two thousand soldiers for training to the U.S. Army School of the Americas (SOA), which had been established in Panama in 1946. Not long after the school moved to Fort Benning, Georgia, in 1984, it began to invite Colombian officers to serve as instructors as well as students. By 1989, although public attention still focused on U.S. involvement in Central America, Colombia had sent more soldiers to SOA—6,552—than any other nation, numbers that would continue to grow in the 1990s and the following decade.[31]

Even though it did not represent a large funding commitment for the United States, the large number of Colombian officers passing through U.S. military courses in the 1970s and 1980s became especially significant as those officers rose in rank to the army's leadership in the following two decades. For example, between 1995 and 2010, eight of the eleven commanders of the army's Seventeenth Brigade, which had jurisdiction in San José de Apartadó, attended a course at the School of the Americas. "Today, U.S. influence [on the Colombian military] is obvious, from structural similarities such as the replication in Colombia of US doctrine with the formation of Joint commands to cosmetic similarities such as uniforms," wrote a U.S. military instructor in 2008.[32]

As the Cold War declined in importance after 1989, U.S. military and police assistance to Colombia steadily grew under the rubric of counternarcotics programs. The Andean Initiative announced by President George H. W. Bush in August 1989 was followed quickly by a $65 million emergency delivery of equipment that included tens of thousands of weapons, warheads, and mortars, part of $127 million in U.S. nominally counterdrug assistance to Colombia that year.[33] Although the military openly acknowledged that its missions were not focused on counterdrug operations, which were carried out by police, more than three-quarters of the package went to the military.[34] A U.S. officer who trained Colombian Special Forces units in October 1992 said, "We were giving military forces training in infantry counterinsurgency doctrine. We knew perfectly well, as did the host-nation commanders, that narcotics was a flimsy cover story for beefing up the capacity of armed forces who had lost the confidence of the population."[35]

While army contacts focused on counterinsurgency, the Drug Enforcement Administration (DEA) handled most U.S. drug war operations in Colombia, in concert with national police. In the early 1990s, those operations were focused on a single objective, at the expense of all else: the capture and ultimately the killing of Pablo Escobar Gaviria. The pursuit of Escobar led

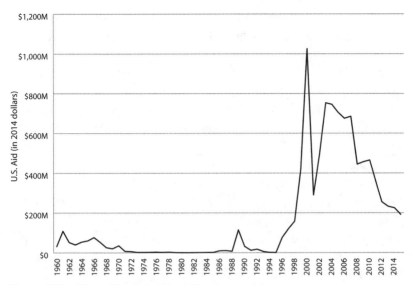

Fig. 1.1. U.S. military aid to Colombia, 1960–2015.

SOURCES: USAID, *U.S. OVERSEAS LOANS AND GRANTS*; SECURITY
ASSISTANCE MONITOR, HTTPS://SECURITYASSISTANCE.ORG.

the United States to collude with forces that subsequently became the war's most violent actors—a new generation of paramilitaries.

Escobar was the notorious chief of the Medellín drug cartel that had unleashed campaigns of terror against public officials who threatened to extradite cartel leaders or interfere with their business. In June 1991 Escobar surrendered to authorities on condition that he dictate the terms of his imprisonment, which was in a compound dubbed "the Cathedral," and from which he continued to carry out homicides and drug business. When he escaped from confinement in July 1992, the hunt for him galvanized a powerful collection of actors, including U.S. agencies, the Cali drug cartel and its professional killers, and the Colombian police and military.

Escobar's relentless violence against both state forces and rivals led to the formation of the People Persecuted by Pablo Escobar (Los Pepes), which conducted a bloody campaign, torturing and killing hundreds of Escobar's lawyers, financiers, and underlings and their family members. The Pepes included other drug traffickers and assassins, many in the pay of Escobar's competitors in the Cali Cartel. These included the Castaño brothers—Fidel and Carlos—and Diego Murillo Bejarano, alias "Don Berna," a former guerrilla in the Popular Liberation Army (Ejército Popular de Liberación, EPL) that operated in Urabá. Both Fidel Castaño and Don Berna had worked in Escobar's organization. (Don Berna in 2005 would control the paramilitary group that committed the massacre in San José de Apartadó.)

Many other people and agencies, both Colombian and U.S., participated in the hunt for Pablo Escobar between his July 1992 escape and December 1993, when he was killed. The CIA deployed a then-advanced airborne intelligence platform that intercepted and located Escobar's phone calls, and the National Security Agency (NSA), Federal Bureau of Investigation (FBI), and Navy Seals were also involved. President George H. W. Bush authorized the deployment of the U.S. Army Special Forces' ultrasecret Delta Force, which trained a Colombian police unit formed in 1992 called the Bloque de Búsqueda (Search Block). U.S. pilots were sent to Medellín to train Bloque pilots and accompanied them on raids.[36]

The Pepes were supporting the Bloque, however, which was giving the Pepes intelligence provided by the United States, according to Lieutenant General Jack Sheehan, who in 1993 directed overseas operations at the Pentagon. Don Berna came and went from the Bloque's headquarters "as if he owned the place," according to a Bloque officer.[37] Cables show that the DEA, U.S. ambassador Morris Busby, and State Department officials in Washington were aware of the collaboration between their Bloque clients and the Pepes, but no one raised an objection. DEA officers reportedly spoke admiringly of the Pepes and wore T-shirts that referred to them.[38] In November 1993 CIA analysts reported that Bloque operatives actually participated in Pepes executions and bombings. Journalist Mark Bowden concluded that the Pepes gave orders to the police, more than the other way around.[39]

The director of the Colombian National Police (CNP) ordered a senior police intelligence officer to "maintain contact with Fidel Castaño, paramilitary leader of Los Pepes, for purposes of intelligence collection," a CIA cable reported in August 1993. A U.S. intelligence profile of Castaño described him as "one of Colombia's most ruthless criminals" and observed that Castaño "is more ferocious than Escobar, has more military capability, and can count on fellow antiguerrillas in the Colombian Army and the Colombian National Police."[40]

Among the Colombian military officers involved in the Escobar hunt was a twenty-eight-year-old army captain, Néstor Iván Duque, who later played a critical role in the 2005 army-paramilitary operation in San José de Apartadó that killed Luis Eduardo Guerra and his family. From 1992 to 1994 Duque was second in command of a U.S. Embassy–supported unit in Bogotá, the Urban Anti-Terrorist Special Forces, when the unit was part of the hunt for

Pablo Escobar, and subsequently in operations against the Cali Cartel. "It was as if it were an American military force, but with Colombian men," he told me, since all its supplies and even an army captain came from the U.S. Embassy.[41]

Escobar's cartel was far from being the only violent group during the period, however, and police and judges were not the only groups of victims. Although popular dramatizations rarely reference the civil war occurring at the time, the Castaños and their gunmen waged a war against the organized Left, especially the Patriotic Union (Unión Patriótica, UP) party. When the DEA and their CNP colleagues and Fidel Castaño collaborated against Escobar's associates and their families in 1992, Castaño had already assembled death squads that had authored the murder of UP presidential candidates, as well as seven massacres in Urabá and Córdoba, where Castaño and other traffickers were buying up land to become a new elite.[42]

When Escobar was killed on a rooftop in Medellín in December 1993, there were several beneficiaries, but perhaps chief among them were the Pepes—who became *autodefensas*: "self-defense" forces, or paramilitaries. "The weapons used by the Pepes were then used by the self-defense forces," said Murillo Bejarano, who became a paramilitary chief and, many believe, successor to Escobar. "Without the Pepes, the self-defense forces would not have existed."[43]

Less than a month after Escobar's death, a sniper killed Fidel Castaño in San Pedro de Urabá. A year later, in March 1995, Fidel's brothers Carlos and Vicente, together with a former army captain, formally founded the Peasant Self-Defense Forces of Córdoba and Urabá (Autodefensas Campesinas de Córdoba y Urabá, ACCU).[44] Their experience in Los Pepes gave the Castaño brothers and Don Berna the contacts and protection they needed to make the paramilitary project into a national federation. But first, they would turn it loose onto the Urabá region, which they conquered using limitless brutality.

War on Drugs or on Insurgents?

As the 1990s progressed, debate heated up among policy makers about the purposes of the U.S. role in Colombia. Official policy dictated that U.S. activities were restricted to fighting the production and trafficking of narcotics, particularly cocaine, and were not to cross the line into counterinsurgency. Some leaders saw the drug war as better terrain on which to establish the legitimacy of a U.S. role than fighting guerrillas, which politically had gone poorly in both

Vietnam and, to a lesser extent, Central America. This official line met with increased resistance from counterinsurgency hawks, especially military officers, both U.S. and Colombian.

By 1996 the U.S. preference for military and police assistance and corporate trade over humanitarian assistance was on display. In March 1996 the State Department did cut some military and police assistance to Colombia for fiscal years 1996 and 1997 because of revelations of the narco-financing of President Ernesto Samper's campaign. The action suspended $33 million of aid for up to seventeen months and cancelled $1.4 million in military training. Nevertheless, Special Forces deployments to Colombia were exempt from the ban.[45]

When U.S. decertification of President Samper's government affected aid programs, officials rushed to prioritize military and police aid. "We need to find a mechanism," former ambassador Morris Busby told Congress in 1997, "which will permit us to express our extreme displeasure with the political leadership of a country such as Colombia . . . but at the same time permit us to go forward with assistance to gentlemen like Generals [Harold] Bedoya [army commander] and Serrano [police chief]."[46]

U.S. police assistance began to climb in 1997, doubling from the previous year. By February 1997, the army agreed with the State Department to field units dedicated especially to counterdrug operations.[47] During fiscal year 1998 the U.S. deployed twenty-four teams of special forces trainers to Colombia, training hundreds of troops in shooting, counterinsurgency, and intelligence techniques.[48] The U.S. Southern Command (SouthCom) apparently deliberately did not review the human rights records of units it trained "because it would interfere with the unit's ability to work together," according to U.S. military officers.[49] U.S. sanctions on the Samper government also did not prevent Colombia from getting delivery of $242 million in sales of U.S. military equipment and services in 1996–99, more than any other Latin American country.[50]

Skeptics said U.S. aid was actually counterinsurgency support disguised as a counterdrug mission, and that Washington should not get involved in Colombia's war against guerrillas, because it would be a costly and drawn out "quagmire," it would put the United States on the wrong side of the war, or both.[51] In fact, opposition in Washington to incorporating counterinsurgency into the missions supported by the United States was always thin. One reason for this was that the drug war only weakly combatted those on the commercial peak of the drug trade's pyramid. Instead, it targeted the least powerful social sectors—peasant growers on one end, and street dealers and users on the other. This skewed the selection of targets for counterdrug operations, biasing them toward the social base of the insurgencies in Peru and Colombia. It also influenced the methods used for counterdrug operations: while some political and economic leaders involved in the business might be shamed out of office, perhaps temporarily, or even imprisoned, those living in areas where coca leaf was grown were subject to aerial fumigation that did not discriminate between coca and other crops or between growers and family members not planting the leaf.[52] But from another, grassroots perspective, the human outcome in communities where the war was taking place was more important than whether the United States was fighting drugs or guerrillas. This was the viewpoint of U.S. citizens who looked for something positive to support in Colombia and sought to do more than just criticize U.S. policy. Such an outlook did not require proving that the United States had ulterior motives to fight a drug war. Instead, it measured the negative impact of escalating war, as well as the results of counternarcotics operations, which were ineffective by any meaningful measure (such as the ease of buying and street price of narcotics and the relative efficacy of treatment).

In addition, this critique required an analysis of who were the actors hurting civilians in communities throughout Colombia, and how they could be dissuaded from committing further harm. It highlighted the finding that paramilitaries committed the bulk of political murders in the mid to late 1990s in Colombia, and that the Colombian Army and police supported by the United States—regardless of their stated mission—were allied with the paramilitaries. It focused on supporting and protecting the massive and growing population of forcibly displaced Colombians, as well as on aiding the smaller but extensive communities and civilian groups that were impacted by the war and articulated an alternative vision to it.

CHAPTER 2
WAR ON THE FRONTIER

Several decades before Luis Eduardo Guerra's murder in San José de Apartadó in 2005, his family was one of thousands who migrated to new settlements in the Urabá region in northwestern Colombia in the 1960s and 1970s, many drawn by the development of banana plantations or driven out of other regions by the widespread interparty violence in the 1950s and its sequelae. The violent conflict that unfolded in Urabá in the decades that followed had complex internal sources. But U.S. companies, especially United Fruit (later Chiquita Brands), both contributed to conditions for conflict and were key to the privatization and internationalization of the violence, which became so severe that communities seeking to escape its logic eventually sought support from outsiders, including U.S. citizen groups.

Urabá includes portions of three Colombian departments: Córdoba on the Caribbean, Antioquia (Colombia's largest and most populous department), and Chocó, which extends to the Pacific. The road from Medellín, Antioquia's capital and Colombia's second largest city, to the town of Turbo on the Gulf of Urabá, begun in 1926, was only completed in 1954, and even then was in poor condition, frequently blocked by landslides.[1] A prison colony established in the 1920s in Ituango, known as Antadó, provided a channel for criminal convicts to come to the area from other parts of Antioquia, and the colony—dissolved in the 1940s—became a refuge for Liberal guerrillas during La Violencia.[2]

U.S. capital investments were central to the region's economy very early in its growth. Frutera de Sevilla, the local subsidiary of the Cincinnati-based United Fruit Company (which later became Chiquita Brands), had in the 1920s established banana plantations in Magdalena Department, to the east of Urabá. In 1959 Frutera de Sevilla offered incentives to local growers in Urabá to plant bananas on land parcels of five to three hundred hectares, leading to the boom in banana plantations throughout the region that would come to define it as a United Fruit enclave, known as the "Banana Axis."[3] The first banana export shipments occurred in 1964.[4] From less than a hundred houses in 1960, the town center of Apartadó grew to a population of nearly eighteen thousand in 1973, and to more than thirty-one thousand in 1985.[5]

But "the particular quality of commercial production did not generate a regional elite living in the area with influence on the state and other sectors," writes María Teresa Uribe in her history of twentieth-century Urabá. Instead, it led to an absent, external, and foreign elite that reinvested its profits outside the area and responded with force to the social conflicts that typically occur as part of this model of development.[6] In addition, the demands of successive stages of banana development attracted different types of banana farmers: internal refugees in the early days of opening jungle; *antioqueño* businessmen who had administrative skills after the sector got going; and in a third stage, outside investors. The process gave rise to complex conflicts between and among laborers and investors over land tenancy and ownership, exacerbated by speculation by land investors, who sometimes appealed to the army to act against settlers on land they claimed.[7]

The municipality of Apartadó was founded in 1968, largely by Liberal Party members from other parts of Antioquia who developed little administrative capacity. Local leaders drew on funds from the U.S. Alliance for Progress, which had supported the construction of Apartadó's first school the previous year.[8] While the banana sector employed many of the newly arrived settlers, many others sought land to work in subsistence agriculture. In addition to land conflicts, they had to deal with career criminals—"bandits"—who also arrived in the frontier region in the wake of La Violencia.

Gradually, drawn by word of mouth from family and friends, in the mid-1960s some families began to move to an area five hours on foot east of the small town center, known as El Mariano. Men came with their families, or came alone and then sent for them after having built lodging and sown their first crops. "It was a very good place since it is in the middle of everything, to move around the area you have to go through it," said one settler.[9]

The early years before crops matured were rough, as there was little day labor available, and most settlers were de facto owners but had no land titles. The National Peasant Association (Asociación Nacional de Usuarios Campesinos, ANUC) organized some settlers to conduct land occupations in the area in the early 1970s, achieving the construction of a road and school and a proposal to buy land for the town center, which the owner rejected. Peasants occupied the land and were evicted by the army, then took advantage of an opening for land titling by the National Agrarian Institute, through which they gained title for parcels up to eight hectares, and established a police post, central square, and chapel. They baptized the town San José de Apartadó, for Saint Joseph, the patron saint of farmers.[10] While Apartadó is a county (municipio) with a city government structure, San José is a territorial district, or corregimiento within Apartadó, which contains more than thirty settlements, or veredas, in its rural mountainous area (see map 2.1).

Moisés and Deora Guerra were from Peque, a rural town between Apartadó and Medellín. They had three daughters there, and Luis Eduardo, who was born in 1968. But when Luis Eduardo was just a few months old, with no place for the family to live, they decided to move to San José, where Moisés's brother had already migrated. There, they settled in the Abibe Mountains, in a hamlet called El Barro ("the mud") near the Mulatos River, and carved a farm from the bush, called "La Montañita."[11] While Moisés was reportedly a hard worker, he also drank sometimes in the San José center, and Luis Eduardo would come to abhor alcohol.[12]

Among the local leaders in San José was Bartolomé "Bartolo" Cataño, an illiterate farmer and Liberal Party militant from España, Antioquia, who had arrived in San José in 1970 and constructed a house and worked the land. Cataño and other leaders worked with women, children, farmworkers, and small business owners to complete the road to San José, drawing sand from the river, sharing food, and sharing the work. When Apartadó's military mayor reneged on a promise to provide trucks for the work, Cataño and others complained to a local ombudsman and Communist Party leader named Bernardo Jaramillo, who scolded the mayor and successfully demanded that he either provide the trucks or pay for private ones so that local people could do the road work.[13] Jaramillo went on to be a national leftist leader and was assassinated while campaigning for the presidency in 1990.

Bartolo led the formation in 1985 of a producer and consumer cooperative in San José known as Balsamar, which eventually had participation from twenty-two different settlements in the area, including farmers in Nuevo Antioquia in Turbo. Farmers contributed 6 percent of their earnings toward

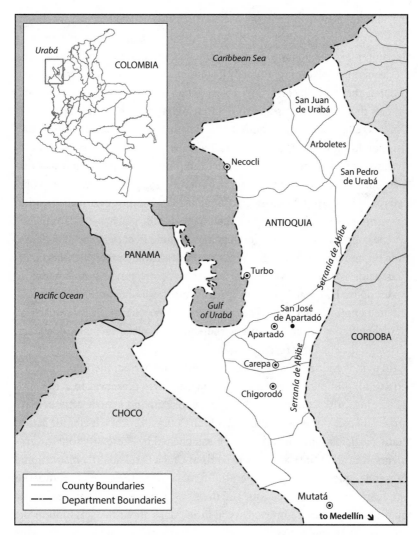

Map 2.1. The Urabá region in Antioquia Department. MAP BY DOUGLAS MACKEY.

the co-op and put in what capital they could, which led to construction of a building in San José's town center to store cocoa and sell household goods. The co-op organized a tree nursery, and timber harvesters in the village of Nuevo Oriente, Turbo, who sold lumber through the co-op then replanted trees from the nursery. In 1990 Balsamar joined forces with other farmer organizations to form a consortium of small and medium producers in Urabá that planted 230 hectares with rice and bought a rice mill.[14] With 1,500 members, Balsamar by 1991 controlled cocoa production and sales in the San José area, had no debts with Urabá's major credit agency, and used local knowledge to improve soil fertility in the area. The co-op's highest decision-making body was a general assembly of all members, who elected a ten-member governing council. Community meetings planned and distributed the work necessary to achieve the co-op's goals—organizational models that would later serve the Peace Community. With the support of a Dutch agency, Balsamar acquired a thirty-four-hectare parcel with a small fish pond, known as "La Holandita," a short walk from the center of San José, which would become the Peace Community's refuge when it was displaced from the town center in 2005.[15] But after 1994 some government officials began accusing the co-op of channeling food to the guerrillas, arresting co-op members and confiscating their harvest.[16]

The cooperative organization had a profound effect on peasant capacity, even though the co-op itself was eventually destroyed in 1996. As one aid official said: "Many things survived from that [co-op] process: in San José de Apartadó we had many peasant councils, mayors and deputies, which contributed enormously to people realizing that they could express themselves, that they had a space to express their ideas, a place to make decisions although they had few resources."[17]

In many rural regions of Colombia during the period, there were and are no meaningful public services, nor a civilian state presence. In areas such as San José, the Communist Party began organizing shortly after settlers arrived, in part through Communal Action Councils, local vehicles for democratic participation, which had been established by National Front governments in 1958. In the rugged rural lands of Urabá that had little institutional presence, guerrilla groups operated freely during the 1970s and most of the 1980s, principally the FARC and the EPL. "One has to recognize that the guerrillas would sometimes give you little books about the situation in the country so you could study," one older San José resident told me in 2015. This "recognition" can be read both that guerrillas were interested in peasants being educated and also that guerrilla perspectives influenced local people. Political education of peasants in Urabá was a consistent part of Communist Party organizing in the region beginning in the 1960s.[18]

The military's response to communist organizing in San José early on included violence against local settlers. In July 1977 an army patrol arrested up to thirty people in Mulatos settlement, not far from the Guerra family; eight young men among them later reappeared dead, while three were disappeared. An army brigade commander summoned three of the dead men to testify in the case of three of the killings, and, unsurprisingly, they did not appear. A military judge then refused to issue a ruling. Meanwhile, the central government appointed military officers as mayors in 1976 in Apartadó, Turbo, Chigorodó, and Mutatá.[19] By 1980 all the towns' mayors were army officers.[20]

The two guerrilla organizations, the FARC and the EPL, operated in different areas and respected each other throughout the 1980s. They took control of two banana worker unions that organized banana farms in the region, and after a period of competition for worker membership, the two merged in 1987 into a single National Union of Agricultural Workers, SINTRAINAGRO, which achieved a number of gains for workers.[21]

Urabá's population was ethnically and culturally diverse, but most residents had arrived from outside the region with no social ties there. With an economy driven by outside actors, corrupt and inefficient local government, and so many newcomers to the area, the Urabá region had few resources to cope with conflict or to weave a healthy social fabric.

Since the banana economy was largely unregulated by the state, its product shipped out of the port in Turbo by multinational traders, it had the quality of contraband, and Urabá the character of a border region. In this respect, Urabá in the 1980s and 1990s was akin to Ciudad Juárez on the Mexico-U.S. border in the first decade of the twenty-first century, with mushrooming cross-border trade stimulated by U.S. capital, a flood of arrivals from other parts of the country drawn by jobs but with no social services, intensive drug and gun contraband, official militarization, illegal armed groups, and social conflict, combining to generate devastating violence. At the same time, the growth of the banana economy made Apartadó and Turbo boomtowns in the 1990s, each growing sizably in population.

The state allowed commercial elites to use migrants as they wished, exhibiting little interest in Urabá for many years, but when it asserted itself, it did so with arms. In addition to assuming mayoralties, the army established the Voltígeros Battalion in Carepa in 1986, and the following year the Eleventh Brigade was established in neighboring Montería to operate in all of Urabá.[22]

Nascent negotiations between the government and guerrillas in 1984 gave birth to a FARC-affiliated political party, the Patriotic Union (UP), which organized successfully in the Urabá region. The governor appointed a UP mayor after the party received more votes than any other in Apartadó legislative elections in 1986. It used this power to support the banana workers union and to award land titles to neighborhood residents who had squatted for nearly twenty years.[23] The party went on to win three Urabá mayoralties in direct elections in 1988, including Apartadó.[24] But this electoral success met with a ferocious backlash from business elites, who organized violent repression.

Peace processes nevertheless proceeded, both regionally and nationally. Most members of the EPL demobilized in 1991, forming a political party, Esperanza, Paz y Libertad, whose members were called *esperanzados*. But after an initial calm, FARC members accused esperanzados of giving tactical information about the FARC to state forces, and then began assassinating EPL members. The most notorious of these killings was a massacre of thirty-four people in January 1994 in La Chinita, an Apartadó neighborhood. The EPL also created an armed militia that killed suspected FARC members and others.[25]

During the conflict between FARC and EPL, Chiquita sided with the FARC, with whom it developed a close alliance. Beginning with monthly cash payments to the FARC in 1989 by way of the FARC-controlled labor union, the relationship included providing weapons, ammunition, and other supplies to the FARC as well as subverting unions controlled by the EPL, which was less accommodating to growers at the time. The FARC, for its part, harassed competing banana growers. The payments to FARC, often made by a former U.S. military pilot who was a Chiquita manager in Colombia, continued through at least 1997.[26]

These changes on the armed Left coincided with the growth of paramilitary death squads sweeping into the region, often with army support, which wiped out UP activists and elected leaders. Many EPL fighters, under attack by the FARC, then joined the paramilitaries. This model for paramilitary expansion in Urabá, and in many cases its personnel, was subsequently exported to the rest of Colombia.

The paramilitaries were organized 1987 in the adjacent state of Córdoba by the brothers Fidel, Vicente, and Carlos Castaño; this group became the Autodefensas Campesinas de Córdoba y Urabá, or ACCU (and subsequently part of the national Autodefensas Unidas de Colombia, or AUC, in 1997). Their first attempts to dominate Urabá's banana region were stymied by guerrilla control.[27] But that did not stop paramilitaries from carrying out a series of massacres, selective killings, and disappearances, especially against banana trade unionists, as the Patriotic Union won electoral victories in the region in 1986 and 1988. In March 1988 the Castaños' gunmen killed twenty-one banana workers affiliated with the UP in Turbo (adjacent to Apartadó), with support from officers in the army's Voltígeros Battalion.[28]

In 1995 the banana companies, including Chiquita Brands, entered into a deal with the Castaños and a new paramilitary unit called the Banana Block that would help catalyze their offensive: the Banana Block and ACCU would serve as antiguerrilla and antiunion enforcers for the companies.[29] The deal was facilitated by a 1994 decree that permitted the creation of "security cooperatives," civilian militias known as Convivirs (literally meaning to "live together" or "coexist") that were ultimately integrated into the AUC paramilitary command structures. The Convivirs were permitted to obtain and use weapons previously restricted to the military, and Convivir members were chosen by army officers, including by the leadership of the army's Seventeenth Brigade in Urabá.[30] They became the principal administrative vehicle for the growth of paramilitary squads during the key period from 1995 until 1997, when Colombian courts made the Convivirs illegal. The governor of Antioquia from 1995 to 1997—and later the president—was a wealthy cattleman named Álvaro Uribe, who became a strong promoter of Convivirs. Banana grower Raúl Hasbun approached him in 1997 to create Convivirs in Urabá; twelve of them were formed there within just a few months.[31]

Chiquita financed paramilitary activity in Urabá from 1995 to 2004, delivering monthly payments that totaled at least $1.7 million during the period. The company claimed that armed groups extorted the payments, but a U.S. prosecutor would later say at a plea hearing: "Defendant Chiquita fails to square its claimed victimhood with the facts. As a multi-national corporation, Defendant Chiquita was not forced to remain in Colombia for 15 years, all the while paying the three leading terrorist groups that were terrorizing the Colombia people."[32]

The company also supported paramilitaries by facilitating the use of its banana shipments as containers for illegal shipments of weapons and drugs. In the best-documented shipment, Chiquita employees at the company port facility in Turbo in November 2001 unloaded three thousand AK-47 assault rifles and five million rounds of ammunition. Although customs declarations for the shipment said they were rubber balls, Chiquita employees used heavy machinery that would not have been necessary for the declared cargo. The AUC had free access to the port, and after two days loaded the weapons onto fourteen of its own vehicles. Chiquita facilitated at least four other weapons shipments to the AUC, including an operation in 2000 that smuggled into Urabá 4,200 rifles disguised in banana fertilizer bags, aboard a ship owned by Banadex, a subsidiary of Chiquita Brands.[33]

The arms shipments illustrate an aspect of why all armed groups saw Urabá as a strategic nexus and corridor: its location on the Caribbean, near the Panama border and canal, straddling mountains and urban centers, with fertile soil and coal deposits. An armed group that controlled the region's territories perceived potential benefits from both legal and illegal commerce.

Chiquita was not the only multinational U.S.-based company selling popular products from conflict-ridden Urabá in the mid-1990s. A Coca-Cola bottling plant in Carepa, adjacent to Apartadó, owned and run by a Miami family, was another scene of labor disputes. Paramilitaries killed two union members in 1994, and then threatened union leaders, when operators reportedly allowed them inside the plant, leading every member of the local union's board of directors to flee in April 1995. The plant manager announced publicly at the time that he had ordered paramilitaries to destroy the union. In December 1996, as the union was negotiating with the plant, paramilitaries gunned down union local president Isidro Segundo Gil at the gates of the plant, then set fire to the local union hall.[34] Gil's killing was followed by visits from gunmen who threatened workers with death if they did not resign from the union. The union ceased functioning in Carepa.[35] Unlike Chiquita's, Coke's executives denied any association with paramilitaries, but the bottling plant owner, Richard Kirby, implicitly admitted the connection, saying later, "Nobody tells the paramilitaries what to do; they tell you." He said he tried to sell the plant after the murders, but Coca-Cola would not let him.[36]

The army's participation in the paramilitary sweep of the region in the mid-1990s was led by the commander of the Seventeenth Brigade in 1996 and 1997, General Rito Alejo del Río. Part of the army's old guard, del Río had attended a course at the U.S. Army School of the Americas in Panama as a cadet in 1967, and viewed the unarmed Left as part of the guerrilla enemy. "As is known," he said in 1997, "the subversion includes an armed branch and a political branch, which includes all of the left and is supported by different bodies which the subversion controls, especially in their areas of influence such as human rights offices which, in turn, receive support from national and international non-governmental organizations."[37]

Del Río reportedly "legalized" paramilitary killings of civilians in 1997 by claiming that the civilians killed were guerrillas, according to a soldier in the Seventeeth Brigade who gave testimony in the late 1990s and was himself killed in 2005. Such "legalization" of executions by making them appear to be legitimate army operations was a precursor to the practice of "false positives" that became widespread several years later.[38]

After guerrillas were expelled from cities in the region, business leaders called del Río "the Peacemaker of Urabá," and U.S. ambassador Curtis Kamman reported in 1998 that del Río's "systematic arming and equipping of aggressive regional paramilitaries was pivotal to his military success" against the FARC.[39] Del Río was typical of Seventeenth Brigade officers who worked with paramilitary commanders in the 1990s. An intelligence officer in the brigade, "Beto" Gutiérrez, was a liaison to national paramilitary leaders, including Carlos Castaño. Successive commanders of the Seventeenth Brigade's Vélez Battalion also collaborated, using paramilitaries as "guides" and informants, according to former paramilitary fighters. In the early 1990s, Captain Bayron Carvajal commanded the battalion, and his men frequently carried out joint operations with paramilitary groups, paramilitary Hebert Veloza García testified. Paramilitary operations were sometimes "legalized," another practice that typified the pervasive "false positive" killings in the next decade.[40]

Peasants in Apartadó and Turbo felt keenly the impact of the paramilitary alliance. In September 1995, paramilitaries killed five leaders in a Turbo settlement. Army-paramilitary operations in the following months patrolled in San José with lists of residents, detaining, torturing, stealing, and killing peasants in several rural settlements. In response to the increased violence, more than eight hundred peasants took over the Apartadó stadium for three weeks in June 1996, leading to an agreement to investigate the violence through a commission formed with representatives of national, departmental, and local government agencies and several local residents. The peasants returned to their lands with a guarantee that the army would not harass them.[41]

San José de Apartadó founder Bartolo Cataño, by then a UP city councilman in Apartadó, was killed on August 18, 1996, as he got into a car to go to San José. Three weeks later, paramilitary gunmen accosted the cooperative's president before dawn and forced him to open the co-op and give them money in the co-op safe, after which they killed him and three other leaders—two of whom had given testimony to the commission. Soldiers from the Seventeenth Brigade patrolled nearby, and some witnesses said soldiers also participated in abducting the victims. Thousands of area residents, including the remaining co-op leadership, fled the region into town centers in subsequent weeks.[42]

As military control of the region shifted from guerrillas to paramilitaries in the mid-1990s, the armed groups made assumptions about the allegiances of who fled and who stayed, subjecting the civilian population to new risks.[43] In a pattern that repeated throughout Colombia between 1999 and 2003, paramilitaries dominated most urban areas, where they made alliances with political and economic elites and accessed legal and illegal commercial activity and public coffers, while guerrillas tended to concentrate in rural areas, closer to their historical peasant base.[44]

Amid bombing, repression, and massacres, peasants in March 1997 established a peace community in San José de Apartadó that refused to support any armed group, including the state's armed forces. Most accounts say the idea came from Apartadó's first bishop, Mons. Isaías Duarte Cansino, who since 1988 had brought together leaders of opposing armed groups to talk in private.[45] But community leaders today say the idea was theirs.[46]

During this period, several indigenous, Afro-Colombian, and mestizo communities promoted neutrality as an expression of their autonomy, ethnic culture, standards of collective behavior, and territorial control. Indigenous leaders of Antioquia in 1996 proposed active neutrality as withholding all support for armed groups—guerrillas, paramilitaries, and the military. They sought the presence of the Church, nongovernmental organizations (NGOs), and international groups, both to be taken more seriously by armed groups and to feel less alone; but doing so in remote areas proved difficult. Governor Uribe, under criticism for his promotion of private armed militias called Convivir, ably co-opted the proposal. Any time that guerrillas attacked civilians in an Antioquian community, Uribe immediately visited and urged the community to adopt "active neutrality" that would support the military.[47]

In early 1997 Uribe participated in a pivotal public meeting in the region to discuss San José's security. In response to the proposal for a neutral community that supported no armed groups, including the army, Uribe urged San José residents to adopt "active neutrality." Participants in the meeting rejected the idea, and Uribe stormed out of the room.[48]

Diverse forces shaped the community's decision to stay in San José in 1996–97. On the one hand, the rural hamlets where peasants lived and worked were the sites of bombing, combat, and operations that targeted civilians. Army troops told peasants that they had no problem with them, but that paramilitaries—known as "head choppers"—would follow. Paramilitaries had demonstrated their intentions through multiple killings in San José, including the September 1996 massacre. The guerrillas urged community members to take up arms, which they would not do. If they did not join the guerrillas or paramilitaries, their options were to flee or face death.[49]

On the other hand, moving to nearby cities did not provide safety. The city of Apartadó was undergoing generalized warfare, and neighborhoods of

UP supporters—the likely destination of San José residents seeking safety—were particularly targeted for paramilitary violence and displacement.[50] Apartadó mayor Gloria Cuartas, believing that peasants displaced from rural settlements in the mid-1990s faced greater danger in San José than in the city, sent trucks to San José to help them move to Apartadó center. But peasants in San José refused the offer.[51] The community's choice of a nonviolent path also constituted resistance against the displacement from their lands that was affecting millions of other rural Colombians.

Father Javier Giraldo, who visited San José in late 1996 and was to play a critical role in its subsequent history, said the destruction of the UP left peasants in the area "politically orphaned," which "challenged them to build a small alternative world, based on principles of solidarity that would bind them together as community in the midst of armed groups that continued to force them to enter the war as combatants."[52] As the community labored to create something new, Giraldo catalyzed support from the national Catholic human rights organizations he founded, the Center for Research and Grassroots Education (Centro de Investigación y Educación Popular, CINEP) and the Justice and Peace Intercongregational Commission (commonly known as Justicia y Paz), as well as international accompaniment of San José that would begin in 1998.

Uribe's active neutrality proposal almost derailed the initiative. "When the people were coming to agree to do that, to declare San José de Apartadó a neutral zone, we didn't do it because neutrality was very discredited," recalled a San José community leader. "Because Alvaro Uribe Vélez talked a lot about neutrality and we saw what happened in Punta de Piedra in Turbo, where there was a neutral zone and the paramilitaries were in command there. . . . For us that was very risky, because this is an area where the guerrillas have influence, the army has a presence, the paramilitaries have a presence. And if we are going to talk about neutrality it should be with all of them." The idea of a peace community thus replaced that of a neutral zone. And instead of stipulating protection of a territory, protection would extend to a population that freely joined this community.[53]

Communities developed these proposals even as combat and the threat of it proceeded around them. On March 26, 1997, three days after peasants in San José publicly declared a Peace Community, the army began bombing and combat operations jointly with paramilitaries in most San José hamlets, leading residents to flee to San José's center, filling its plaza.[54]

As sick and hungry peasants gathered in the San José center in the weeks following the assault, some of their leaders approached Giraldo with an additional proposal: If the Church-based groups committed to accompany the community day and night, a large number of peasants would stay. If the human rights groups left, the majority of peasants would flee.[55] The die was cast: the Peace Community would stay, and so would human rights accompaniers.

CHAPTER 3
HOW PLAN COLOMBIA WAS SOLD

As the drama in San José de Apartadó unfolded, binational policies and events in the 1990s and the following decade shaped its context, including increased U.S. engagement in the war against guerrillas and drug traffickers in Colombia. This escalated U.S. military involvement was not inevitable. U.S. and Colombian actors constructed a multibillion-dollar commitment in response both to arguments and interests of those actors and to developments in the conflict itself.

The armed conflict in Colombia underwent important changes in the late 1980s and early 1990s. Negotiations with guerrilla organizations in 1987–91 led to the demobilization of some guerrillas, the creation of new political parties, and a constitutional assembly. The establishment of the Patriotic Union by the FARC in 1985 drew support from FARC supporters and participants, as well as other activists and voters. But the leadership and members of parties created out of the EPL and FARC were systematically massacred in the 1980s and 1990s, many by right-wing paramilitary organizations formed by drug traffickers, landowners, military officers, and political elites.

The result was to strengthen the militarization of all armed groups. The paramilitaries and army took up spaces left by the Left and displaced communities, in some cases with the participation of ex-EPL members who became paramilitaries. And without political options, the FARC consolidated around its most war-oriented leaders.

President César Gaviria (1990–94) initiated policies of structural neoliberalization of the Colombian economy, privatizing public entities, applying structural adjustment, and prioritizing foreign capital. The economic crisis generated by these policies led many in the population toward the illicit economy, and made political leaders even more vulnerable to the external demands of international financial institutions and of Europe and North America.[1]

At the same time, the end of the Cold War affected the regional strategy of the United States, which sought to legitimize its military actions in the war on drugs. Antidrug operations in Peru and Bolivia—where the majority of coca leaf was grown in the 1980s—pushed the core of coca growing toward Colombia, where traditional drug traffickers, the paramilitaries, and guerrillas adapted and found in it new sources of maintenance and expansion.[2]

Colombian paramilitary groups consolidated in April 1997 into the Autodefensas Unidas de Colombia (United Self-Defense Forces of Colombia, AUC). Paramilitaries drew support from drug traffickers; elements of the Colombian military, police, and politicians; and landed elites, especially those impacted by guerrilla aggression. The AUC would become the worst violator in the conflict and the beneficiary of the massive land transfers represented by the forced displacement of more than five million people. It was not, typically, a direct recipient of U.S. assistance.[3] But because it was an ally to Colombian armed forces and civilian leaders supported by the United States, it benefited from the U.S. project in Colombia.

In the United States, Canada, and Europe, human rights movements and the influence of NGOs grew in the 1990s as well. The United Nations High Commissioner for Human Rights opened a monitoring office in Colombia in 1997. The same year, the U.S. Congress approved an amendment, which became known as the Leahy Law, that prohibited assistance to military and police units of other countries if the State Department has credible information that they have committed gross human rights abuses. Though today it is global in scope, the Leahy Law initially applied to counternarcotics aid only.[4]

The U.S. Drug War Ramps Up in Colombia

During the 1990s, the principal branch of the Colombian armed forces that received U.S. assistance was the Colombian National Police (CNP)—protagonists in the hunt for Pablo Escobar and other Colombian counterdrug operations—leading to what one military historian called the Colombian Army's "envy" of the CNP's air mobility, in the context of already intense interservice rivalry.[5] Rep. Benjamin Gilman of New York, who chaired the House International Relations Committee in the 1990s, was a key champion of the CNP. The police became heavily infiltrated by Escobar's enemies in the Cali Cartel and by others who became the core leadership of paramilitary organizations.[6] The CNP's operations were primarily urban, while the war between the army and guerrillas, especially after the demobilization of the M-19 guerrillas in the late 1980s, was mostly rural.[7]

In 2000 the United States expanded its Colombia assistance to the army, bringing U.S. resources to the war in the countryside and shifting the war's calculus. The official logic of the shift was to eradicate coca crops planted on increasing amounts of land, especially in the southern Colombian department of Putumayo. This "Push into southern Colombia" operation aimed to reduce the amount of land planted with coca by 50 percent by 2005.[8] The U.S. policy for this shift was expressed in a bilateral program known as Plan Colombia, inaugurated by a $1.3 billion package signed by President Bill Clinton on July 13, 2000. More than three-quarters of the funding was to aid Colombian military and police.[9]

For Plan Colombia's counterdrug operations, pilots from Virginia-based DynCorp flew aircraft that sprayed glyphosate, an herbicide marketed in the United States as Roundup, produced by Monsanto Corporation. DynCorp's contract with the State Department gave "command and control" authority to its personnel in the field, who were reported to participate in combat operations.[10] Because many coca fields were in territory controlled by the FARC, which sometimes fired on aircraft, the spray planes were to be accompanied by military aircraft provided by the United States under Plan Colombia. Roundup, however, was never meant to be administered from the air, as Monsanto itself warned at the time.[11]

State Department planners knew in advance that the aerial spraying and combat generated by the push into southern Colombia would displace rural farmers on a massive scale—itself a serious violation of human rights. In fact, they *budgeted* for the forced displacement of thirty thousand residents.[12] The initial Plan Colombia package included $15 million for "emergency resettlement and employment of persons displaced by the Push into Southern Colombia program."[13]

The political imperative in Washington to support supply-side counterdrug programs in 1999 may have been sufficient to engage the Clinton administration and Congress. Before the advent of medical marijuana reforms and increased cynicism about the drug war's effectiveness in the early twenty-first century, the drug prohibition narrative and plans to "go to the source" of cocaine production still appeared politically impregnable. General Barry McCaffrey, as director of National Drug Control Policy from 1996 to 2001, was also vociferous in urging policy makers to support a military push in Colombia.[14] Throughout the presidency of George W. Bush and Barack Obama's first term, fighting drug traffic would continue to dominate the discourse of the U.S. Southern Command (SouthCom) about its mission in the region: it was the only issue that SouthCom chiefs addressed in every single posture statement before Congress from 2000 to 2014.[15]

But other factors—apart from drug war goals—played important roles in Washington's decisions in 1999–2000, and after that time as well, to dramatically increase U.S. military involvement in Colombia. Chief among these were U.S. interests in Colombian oil, and vendors of Plan Colombia's products and services. The Pentagon's use of private contractors for military functions, which would grow exponentially under Defense Secretary Donald Rumsfeld, was already on the rise. Bureaucratic imperatives to protect institutional mandates and budgets were also important.[16]

Military hardware suppliers played a key role in gaining Clinton's and lawmakers' support for a military package. "Despite the drug czar's warnings," *Newsweek* reported in 2000, "few in the White House paid much heed until last September [1999], when Democratic pollster Mark Mellman showed up with worrisome news: the public perceived that 'drug use' was on the rise and was inclined to blame Democrats." Mellman's poll asked eight hundred respondents whether they supported a $2 billion spending increase to fund "tracking planes to be flown in drug producing areas"; 56 percent said they would. The poll, it turned out, was commissioned by Lockheed, which produced the P-3 radar aircraft used to interdict trafficking planes.[17]

Two leading helicopter manufacturers, Sikorsky Aircraft Corporation and Bell Textron, also actively lobbied for budget outlays from Plan Colombia. The companies gave free helicopter rides over Washington to Congressional staffers, and Textron even hired a former Colombian ambassador to lobby.[18] They needed a financial boost. "The market for military equipment abroad is not great these days, and obviously these companies have to sustain their production base," Army War College specialist Gabriel Marcella told the *Los Angeles Times* in 2000.[19] Emissaries from the Colombian Army and police, long in competition with each other, also vied to urge legislators in Washington to purchase the helicopters. Twenty-two Congressmen from Texas, where Textron is based, wrote a "Dear Colleague" letter in 2000 to support buying Textron's Huey UH-1H helicopters. Two members who led this effort, Democrat Martin Frost and Republican Kay Granger, represented

Fort Worth, where Textron built the Hueys, and each had received more than $30,000 in campaign contributions from Textron from 1995 to 2000.[20] Senate appropriators in May 2000 changed the Clinton administration's proposal for thirty Blackhawks to instead purchase seventy-five cheaper renovated Hueys.[21]

Senator Christopher Dodd, normally a skeptic of U.S. military involvement in Latin America, proposed dedicating funds to purchase Blackhawk helicopters produced by Sikorsky in his home state of Connecticut. Dodd had received $38,000 in campaign contributions from Sikorsky's parent company, United Technologies. In June 2000 Dodd offered a speech on the Senate floor and an amendment that would give the decision about helicopters to Pentagon and Colombian military officers–who had made clear their preference for Blackhawks.[22] In the end, the House-Senate conference committee split the difference in June 2000, approving the purchase of eighteen Blackhawks and forty-two Hueys, most of them for the military.[23]

In 2010 Congresswoman Granger became chair of the House Appropriations Subcommittee on State and Foreign Operations, which—with its Senate counterpart chaired by Senator Patrick Leahy from 2010 to 2014—controlled $40 billion in foreign assistance annually channeled through the State Department. Granger's committee has jurisdiction over the purchase of helicopters and other military equipment provided to Colombia and other countries, including Mexico and Central America. One of the principal vendors for those helicopters was located right in Granger's Fort Worth district—Textron, which produces Huey helicopters. Textron contributed $10,000 to Granger's campaign in 2010 and employed nearly four thousand people in Fort Worth and thousands more in the surrounding county.[24]

Another key Congressional actor who represented a major beneficiary of Plan Colombia was Frank Wolf of Falls Church, Virginia. DynCorp International has a major office in Falls Church and contributed $3,000 to Wolf's campaigns in 2007–8. (DynCorp also contributed $10,000 to Kay Granger's 2010 campaign.)[25] In 2005–6 Wolf chaired the State and Foreign Operations Subcommittee that appropriated $164 million for DynCorp in 2006 alone, and he was the subcommittee's ranking Republican in 2007–8.[26] Wolf gave particular credibility to Colombia spending, since he also was appointed to co-chair the Congressional Human Rights Caucus in 2001.[27]

One result of the political jockeying for Plan Colombia funds to go to U.S. companies was that the military officers on the receiving end often found the actual benefits of aid deliveries to be minimal. Of $820 million in military assistance, about half of that was for helicopters. "They were tin cans.

It was a struggle between those from Connecticut and the House Speaker," said a high-ranking Colombian officer who served on one of the work groups that designed the package. "The [helicopters] arrived and within a year they were no good," said another officer. Of the other $400 million, the first officer said, $200 million was for "buildings for the gringos," constructed at inflated rates. "My thesis was that the assistance was a lie," he told me. "The important thing there was the institutional support, the international support from the United States."[28]

In September 2000 the United States and Colombia signed technical agreements for implementing the assistance, which included language guaranteeing that "all goods and services acquired with U.S. Government funds . . . will be acquired in the United States and sent from the United States" unless another arrangement was agreed. What's more, the United States retained title to the helicopters and other aircraft that were part of the package. These arrangements made it nearly impossible for Colombia to audit the resources from the United States used for Plan Colombia. Colombia's audit agency found in 2004 that, in most cases, officers in each of the military branches were unaware of U.S. funding amounts or sources used to legally commit the funds, and that the Defense Ministry had no record of environmental impact studies for U.S.-sponsored construction in Colombia. Plan Colombia was in the hands of the United States.[29]

Failure of Colombian Negotiations

Plan Colombia was initially framed as supporting negotiations between the government in Bogotá and the FARC that began in 1998 in southern Caguán municipio. But changes in both countries shifted the plan's rhetoric and substance. The Bush administration's declaration of a "global war on terror" in response to the September 11, 2001, attacks opened the way to turn Plan Colombia into an openly counterinsurgent commitment. In 2002 any funding proposal in Washington with the name "antiterrorist" was likely to receive all that was requested. The suspension in the United States of even superficial interest in peace worldwide coincided with renewed warmongering in Colombia, as paramilitary rampages and guerrilla attacks pushed already anemic negotiations between the FARC and the government over the edge.

Promilitary observers frequently note that the FARC used the period of negotiations between 1998 and 2002 to intensify and gather more resources for warfare.[30] While this is true, the Colombian Army also used the period to rearm, and Plan Colombia was central to this rearmament. Nazih Richani argues that Washington's commitment to the war saved Colombia's elite from a negotiated solution to the war, which they had generally favored in the late 1990s.[31] When negotiations were finally broken off in February 2002, the United States helped supply coordinates for Colombian air strikes with hundreds of bombs against eighty-five FARC locations, launched from an air base in Meta Department.[32] When hardliner Álvaro Uribe became president six months later, the country was fully back at war.

In November 2002 National Security Presidential Directive 18 formally expanded the uses of Plan Colombia to include counterterrorist objectives as well as counterdrug missions.[33] The following year this executive action was solidified into legislation to support "a unified campaign against narcotics trafficking, illegal armed groups, and organizations designated as Foreign Terrorist Organizations." This legislative language was repeated every year afterward.[34] That decision was critical to what followed. While previously counterinsurgency goals were typically subordinate to drug war objectives, now the reverse would be true: counterdrug goals were secondary to fighting the FARC. It also meant that the United States would support Colombian military units throughout the country, not only those that had counterdrug missions, thus expanding the geography and purposes of U.S. assistance. In the words of one U.S. advisor, in 2003, "there [was] a directive to sync our aid to the [Colombian military's] strategy."[35] It also meant that the United States would measure the success of its own policy and investment not so much by the metrics of coca eradication and cocaine seizures as by the progress of the war against the guerrillas—which would lend itself to the military's "body count" benchmarks of success.

In a subsequent semifictionalized account of the counterdrug base in Tres Esquinas where General Mario Montoya was commander in 2001, another U.S. advisor quoted a general he called "Montalvo" as saying: "Colonel, read my lips. . . . I want guerrilla base camps. . . . I want body counts." "As far as I'm concerned," the advisor wrote, "the host nation should rely on whatever works for them."[36]

Oily Policy

In addition to counterinsurgency goals, U.S. interests in oil also shaped the Plan Colombia agenda. U.S. and other international oil companies have a long history of involvement in Colombia's turbulent internal affairs. Texaco began operations in the Magdalena Medio region of Colombia in 1926, and its questionable land acquisitions formed the basis for considerable conflicts in the region in later decades.[37] In the 1980s Texaco paid army battalions in the Magdalena Medio to carry out an antiguerrilla campaign, which was also financed by the Medellin Cartel's second most powerful capo, Gonzalo Rodríguez Gacha, whose daughter had been kidnapped by FARC guerrillas. The traffickers financed paramilitary death squads, and thousands of persons were killed in the campaign between 1982 and 1985.[38]

The Colombian Army made protecting the oil industry part of its core mission in the 1990s, a commitment that continued during Plan Colombia. In 1992 foreign oil companies began paying the Colombian Army a dollar per barrel in a special tax to protect their facilities in Colombia. An army commander estimated in 1996 that half of all troops were engaged in protecting oil and mining properties.[39] The army commander installed in 1998 on the United States' recommendation, General Jorge Enrique Mora, increased the size of the conscript army in order to relieve professional soldiers guarding infrastructure, who would be redeployed to counterinsurgency operations. In 2001 some ten thousand professional soldiers were transferred to newly created mobile brigades supported by the United States, and they were replaced by regular conscripts in eight dedicated Energy and Roads battalions (increased to eleven in 2003). Dedicated U.S. funding of $4 million for infrastructure security continued annually through 2007.[40]

In 1996, after evidence came to light of the presence of narco-dollars in President Ernesto Samper's 1994 campaign, the Clinton administration "decertified" Colombian cooperation in drug control, which put at risk but did not suspend U.S. assistance to Colombia. In the wake of that decision, eleven blue chip multinational companies, including Occidental Oil, Bechtel, Caterpillar, Enron, Colgate-Palmolive, and BP Amoco, formed the U.S.-Colombia Business Partnership to promote U.S. business interests in Colombia. Initially focused on countering the impact of decertification on U.S. exports, the partnership rapidly turned its energies to increasing U.S. military and police assistance, for which it lobbied intensively.[41] Southern Command chief General Charles Wilhelm testified in 1998 that oil discoveries in Colombia increased its strategic importance.[42]

In 1999 Occidental Oil became the partnership's lead company to lobby for the Plan Colombia assistance package. Occidental held a controlling interest in the Caño Limón-Conveñas oil pipeline that runs from oil fields in Arauca, at the Venezuelan border, to the Caribbean coast, and was providing helicopters for the army's use in Arauca.[43] Vice President Al Gore also had extensive family stock holdings in the Los Angeles–based Occidental, which contributed $1.5 million to Congressional and presidential campaigns and spent $8.7 million lobbying U.S. officials—mostly regarding Colombia—between 1995 and 2000.[44]

Occidental's vice president, Lawrence Meriage, testified before Congress in February 2000 to support the aid package for the Colombian army and police. Meriage said that "oil development operations . . . are fundamental to the success of Plan Colombia," and he urged lawmakers not to limit the aid package to units operating in southern Colombia. Putumayo, he said, is far from "the northern regions where the bulk of existing and prospective oil development takes place," and concentrating forces there might push guerrillas into neighboring Ecuador, where Occidental "has operations . . . some 40 kilometers from the Colombian border."[45]

Meanwhile, Gore's opponent in the 2000 presidential election, George W. Bush, had his own Colombian oil connections. Bush's company, Harken Energy Corporation, and its predecessor Arbusto Oil had not done well for their investors in the 1980s, but Bush's connections served them and him well. "I learned the value of personal diplomacy from seeing my father make friendships and relationships with foreign leaders," Bush said. He owned 345,426 shares in the company by 1993, when he sold them in preparation for his campaign for governor of Texas.[46]

George W. Bush met Rodrigo Villamizar in the late 1960s at Harvard Business School, and Villamizar became a key Latin America advisor to Bush. When Villamizar was tapped to be Colombia's energy minister in the mid-1990s, he adjudicated three oil contracts for Bush's Harken Energy with Colombia's oil company Ecopetrol.[47] Villamizar would later be sentenced to four years in prison for an act of corruption.[48] In October 1999 President Andrés Pastrana met in Austin with Governor Bush, who introduced him to a group of oil executives and investors. According to Pastrana, Bush said at that time that he still held stock in Harken.[49]

The declaration of the "global war on terror" in late 2001 pushed the protection of oil production in Colombia out into the open as a policy objective. The rationale was that the new war made Middle Eastern sources of oil less stable, so that the flow of oil from Colombia—then the eighth largest supplier of oil to the United States—was more critical. In addition, guerrilla attacks on multinational oil facilities in Colombia were affecting their profitability, while paramilitaries frequently stole oil from the pipelines.[50]

Moreover, according to one oil company president in 2004, Colombian political leaders were then "desperate" that the country could return to being a net oil importer if it did not develop untapped oil wells, some of which were located in conflict regions. The state oil company, Ecopetrol, in 2001 reduced its mandatory share of joint oil ventures from 50 percent to 30 percent, providing further incentive to U.S. companies to push for oil exploration and production.[51]

As stalled negotiations between the Pastrana government and FARC were about to break down in January 2002, Colombian officials lobbied in Washington to expand the mandate for U.S. military assistance beyond counternarcotics missions.[52] In February U.S. ambassador to Colombia Anne Patterson announced that President Bush would request an additional $98 million to train and equip the Colombian Army's Eighteenth Brigade to protect the Caño Limón pipeline owned partly by Occidental, located near the Venezuelan border, against guerrilla attacks. "There are more than 300 infrastructure points in Colombia that are strategic for the United States," Patterson said.[53] Congress subsequently approved funds for the resulting Infrastructure Security Strategy (ISS) for 2003 and 2004.

The cozy relationship between the U.S. Embassy and Occidental in particular was demonstrated in late 2002, during a conversation I had with the embassy's human rights officer, Stewart Tuttle. The U.S. peace organization Fellowship of Reconciliation had been urging Tuttle to visit San José de Apartadó after a paramilitary raid on the settlement of La Unión had prompted residents to flee a few months before. Tuttle cheerfully explained that his schedule had been freed up because he was going to be visiting Arauca in an Occidental helicopter, but the trip had been canceled.

Visions from Below

Once Plan Colombia was approved in 2000, and the neoconservative-fueled global war on terrorism was in full swing, the burden of proof for changing policy shifted, weighing heavily on critics of the funding. Drug war ideology, material interests, and anti-Communism determined the dominant discourses of U.S. policy regarding Colombia. But grassroots voices consistently challenged those narratives by highlighting the contradictions in the dominant story and the unannounced failures in the lives of people victimized by the policies, in both Colombia and the United States.

A key challenge to the dominant narrative came from School of the Americas (SOA) Watch. Father Roy Bourgeois founded SOA Watch in 1990, initially in response to the killing in November 1989 of six Jesuit priests, their housekeeper, and her daughter by Salvadoran soldiers, who had received military training at the SOA. The movement organized a weekend-long vigil at the gates of Fort Benning, Georgia, on the anniversary of those murders each November. Through much of the 1990s, the movement focused heavily on the SOA's client military in El Salvador, reflecting its base of Central America activists and its orientation to Catholic martyrs, which included Salvadoran Archbishop Óscar Romero and four American churchwomen, also killed by SOA graduates, in 1980. This shifted during the second half of the 1990s, as the United States became more militarily involved in Colombia and the Cold War conflicts in Central America concluded. The ritual reading at the vigil of thousands of names of victims of SOA graduates—many increasingly from Colombia—also impacted activists at the vigil. Revelations in 1996 that the school had used interrogation manuals that countenanced torture and assassination received mainstream attention and fueled the movement.[54] By 1998 more than seven thousand people showed up at the vigil against SOA at Fort Benning and two thousand of them committed civil disobedience.[55]

In the fall of 2000 Congress nominally closed the School of the Americas and created the Western Hemisphere Institute for Security Cooperation (WHINSEC) in its stead with an expanded human rights curriculum at the same location. Though little changed in the school, the closure represented at least a symbolic victory for the protest movement that gathered every November at Fort Benning.

Promoting Human Rights as a Selling Point for Commitment to War

In the development of U.S. policy, self-interested corporate and political motives cohabited with loftier goals to promote respect for human rights. And human rights legislation such as the Leahy Law gave critical political cover to liberals to support military packages they otherwise might have opposed. The Leahy Law requires the State Department to exclude from assistance foreign military and police units for whom there is credible evidence that members have committed gross rights abuses, unless they have been brought or are being brought to justice. But the law is only implemented *after* Congress has decided on foreign aid packages, whose overall amount is not affected by the exclusion of units.

Independent of the Leahy Law and specific to Colombia, beginning in 2000, Congress required the State Department to certify, before each "tranche" of deliveries of U.S. assistance, that the Colombian armed forces and government were fulfilling several human rights conditions, including severing the military's ties with paramilitary groups and advances in the investigation and prosecution of human rights crimes. As part of the certification process, which applied to a percentage of the overall package, the State Department was also required to consult with human rights organizations in both Colombia and the United States. It was liberal Congressional members, though, in the final Congressional debate on Plan Colombia, who inserted a provision for a presidential waiver of the human rights conditions for "national security interests."[56] During the first cycle of human rights certification, in 2000, the Clinton administration waived the conditions.[57]

At the time, established human rights groups were reporting that paramilitaries were responsible for 79 percent of the twenty political killings that occurred daily on average in Colombia.[58] The resulting message, then, was that U.S. national security was indifferent to massive human rights violations by paramilitary groups. At the very least, it threw into doubt the stated Plan Colombia objective of increased respect for human rights in Colombia.

Both the Leahy Law and the certification process were subject to interpretation by the executive branch, and nongovernmental groups had no control over their implementation. Those groups presented compelling evidence that Colombia had not met certification requirements, and that the United States was aiding military units that carried out extrajudicial killings, in violation of the Leahy Law.[59] But in its statements and human rights reports, the State Department claimed progress by Colombia in respect for human rights, ignored paramilitary-state collaboration, and highlighted guerrilla groups' kidnapping, recruitment of children, and harms from guerrilla landmines.[60] Some human rights advocates supported the certification requirement as a mechanism to pressure the Colombian state to reduce violations and advance human rights cases in the courts, because it periodically required the State Department to directly engage human rights groups and concerns. The laws added to the tools for dissuading human rights violations. But one overall impact of the certification process was to narrow measurement of respect for human rights to a few emblematic cases on which NGOs focused their pressure for change.[61]

A similar dynamic came into play when members of Congress submitted "Dear Colleague" letters on Colombian human rights to the executive branch. Liberal legislators who were unwilling to challenge Plan Colombia's military focus and funding could appeal for progress on specific cases or communities, and NGOs with close relationships with those communities worked with those legislators to generate wider awareness and support in Congress. In April 2001 thirty-eight Congressional representatives, led by James McGovern and Janice Schakowsky, wrote to Colombian president Andrés Pastrana to express concern about the March 5 paramilitary attack on San José de Apartadó as well as the larger history of violence against the community.[62] Twelve of the signers had voted for Plan Colombia funding in 2000.[63] Subsequent "Dear Colleague" letters in 2002 and 2004 focused on paramilitary killings in San José and threats to deport international groups accompanying the Peace Community, signed by several dozen legislators, again including members who voted for the Colombia military assistance package.[64]

Most Congressional letters after 2005 were directed at administration officials in Washington and more directly urged U.S. policy determinations, especially refraining from issuing a human rights certification, though the appeals were still generally framed around specific human rights violations. By then, military funding by Congress for Plan Colombia was on autopilot. It would take much more than letters from Congressional Democrats to change either policy or facts on the ground.

CHAPTER 4
"WE WANT A WITNESS"

ACCOMPANIMENT IN SAN JOSÉ DE APARTADÓ

In response to a nomination by the Colombia Support Network (CSN) based in Madison, Wisconsin, the Fellowship of Reconciliation (FOR) in 1998 awarded its annual international peace prize to the Peace Community of San José de Apartadó. As a pacifist organization using nonviolence to resist war and injustice, FOR was inspired by the community's courage and values. A representative of the community, Gildardo Tuberquia, traveled to Madison, Wisconsin, in December 1998 to receive the award from FOR's director, Father John Dear, who was very impressed with Gildardo. In January 2000 the community sent an invitation to FOR to join the third anniversary commemoration of declaring themselves a peace community in March 1997.

As coordinator of FOR's Latin America program, I received the invitation on our fax machine in San Francisco, and I thought it would take too much time to go. It was not possible for a visitor to arrive in San José in even a long day of travel: instead, you needed to fly to Medellín, stay overnight, then take another flight to Carepa, get from there to the Apartadó bus station, then take an open-air *buseta* an hour and a half up the road to San José. It seemed like a lot just to respond to an awardee's invitation.

But a month after I received the community's fax, shortly after darkness fell on Saturday, February 19, armed men entered the San José town center with a list of names in hand. During that day, army troops had detained several residents at a military roadblock set up on the single road leading into the town center, a few minutes away. Some people saw about twenty uniformed armed men gathered at a farm on the same road during the day. After 7:00 p.m., the men entered the soccer field, divided into three or four groups, and calmly walked into town. As people ran, they said, "Don't look at us or we'll kill you."

The gunmen went to the small town's phone switchboard and cut cables (to the loudspeaker, possibly thinking they were phone lines). In the central plaza with its basketball court, Albeiro Montoya fled and was cut down by gunfire. The men then proceeded to little shops and, one by one, killed four other local merchants because, they said, they sold goods to guerrillas. One of them, Mario Urrego, said to his neighbors, "Don't worry, it's the army," before they shot him in front of his family.[1] He had reportedly recognized one of the gunmen, who wore army insignia on their uniforms. Two hooded men, one of them recognized by community members as a guerrilla who had surrendered to the army the previous month, pointed out victims.[2]

In a statement the following day, the Colombian Catholic human rights group Justicia y Paz said the killings were foretold by a military "intelligence report" disclosed in the media the previous month. The report said that peace communities—specifically naming San José de Apartadó—were being used by the FARC for their attacks.[3] Residents slept for days afterward in a community granary, instead of their houses, because of their fear.

Observers from the human rights group Peace Brigades International (PBI) who witnessed the February 19 paramilitary incursion called their colleagues every few minutes during the attack, setting off a chain of calls to national and international organizations before the gunmen had even departed. I spoke with one of the PBI witnesses, Andrew Miller, when he returned to Washington. Andrew was understandably shaken up, but undeterred. In light of the massacre, I did not feel I could turn down the community's invitation, and so I booked flights to go to Apartadó.

On the plane from Miami I sat next to Carlos, a young U.S. Army Ranger on his way to serve in Colombia. He served a stint in Colombia in 1997–99 and had recently come from Kosovo, where two months before a soldier in his unit had lost it, raping and then killing an eleven-year-old Albanian girl.[4] Other soldiers had committed abuses in Kosovo—five men in the same unit were disciplined for abusing civilians—but Carlos's buddies were in shock. Carlos was concerned with the military's economic legacy. "Will they remember that we established a market system, all the good things we did?" he asked.

Carlos thought the United States should not get more involved in Colombia because the people would end up hating Americans. Colombian soldiers, he said, were afraid of losing their jobs, and "half of them join the paramilitaries" if they get kicked out. "It's all about money." Despite his fear that Colombians would hate us, he believed that people want to be with Americans because "we're the big guy on the block, we kick ass."

For its third anniversary in March, the San José Peace Community had organized a three-day collective walk to visit its settlements in the Abibe Mountains. San José is a *corregimiento*, or district, part of Apartadó, whose mayor a few weeks before my arrival had been arrested for participating in a paramilitary organization.[5] Those of us who took part in the walk included dozens of community members, representatives of peace communities in Dabeiba and Cacarica, international volunteers from PBI, a woman from Pax Christi in Belgium, a Canadian priest named Brendan who had previously lived in San José, me, and, on the third day, officials from both the Canadian and U.S. embassies.

Before departing, community leaders sat with us in the community building's second-floor room, shared a meal prepared by nuns living in San José, and talked about the region's history. The main exponent of this history was a thirty-one-year-old soft-spoken peasant named Luis Eduardo Guerra. Guerra pointed out that the army killed peasants in the 1970s before paramilitaries ever arrived in the region. The absence of any state presence except the army compelled residents to organize their own schools, health clinics, and agricultural economy.

Most combat occurred in the rural hamlets, not in the town center of San José. The first massacre inside the town itself was in September 1996, when paramilitaries killed the co-op leader and three others. Soldiers departed that evening; the same night paramilitaries came in. "So-called paramilitaries," Guerra said, "because some peasants said that they recognized them" as soldiers.

Some five hundred people signed the Peace Community declaration on March 23, 1997, by which they agreed to a set of principles. They would not support any armed group—materially, with information, by selling food, or by taking up arms. They would not ask armed groups to resolve conflicts. They would not drink alcohol. They also would oppose injustice and impunity for political violence. They agreed to elect a seven-member internal council that would lead the Peace Community. And they would collaborate in community work days, which was also a safety measure.[6] "The truth is, when we declared the peace community, it was from fear," Guerra said.

During the same period, the AUC continued to consolidate its hold on most of Urabá. Supported by Chiquita Brands and local banana growers as

Fig. 4.1. Luis Eduardo Guerra. PHOTOGRAPH BY JUTTA MEIER-WIEDENBACH.

well as the Seventeenth Brigade, the AUC's Banana Block exercised control in the towns, including Apartadó and Turbo, as well as the road between Apartadó and San José, while the FARC continued to operate in the Abibe Mountains.[7]

Within the first year of the Peace Community's founding, forty-eight of its members were killed, despite the support of Bishop Duarte and the Church's human rights group Justicia y Paz. Guerrillas murdered five people, but most of the killings that year and later were carried out by a combination of army and paramilitary forces.[8]

In April 1999 a group of hooded paramilitary gunmen came into town and murdered community cofounder Anibal Jiménez and two others. The attack strongly marked the community, particularly because Jiménez was an important leader, who had composed the Peace Community's hymn and was responsible for its educational programs.[9] Among the witnesses to this killing were Luis Eduardo Guerra and his stepbrother, Wilmar Dario Tuberquia Valderrama. Dario gave testimony in 2000 to judicial investigators about the massacre, though he could not identify the hooded men.[10]

Luis Eduardo traveled to Bogota in March 1998 to participate in a workshop also attended by two Spanish representatives of PBI. He described to others present how the army attempted to legitimize its presence in San José through psychological operations, by offering games to children, giving away kitchenware, and sending dentists, but that community members decided to exhibit social indifference, simply refusing the military's gifts. And the military departed.

After deciding in 1997 to stay in San José, leaders had planned a new cooperative store in an attempt to restore the community's economy. News of the plan reached guerrillas in the mountains, who came down to confirm the news. That October, guerrillas killed three Peace Community leaders, including one of the most respected, Ramiro Correa. "The decision had already been made," wrote PBI's Carlos Beristain. "When they killed the three leaders, the community was mute and in rage."[11]

Safety is relative. For Apartadó in 1997, which had seen seven massacres of civilians the previous year,[12] the killing of forty-eight community members in a year was a terrible loss. But it probably still represented greater relative safety than the alternatives of fragmenting and dispersing themselves to nearby cities or other lands.[13]

By 1997 community members already had profound distrust of the Colombian institutions responsible for protecting them and bringing armed groups to justice for crimes against campesinos. Instead, they increasingly appealed to the international community, including the Inter-American system of the Organization of American States (OAS). After the many murders in the first year after their declaration, community leaders worked with Justicia y Paz to bring their case before the OAS's Inter-American Human Rights Commission, which visited San José de Apartadó and issued precautionary measures (an advisory ruling) in December 1997, while also recommending that the Inter-American Human Rights Court issue "provisional measures"—a ruling binding on the Colombian state.[14] The community effectively used its victimization by state forces, allied paramilitaries, and guerrillas to mobilize international support and solidarity, and used that support to deter further aggression and impunity.

The Inter-American Human Rights Commission is based in Washington and represents states, although its members and staff typically are professional human rights attorneys. The Peace Community was thus implicitly appealing to an external agency that was "above." The involvement of the Inter-American Commission would lend important institutional legitimacy to the community's claims of violations, of its nonstate project, and of the need for state protection.

After Luis Eduardo's talk, we set out on the morning of March 20. Other community leaders had just met with a representative of Colombian vice president Gustavo Bell. "We expected more," one of them said of the conversation. The air was still cool, with international visitors and several others on horseback, the rest on foot. Father Brendan insisted on walking; he said he preferred it. I rode a horse belonging to a community leader known as El Negro, but my long legs made my feet and the stirrups scrape frequently against the many rocks on the muddy path. We climbed up into cloud forest, passing bright reds in the flowers, tropical birds, and the cocoa pods ripe on the low trees. The horses and mules worked hard carrying us and themselves up and down the hills, eating and dropping manure as they went, once in a while galloping on a straightaway or across a tiny ravine. The visitors from North America, Europe, and Afro-Colombian river communities of the Atrato region, not accustomed to riding horses, were tired.

We spent the first night, after five hours of rough climbing, in La Esperanza, one of the Peace Community's settlements to which families had recently returned. The visitors must have outnumbered those living in the settlement, but the organization of food and sleeping places was impressive. Everyone was taken care of, and a group of campesinos played guitar, sang country songs, even danced.

After dinner, community members symbolically reenacted their displacement and the founding of the community. Kids struggled to read aloud from handwritten texts, one of which was an ideological tract about imperialism and the Patriotic Union party. Others were more straightforward: how the families lived in the woods with nothing to eat and nothing to give their children when they cried. How they, too, cried. "This is the word of God," they read at the end of each passage.

The following day, we descended from La Esperanza to La Unión, where we stayed the night. Both are settlements or *veredas* within the San José de Apartadó district. Residents had fled La Unión and other veredas in early

1997 but had returned en masse in March 1998, on the first anniversary of the Peace Community's declaration. In a house occupied by nuns from the graphically named Sisters of the Slaves of Jesus, we commemorated the occasion by painting our names on a banner that the community would later keep intact and display for years.

The next morning the group was joined by Michael Fitzpatrick and Nicholas Coghlan, diplomats from the U.S. and Canadian embassies, respectively. Coghlan had visited La Unión the previous year. "In La Unión, it was evident that the concept of the Community of Peace worked, and worked well," he later wrote. "This was partly because the place was small enough for regular village meetings not to be too onerous and for solidarity to be easily maintained."[15] As we headed back to the San José town center, Fitzpatrick rode his horse with confidence and flair; he told me he had come to San José "to get out of the office."

That night, Luis Eduardo, other community leaders, and visitors addressed more than one hundred people gathered on the square. When it was his turn, Mike Fitzpatrick said he hoped "those in Caguán" (i.e., the FARC, concentrated for negotiations in San Vicente del Caguán in southern Colombia) were listening to this message of peace. Coghlan said that people cannot imagine how cold it can get where he comes from, but he expressed solidarity with those in the square.

The North American diplomats and I talked during the event at the edge of the dark plaza. Fitzpatrick recalled a soccer star who publicly got on his knees to thank the Rodríguez Orejuela brothers, who sponsored his team and were responsible for many deaths from the tons of cocaine they trafficked into the United States. There was no condemnation of the soccer star. "It shows how far this country has to go," he said.

"This might be polemical," I said, "but Madeleine Albright, when she was interviewed about the sanctions on Iraq, was asked about the World Health Organization estimate that 250,000 kids have died as a result of them, and she said, 'It was worth it.'" There was no opprobrium of her by President Clinton. "This is not the only country with a long way to go," I said. Fitzpatrick nodded quietly.

The following morning, a large group marched around the San José town center under the burning sun, stopping at each place where five men had been killed on February 19. Then there was a Mass, and then the terrible news: two members of the peace community in nearby Cacarica had been killed the day before in the port city of Turbo, where hundreds of displaced community members were living in the stadium until they could negotiate safe conditions for their return. Otoniel Bautista, who lived in one of Turbo's barrios, was killed in his home; the gunmen then walked casually into the street, showed schoolchildren their weapons, and said, "You didn't see anything, you know nothing, you don't know us."[16] Another Cacarica community member, Ricardo Goez, attended Otoniel's wake in the evening, returned home, then was killed while watching television. Ana, a Cacarica community member, told me about the deaths, then began to cry.

I accepted a ride leaving San José and met up with the PBI team at their house in Turbo. There, members of the PBI team asked me how I was. "Sad," I said. They told me they were going to the burial and did I want to go? Yes, I did.

At the church, the priest blessed the Eucharist; a hundred or so people sat in the pews, with the coffin in the center aisle. Then we marched solemnly to the cemetery. I had brought my camera, and raised it to take a picture as the mourners left the church, but I couldn't. It might give offense, or provoke fear. But on the way, a member of Justicia y Paz told me that the family wanted me to take photos of the funeral march, of the coffin, and of Oto's face. Okay, I said.

We entered the cemetery, and the pallbearers laid the casket on a bench under a kiosk. The top was raised to show Oto's face, and family and friends, crying, pushed close to see him, sobbing, one woman near collapse, a boy saying, "Papi! Papi!" Old and young, women, men, boys all wailing, others trying to ensure everyone had a chance to see.

Men brought the coffin out into the cemetery to slide it into its place in a crypt, and the pitch of crying rose again, one woman throwing herself on the casket, not wanting to see it go; another woman who had earlier been so composed, his eldest daughter, had tears pouring from her face; and finally the casket was put into the wall. A man took the bricks and mortar to close up the wall, the cries subsiding, a young boy throwing a last rose into the hole onto the casket. There was quiet when the burial was over and done. Then we walked back through the town to the Justicia y Paz house. The next day, March 24, I returned to the United States.

From the moment of arriving in San José de Apartadó's dusty center to walking sadly through Turbo after the funeral, I struggled with a singular question: How can we make a positive difference for these people from back in the United States? It was hard to remain indifferent to the kind of suffering I had seen. Several days after returning to California, I spoke with Michael Schiffer, Senator Dianne Feinstein's foreign policy director in Washington, who said he did not see the enormous military aid package known as Plan Colombia as an escalation of war. His response underscored that what seemed to be common sense to me and others I knew would not by itself be persuasive among Democrats in Congress who supported a military approach. I decided to organize a group to return to San José de Apartadó.

Two subsequent events in 2000 marked the community as well as international involvement in its fate. On July 8, masked paramilitary gunmen entered the San José Peace Community settlement of La Unión and ordered six men, community leaders, into the settlement's central clearing, as women and children watched. While a helicopter believed to be the army's flew overhead, the paramilitaries executed the men, then told those remaining that they must leave La Unión. But they did not leave.[17]

In November the Inter-American Human Rights Court issued provisional measures—a binding ruling—that mandated the protection of members of the Peace Community. The ruling applied to all members of the Peace Community, even if they were not identified by name in the ruling, and required the participation of the Peace Community and their representatives (at that time, Justicia y Paz) in the planning and implementation of any measures to protect the community and its members. It also required the government to investigate the many crimes that led to the ruling, bring those responsible to justice, and inform the court of progress every two months.[18]

Around the same time, a secret report by the Seventeenth Brigade's intelligence unit (B-2), later disclosed in court documents, reflected how threatening the military believed this and other peace communities to be. The report discussed Cacarica and other Afro-Colombian peace communities along the Atrato River basin in Chocó but dedicated considerable attention to San José, detailing its history, organization, and international support, and naming eleven other settlements seeking to become peace communities. "The FARC has ably infiltrated these settlements," the report said. "The Peace communities, with their active neutrality, would become complicit with the delinquent and a State Within the State." It called on the brigade commander to "regulate and condition requests" to recognize "peace territories."[19]

An international activist delegation visited San José de Apartadó in March 2001, co-organized by FOR and the human rights organization Global Exchange, which had hired a young Colombian American organizer named Sandra Alvarez. The two organizations shared an office in San Francisco's

Mission District, and we reached out to activists and others to participate. The Peace Community's U.S. profile grew when the *Boston Globe* reported on February 21 about a visit to San José by Congressional representatives Jim McGovern and Janice Schakowsky. The *Globe* quoted Luis Eduardo Guerra: "The only weapon we have to survive is our neutrality and transparency."[20] Moved and impressed by the community's peace commitment, McGovern and Schakowsky mobilized when, two weeks after their visit, paramilitaries burned several houses in San José and threatened international volunteers. The two Representatives organized a letter signed by thirty-eight members of Congress, urging President Pastrana to respond to the attacks.[21]

During the three days that the delegation accompanied the community, our group saw the place where a young man lost his leg to a landmine left by the army. While the man cried, troops nearby not only did not seek help but laughed, an indication of how far the war had dehumanized its participants. We talked with a young man to whom the army had offered money the previous month in exchange for information, and more money for other assistance. "Together with the paramilitaries we have to finish off those dogs," they told him. "By blood and fire, sooner or later we will take San José." The man said he refused their offer.

On a Sunday afternoon, while the group watched boys catch catfish in the little river that runs down from the peace community settlement of La Unión, soldiers reportedly told community members farther up the path returning from the town that they would leave orphans like the last time, referring to the massacre in La Unión the previous July.

After dinner one evening during our visit to San José, we gathered with the community's Internal Council on the second floor of the bodega. Eduar Lancheros, a seminarian with Justicia y Paz who had worked with the Peace Community since its founding, did most of the talking. He told us that the government had established an interagency commission, in response to the July 2000 massacre in La Unión, to investigate who was responsible for this and other crimes. The commission was to include representatives of the attorney general's office, inspector general, vice presidency, and observers from the United Nations, but the community had no confidence that it would lead to identifying or punishing those who had attacked the community, or even preventing further violence. Of more than sixty murders of Peace Community members up to that point, there had been no justice for any of them. "All of the previous massacres were announced by the army, and were carried out," Eduar told us. "We know there will be another massacre, we know we will go down, though we don't know when or who will fall. We ask that you be with us and keep the memory of this experience alive. We want you to be a witness to our process."

The community wanted FOR to come to Apartadó every six weeks when the commission met. We said it might not be practical to come all that way every six weeks, that it might be more feasible to have someone stay in San José. In fact, with the protective accompaniment of PBI in mind, we believed that such a presence might mean more than just being a witness. Maybe, through an international team backed up by a network of institutional support for the civilian population's rights, the Peace Community would not go down, not this time.

The same day of our meeting with community leaders in the community center, the United Nations reported on human rights in Colombia in 2000, stating that its personnel had received direct testimony of the military's participation in the February 19 massacre, as well as evidence of army censuses and paramilitary roadblocks in San José.[22]

When our delegation returned to the United States, we set about responding to the community's request. We would not be the first international organization to provide protective accompaniment in San José de Apartadó—PBI volunteers had accompanied the community since 1998, when it established a team in Urabá, with an office and house in the adjacent port city of Turbo, and had initiated its international accompaniment project in Colombia in 1994, with teams in the cities of Bogotá and Barrancabermeja.

———

Protective accompaniment seeks to strengthen the security of activists, organizations, and communities threatened with political violence, through a physical presence of foreign citizens who are backed by an international network of support and advocacy for human rights. It seeks to intervene in the chain of influence on perpetrators of political violence, using the international community's power and the interests that both national and international actors have in respecting human rights.[23]

In this respect, accompaniers are not "human shields" as some accounts have suggested. No one believes that foreign nationals can stop a bullet, once the decision is made to fire it, any better than can the activists whom the foreigners are accompanying. But accompaniment uses physical presence as both a signal to potential perpetrators and as a witness and observer of risks faced by activists, in order to affect—in advance—the decision to fire a bullet or commit other abuses. In political violence, a triggerman—they are nearly always men—never decides alone to commit aggression. He is tied to organizations that have links to state actors, are sensitive to their international standing, or both. Accompaniment organizations engage and work to build international and national networks of awareness of the groups they accompany and the dangers they face. They do this through contact with government officials from the accompaniers' countries—legislators, embassies, foreign ministries—with other international bodies such as United Nations agencies, and with grassroots networks, churches, and nongovernmental organizations.

For PBI, the emphasis on protection of human rights defenders is based on a premise that those people represent a core of organization for social change. Even if other parts of the organization are exiled, weakened, or even destroyed, the survival of that core would make possible the continuity of work for social changes toward a country in peace with social justice. In that sense, the goals go beyond protection itself. And the process of reflection about what are the core points or individuals of an organization or community occurs jointly and in coordination with the accompanied group.[24]

At least a dozen international organizations have provided unarmed civilian protection—or accompaniment—in Colombia since 1994. The first request to PBI for accompaniment in Colombia was from the Association of Family Members of Detained and Disappeared in Colombia (Asociación de Familiares de Detenidos y Desaparecidos, ASFADDES) in 1990, but PBI was not then in a position to assemble a project. It was not until early 1993, when ASFADDES, Justicia y Paz, and the Regional Committee for the Defense of Human Rights in Barrancabermeja separately sent requests to PBI that the organization assembled a committee and exploratory team. That team was made up of four people with PBI experience in Guatemala and El Salvador, who brought what they had learned from accompaniment there during a two-month visit in May and June 1993. After fundraising and extensive internal decision-making, PBI established a project in Colombia in October 1994, with teams in Bogota and Barrancabermeja. It would expand with teams in Urabá in 1998 and Medellín in 1999.[25]

In many ways, PBI opened the way for other accompaniment organizations in Colombia, demonstrating that the methods they used worked. Other accompaniment projects—religious and secular, North American and European—followed PBI in the 1990s and the following decade. Some had permanent teams, while others organized shorter presences. Some focused on specific regions and partners, while others spanned broad reaches of Colombia's geography. Most were small, with teams of no more than ten people.

International accompaniment in Colombia is a form of unarmed civilian protection and has several features. As some people use the word "accompaniment," it is a religious and Christian concept, tied to human solidarity, to the Catholic social justice principle of "the preferential option for the poor," and to the apparently simple act of *showing up*. Together with the complexities of living in a conflict zone, this physical act helped accompanier Peter Cousins to keep his faith "incarnational, not in some pious construction . . . rather than lofty, priestly sermons from the pulpit, the Peace Community— and circumstances generally—preached their own homily to me."[26] In a similar sense, accompaniment often includes emotional support and the legitimization of narratives of those who are accompanied, which can be critical in a conflict where public opinion has been hostile or indifferent to those narratives. In Colombia, accompaniment can also refer to support or collaboration: a human rights defender, for example, who has a legal case or litigation for a human rights violation is "accompanying" the process.

The concept in Colombia is also tied to the *dissuasion* of violence, and to the analysis that indicates that international presence has dissuasion against violations committed by the armed forces and paramilitaries, but not as much against violations by the guerrillas. As such, this dissuasive presence is not so much an *interposition* between armed groups as *standing at the side of* an unarmed group that is under threat of violence.[27]

A premise of accompaniment as a conscious strategy is that the Colombian government has been sensitive to its international image. Although that sensitivity has varied over time, it is a prerequisite for accompaniment to function well as protection. This also means that international accompaniment attempts to leverage power above—primarily the power of European, U.S., and Canadian governments and of international bodies such as the UN— to affect conditions on the ground. The perceived race of accompaniers— usually but not always white—is also a signifier that is used to help dissuade perpetrators. "The communities that are resisting or returning from displacement tend to be in the racialized 'frontier' regions, and as such the whiteness of accompaniers stands out there all the more as 'out of place,'" writes Sara Koopman in her study of accompaniment and privilege in Colombia. "The war is driven by desires for capitalist development and 'modernity,' which is imagined as white. But accompaniers are not in these regions to 'develop' them, but rather standing with those who are struggling for a different vision of development."[28]

Those with greater race and passport privilege standing "at the side of" those targeted with political violence can both employ and subvert the categories of "above" and "below," by highlighting the experience of those "below" as protagonists in the narratives circulated among those "above," and by locating representatives of people from "above" and "below" in the same physical space. But by leveraging the power of both racism and of states (especially the wealthy and militarily powerful states of Europe and North America), international accompaniment also runs the risk of reinforcing the inequalities in security that it is attempting to address. Some groups intentionally counter this potential for reinforced inequality through selection and preparation of volunteers and emphasizing that the human rights defenders and communities they accompany are the protagonists and speak for themselves.[29]

An international presence does not function to dissuade every kind of threat, according to accompaniers I interviewed in Colombia in 2015. "With the guerrillas, I doubt that our presence has an effect. The presence of foreigners has never been a force of dissuasion in those cases," observed a Canadian accompanier. Moreover, said a PBI member, "in an area with open conflict, where there are guerrillas, together with the armed forces, our presence can become a military target." Someone else from PBI stated: "Sometimes, you have to say, sorry, but international presence won't stop that kind of threat." But, according to another PBI member, there was some dissuasion with the guerrillas, even though establishing direct communication with them was illegal: "International presence affects the guerrillas' attitude: they won't be as authoritarian [or] visible with an international presence. It is clearly not the same . . . but they are also sensitive to their international image."[30]

The overall level of risk or of violence also impacts the effectiveness of accompaniment. PBI arrived in Colombia five or more years before other international NGOs, in conditions where accompaniment was more novel but also more risky. Perhaps for this reason—and because of the comparatively greater quantity of its accompaniment—before 2001, PBI experienced several serious violent incidents against those it accompanied.[31]

In the 1990s the Urabá region experienced extremely high levels of violence carried out by state forces, guerrilla groups, and paramilitary gunmen, devastating people both in cities and in rural areas such as San José de Apartadó. "At that time it was not advisable for a North American to go around here permanently. He would be a military objective of the armed groups," a church representative in Apartadó told me. In those conditions, accompaniment occurred on visits or delegations to Urabá—for example, U.S. Presbyterian leaders visited three times in 1997, but the visits provoked more fear of potential attacks on the visitors than they provided protection.[32] Nevertheless, in 1998 PBI established a team in Urabá to accompany San José de Apartadó and the Afro-Colombian peace community in Cacarica. The following year, the number of killings in San José dropped by more than two-thirds, even as the homicide rate in Apartadó as a whole increased.[33]

The Fellowship of Reconciliation team arrived in San José de Apartadó in early February 2002 to a lively community welcome. Unlike PBI's visits to the center of San José, the two-person FOR team would live full-time in rural La Unión, which is located a ninety-minute hike from the town center, and effectively served as the agricultural hub of the Peace Community. Wearing FOR T-shirts and caps and equipped with a satellite phone, the inaugural team was two young U.S. volunteers who signed up for six-month stints, Chris Moore-Backman and Lily Ray.

The FOR had prepared for establishing a team as best we could, including two additional visits to the community—one of them coinciding with the World Trade Center attack on September 11, 2001. In July 2001, hundreds of paramilitary troops carried out an incursion into La Unión, and seventeen-year-old Alexander Guzmán was killed as he fled, heightening our sense of urgency. We recruited volunteers, conducted training, raised funds, hired a coordinator, obtained work visas, and established a committee, a project mandate, and communication protocols. Before traveling to Colombia, Chris, Lily, and coordinator Jutta Meier-Wiedenbach met with dozens of Congressional staff members, many of whom pledged to serve as emergency contacts. But the realities of rural Colombian conflict would show the shortcomings of our preparation.

For one thing, peace negotiations initiated three years earlier between the FARC and Colombian government, already stalled by lack of political will, broke down completely on February 20, when the FARC hijacked an airliner and kidnapped a senator. President Andrés Pastrana, under heavy criticism for the peace talks from presidential candidate Álvaro Uribe, immediately ended the negotiations, and the military began a full-scale attack on the area in southern Colombia where FARC troops were concentrated, and where talks had taken place. Though this was far from San José de Apartadó, conditions were not propitious for respecting a civilian zone that rejected all armed combatants.

In one early incident in March 2002, word circulated in La Unión that an armed group was approaching the settlement. Believing the group was paramilitary, many residents ran, but others stayed behind, and the FOR team stayed with them. A dozen gunmen arrived in the hamlet tired and thirsty, not seeking to attack. They asked the young FOR volunteers for water, to which the volunteers quickly assented. One team member called the U.S. office, and was reminded that giving water to an armed group went against the community's neutrality, but it was too late. They gave the armed men water. Some guerrillas were fascinated with the gringo foreigners in this remote area. A commander briefly became concerned when he heard that a woman—who was an FOR volunteer—was on the phone with the outside world. He said the community used to support them, and didn't understand why it did not any more. After several hours the guerrillas left. The event ended peacefully, and giving water to an armed group had no demonstrable effect, but it demonstrated the need to prepare for more contingencies.

The same month, paramilitaries initiated attacks on civilian transport vehicles on the only road between Apartadó and San José, which was just seven miles long, effectively creating a blockade of goods to and from the community. On March 27, guerrillas attacked an army checkpoint on the road, killing two soldiers.[34] Paramilitary reprisals against the community predictably followed. On the morning of March 30, the day before Easter, Peace Community members Gilma Graciano and Orfilia Sánchez were riding in the chivero—an open-sided public transport along the rough road between San José and Apartadó—when the driver was stopped by armed paramilitary gunmen, about five hundred yards from a military checkpoint. The men took Graciano and Sánchez aside from other passengers. Graciano had given testimony to judicial investigators about the July 2000 massacre in La Unión carried out by paramilitaries.[35]

News reached the FOR coordinator Jutta Meier-Wiedenbach in California, who initiated a rapid series of calls to army, police, civilian, U.S. Embassy, Congressional, and NGO offices in Colombia, to both gather information and urge intervention. The first call went to the army's Seventeenth Brigade commander, for whom she left messages with several subordinates. Next was the U.S. Embassy's human rights officer, Mari Tolliver, who agreed to make her own calls. A Seventeenth Brigade officer would reportedly tell Tolliver that the army had no checkpoint on the road that day.

We learned the next day, which was Easter, that at the moment of the kidnapping, Graciano cried and held on to a nun who was in the same vehicle. With the gunmen distracted, Sánchez was able to run away and survive. But that Sunday morning, Graciano's body was found in the city of Turbo, with signs of torture and a shot to the head. Though two international volunteers who had recently arrived up the mountain in La Unión and were physically removed from the events on the road could not be expected to deter such a killing, it was nevertheless devastating and discouraging.

Between April 9 and 16, paramilitaries killed three chivero drivers who worked the Apartadó–San José route. Chivero service ceased entirely from then until the first week of May. The paralysis of public transport and targeting of community members on the single road in and out of San José had a material and substantial impact on the Peace Community's economy: they relied on it to bring up supplies to live on and farm, as well as to bring their own products to market. Schoolteachers and health workers also could not reach the town center or settlements in San José. Community leaders called it a blockade, and said it was generating hunger among San José residents. Even the International Red Cross was not taking supplies up the road.[36]

When FOR and PBI contacted Congressional staff, they agreed to circulate a letter about the blockade of the Peace Community in the House of Representatives. The year before, several dozen Congressional representatives had already written a letter about the Peace Community. The May 24 letter from forty members of Congress urged Colombian president Andrés Pastrana and his government to dismantle the paramilitary checkpoint on the road to San José and investigate threats and attacks on community members, highlighting the killings of Gilma Graciano and the chivero drivers and referring to the presence of PBI and FOR teams. The legislators also expressed direct support for the Peace Community's "effort to build a nonviolent alternative to the conflict."[37] In June the Inter-American Human Rights Court expanded its ruling for protection of the Peace Community to include those providing services to the community, especially drivers along the Apartadó–San José road.[38]

Apartadó bishop Germán Garcia personally challenged the blockade as well. By one account, he drove a vehicle up to San José and was stopped on the way by paramilitaries. He asked them by what authority they were stopping him, challenging their legitimacy.[39] The bishop's confrontation, Congressional letter, and Inter-American Court ruling were powerful signals, and by June the blockade was effectively ended. The outcome also appeared to demonstrate, again, that paramilitary conduct could be impacted by international pressure on the Colombian state.

The army-paramilitary alliance was not the only deadly force in the area of Apartadó. On April 4, guerrillas set up a rendezvous with two women in San José for the release of a kidnapped family member. The women left without the captive, whom the guerrillas later killed. Later that month, in an Apartadó neighborhood, guerrillas attacked a banana plantation and opened fire, killing nine banana workers.[40] The highest death toll in a single action in the war occurred the following week, on May 2, in the Afro-Colombian community of Bojayá in neighboring Chocó Department. There, guerrillas fired a pipe bomb toward paramilitaries hiding behind a church, but the bomb fell instead on the church where three hundred civilians had taken refuge, killing ninety-eight people, including forty-eight children.[41]

Guerrilla activity in Urabá was the most immediate focus of the U.S. Embassy and its Colombian military allies during this period. On May 13, I received a fax in my San Francisco office from U.S. ambassador Anne Patterson urging me to withdraw the FOR team from San José. She noted that, despite the State Department's travel warning about Colombia, some U.S. citizens "including volunteers with your organization" choose to travel there. "As a result, a number of Americans have died at the hands of insurgents and criminals." The letter said that FARC shipments were going through the San José area, and that paramilitaries make no distinction between these and supplies of food for civilians. She invited us and our field team to meet with her in Bogotá for a security briefing.

The FOR Colombia team and coordinator Meier-Wiedenbach met for an hour and a half on June 4 in Bogotá with Patterson, together with a cluster of U.S. military and civilian officials, some of whom did not identify themselves. Patterson claimed to have evidence that San José was a logistical center for the FARC, whom she said received shipments there. "We have photos of eight-ton trucks in the town center, campesinos gathering food and putting it on mules. We have other evidence we can't share with you." Embassy personnel said the photos were not from the army, that "we don't have to be there to take photos"—in other words, they were U.S. satellite images from above.

The FOR team members spoke of the community's regular mule-laden legitimate shipments of supplies for and harvest of the banana crop. When FOR said its team would know about large shipments going through the community, Patterson responded, "It seems strange to us that you wouldn't know," implying that FOR was either aware of guerrilla logistical operations or idiots. Patterson also said she would share information about the shipments with Congressional representatives who had signed the letter on San José ten days before.

Asked about the embassy's communication with other NGOs working in Urabá, a U.S. official present said their first priority was U.S. citizens, to which Meier-Wiedenbach responded that FOR was there because it valued Colombian lives as much as U.S. lives. A security officer became upset at this, saying they did value Colombian lives as highly, that they wanted to make the Colombian army and police like their American counterparts, serving the people instead of oppressing them. By supporting the community's refusal to have the armed forces present, he implied, we were undermining that goal.

Patterson disputed the essential logic of the Peace Community, which she critically dubbed "the so-called peace community." In light of the activities of guerrillas and paramilitaries in the area, she wrote, and "the limited manpower and mobility of the Army and the police in the region, we are skeptical that the Colombian government can protect San José de Apartadó without the presence of a government representative in the community." This logic, which ignored Colombian agencies' lack of political will to protect civilians in the area—indeed, the participation of some in attacks on civilians—led to focusing U.S. offers of assistance on helping resettle fleeing residents in the United States, on the one hand, and increased police and military capacity, on the other.

The FOR members and allies saw the embassy's actions as attempting to limit support for human rights work by denying responsibility for security of U.S. citizens in the community. One international human rights advisor in Colombia consulted by FOR said that if the embassy had information about possible attacks, it should share it. Short of that, he said, it would be setting up the community for a massacre.

CHAPTER 5
MAPPING OUR WAR

WHERE DID U.S. AID IN COLOMBIA GO?

The United States had interests in Colombia much larger in scale than a rural community like San José de Apartadó. The same Monday when the two families were killed in San José in February 2005, Florida governor Jeb Bush led a cohort of 185 businessmen and women representing more than 60 U.S. firms on a commercial visit to Bogotá, where they met with President Uribe, cabinet officials, and Colombian business leaders. A press release noted that Florida's trade with Colombia came to $3.9 billion annually.[1]

San José de Apartadó is a small community in a large country, millions of whose people were affected by the war, and the area was not even a focus of U.S. assistance, military or civilian. Yes, the Peace Community was a canary in a coal mine. But in order to understand what impact the United States had on the war and human rights in Colombia, our lens needs to be widened considerably.

Through embedded assumptions about the legitimacy of allied states, the United States exercised judgment regarding which forces in the conflict were the "good guys"—the armed forces. This decision was also based on goals shared with the Colombian military, such as weakening the FARC, and led to decisions to strengthen that force's capacity, rather than intervening in the war's operational decisions. That is, it implied a level of trust that did not require the United States to carry out military activities itself, nor closely coordinate Colombian military actions. The Bush administration expressed its support for the Colombian military at high levels, publicly and repeatedly from

2001 to 2009. At least until 2007, this had the effect of signaling that human rights abuses would be glossed over and not put U.S. support at risk.

The United States has many diverse reasons, rationales, motives, and explanations for appropriating military assistance to its allies. Generally, each of these rationales generates a program and a funding stream, with respective agency bureaucracies, leadership, and prerogatives. Counternarcotics funding goes through the State Department's Bureau of International Narcotics and Law Enforcement and the Defense Department's Section 1004 program, among others. Counterterrorist funds pass through Foreign Military Financing, Joint Combined Exercises and Training, and other Pentagon programs. Human rights resources pass through the International Military Education and Training program and staffing of the State Department's Bureau of Human Rights, Democracy and Labor. Military equipment produced by U.S. firms and transferred to another country could go through a grant (through one of several accounts), a commercial sale, or a subsidized government-to-government sale. Some military cooperation occurs through assistance, while other cooperation is embedded in funds for the U.S. military's own training or operations. Military and police training can be conducted by U.S. active duty or reservist soldiers, by private contractors, or through a third country. Training for Colombian personnel can occur on any of dozens of military facilities or civilian schools in the United States, on a Colombian military base, or at a U.S. base in the region. Anthropologist Winifred Tate suggests that this diverse range of rationales and agencies helped enable the passage and political support of Plan Colombia.[2] A key military client like Colombia receives U.S. assistance through many of these programmatic vehicles, personnel, and locations.

Once Plan Colombia was approved in 2000, and after its mandate was extended in 2002 to include support for counterinsurgency missions as well as counternarcotics, the policy in Washington was largely on auto-pilot, with little space for consideration of alternative policy frameworks. Control of the White House and both chambers of Congress by leadership committed to the military approach to Colombia compounded the automatic nature of policy direction.

As U.S. aid was synchronized with the Colombian military's strategy, its geographic reach also expanded beyond coca-growing areas in southern Colombia, to include aid of some kind to fifteen of the army's twenty-five territorial brigades at the height of assistance in 2007, and a growing number of mobile brigades.[3]

In the first years after 1998, when the Leahy Law was established, embassy staff had primary responsibility for its implementation, and in Bogotá the embassy developed lists of military and police units vetted for assistance, which would grow by 2005 to more than 250 units. However, because individuals nominated for training were considered "units," many other unvetted battalions and other units from which those individuals were drawn also received assistance: personnel from more than 50 unvetted units received U.S. training in 2006, for example.[4]

The U.S. Embassy in Bogotá was the largest in the world in 2003, with 4,500 employees and contractors.[5] But in a country as large as Colombia, and an institution as big as the Colombian Army, the United States attempted to extend the influence of that presence through several multipliers: helicopters for better and more offensive mobility; promotion of U.S. doctrine among military leaders; training the trainer and support for military schools; the cultivation of rising officers; and making U.S. technology standard issue for the military, leading to "interoperability" between Colombian armed force branches and units.

In Colombia, building capacity included an extensive program of constructing military facilities. "War is very expensive," General Leonardo Gómez Vergara told me in a 2013 interview. It requires specialized, costly, and extensive infrastructure and equipment. "But let's be realistic. In Plan Colombia, 90 percent of the money went back to the United States. It was a circular business."[6]

The Helicopter War and Its Myths

The biggest ticket item in that circular business was helicopters, representing $328 million in the initial package in 2000.[7] Beyond production and delivery, such aircraft required maintenance, fuel, replacement parts, and training for pilots, mechanics, and other operators. Most of the helicopters delivered in the 1990s and in Plan Colombia's early years required repairs. Colombia, which had recently emerged from a steep recession, was not prepared to finance the helicopters' repair and maintenance. When the Colombian Air Force sent several of its own planes to the United States in 2001 for refitting, logistical problems delayed their return.[8]

Other equipment sent by the U.S. demonstrated similar problems. According to military historian Robert Ramsey, eighteen Vietnam-era trucks "arrived in such a dilapidated condition—rusted bodies, batteries and engines so old that the [Colombian military] had ceased using them a decade earlier, heaters and ignition systems suitable for subzero conditions—that the Colombians, who estimated it would cost roughly $53,000 to make each truck serviceable versus just over $67,000 to buy a new one, refused to accept them."[9]

The initial Plan Colombia package was supposed to remedy issues of aging helicopters. But several Colombian military officers emphasized to me in interviews that at the beginning of Plan Colombia, the U.S.-provided helicopters were not authorized for use in repelling guerrilla violence, even in the most dire circumstances. Some told a story about a FARC attack in Tolima Department in which more than a dozen police fought and died, while close by a U.S.-provided helicopter sat paralyzed because it was only authorized for strictly counterdrug operations. A 2014 account produced for the U.S. Joint Special Operations University (JSOU) told it this way:

> American-funded aircraft were often prevented from assisting Colombian security forces that were in contact with the FARC or other insurgent groups, even when their employment could plainly spell the difference between life and death. An especially poignant example occurred in July 2000 during a guerrilla attack on a small Colombian police outpost. The 14 policemen held 300 attackers at bay for more than a day while radioing for help. Three Black Hawk helicopters sat at a base only 20 minutes away by air, but did not receive permission to assist the outpost because the United States had provided the helicopters for counter-narcotics purposes whereas the policemen were under attack by insurgents. The policemen ran out of ammunition after 27 hours, at which point they surrendered to the guerrillas, who promptly executed them.[10]

The July 14, 2000, guerrilla attack on Roncesvalles in Tolima Department recounted by JSOU was indeed tragic and brutal, but there is substantial evidence that it did not occur as later told in military narratives and that the policemen's murders could not have been prevented by freer use of U.S. military aid. The JSOU study and another U.S. military history cited a contemporaneous *U.S. News and World Report* story with the same details.[11] But Colombian court documents based on a lawsuit by three slain policemen's families, and even contemporaneous accounts in the Colombian media, tell a different story. Those accounts established that the fighting lasted for thirteen hours (not twenty-seven), and during most of that time, an AC-47 fighter plane and two Blackhawks from the Colombian military operated above the town. A military log from the night conveys the desperate situation. Some two hundred guerrillas initiated the attack at 8:15 p.m. by launching cylinder bombs at the police station, probably immediately killing several of the fourteen policemen deployed there and cutting off most radio communication.

By 11:20 p.m., three Blackhawk helicopters and the AC-47 were dispatched from a nearby base. The plane's pilot reported cloud cover and departed briefly. Police reported that the attack diminished as a result of helicopter fire at 12:50 a.m. and again at 2:18 a.m. But the helicopters did not land, while not far away army troops waited for dawn before moving by road into the town. By 8:00 a.m., pilots reported that guerrillas had moved civilians into the street as human shields against attack from the air. An hour later, the policemen were dead. The courts awarded a million dollars to three surviving families for the state's negligence in ensuring the police had adequate protection, but it was not a restriction on counterdrug aircraft that exposed the police and led to their deaths.[12] In contrast to what these detailed accounts showed, the U.S. military used a distorted narrative to claim that U.S. technology could save the lives of "good guys," if only political constraints—specifically, the restriction on U.S. military assistance to counterdrug aid—were removed.

Once U.S. assistance formally expanded in 2003 beyond counternarcotics programs, a principal focus of its resources, including the provision of helicopters, fuel, and maintenance, was a fifteen-thousand-soldier force operating in southern Colombia, called the Joint Task Force (JTF) Omega. The United States established JTF Omega that year as its primary instrument to support Plan Patriota, which over three years sought—with little success—to destroy the FARC's leadership, take territory, and gain strategic advantage in rural areas dominated by FARC in southern Colombia. The offensive was hobbled by jungle diseases, land mines, and by its purely military approach: once army units dislodged guerrilla fighters, the military moved on, and guerrillas returned. JTF Omega "absorbed almost everything" of U.S. aid, according to an army officer involved in logistical planning.[13] In 2004 the United States assisted two dozen battalions in JTF Omega; by 2006 it assisted more than forty; by 2009 it approved aid to more than sixty. U.S. assistance for JTF Omega fuel and helicopter flights alone totaled between $12 million and $24 million annually from 2004 through 2010.[14]

Aiding Intelligence and "High-Value Targets"

The U.S. counterguerrilla strategy in Colombia included extensive intelligence activities, military officers told me. In February 2003 the FARC downed a Cessna plane and seized the three surviving crew members, who worked for a U.S. company contracted by the State Department.

Shortly thereafter, CIA analysts and contractors established an intelligence cell in Colombia that helped create regional intelligence centers to push tactical intelligence to local commanders—Army Regional Military Intelligence Units (Regional de Inteligencia Militar del Ejército, RIMEs)—and "taught the art of recruiting informants to Colombian units," according to a 2013 *Washington Post* investigation.[15] The RIMEs supported by the United States were located in several divisions, including at the Fourth Brigade in Medellín (which was otherwise largely excluded from direct assistance).[16] According to Colonel Juan Carlos Piza, who served in the Fourth Brigade's command staff from 2002 to 2007, "The RIME gave information to the Seventh Division and the Fourth Brigade, first-hand."[17]

The Seventh Division, which operated from the same military base as the Fourth Brigade, had two to four intelligence advisors as part of the RIME who helped the brigade create cells focused on guerrilla leaders—the army's "high-value targets." The army had tried to kill such leaders beginning in 2004, without much result. "The RIME was huge. It had a lot of capacity, technical capacity that the United States gave," Piza told me.

Beginning in 2006, the United States provided laser-guided bombs to go along with real-time intelligence about the locations of guerrilla leaders, in order for Colombia to bomb and kill them. With the help of U.S.-supplied Paveway bomb guidance kits purchased from Raytheon, the attacks killed forty-five FARC and ELN leaders over the next seven years. Bombing operations generated from U.S.-Colombian target selection, technology, and tactics included killing anyone who moved near the target. U.S. and Colombian personnel jointly developed bombing tactics that included "blast pressure [that] would kill anyone else close in" and "shooting the wounded trying to go for cover."[18]

War through Building Things

The war's expansion required the construction and expansion of military and police facilities in Colombia, and the United States and Colombia advanced this construction through a series of secret agreements, annexes, and appendices, which in turn were based on bilateral agreements signed in 1952 and 1974. Commanders of the Colombian Army and Air Force and the director of the U.S. Embassy's Narcotics Affairs Section signed twenty-five such agreements in August 2001 for more than $30 million worth of construction that occurred at several bases in southern Colombia—mostly at Tres Esquinas and Larandia, Caquetá—and that the U.S. Army Corps of Engineers coordinated.

The work included construction of a riverine base, helicopter landing pads, flight operation buildings, fuel storage tanks, barracks, weapons and ammunition storage buildings, hangars, a sewer system, bunkers, roads, towers, fencing, and an airfield upgrade for A-37 aircraft. It also encompassed "force protection" measures at other bases in Marandua, Vichada; Apiay, Meta; and Bogotá. Two months later came an agreement to build a naval facility in Buenaventura, on the Pacific coast. In September 2002, the two governments signed agreements to build a "floating maintenance facility" in La Tagua, Putumayo, and a hangar for C-130 aircraft in Bogotá. In 2003 more construction commenced in the departments of Caquetá and Tolima and again in Buenaventura. Subsequent years saw agreements to build military infrastructure in the departments of Atlántico, Bolívar, Caquetá, Cundinamarca, Nariño, Putumayo, San Andrés, Tolima, and Vichada.[19] A report in May 2002 by U.S. ambassador Anne Patterson on counternarcotics aid focused on the material upgrading of facilities, including the Colombian Army intelligence school and other installations, more than on what occurred there.[20] U.S. construction on military bases in Colombia continued in 2009–10, though at a somewhat reduced level.

Military Facilities as a Regional Platform

The Pentagon's Latin American intelligence and operations, primarily for counterdrug programs, functioned from a small network of facilities in the Andes and Caribbean, established after U.S. bases in Panama were closed at the end of the 1990s, in compliance with the Panama Canal Treaties. A key facility was the air base in Manta, Ecuador, which hosted U.S. military aircraft, soldiers, and contractors who conducted air surveillance in the Pacific Andean region, as part of a ten-year lease that would expire in 2009. When Ecuador's President Rafael Correa, elected in 2006, pledged not to renew the lease—famously saying he would do so only if Washington permitted an Ecuadorean military base in Miami—the United States sought another site for the air operations. Colombian Defense Ministry officials broached "the possibility of a U.S. air base in Colombia to replace Manta" as early as June 2007.[21] That October a U.S. military team surveyed a commercial airport in Barranquilla and a military base in Palanquero, which they recommended as "without question the best location to conduct full spectrum U.S. military and interagency operations."[22] The U.S. Army defined such "full spectrum operations" overseas as the application of combat power offensively, defensively, and for stability to "defeat enemies and simultaneously shape the civil situation."[23]

Colombia and the United States negotiated the subsequent agreement for U.S. use of seven Colombian military bases, signed in October 2009, during heightened isolation of Colombia, in the wake of a March 2008 cross-border attack on a FARC camp in Ecuador that killed the guerrillas' leading international spokesman, Raul Reyes. Many suspected U.S. participation in the operation, which presidential candidate Barack Obama publicly supported. As base negotiations proceeded in July and August 2009, tensions between Colombia and Venezuela escalated, while Venezuelan president Hugo Chávez cut diplomatic ties and turned to other South American countries to replace Colombian imports.[24]

The base agreement, which a Colombian court ruling eventually overturned, demonstrated how little the Pentagon's strategic vision for the region had changed, despite the new Obama presidency and South America's movement over the previous decade toward greater autonomy from Washington. The agreement would have codified a U.S. military presence in Colombia with considerably greater capacity than the facility at Manta, including the deployment of C-17 cargo aircraft—which are not used for counterdrug operations but can airlift heavy equipment such as tanks—with a range over most of South America. President Obama's first budget request in May 2009 sought $46 million for construction on Colombia's Palanquero Air Force Base "for conducting full spectrum operations throughout South America."[25]

Colombian interior minister Fabio Valencia Cossio said in July 2009 that the agreement sought to "deepen assistance in areas such as: interoperability, joint procedures, logistics and equipment, training and instruction, strengthening monitoring and reconnaissance capacity, combined exercises and especially exchange of intelligence information." There would be an attempt to "expand training offered to other countries in the region through instruction of helicopter pilots and in human rights and international humanitarian law." Colombia was already imparting military training to jungle commandos and naval forces of other countries, Valencia said, and planned "to continue doing so with low-cost training and of the same quality as that offered by countries such as the United States and United Kingdom."[26]

The locations of U.S. troops on bases named in the agreement also would have been more oriented toward the Caribbean and Venezuelan side of Colombia, instead of the south, where U.S. aid to date had been concentrated. Uribe was staking much of his regional foreign policy on the antagonism with Chávez and Venezuela, and "was looking for" reactions from Venezuela and Ecuador to the base agreement.[27] By pursuing the base agreement with Uribe, Washington was still "syncing" its strategy to Uribe's. For his part, Uribe sought to demonstrate he had U.S. military support in the conflict with Venezuela.

The base agreement would have established a more permanent infrastructure for U.S. military involvement in Colombia and the region. It would have meant "more equipment, more budget," according to a U.S. intelligence operative I spoke with in 2016, and "larger buildings, more of them, more people, more facilities. It would look more like any major U.S. military installation in Western Europe."

The agreement provoked regional condemnation because of extraterritorial aims that it outlined for the U.S. presence, and opposition inside Colombia to the imposition on national sovereignty in provisions for U.S. soldier immunity from prosecution for crimes. Despite a seven-nation tour by President Uribe promoting the deal, only Peru openly supported the proposal, and two meetings in August 2009 of presidents from the Union of South American nations hotly debated the issue.[28] "Besides the problem of national sovereignty," more than a hundred Colombian organizations and leaders wrote in August 2009, "this kind of agreement generates risks to the region's security and stability, prolongs failed anti-drug policies, creates incentives for the arms race and aims to expand and prolong an internal armed conflict of which we are sickened."[29] Colombia's broken relations with Venezuela had a disastrous economic effect on its exports: bilateral trade plummeted 77 percent between 2008 and 2010.[30]

A Colombian human rights group, the José Alvear Restrepo Lawyers Collective, filed suit in February 2010 against the accord, and the Colombian Constitutional Court ruled in August 2010 that the agreement was a treaty that required Congressional approval, before reconsideration of its contents by the same court.[31] Juan Manuel Santos, inaugurated as president the same month, did not pursue the project, instead reestablishing relations with Venezuela.

The defeat of the base agreement was a major achievement of Plan Colombia opponents, but it did not end U.S. military involvement. The lack of an agreement, for example, had not prevented the United States from providing ten aircraft to the base in Palanquero in 2008–9.[32] Subsequently, U.S. military agencies in 2010 signed contracts for construction at three bases in Colombia worth nearly $5 million, including two contracts for an "Advanced Operations Base" in the large army base at Tolemaida for use by U.S. Special Forces.[33]

■ Sites of U.S. Military Presence, 2000–2010
— Departmental Boundaries

Map 5.1. U.S. military presence in Colombia, 2000–2010. In most locations U.S. military personnel led training courses or advised Colombian units but were not stationed throughout the decade. MAP BY DOUGLAS MACKEY. SOURCES: RODRIGO RIVERA SALAZAR, UNPUBLISHED MEMO, FEBRUARY 21, 2011; U.S. DEPARTMENT OF STATE, "FOREIGN MILITARY TRAINING REPORTS," FISCAL YEARS 2001–10.

War through Military Protégés

Plan Colombia also expanded existing U.S. military training to large numbers of officers and foot soldiers in a wide range of skills. Between 2000 and 2010 the United States funded the military training of 77,276 Colombians at a cost of $151 million. Most Colombian Army officers, especially those who rose in rank, received at least some U.S. military training. In many cases, according to a former army personnel officer, training in the United States was more a reward for past conduct than preparation for future military roles, but the range of training given was vast. Most of the training occurred in Colombia—which was much cheaper than bringing soldiers to the United States—including large groups of infantry training taught by U.S. Special Forces officers. Higher-level, specialized, and technical courses were typically given in the United States. The United States also sent hundreds of Colombian soldiers to courses in eight other countries from 2000 to 2010, including senior officers for counterterrorism training in Germany.[34]

More than a thousand soldiers also took civil-military relations seminars in Colombia during this period. Another 121 Colombians got training in how to purchase equipment through the U.S. military sales system. Many more studied helicopter and aircraft maintenance, electronics, and repair; corrosion control; air intelligence and operations; flight safety; supply and logistics; medical assistance; and budget preparation. Some studied computer literacy and English, presumably to communicate more effectively with their U.S. partners and teachers. Smaller numbers of Colombian personnel are reported to have taken courses in special operations, army intelligence, and counterterrorism. Dozens took courses for army instructors. A few attended West Point. More than 900 soldiers got physical training at Randolph Air Force Base in Texas. Nearly 3,400 Colombians attended the former School of the Americas in Georgia during the decade, including more than 500 at a course for cadets, another 200 officers at a course for army captains, and more than 300 at a counterdrug operations course. The data on training of more than 25,000 Colombians out of the 77,276 has been classified; most of the classified training was Pentagon-funded counterdrug training.[35]

In 2003 the United States also spent $25 million in its Antiterrorism Assistance Program to train army and police anti-kidnapping units, Grupos de Acción Unificada por la Libertad Personal (Unified Action Groups for Personnel Rescue, or GAULA), which were distributed throughout Colombian Army brigades.[36]

Training occurred at more than sixty locations in the United States, and at dozens more in Colombia. Between 2009 and 2011 alone, U.S. military personnel operated in twenty-four different locations across Colombia. The Colombian military in 2011 recognized the presence of 388 such personnel, most of whom were likely engaged in training.[37]

The operational impact of training might be relatively short, but the impact of doctrine—the principles that guide military action and are embedded in training and organizational culture—is long-term, according to officers I interviewed. As a result, changes in doctrine have a longer duration of effect than changes in training, since officers trained and formed in the framework of a doctrine will be influenced by it for their entire careers. The long-term education and cultivation of Colombian officers meant that they understood how the United States operated, its military and even civilian systems, and easily interacted with it. This was "soft power" of relationship-building at work, so that when the military "hard power" of Plan Colombia came into play, the Colombian military establishment was ready.

When Colombia launched Plan Patriota in 2003, the Military Group based in the U.S. Embassy in Bogotá initiated a program to embed about sixty U.S. military advisors in Colombian brigade and division headquarters, including the division command in Medellín responsible for the Seventeenth Brigade in Urabá. Most advisors stayed for a year. A U.S. advisor "can empower a Colombian senior officer by making him successful," according to Douglas Porch of the U.S. Naval Postgraduate School.[38] U.S. advisors posted with brigades or divisions could circumvent bureaucracy for material requests from commanders, for example. As operations in the Middle East siphoned off active duty U.S. soldiers after 2002, however, many of the advisors sent to Colombia were part-time Reserve and National Guard soldiers.[39] The United States even sent a school bus driver, a reserve officer, to Colombia as an advisor. "That kind of thing caused problems," one U.S. military instructor remembered.

Moreover, U.S. soldiers sought the Colombians' trust, but individually and institutionally they themselves had limited trust in their Colombian counterparts. "I also realized that our best opportunities to connect with the students was [sic] outside of the classroom, so we took advantage of any chance we had to hang out with them," wrote one visiting instructor, showing how informal messages could be as important as formal instruction.[40] An advisor from 2002 to 2006, however, said "the most likely risk" was "from the close relationship that develops" with Colombian soldiers, since insurgents might have infiltrated the Colombian unit. As a result, the two countries agreed early in Plan Colombia to build separate housing for U.S. personnel.[41] As of early 2016, the United States still maintained a military intelligence brigade in Barranquilla, according to a U.S. intelligence operative, who told me it was separate from Colombian forces, because "the U.S. military intelligence and law enforcement community views most members of the Colombian military and police as security risks."[42]

This distrust by advisors on the ground and the vote of confidence expressed by high-level support and aid packages appear to be contradictory. But both had the effect of creating a hands-off approach to Colombian operations, which in turn distanced both groups of U.S. officials from awareness of human rights problems.

The Colombian military "has an emotional dependence on U.S. support," according to a U.S. military mission chief in Bogotá quoted in 2007.[43] I witnessed this dependence while interviewing a retired Colombian colonel who worked as a contract advisor to Task Force Omega and to whom I had introduced myself as a researcher. He asked if I would intervene with U.S. officials to support the promotion of an officer, his mentor, to command the army. In another example, Colombian defense minister Camilo Ospina even told U.S. officials that he was Pentagon chief Donald Rumsfeld's deputy in Colombia, "coordinating his . . . third front of the war on terrorism."[44]

U.S. Aid as a Signal

Some army units received assistance whose concrete purpose and mission was not clear. One glaring example was the Eleventh Brigade, which operated in areas that became the center of paramilitarism in the late 1990s—the Caribbean departments of Córdoba and Sucre, as well as the Bajo Cauca area of northeastern Antioquia. Paramilitary chief Carlos Castaño said as early as 1997 that Córdoba was a "liberated area."[45] There was scarcely any guerrilla activity in the department for the army to fight. So it was curious that the United States chose to aid several army units operating in the department. According to State Department records, the United States gave assistance to the Eleventh Brigade command staff and three of its battalions in 2005, 2006, and 2007.[46] Yet paramilitary leaders in Córdoba and Sucre established training camps, operated freely, and established alliances with local business and political elites, twenty-six with whom they had signed a pact to "re-found" the nation in 2001. By 2005, although Don Berna's paramilitaries who "demobilized" that June continued to produce cocaine, the military was not conducting counterdrug operations against them.

In December 2005, under the watchful eyes of Eleventh Brigade soldiers, paramilitary chief Salvatore Mancuso—who ultimately confessed to responsibility for thousands of murders—threw the "wedding of the year" for himself and his bride in Puerto Escondido, Córdoba. On a farm Mancuso purchased for the occasion, with some five hundred armed bodyguards ringing the property, hundreds of guests from the region's high society enjoyed the finest whisky and champagne, with three elaborate menus, and well-known musicians, all dressed in the finest clothing. "If Mancuso had not existed, we would have had to invent him," a well-known lawyer said of the groom.[47]

When U.S. assistance to Colombia was approved in the fall of 2005, the Eleventh Brigade's commander was Colonel Javier Fernández Leal, who had just returned from a course at the U.S. Army War College in Pennsylvania, where he wrote a paper about the costs of war in Colombia.[48] When I interviewed him in 2014, Fernández Leal told me in measured tones that he set up three roadblocks "to see who was going" to the paramilitary wedding, and that many people covered their faces as they went through. However, the roadblocks also served to protect Mancuso's party from interlopers.[49]

Fernández Leal said he was uncertain what U.S. assistance to the brigade consisted of during the eighteen months he was in command there. But if unit-level assistance was sometimes invisible on the ground, high-level U.S. statements of support and confidence in the Colombian military were more visible, and often meant more to army leaders. In April 2004, for example, the U.S. representative to the UN Human Rights Commission in Geneva responded to a UN High Commissioner on Human Rights report describing Colombia's "critical" human rights situation by saying publicly that Colombia had "significantly" improved its human rights record, as measured by the reduced official numbers of homicides, kidnappings, and forced displacement overall in 2003.[50] U.S. praise continued after extrajudicial killings became a national scandal in 2008. Colombia made "important advances in human rights cases," the State Department said in its 2009 human rights certification.[51] In 2010 Secretary of Defense Robert Gates said that Colombia "has gotten to the point where it should play not just a regional role, but a global role."[52]

Protecting the Flow of Oil

"After September 11, [2001], the issue of oil security has become a priority for the United States," U.S. ambassador to Colombia Anne Patterson told an interviewer in early 2002.[53] Later that year, Congress approved $98 million of assistance for the Infrastructure Security Strategy (ISS), which was pro-grammed to be spent in 2003 and 2004, principally to protect the Coveñas-Caño Limón oil pipeline running through Arauca Department in eastern Colombia: $71 million for ten helicopters, $15.4 million to train troops, and $12.7 million to equip the army's Eighteenth Brigade.[54] From December 2002 to April 2003, seventy U.S. trainers of the Seventh Special Forces Group and the Fourth Psychological Operations Group were in Saravena and Arauca municipalities, training nine hundred troops in light infantry tactics at a cost of $9 million.[55]

Arauca Department was a center of Colombia's oil production, but it was also a center of both unarmed Leftist electoral activity and guerrilla actions. Shortly after his inauguration in August 2002, President Uribe issued direc-tives that created "rehabilitation zones" in Arauca and a Caribbean coastal region, suspended some civil liberties, and gave military commanders spe-cial authority. In Arauca, the edict applied to three municipalities that bor-der Venezuela where the Eighteenth Brigade conducted operations. During a brief four months in 2002, the military used its powers to arrest more than two thousand people in Arauca Department, and the following year arrested virtually all opposition candidates for governor and Arauca County local posts.[56] The crackdown coincided with the presence of U.S. advisors work-ing with army battalions in the same areas. Whether or not it was intended, the U.S. military presence helped to legitimize Uribe's repression.

U.S. trainers returned to Arauca in 2004 and 2005 to train smaller groups of soldiers from the Eighteenth Brigade and Fifth Mobile Brigade, includ-ing courses on "narco-terrorist organization."[57] The delivery of helicopters and other equipment was delayed, much of it only arriving in mid- to late 2005.[58] By 2008 the resources of ISS had been spent, and the United States ended direct assistance to the Eighteenth Brigade but continued to aid the Fifth Mobile Brigade. The command staff and four counterguerrilla battal-ions of the Fifth Mobile Brigade, with operations in Tame municipality, also received U.S. assistance at least from 2003 until 2009.[59]

The United States also built lasting facilities for the army in Arauca. In February 2005 the U.S. finished construction of a hangar for ten helicopters, fueling station, munitions depot, and barracks for 120 U.S. soldiers and contract personnel. By 2013, when I interviewed an army commander in Saravena, the U.S. personnel were long gone, but the U.S.-built facilities re-mained in use.[60]

U.S. assistance to areas strategic for oil, coal, and gold was not limited to Arauca. The initial push of Plan Colombia in 2001 concentrated on counterdrug operations in the southern department of Putumayo, where Houston-based Argosy Energy had fifteen wells. The Canadian company Gran Tierra purchased Argosy for $41 million in 2006, and by 2013 Gran Tierra controlled hundreds of thousands of acres in Putumayo, Cauca, and Norte de Santander.[61] The Putumayo wells were making a profit and expected to produce into the 2030s.[62] Another Canadian oil company, Petrobank Energy and Resources, bought the largest and most productive field in the Putumayo basin in 2001, and by 2006 it held more than 2.5 million acres in Putumayo and the savannah region north of it, making it one of the largest land owners in the country.[63] Pacific Rubiales purchased the company's Colombia assets in 2013, after Petrobank's shareholders had made $150 million in dividends since 2002.[64]

Pacific Rubiales's operations in Colombia outstripped all other foreign companies by 2012, mostly because of its wells in Meta Department, which produced nearly half of Colombia's crude output that year.[65] Beginning in 2007 the U.S. military concentrated heavily on "consolidating" state control in Meta Department, especially in La Macarena. Although the ISS funds had reportedly all been spent, SouthCom and USAID spent heavily in Meta in an effort to generate greater stability and governance in the area.[66]

Adjacent to Arauca, to its southeast, is Casanare Department, where Harken's oil fields were concentrated. There, the army established the Sixteenth Brigade in 1992; it began receiving U.S. assistance in 2005, and did so for three consecutive years, focusing on four combat battalions.[67] During the 2000–2010 decade, the Colombian Army created new units dedicated specifically to protecting pipelines and other energy infrastructure.

One Officer's Story

The impact of diverse U.S. military programs in Colombia becomes more clear through the stories of individual army officers. Lieutenant Colonel José Octavio Duque served as deputy commander of the Western Hemisphere Institute for Security Cooperation (WHINSEC, the former U.S. Army School of the Americas) from 2004 to 2006, his last active duty assignment. After that, he served as dean of the army's engineering school, and then as director of the communications division of the Nueva Granada military university. In September 2014 I called him there, said I was writing about U.S.-Colombian military relations, and was interested in talking with him about his WHINSEC experience. He graciously accepted.

We met on the university campus and talked in his cubicle office over coffee. "I have always been an academic beneficiary of the United States," he said. "I adore the United States." His father, also a Colombian army officer, fought alongside U.S. forces in Korea and received a bronze star.

His own love relationship with the United States began at age seventeen, Duque said, when he took courses in Panama at the School of the Americas and the airborne school at Fort Sherman. He spent ten months at the U.S. Army Engineering School in Fort Belvoir, Virginia, and later studied psychological operations in multiple courses with U.S. Special Forces at Fort Bragg. He founded the Colombian Army's school of civil-military relations, which brought him in frequent contact with the U.S. Southern Command and Fort Bragg. Specializing in communications, he also studied at a U.S. military radio facility in Hawai'i. He took dozens of U.S. human rights courses, beginning in the 1990s. And in 1993 he served as a military observer beside U.S. troops in Yugoslavia, where he was taken prisoner by Serbs for two months.

Though Duque did not say much about it, from January to November 1999, he commanded the Bejarano Battalion of the Seventeenth Brigade—the same battalion his brother Néstor Iván would command five years later.[68] During that period, late on April 4, 1999, paramilitaries passed an army checkpoint within the battalion's area of operation on the road to San José de Apartadó—the sole vehicular access into the community, usually patrolled by the Bejarano Battalion—and murdered three members of the Peace Community of San José, including its cofounder Anibal Jiménez, and a sixteen-year-old boy, Daniel Pino, who bled to death after his stomach was cut open with a machete.[69] Luis Eduardo Guerra and his stepbrother, Dario, were witnesses.

Army collusion with paramilitaries and actions with devastating psychological effects continued. Less than a week after the April 4 massacre, several human rights workers traveled with a community member to San José, in a public buseta (small bus). Shortly after a brief search at an army checkpoint, they were stopped by a pair of paramilitary gunmen, who spoke with someone by radio, to receive instructions, and got on the transport with the group. The gunmen went with them a little ways, then got off. That night, at 1:00 a.m., the group heard explosions in the surrounding hills. In the wake of the killings days before and ongoing paramilitary presence, community members were terrified. The human rights group called the Bejarano Battalion commanded by Duque to report the bombing and ask what was happening. The military officers replied that, not to worry, it was the army, carrying out a demining exercise—at one in the morning.[70]

In 2004 Duque was invited to serve as deputy director of WHINSEC in Georgia, a kind of "chief of the foreigners" at the school. While there, he recommended that the number of Colombian instructors be increased, which in effect occurred. Among the sixteen Colombian instructors serving while Duque was there in 2005 was Colonel Santiago Herrera Fajardo,[71] who in 2008 was relieved of his post by army commander Mario Montoya, and subsequently imprisoned for his role as commander of the Fifteenth Mobile Brigade in northeastern Ocaña, which had one of the highest levels of reported civilian killings. "Herrera Fajardo comes from a very distinguished family here in Bogotá," Duque told me. Herrera commanded the mobile brigade or battalion with the highest number of reported executions documented under his command—thirty-seven.[72] According to the court ruling against another officer in the brigade, the killings were committed in concert with a paramilitary group, who turned over what were called "gifts"—persons to be killed—in exchange for information on army movements (to stay clear of them) and for being allowed to commit its own crimes.[73]

I commented to Duque that his brother, Néstor, had had to deal with accusations of rights violations. In fact, Néstor was a key player in the operation that led to the 2005 massacre in San José de Apartadó. José Octavio said yes, but that his brother was very organized and had filed suit against Father Javier Giraldo, the priest who was so important to the San José Peace Community. We went on to talk about other aspects of human rights in Colombia and U.S. policy. Before we parted, I asked if he thought his brother would talk with me about his experience. He said it had been painful for him, but why didn't he ask? He picked up the phone and called Néstor, explaining that he was with a U.S. researcher and asking whether he would talk with me. His brother agreed and suggested I come over to the Military Club, a half-hour cab ride away. I did.

U.S. military involvement in Colombia from the inception of Plan Colombia in 2000 to its peak in 2007 expanded its purposes and grew dramatically in scale and geographic reach. This occurred through Washington's investment in the Colombian military's doctrine, schools, infrastructure, officers, and battlefield success. As Colombian officers trained by the United States moved in and out of army brigades around the country, U.S. influence also spread. It is thus difficult to isolate a part of the Colombian Army exempt from that influence, including the Seventeenth Brigade, which was deeply implicated in a relentless series of abuses in San José de Apartadó, including the massacre there on February 21, 2005.

CHAPTER 6
KILLING THE FUTURE

San José became a pilgrimage site in the early twenty-first century for people all over Colombia and beyond. Beginning in 2003 a network of Colombian rural communities resisting the war brought representatives of groups and communities in Cauca, César, Caquetá, Arauca, Guajira, and Medellín to San José for month-long sessions of a "peasant university."[1] The Fellowship of Reconciliation (FOR) and the Colombia Support Network (CSN)—which had established a sister-city relationship between Apartadó and Madison, Wisconsin—organized international delegations throughout the decade. Academics came to study the community, and diplomatic visitors came to meet and get a sense of the human rights situation. Accompaniment organizations Peace Brigades International (PBI) and FOR had a permanent presence. External attention and support appeared to have an impact: in 2003, the year after local and international advocacy led to the lifting of the paramilitary blockade on the San José road, the number of San José residents killed dropped from twenty-one to one.[2]

Peace Community leaders also traveled abroad. Luis Eduardo Guerra visited Italy in October 2003 on a solidarity tour, participating in a peace march from Perugia to Assisi. As he sat down to rest during the march, an Italian marcher teased him, saying she had never seen a tired campesino. "Tired, but not defeated," he replied. An Italian solidarity group invited him to stay longer with the aim of protecting him from threats he was receiving in Colombia, but he returned after the march.[3]

Within Colombia, the community was also a central part of a network of communities and groups that resisted the war and sought to create autonomy from its diverse actors and mechanisms. In December 2003 San José was one of eight communities that formed the Network of Communities in Resistance (Red de Comunidades en Ruptura y Resistencia, RECORRE).[4] Four of these communities declared themselves in "rupture" with Colombia's criminal justice system, meaning that, if their members were arrested, they would declare themselves prisoners of conscience.[5]

The communities' declaration responded to the failure of that system to prosecute crimes against community members by soldiers and paramilitary gunmen, while at the same time charging a wide array of community leaders and members with membership in guerrilla groups, conspiracy, and terrorism, based on what the communities said was false evidence. They pointed to a September 2002 official report alleging fifty-four lines of phone communication between paramilitaries and judicial investigators that were never investigated, as well as to the fact that judicial investigators (who also serve as prosecutors) often work within military bases and "conceived of their function as a simple annex to military power." In announcing their conscientious objection to this system, the communities asked for support from other governments and their embassies in Colombia to exert "moral and political pressure for Colombia to reconstruct its justice system" in a way that "respects fundamental ethical and judicial principles."[6]

But the community also had attracted enmity from diverse powerful actors—not just the army and paramilitaries. On March 12, 2004, a prosecutor and the army came to the San José town center and arrested two men and two sisters, without showing a judicial warrant. The women, including Peace Community leader Diana Valderrama, were released shortly after soldiers realized they had mistaken her identity, but not before Colonel Néstor Iván Duque reportedly told them that he had plans to attack the community with "heavy machinery" and had a team of ten men for the job.[7]

The two arrested men, Elkin Tuberquia and Apolinar Guerra, were both campesinos who previously had agreed to serve the guerrillas as milicianos—civilians who lived at home but kept a radio and weapons. But they had left the guerrillas years before their arrest, they told an official who visited them, after which they sought to distance themselves from the FARC in the town center, where they were arrested and brought to the Seventeenth Brigade's base. Under pressure from a physical beating by Duque, they confessed to being guerrillas and were assigned a public defender, but she did not bother to visit them after hearing about their confession. The local ombudsman realized that someone should hear their side and went to see them, initially at the military base. There, he spoke with Elkin only in the presence of Duque, and he was not permitted to see Apolinar, who had been beaten. After they were transferred to a local jail, however, they told the ombudsman they had been beaten, threatened, and forced to sign a confession. The ombudsman then filed a habeas corpus petition, and the two men were released on March 31. The judge imposed as a condition for their release, however, that they sign a document admitting the charges against them, setting in motion a process that would lead to their rearrest and service as army informants months later.[8]

Also in March, community members found an explosive artifact—probably a grenade—in a banana field in La Unión. By the community's account, they contacted the ombudsman's office in Apartadó to ask the authorities to remove the artifact from the community. A community member brought it to San José, where the ombudsman staff took photos of the object, saying they would consult about how to dispose of it, but no authority ever did. Instead, ombudsman staff told community members that it was a smoke grenade that they would pick up at a later time. So the community placed it in an uninhabited house in San José, where it was forgotten for months.[9]

On Saturday, May 22, a bomb exploded in a discotheque in Apartadó, killing five people and injuring ninety-three.[10] In response, President Uribe convened a security meeting on May 27 in adjacent Carepa, where he demanded that the military or police establish a presence in San José to detect "unscrupulous persons." He also accused Peace Community leaders of obstructing justice, and added: "I wish to remind the internationals in San José de Apartadó that in Colombia there can be no impunity for either Colombians or for foreigners. If they come here, they come to help our communities, not obstruct justice. . . . I respectfully reiterate my suggestion to DAS [Departamento Administrativo de Seguridad (Administrative Department of Security), Colombia's equivalent to the FBI] and to the police that if these people again obstruct justice, they put them in jail and if they have to be deported, to deport them."[11] This was a direct threat to the accompaniment of groups such as PBI, FOR, and Navarra Nuevo Futuro, a Spanish NGO with a presence in San José that assisted with housing.

On June 2, soldiers from the Bejarano Battalion and agents of DAS came into San José and sought out the PBI volunteers there at the time—an Italian man and a German woman—purportedly to verify that they were acting within the limitations of their work visas. Detectives obtained bank statements of the community and its leaders for all of 2004, as well as Luis Eduardo Guerra's bank account from 2001, after which he had closed it.[12] In November DAS agents would ask for a list of all community members' names, purportedly to provide security, as well as all foreigners' names.[13] Intelligence reports on the Peace Community alleged, without citing sources, not only that the Peace Community's principles were a "façade," that it stored and transported supplies for the guerrillas and denounced army bombings of its houses, but that the guerrillas had instructed them to do so. One such report said the community was supported economically by international organizations, ignoring the community's production economy.[14]

These intelligence operations were part of an extensive national program by DAS, at its peak in 2004–5, to illegally spy on and harass Colombian and international human rights organizations, journalists, peace groups, Supreme Court justices, United Nations staff, and political opponents of President Uribe, who had command authority over DAS. The DAS surveillance was especially concerned with international activities that reflected on Colombia's human rights image, and included creating the appearance of links between guerrillas and the targets of surveillance.[15]

———————

Luis Eduardo became the community's principal spokesman after 2003, living for much of the time on a farm owned by the community that was close to Bogotá, where he could participate more easily in official meetings. He also had received a number of threats in San José, and the farm was a safer location. By mid-2004, however, he had moved with his wife, Luz Enit, and four children back to San José, where they settled into a house in the town center. Luz Enit was also the daughter of Luis Eduardo's stepmother, Miryam.[16]

On the morning of August 11, sixteen-year-old Luz Helena Torres saw a shiny object tucked into a shelf in a home in San José, picked it up, and showed it to Diener, at ten years old the oldest of Luis Eduardo's and Luz Enit's children. Luz Helena brought the object outside to show to Luz Enit, who was saddling a horse with a neighbor.[17]

The explosion was audible all the way up the mountain in La Unión, and severely injured Luz Helena, Luz Enit, and Diener, who were brought to the hospital in Apartadó.

In the hallway outside Luz Enit's hospital room, a young policeman approached Luis Eduardo. FOR team member Sarah Weintraub recounted the exchange that followed.

"Excuse me, I need to see your ID," the policeman said.

"I already showed it to your colleague," responded Luis Eduardo.

"I need to see some ID."

"Look, you have already asked me for it three times and I've showed it, alright?"

"Well, I need you to show it again."

"I'm not going to show it again. Ask your friend."

"Why don't you want to tell me who you are?"

"Look, my wife is dying in the other room. Can you just leave me in peace?"[18]

At this point, another international accompanier intervened, asking for the name of the policeman and his commander, and he stopped harassing Luis Eduardo.[19] Colonel Duque also questioned Luis Eduardo in the hospital, claiming that the explosive was homemade (an assertion also made publicly by a police official). Doctors said that Luz Enit needed to be flown to Medellín to receive adequate attention; use of a helicopter had to be authorized by police. Luis Eduardo told FOR accompaniers that Duque pressured him to sign a document saying that the explosive was made by community leaders, which Luis Eduardo refused to do. The helicopter was not authorized, and Luz Enit died the next day. The young Luz Helena died as well. Luis Eduardo's son Diener's leg was severely damaged, and he spent weeks in recovery in a Medellín hospital, accompanied by Luis Eduardo.[20]

Coincidentally, Vice President Francisco Santos visited San José on August 13, two days after the explosion, to hear from community members in a meeting that had been previously scheduled. He first held a meeting with local and national officials in Apartadó, where he reportedly said that the community's version of an abandoned grenade was "a liar story." He then flew by helicopter the few miles to San José, where he said again that the evidence suggested that the explosive was not the same grenade the community had denounced. Community members told him the government had failed in their responsibility by not protecting them from the grenade, which they had been told was a smoke bomb. Investigators subsequently concluded that it was, indeed, a grenade.[21]

In a meeting with international volunteers several months later, Duque would mimic what Luz Enit looked like, with the tubes in her nose and spread on the bed with her mouth open. On November 16, Colonel Duque spoke on an Apartadó radio station. Asked about the Peace Community, he said residents were "finally losing their fear of giving information to the military" and that important members of the FARC had deserted with help from the community—which he said was supporting the military "so that no one thinks it's a criminal community, of guerrillas, no never!"[22] The statement implied both that the Peace Community was guerrilla-affiliated and that this affiliation was losing its grip, an assertion that would reappear in later narratives influenced by Duque.

———————

Paramilitary and guerrilla movements during the same period were also changing the violence in Urabá and its impact on San José de Apartadó. As part of the paramilitaries' negotiations in 2004 with the national government to demobilize, many of the AUC's commanders and members were concentrated in Santa Fe de Ralito, in Tierralta, Córdoba, just over the mountains east of San José de Apartadó. Yet despite fanfare about the demobilization, paramilitaries and their successor groups continued to kill hundreds of civilians a year across the country, including more than eight hundred in 2004.[23]

On November 25, 2004, the paramilitary unit known as the Banana Block formally laid down its weapons, and demobilized fighters were gathered in a Turbo settlement, called El Dos, under the supervision of the High Commissioner of Peace.[24] Banana Block gunmen had committed many crimes along the road between Apartadó and San José. Of 447 Banana Block members who demobilized, 57 had belonged to the army.[25]

From the other side of the Abibe Mountains, in Córdoba, the Bloque Héroes de Tolová continued to operate, led by drug capo Diego Murillo Bejarano, alias "Don Berna." In December, command of the block, which had grown to three hundred troops after the Banana Block's demobilization, was assumed by twenty-five-year-old Uber Darío Yáñez Cavadías, alias "21" or "Orejas," a bodyguard of Don Berna.[26] The block also included a fifty-five-year-old military instructor, Manuel Arturo Salom Rueda, known as "JL," who had trained thousands of paramilitary troops all over the country since the 1980s. He had been a sergeant for more than twenty years in the army, where he first worked with paramilitaries in the Middle Magdalena region.[27]

Like other paramilitary groups, the "heroes" of Tolová did not discriminate much when they decided to target individuals for killing. "Within the little or no work of 'military intelligence' done by these paramilitary groups to select their 'objectives,' it is evident that to determine them, many times an accusation that a citizen was reportedly a subversive was enough, without any additional verification, to end his existence by all means," concluded a judge in a study of the Heroes of Tolová Block.[28] They also recruited children—many of them within days after Yáñez's arrival as commander in late 2004. More than twenty minors would participate in the February 2005 operation under Yáñez's command in San José de Apartadó.[29]

In November 2004 combat in the secluded and vulnerable San José settlement of Mulatos led several families to flee into the San José center. On November 17, guerrillas abducted Amador Delgado from his home in another settlement of San José, and his body was found the following day. The Peace Community denounced the killing.[30] On the afternoon of November 22, FOR team member Brad Grabs heard explosions and gunshots in the direction of Mulatos, which continued on and off. By 11:30 p.m., the combat had moved closer to La Unión, a half-hour walk away, erupting every twenty minutes or so. Grabs called me in San Francisco, and I called the Seventeenth Brigade, speaking directly with Colonel Duque. The aim of the conversation was to remind him that civilians, including international observers, were in the area where combat was taking place, so that the army at least might ensure not to target those civilians. Duque asked me why I had not called the month before, when the FARC had killed a civilian. I said that there had not been combat at that time.

On December 6, ten gunmen raided a meeting in the Embera Katío indigenous community located on the road between Apartadó and San José, and took three leaders out and beheaded them by the river, threatening community members if they removed the bodies. The Embera community had attempted to stay out of local conflicts, and it was at first unclear who committed the murders.[31]

Four days later, community leaders again met with Vice President Santos, who had once been kidnapped by the FARC himself. The community and national government were negotiating the positioning of a police post, which the community wanted to be placed outside the town limits because, they said, armed attacks came from *outside* the town center, and placement of an armed contingent inside the center would make it a target for guerrillas. But the government had stalled, postponing meetings even after San José leaders had flown to Bogotá, according to a community ombudsman at the time.[32]

On the way to Apartadó on December 13 for their flight to Bogotá, the leaders were stopped at a military checkpoint to show their identification. There, a man in army fatigue pants with a fresh wound under his eye began to question Luis Eduardo aggressively, asking what role he played in the community, according to others in the meeting. Luis Eduardo would not answer, and asked the man his name, but the man refused to give it.[33]

Three days later, FOR team members met with Colonel Duque at the base of the Seventeenth Brigade in Carepa, south of Apartadó. Duque's Bejarano Battalion had jurisdiction over the road between Apartadó and San José, where the army presence had grown larger and included troops from the Thirty-Third Counter-Guerrilla Battalion and national police as well as members of the Bejarano Battalion. These units frequently had checkpoints that stopped and searched chiveros and their passengers. When members of FOR asked him about the presence of uniformed men with no nametags at the checkpoint, Duque replied that probably the soldiers did not have enough money to buy the name patch, since they had to buy their own uniforms.[34]

Duque told FOR that he liked war and combat, but only when it was necessary. He listed other army units that operated in the area, and singled out the Thirty-Third Counter-Guerrilla Battalion, saying they were "killing machines" and had several complaints against them. He also said the Thirty-Third helped him when he needed them to fight guerrillas.[35] A community member would say four months later, "'Everyone knows that the counter-guerrilla battalions are the craziest of all the soldiers. They are recruited for craziness.'"[36]

At a checkpoint on the road to San José on December 18, FOR team member Brad Grabs encountered the same unidentified commander with the cut on his eyelid, and after some pleasantries asked his name. The man did not respond. The awkward silence, Grabs said, was the most frightening experience he had in Colombia, even though no tense words were exchanged. A commander's refusal to identify himself, on a road where paramilitaries frequently operated, after a local paramilitary block had supposedly demobilized, suggested that the army and active or former paramilitaries were patrolling the road together, and that was scary enough.[37]

During the same period, army soldiers arrested Alfonso Bolívar Tuberquia of La Resabalosa settlement, holding him at least one night before releasing him. It was not the first time he had been detained, nor would it be the last.[38]

In January the DAS subpoenaed bank account information for Luis Eduardo Guerra, Father Javier Giraldo, and fifteen other Peace Community leaders and members, which was provided to the DAS office in Apartadó on February 2. The DAS memo said that the agency should coordinate its actions with the army to avoid "problems as occurred in the past."[39] Luis Eduardo must have been unaware of the actions taken by DAS but presciently told an interviewer on January 15: "Our project is to continue resisting and defending our rights. We don't know how long, because what we have lived during all this history is that today we are talking; tomorrow we could be dead. Today we are in San José de Apartadó; tomorrow most people could be displaced."[40]

An FOR team risk assessment in January noted that "the military-paramilitary maintains a region of control in the form of checkpoints on the road to Apartadó and trail to La Union" and that "there is a general sense that the FARC is capable of mounting activities in the region." FARC members passed through La Unión several times in January and early February.

El Porroso is an Emberá indigenous hamlet in Dabeiba County, south of San José and Urabá's banana zone, and the Voltigeros Infantry Battalion went there on February 8 looking for combat, thinking they would be on the offensive. The Voltigeros Battalion belonged to the Seventeenth Brigade, which had operational jurisdiction throughout the Urabá region. Upon arriving in El Porroso, the soldiers attacked the guerrillas to prevent them from taking over the hamlet, and reportedly killed eleven guerrillas. The soldiers were excited; "you get carried away thinking that the enemy is done," one soldier said later.[41]

But then the combat turned. The soldiers moved higher up in the village where there were more guerrillas, and an intense firefight ensued. As the soldiers crossed over the Porroso River, the guerrillas received reinforcements. "There were even children firing bullets at us," Edison Osorio, a professional soldier, told journalists. Nineteen soldiers died in the confrontation, and five more were wounded. A guerrilla medic who helped the wounded survive said she was "healing them so they'd go tell how the [guerrillas] had killed their friends."[42] If the military's own losses were measured in deaths, why wouldn't they measure their victories over the guerrillas in deaths? Did the guerrillas use children to kill soldiers?

The combat was part of a series of guerrilla actions in the region. Only forty-eight hours after the killings in Porroso, at shortly after 7:00 p.m. on February 17, three armed men stopped a small public bus traveling in Dabeiba. They took eight passengers off the bus and marched them several hours into the brush. The kidnappers released the children and several adults, who then walked all night back to the road, while retaining two men and two women. Newspapers at the time said the FARC was responsible.[43] Only a few days before these events, in a joint FARC-ELN operation, guerrillas had attacked a navy base in Iscuandé, Nariño, in southwestern Colombia, killing sixteen soldiers and wounding twenty-five.[44]

The media covered the guerrillas' actions extensively, emphasizing community fears of more violence. "For the last ten years the FARC's presence in the Gulf of Urabá area . . . has been minimal due to the arrival of the self-defense groups [paramilitaries] which forced the guerrillas to retreat and find refuge in the neighboring northern Chocó and Abibe Mountains in northern Antioquia," El Tiempo reported.[45] The implication of this reporting was that paramilitaries and the army's presence reduced violence, while the guerrillas made it worse.

The army's disaster in El Porroso led its leadership to accelerate a plan for a large offensive operation in response. Brigade commander General Héctor Jaime Fandiño was ordered back to Bogotá and replaced by General Luis Alfonso Zapata Uribe, recently head of the military's joint special forces command. When Zapata Uribe relieved Fandiño on February 10, Fandiño told him that "since some time before a brigade operation was in planning with participation by the command staff and tentatively called 'Phoenix,' which would be carried out in February." Fandiño showed Zapata Uribe a draft of the operational plan.[46] Division commander General Mario Montoya flew to the Seventeenth Brigade headquarters in Carepa to meet with Zapata Uribe and other officers who were planning Operation Phoenix.

Most of the principal commanders in the room had received a course at the U.S. Army School of the Americas (SOA), in either Panama or, after 1984, Fort Benning, Georgia. Colonel Duque had attended for two weeks in 1984 and was responsible for operations along the San José–Apartadó road. He was named the commander of Phoenix in the operational order. General Zapata Uribe attended SOA for five weeks in 1976. General Fandiño attended the SOA during the same five weeks in 1976. Lieutenant Colonel José Orlando Acosta Celi, head of operations for the brigade, attended for two weeks in 1983. Vélez Battalion commander Colonel Orlando Espinosa Beltrán attended for a month in 1986. General Montoya, the highest-ranking officer present, had been an SOA instructor for a year in 1994.[47]

A key point in the meeting was the decision to use "guides," who could be local civilians or demobilized combatants, or—if used euphemistically by army officers—paramilitaries. Espinosa reported that General Montoya told the brigade officers: "If there aren't guides, don't do the operation."[48]

"At that time guides were allowed and everyone used guides," Montoya told me when I spoke with him in 2013. "That I gave instruction or said there needed to be guides, I don't deny that. . . . I can't say that I said it, because there is no recording. But it is very probable that I said it." But he insisted that he did not order that the guides be paramilitaries.[49] A few days after the army meeting in Carepa, on February 22, Colombia's Council of State, a quasi-judicial body, would issue a ruling that peasant soldiers—who might include guides—and police could not enter combat zones.[50] The decision of what guides to include could have been made by one or several officers: General Fandiño; the brigade's intelligence officer, Colonel Fernando Augusto Castro; its operations officer, Lieutenant Colonel Acosta; or Lieutenant Colonel Duque, as coordinator of the operation.

Another key decision related to the geographic objectives of the operation. "There was never any real intelligence" about where the guerrillas who attacked in Porroso went afterward, Duque would later say. They could have gone to several locations—Rio Blanco; Rio Esmeralda, located in the Nudo de Paramillo; or Mulatos Canyon, in San José, he said. The brigade officers chose to take the operation to Mulatos. "It was planning by intuition, we could say," Duque recalled.[51]

Captain Guillermo Gordillo Sánchez was ordered from Capurganá, a small resort town near the Panama border, where he was leading a company in a military competition. On the evening of February 17, he arrived in Nuevo Antioquia (a district adjacent to San José), where he took command of Bolívar Company in the Vélez Battalion, whose soldiers had been there already for a month.[52]

While Operation Phoenix got under way, on Friday, February 18, the Peace Community issued an announcement: the following month, on the anniversary of its declaration as a peace community, it would establish "humanitarian zones" in eight settlements in the San José district that had suffered heavily from the war, where families could take refuge in case of combat or bombing, and the community demanded that armed groups stay out. The sites would have communication equipment to convey civilians' experience and seek respect for their neutrality in the midst of conflict, and people there would not collaborate with the armed groups. In other words, civilians would resist the use of these communities by the army as well as by the paramilitary and guerrilla combatants operating in the area.

The community denounced "the paramilitarization not only of Urabá but of the whole country," saying that the military's bombing, burning, killing, and torture had reduced the Mulatos settlement from ninety-eight families to only eleven in the previous year. Paramilitaries had taken over Rodoxali, adjacent to Mulatos, the community said, "and have announced that the next settlement to take is Mulatos."[53]

The humanitarian zones initiative was an attempt to prevent the forced displacement of civilians in the face of combat. The community also envisioned the humanitarian zones as sites with pavilions for the education and organization of the settlements, making it easier to procure respect for civilians' crops, possessions, and homes. It invited people from Colombia and worldwide to join the community for the inauguration of these zones on its anniversary, March 23. Families would also return that day to La Esperanza settlement, which had been organized by the Peace Community but displaced by combat and threats. One member of the peace committee set up to form a humanitarian zone in Mulatos was Alfonso Bolívar.[54]

Throughout the area, residents saw army troops and equipment engaged in operations. On the road between Apartadó and San José, the army withdrew its normal roadblock from February 19 to 22, according to local observers, presumably because the soldiers were participating in Operation Phoenix. On Saturday, February 19, army soldiers reportedly told someone in La Esperanza settlement, "Go to San José now. You can't stay here."[55] Luis Eduardo arrived at Miryam's house in the Mulatos settlement that same day, with the aim of harvesting cacao with his stepbrother, Dario, on Sunday. He was traveling with his son Diener and his seventeen-year-old girlfriend, Beyanira Areiza, with whom he had begun a relationship several months before. But the sound of combat and helicopters in nearby Nieves led Luis Eduardo and Dario to delay their work until the following day.[56] A neighbor told them that the army was all over the area. Instead, they stayed close, cutting plantains and fishing in a river near the house until seven in the evening.[57]

On Sunday, just after 11:00 a.m., two helicopters repeatedly flew close to La Union, where FOR volunteers learned there had been fighting in the nearby settlement of Las Nieves. In Las Nieves, soldiers questioned Roberto Elías Monroy in his home with his family. Soldiers had detained and interrogated him two months earlier at the Seventeenth Brigade headquarters.[58]

Just after noon on Sunday, the hospital in Apartadó received a wounded soldier, Oscar de Jesús Sepúlveda Altamiranda, a wounded four-year-old girl, and the body of a man, apparently the father of the girl. The hospital reported that they came from Las Nieves. Yet Sepúlveda appeared on a list of five wounded and four dead soldiers in Dabeiba, another county in the region, from the night before.[59] That night, Caracol Radio reported that the army had killed a guerrilla militia leader known as Macho Rusio in Las Nieves, evidence that army soldiers were in the area.

The man who accompanied Luis Eduardo on Monday morning was his stepbrother, Wilmar Dario, nicknamed El Gurre—"the armadillo"—because of his ability to slip away. Just twenty-three years old, he later told visitors he had escaped death four times. Together with Luis Eduardo, he had witnessed the paramilitary killings of community leaders in 1999.[60]

Luis Eduardo's farm was an hour's walk from his stepmother Miryam's house, in a place called Cantarana. He had told her that he would buy land closer to the town center, and she could work his farm in Mulatos.[61] Someone Luis Eduardo saw on Saturday believed the army would be in Cantarana.[62]

Miryam later said she pleaded with Luis Eduardo not to go out to pick cocoa: "We knew that they were doing a military operation. I did all but plead with him to head back to San José. . . . He didn't pay attention to me because he wasn't afraid. Besides, he needed the money from the harvest to take his son in to the doctor."[63] The family let him go, and waited.

Dario later said he told Luis Eduardo, "If we see the Army here I am not going to Cantarana. If they surprise us, I will be quiet."[64]

Luis Eduardo, Beyanira, Diener, and Dario moved along the Mulatos River at midmorning, laughing and talking. Then, Dario saw a soldier coming upstream toward them and told Luis Eduardo it was the army; Luis Eduardo said they would go toward them. The army and paramilitaries were patrolling together along the river, with a heavy paramilitary, known as "Cuatro Cuatro," in front, on point. A soldier raised his rifle and yelled, "Stop, don't run!" Dario told Luis Eduardo he would not run, and Beyanira asked him what he would do. As the soldiers got closer, Dario saw they had green berets, typical of the army, and changed his mind.

Dario then jumped off his horse and ran in the other direction into the bush. Cuatro Cuatro ordered his men to detain them, according to testimony by the Heroes of Tolová paramilitary commander Yáñez Cavadías, alias "21," who said that Captain Gordillo of the Vélez Battalion was with them. The soldiers began to interrogate Luis Eduardo about where they had come from, where they were going, and whether they belonged to the guerrillas. It was then, according to Yáñez, that Gordillo and three paramilitary commanders decided to kill them, "because they were supposedly guerrilla informants, and if we let them go they could tell the guerrillas about us."[65]

Dario, as he ran, heard someone yell, "Ay! Ay!" as if they were being beaten. He kept running through the hills.[66]

Yáñez testified that Cuatro Cuatro and two other paramilitary troops brought Luis Eduardo, Beyanira, and Diener out of the riverbed and killed them with machetes in the brush. The men shot and beheaded Diener, whose skull would be found by the river, away from the bodies. One of them forced Beyanira's head into the water.[67] They also took Beyanira's gold earrings and US$300 she had hidden in her underwear.[68] The paramilitary-army troops departed, leaving the mutilated bodies of the three in the open, near the old Mulatos health center. Commander "21," Captain Gordillo, and their men headed away from the river, taking Luis Eduardo's horses with them.[69]

At about 1:00 p.m. on the same day—Monday—several residents heard explosions from the direction of a settlement known as La Resbalosa ("The Slippery"). La Resbalosa was high in the mountains, right on the border between San José de Apartadó and Tierralta municipality, part of neighboring Córdoba department. Soldiers in the area heard the explosions, too, though they later testified they did not know where they came from.

According to Dario's account, he arrived at the Bolívar farm in Resbalosa at about 2:30 p.m., while Alfonso was eating lunch with Alejandro Pérez Castaño and other workers. Dario warned them that the army was coming, and after Alejandro walked out of the house, shooting began. Alfonso, Dario, and others then ran into the bush, the soldiers shouting after them. When they met up again, relieved they had not been killed, Alfonso told the others he had seen his wife, Sandra, on the floor of the house, covered in blood, and he decided to go back to the house to see what happened. Dario and the others stayed in the hills.[70]

When the shooting ended, and the soldiers and paramilitaries had chased Alfonso and the group in vain, Jorge Luis Salgado, alias "Kiko," was among the paramilitaries who approached the house, outside of which he saw Alejandro's body, the head and stomach destroyed, and he began to vomit. Another paramilitary picked up an AK-47 rifle by the body and turned it in to his commander, for which he would be rewarded. Members of the unit then discovered two small children in the house, hiding under a bed: Natalia, six, and Santiago, less than two years old. Kiko testified that some of the gunmen proposed turning the children over to a neighbor or to the family welfare agency but that their paramilitary commanders refused.

> The [commanders] came to the conclusion that these children would be a threat in the future in that they would grow and become guerrillas and there would be a day when one of them would see [the commanders] and accuse them. For that reason it was ordered for the troops or some designated men to execute them in silence, but none of us wanted to follow the order, refusing to follow it. It was in that moment that the father of the children appeared. . . .

When he arrived the kids shouted "Daddy," scared, since Alias 36 had them. He told them nothing would happen to them. He begged our commanders to please not kill the children, that if they wanted, to kill him but to let the children live. . . . He was on his knees with his hands behind his neck as they had told him. The children ran toward him, talking, he told them not to worry, and other things I don't remember. But one thing I remember is when the father, aware of what would happen, said to the boy that they were going on a long trip and possibly they would not return. That is when the girl got some clothing for the boy and gave it to him, saying goodbye, in Alias 36's arms, saying goodbye with her hands.

Paramilitaries carried the children away. Then one of the commanders, known as "Cobra," struck Alfonso in the back of his neck. His execution followed. Salgado said he walked away from the house, and when he looked back, he saw "Cobra" holding Natalia, "then he took her by the hair from above her head and ran the machete across her throat, he let her go and the girl fell to the ground. And seeing that, I went on walking to my unit."[71]

The same Monday afternoon, dozens of soldiers from the Thirty-Third Counter-Guerrilla Battalion arrived at Miryam Tuberquia's home in El Barro, Mulatos, from which Luis Eduardo had departed that morning. They kept her family and neighbors who had taken shelter in the house and one next to it, including her brother, five children, a young girl, and a neighbor, captive there for the next six days.[72]

According to Miryam's account, two of the uniformed men who held them captive were very aggressive. One, whom the others called Melaza ("molasses"), asked about the guerrillas, saying a person would die for not telling the truth. Miryam replied, "What truth am I going to tell if I don't know anything?" The soldiers accused Miryam of being a nurse to the guerrillas. Another soldier, called Saisa, took her food, ordering her to milk some cows. She said not to take her food, and he told her to go ask the guerrillas for some. She said they should go look for armed groups, as she had nothing to do with that. Saisa said that because no one would talk, people were dying and the soldiers had to clean it up, to "make it healthy." Miryam told them: "Doesn't it make you sorry to kill poor people who when you arrive are always working, who you never found with weapons?" One soldier told a family member that he was not in the army to kill people but to receive a salary.

One soldier told Miryam, "The paramilitaries are up there in the hills and they will get you. They will sweep clean. They will burn all your houses and cut off everyone's head." According to a witness, during their house arrest, a girl being held captive went out to get water for cooking, and one soldier said to another, "Could you cut off this little girl's head?" A soldier with him reportedly said, "Sure, if they tell me to, I will." Miryam said that Melaza told them they would finish off everyone in the Peace Community, and that if they had to they would get the foreigners, too. A family member said that one of the soldiers showed the group a machete and threatened to cut off their heads.[73]

An army officer asked Miryam who Luis Eduardo Guerra was. She replied that he was her son, and asked if they were killing the people. "What people?" responded a soldier.

On Wednesday, another soldier ordered men to dig in the rooms of the home, for weapons, he said. "You can tear down the house, we don't have weapons," a family member said. They did not find any. Believing the military would kill them, scared family members prayed and read their Bibles. "We thought we were done for," one said.

One soldier asked Miryam if she knew Luis Eduardo and Alfonso. When she said yes, he told her, "What a pity, we've killed Alfonso, we killed him with the whole family." She was quiet; Alfonso was her first cousin. The soldier also said they had killed Luis Eduardo with his family.

Miryam responded sarcastically: "You are doing things so well, because you are killing little boys, just born." The soldier began to cry.

The soldiers initially said that they had killed Luis Eduardo, Beyanira, and Diener, but after Miryam said they were civilian family members, they insisted that paramilitaries had committed the killings.[74] The change in narrative was a common practice in what came to be known as "false positive" killings: the identification of army and paramilitary together as "we"; taking credit for paramilitaries' operational "successes" until the victims of such success were shown to be obviously civilian.

While soldiers held families in Barro captive, combat went on nearby. On Tuesday, February 22, army helicopters fired on sites in the San José settlements of Bellavista, Buenos Aires, and Alto Bonito, killing several farm animals. After the bombing, some one hundred military troops entered houses in Bellavista, one of them reportedly saying of the residents, "Here they are, let's kill the sons of bitches." The residents fled; upon returning, they found all their chickens gone.[75]

That morning, Dario and the men with him went back to the Bolívar farm. They found a lot of blood in the house, and Luis Eduardo's horses, leading Dario to believe that the same soldiers he had seen along the river had come to the Bolívar house. After searching for some time, they saw an oddly high stack of cocoa branches and freshly moved soil, and realized that there were bodies buried there. Scared, they went back up into the hills, sleeping in an abandoned house.[76] The following day, some of these men told members of the Peace Community what they had seen.

When Peace Community council members received information on Wednesday about the killings, they immediately requested that the attorney general's office, called the Fiscalía, come to the Bolívar farm in Resbalosa to exhume the remains as part of an official investigation. They also organized a community search committee for the seven-hour walk up to Resbalosa, through the dense forest and over the foggy mountain peak known as Chontalito, departing shortly after 5:00 a.m. on Friday morning, February 25. The committee included women, men, children, older people,—a hundred in all—as well as international accompaniers from FOR, PBI, and a U.S.-based community health group called Project Concern. The FOR accompaniers were Renata Rendon, a Colombian American from New York, and Trish Abbott, recently arrived from England. They all hiked some seven hours to Resbalosa, near the edge of Córdoba state.

When the first group in the committee arrived at Alfonso Bolívar's farm in Resbalosa, in the early afternoon, they found the site where cacao branches and cacao shells had been piled up over where bodies were buried, emitting a strange but not overpowering smell. At the house, Rendon and Wilson David saw big black tarps with blood on them, things knocked over, and on the outside, two small bloody footprints on the wooden floor. A pig was eating corn. Amid the ransacked house, there were machete cuts in the mattresses and furniture. Rendon began to film.

Down the hill from the house, dozens of community members without foreigners encountered some fifty soldiers, who pointed their rifles at them. Someone in the group yelled that they were civilians with babies and old people. Rendon and a PBI volunteer approached the soldiers, whose commander—a Captain Gordillo—appeared out of breath and sweating. Rendon explained to Gordillo that international observers from the United States, Canada, France, England, and Spain were present. Gordillo told the soldiers to release the community members.[77]

Fig. 6.1. One hundred community members hiked seven hours to the massacre sites before judicial investigators arrived. PHOTOGRAPH BY JESÚS ABAD COLORADO.

Later that afternoon, helicopters that were provided by the U.S. Embassy's Narcotics Affairs Section brought the Fiscalía's team of forensic investigators to La Resbalosa for the exhumation.[78] The team began work the same afternoon. Dressed in light-blue jump suits and long gloves, the half-dozen investigators began to uncover the bodies buried under the leaves and shallow soil. The smell was intense. They pulled out a torso, its intestines visible, then another torso, then a child whose arm had been cut off. Then what looked to Rendon and Abbott like a penis.

As this was occurring, soldiers from the Vélez Battalion sat nearby, one of them writing in a notebook. Some of them were laughing. They took many pictures of themselves flashing victory signs outside the Bolivar house. Captain Gordillo stood nearby, talking with a relative of one of those killed.[79]

Hearing that the bodies of Luis Eduardo, Beyanira, and Diener had been discovered an hour's walk away, most of the community group and accompaniers descended down to the Mulatos River. There, a young woman who had fallen behind the main group had come across the three bodies in the open air, then made her way back to the group. The community's attorneys immediately informed the Fiscalía and vice presidency of the bodies' location. The group saw the Fiscalía team fly away from Resbalosa in helicopters as they walked just after dark. They slept outside in the moonlight.

Early the next morning, a group of forty walked along the Mulatos River until they saw vultures flying over the second massacre site. First they saw on the riverbank what was left of Diener's head, the flesh already eaten by animals. Less than twenty feet away, a machete had been thrown into the weeds. About fifteen yards away were the bodies of the three, still clothed, though Beyanira's sweatpants had been pulled down to her knees. Slightly downriver were Beyanira's boots and another machete. No one spoke. No one cried, at first. Eventually, Elkin Ramírez, a human rights attorney who represented the community, urged everyone not to touch anything because it was evidence.[80]

The PBI accompaniers called from their satellite phone to convey the site's location so that the Fiscalía investigators could get there. Young men used slingshots to throw rocks at the vultures that circled above and perched on nearby trees, and to keep away pigs. The group waited for the investigators, but they did not come. At 4:00 p.m. they heard two helicopters and rushed to the old health clinic to wave white shirts at the pilot, shout, and start a fire, but the helicopters instead ascended to Resbalosa, picked up troops, and flew over again as they descended, letting out troops nearby. The group witnessed this operation four or five times.[81]

In the late afternoon, a group of soldiers arrived on foot at the site. One of the soldiers with no name tag picked up the machete close to Beyanira's boots, wiped it in the sand, washed it in the river, then walked with it past the group, making a gesture to show a throat being slit, and said, "This was the beheading machete." The soldier walked away and kept the machete, which would not be seen again.[82]

As in Resbalosa, investigators had to be sent by helicopter to Mulatos to exhume the remains of the massacre victims. The community's attorneys and FOR communicated the exact location of the site in Mulatos to the vice presidency and the local ombudsman, respectively. An official in the vice presidency stated that the helicopters could not go in because of weather conditions, though it was clearly not true. A Fiscalía official reportedly told the vice presidency that the investigators could not get to the site because the army would not allow them to go.[83]

The group had passed Friday night in a nearby house. International accompaniers updated their offices in Turbo and Bogotá throughout Saturday, but by nightfall on Saturday, they were running low on food and had had little sleep, and the internationals' satellite phone was out of battery. The delay prompted a flurry of high-level contacts by PBI, FOR, and the community's legal representatives in Medellín to press the Fiscalía to action—which also served to alert the U.S. and European embassies, UN officials, and Colombian agencies of events as they unfolded. Desperate at the inexplicable failure of investigators to arrive, community leaders decided they would bring the bodies down themselves if the Fiscalía did not appear by the next morning. The action would be illegal, and it presented a dilemma for the international volunteers, since accompanying the act might also be viewed as illegal and grounds for deportation. Eventually, the investigators arrived in Mulatos early on Sunday morning and removed the remains of the three people.

On Sunday, part of the Peace Community and international delegation hiked to El Barro after leaving the Mulatos massacre site, carrying the community's flag. On arriving, they saw three wooden houses. On the first, which was empty, someone had written with a burnt stick: "Out guerillas, it's your worst nightmare telling you so—El Cacique," and above that: "The Scorpion BCG 33." The words referred to the Thirty-Third Counter-Guerrilla Battalion "Cacique Lutaima," the "killing machine" with whom Duque said he was working.

At one of the other houses, an older man sitting on a bench was reading a Bible, and he smiled when he saw the group approach. Miryam came out of the house and expressed her relief that their ordeal was over. But when the community confirmed that they had found the bodies of Luis Eduardo, Beyanira, and Diener, her eyes filled with tears.

There were at least three soldiers posted at the houses when the group arrived, but they did not stop Miryam and the family from leaving. Relieved, the family prepared to depart with the group, leaving home and belongings behind. Jesús Abad Colorado, a photographer in the group that arrived, spoke to one of the soldiers about the campesinos' pain, which had

Fig. 6.2. Miryam Tuberquia (*left*) and family members fled after being held captive by soldiers during the massacre. PHOTOGRAPH BY JESÚS ABAD COLORADO.

him overwhelmed. Visibly disturbed, the soldiers responded, "It's always the campesinos that lose everything. Just look, this family is going to leave even their pigs." By the time the group left a few hours later, the soldiers had erased the graffiti on the first house.[84]

No one yet knew how many people had been killed, and rumors flowed of missing families and even bodies in other settlements, including Las Nieves and La Esperanza. So on Tuesday, March 1, community members and international volunteers again hiked in search of the missing. In La Esperanza they found the missing family; in Las Nieves, where Macho Rusio had been killed, a group of five had been in hiding for several days. A father in the group later testified that the military had tortured his son and threatened to cut out his wife's eyes and tongue, until he agreed to lead them to the guerrilla militia leader's house, but that after Macho Rusio's death, they heard soldiers preparing machetes. Believing the soldiers would kill them, they fled into the bush. When community members and FOR accompaniers arrived, the family came out of hiding and fled with the community, still terrified of military operations.[85]

Meanwhile, community members awaited the release of the remains of Luis Eduardo, Beyanira, and Diener from the Fiscalía in Apartadó. Luis

Eduardo's hands, however, were so decomposed that they could not identify them with fingerprints, and they had no dental records. They finally managed to identify him and release the bodies late Sunday evening, and the community brought them to San José in coffins mounted on the *chiva* vehicles. The driver of the chiva that carried Luis Eduardo's body received death threats, and a few days later he fled the region.[86]

CHAPTER 7
PROJECTS OF LIFE

Outsiders frequently imagined San José de Apartadó, or even Colombia as a whole, as being in a condition of total and permanent war. I often heard this in the United States when I told people that I was going to visit Colombia. Media reports on the war and human rights alerts that focused exclusively on acts of violence such as the massacre of February 2005 frequently reinforced this mistaken perception. The myth of ongoing and all-encompassing violence in a place, even if unconsciously held, yields easily to the idea that the only way for outsiders to engage a conflict there is by supporting the violent actors who are the least objectionable.

Yet since the 1990s, when Plan Colombia was conceived, and the following decade, when it was executed, Colombia gave birth to hundreds of unarmed initiatives across the spectrum of social sectors, national geography, objectives, and methods—initiatives that typically were little known or invisible to U.S. policy makers and the general public. When they were aware of these unarmed initiatives, U.S. policy makers in theory had at their disposal a range of potential actions to support them, principally by pressure on Colombian authorities to prevent acts of violence against activists and unarmed groups and bring to justice the perpetrators of these acts. Because the United States was a major patron during this period of Colombian military, police, and judicial agencies, it had considerable leverage.

Grassroots groups and human rights organizations in the United States, while they had less power and resources than U.S. officials, nevertheless had a wider range of options available to support Colombian peace initiatives. And when the levers of governmental power became less amenable to direct grassroots advocacy, groups from below in both the United States and Colombia increasingly turned to other means to pursue their goals of peace, equality, and justice. Cataloging the range of Colombian initiatives and U.S. grassroots support projects helps us understand both the efficacy and the limits of local, national, and transnational responses from below to state violence.

Rural Farmers Resist

Before, during, and after the February 2005 massacre, as the Peace Community in San José de Apartadó struggled to deal with state, paramilitary, and guerrilla violence as well as with the devastating impacts of that violence, its members also conducted constructive activity. They produced crops and built alliances with other communities in Colombia and beyond that resisted violence, displacement, and impunity. In August 2004 the Peace Community hosted a "peasant university" that supported food sovereignty for ten rural communities from across Colombia resisting control by armed groups. Topics included organic agriculture, diet, preparation and analysis of soil, geopolitics of food, irrigation, and religious celebrations. "Our search to be able to weave solidarity and build together," the community wrote, "is born of a desire to be able to maintain and secure spaces of civilian resistance that allow communities and the civilian population to live in the midst of the war."[1] The project was conceived as radically different from ordinary academic universities, which the communities viewed as based on formal degrees, knowledge used for exploitation and exclusion, and the logic of consumerism.[2]

The peasant university grew out of a gathering and network of Colombian communities in resistance, RECORRE, initiated by the Peace Community in August 2003. The first university lasted for a month, and a second occurred barely a month after the 2005 San José massacre, with participants traveling for up to seventy hours to one of the communities in southern Caquetá Department.[3] The RECORRE members included Nasa and Wiwa indigenous communities from the departments of southwestern Cauca and northern César, Afro-Colombian communities in western Chocó, as well as peasant communities from southern Bolívar and eastern Antioquia. The network's members undertook a radical rejection of the state, including of its judicial entities, which would have important ramifications for both the

Peace Community and for its international supporters. They called this rejection "rupture."

But this network of more than a dozen communities represented only one set of many nonviolent initiatives in the midst of the war, which took many forms and constituted responses from below to war and human rights violations. They included both rural and urban experiences; church-based peace projects; initiatives that resisted war or that sought to establish local democracy; projects based on the identities of Afro-Colombians, indigenous, or peasants, of women and youth. These initiatives represented key alternatives within Colombia, but their existence also demonstrated that the options both for U.S. policy and for grassroots activists were not limited to supporting the state or armed resistance to it. They upended the narrative that there were no protagonists with whose values non-Colombians could identify, and that outsiders could only denounce crimes of political violence.

Such projects included a nonviolent community defense force in Cauca Department, called the Indigenous Guard; conscientious objection by youth to participation in any armed group; Afro-Colombian peace communities; trade unionist protests; and feminist mobilizations against war. The Colombian political Left was the foundation for one of the most developed human rights movements in the hemisphere. By 2005 more than two hundred local and national human rights organizations were grouped in the Colombia-Europe-U.S. Human Rights Observatory (Coordinación Colombia–Europa–Estados Unidos, CCEEU). These organizations became expert in bringing human rights cases and issues to the Inter-American and United Nations systems and to Washington.[4] They also documented many thousands of violations of human rights and compiled this documentation more effectively than groups in almost any other country. This coordinated documentation facilitated the work of international human rights advocates.

Art, theater, and dance also were important media for telling grassroots movements' stories, conveying resistance to war and violence, and imagining alternatives. Making art was often conceived as the antithesis of making war. Such cultural expression was also an important container for identity, rarely conveyed in the dry statements of government policy. Art may come from young people or may be made by older community members seeking to pass on identity and stories to youth.

Most participants in these initiatives did not set out to become activists; the issue came to them. Often this was because of one of the innumerable tragedies of the war—a family member or a friend threatened, disappeared, killed, or raped. Others belonged to communities whose leaders envisioned and organized collective resistance to war and its violence.

Antimilitarist Initiatives

The national mood in Colombia in 2002 favored war, but only five years before, millions of Colombians mobilized for peace. In 1996 a national coalition asked Colombian children to vote on peace, followed in October 1997 by a referendum for peace in which ten million Colombians participated. Journalists, academics, and businessmen formed groups for peace. A large gathering in 1996 of NGOs from all over Antioquia, Colombia's most populous department, supported rural communities' posture of active neutrality. Large local and national mobilizations for peace continued through 1998 and 1999, including marches by more than two million Colombians against kidnapping.[5] This upsurge created the conditions for peace negotiations that took place between the government and the FARC from 1998 to 2002.

Those talks collapsed because "none of the parties could overcome the logic of war with a political logic," according to Ana Teresa Bernal, who was part of a working group in the negotiations and led the National Network of Initiatives Against War and for Peace (Red Nacional de Iniciativas Ciudadanas por la Paz y contra la Guerra, REDEPAZ). "All of the negotiations did not focus on more than the procedural, on whether planes would fly over [the demilitarized zone] or not. It was a logic of war and it dealt with war's actions."[6]

Young men and women who opposed the war or could not in good conscience participate in it also organized to support each other. The most prominent of these groups, the Medellín Youth Network (Red Juvenil) and Colombian Collective Action of Conscientious Objectors (Acción Colectiva de Objetores y Objetoras de Conciencia, ACOOC), resisted participation not only in the Colombian Army but in illegal armed groups. Paramilitary and guerrilla groups forcibly recruited youth in the city's poor and working-class neighborhoods that in some cases those groups controlled. "No army defends us," said the Red's youth, many of whom were stigmatized by the larger society as presumed gang members, as violent, as objects rather than subjects of policy.

In Colombia, young men who have done military service or been exempt from it receive a military-issued card; the army frequently conducts round-ups of young men found without these cards. Red and ACOOC members directly challenged the army's actions to forcibly recruit on the street, which were declared illegal by Colombia's Constitutional Court in 2009, by going to where they occurred and disrupting them.

Red members also conducted workshops in poor neighborhoods or at their rambling house in Medellín. They used play, art, confrontation, writing, and humor in these workshops to question and deconstruct armed authority. They helped young men targeted for recruitment by paramilitary groups to set up community networks that publicly supported their decision not to join. They organized free concerts in the park by popular bands whose followers were sometimes in conflict, and used the occasion to keep the peace. They organized international gatherings of war resisters. They denounced illegal roundups of youth, protested at military bases, and provided legal defense for conscientious objectors and others held against their will by the military.

Other antimilitarist initiatives mobilized women from across the country, drawing on feminist solidarity and analysis of armed conflict. In late 1996, as San José de Apartadó was undergoing one of its most severe trials, a nun told a public gathering in Apartadó that 95 percent of the women in one community in the region had been raped. When a group of feminist women in Medellín heard this, it ignited an idea: to bring women from around the country to Apartadó to embrace women who had suffered war's violence and humiliation. Thus was born La Ruta Pacífica de la Mujer (The Women's Path to Peace), which organized 1,500 women in a caravan of buses from remote areas of the country, some of whom left their communities for the first time, traveling several days to reach Urabá.

The Ruta Pacífica organized several more national caravans to marches in conflict areas in Bolívar, Cartagena, Barrancabermeja, Bogotá, and Chocó to express solidarity with and accompany women impacted by the war's violence, often on November 25, the International Day Against Violence Against Women. In 2003 the Ruta led 3,000 women to southern Putumayo Department, the epicenter of the U.S.-led military offensive against coca growing and FARC guerrillas. Hundreds of women's groups across the country endorsed the Ruta's statement against the "militarist policy of the current government, which favors the use of weapons and force to treat problems that are rooted in and generate poverty, historic expropriation, marginalization, and disorder."[7]

A number of more local initiatives also made a claim to unarmed means for social change. Faced with bleak prospects for peace at the national level, these community efforts sought to create democratic processes and a new political culture. Afro-Colombian communities located along the Atrato

River in Chocó Department, southwest of Apartadó, had historically been ignored by the state—many were literally not on national maps. Guerrillas established a presence in the Atrato River basin in the 1980s, so when paramilitary groups made their westward sweep in 1996 from Córdoba into Urabá, the communities lay directly in the path of conflict. Subject in early 1997 to blockades of food, massacres, forced disappearances, selective killings, and even bombing by the army, nearly five thousand residents of remote settlements displaced to the town of Pavarandó, Antioquia, many of whose residents themselves had fled. With support from the Catholic Church, the displaced communities in late 1997 declared themselves the San Francisco de Asís Peace Community, planned a return to their lands, and negotiated a commitment of respect from the armed groups in the area and of support from the state. Other communities that had displaced to the nearby city of Riosucio followed suit that year, and combined to establish two other peace communities, Natividad de María and Nuestra Señora del Carmen. United Nations agencies and international NGOs supported the communities' continued negotiations of commitments from Colombian state agencies.[8]

Other Afro-descendant communities established humanitarian zones in Cacarica on the lower Atrato River, and Jiguamiandó, in the middle Atrato, similar to the model of San José de Apartadó. They had to confront long-term paramilitary harassment and threats but continued nonviolent resistance for more than a decade, accompanied by Justicia y Paz and PBI.

Other communities worked within local government structures, while remaking them. In Mogotes in Santander Department, a town of thirteen thousand people, guerrillas of the ELN kidnapped a corrupt mayor and killed two civilian town officials in late 1997. The community responded with a regional mobilization that supported the local reassertion of sovereignty by a Municipal Constituent Assembly, which demanded that the ELN release the mayor, which it did. The assembly then dismissed the mayor by an overwhelming majority. It also organized more than 150 delegates from village assemblies, neighborhood action groups, and associations of teachers, health workers, religious groups, and trade guilds into a permanent forum that traveled from remote settlements each month to discuss and reach consensus on local issues. As in the peace communities in Urabá, the Catholic Church and Christian principles were key to catalyzing the initial organization of the assembly. Subsequent mayors and a parish priest later criticized the process, leading to its reduced influence. But it demonstrated that democratic nonviolent organizing could have an impact.[9]

One result was that other communities followed Mogotes' example. One of them was Tarso, Antioquia, a town of 6,300 that similarly formed a municipal constituent assembly in 1999. Producing mostly coffee and cattle in an area with both a high concentration of land ownership and the influence of liberation theology, Tarso peasants had organized land takeovers in the 1970s. By 1999, as the coffee economy tanked, the municipality was experiencing a debt crisis, corruption, an inability to even pay public employees, and violence from both ELN guerrilla and paramilitary groups. Faced with a lack of public participation, activists put together working groups with broad representation to address jobs, social spending, education, and human rights and duties. The advent of acute crisis, collective organizing experience, leadership by a trusted activist, space for participation, and support by the Catholic Church and other outside actors once the process began were important ingredients in the initiative's success.

The Tarso process was most explicitly focused on democratic participation, but some of its leaders had earlier joined the guerrillas and demobilized because of their conclusion that the armed struggle prioritized military over political activity. When those leaders promoted the idea of a peace community in 1997, an ELN squad accused members of collaboration with paramilitaries, publicly killing one of the leaders. After Tarso organized its municipal constituent assembly in 2001, paramilitaries raided the town and threatened leaders who had demobilized from the ELN, forcing them to flee for a year.[10] But the assembly used the leaders' absence to develop relationships with government funding agencies in Medellín and Spain, to diversify its agricultural economy, and to demonstrate to the paramilitaries that their threat made no sense.[11]

By 2007 dozens more constituent municipal assemblies had been established, but faced with the tension between confronting and evading the threats posed by armed groups, most did not explicitly reject or resist the war.[12] Mogotes and Tarso, on the other hand, were among the Hundred Municipalities for Peace project initiated by REDEPAZ, a Colombian peace network formed in 1993.

Some communities organized to protect civilians threatened by armed groups by establishing dialogue with them. The Peasant Workers Association of Carare River (Asociación de Trabajadores Campesinos del Carare, ATCC) is organized in thirty-two villages in Santander Department, home to five thousand people. Since threats from armed groups generally preceded most violence against civilians in the area, in 1987 the ATCC was formed to mediate responses to the threats. Threats typically were based on accusations that the civilians were informers for opposing groups, so the ATCC investigated the accusations, using up to ten different means, including consulting neighbors, surveilling the accused, asking for a "second chance," guaranteeing the demobilization of the accused, and using its own moral authority to urge respect for civilians. To guarantee transparency, the leaders tape recorded their meetings with armed groups and played the recordings from a loudspeaker in the plaza during public gatherings. Many political scientists frame control of political violence as a function of armed groups, but residents interviewed by the researcher Oliver Kaplan "naturally responded that the 'actor' who had control was not any armed group but in fact the civilian ATCC."[13]

Other efforts worked to establish restorative justice at the interpersonal and community level, such as the Schools for Forgiveness and Reconciliation in fourteen cities, initiated in 2000 by Father Leonel Narváez. They sought not to forget violence but to "remember with different eyes" and create positive social capital to use in negotiation of conflicts.[14]

Many of the broad array of initiatives were vibrant for a time and became less active after a year or several years. In Mogotes, for example, tension arose in 2004 between the Constituent Assembly and the formally elected government, and confusion about the roles of each.[15] A project in Samaniego, a community in southwestern Nariño, to establish a peace territory and a local peace pact reduced violence, though participation grew and diminished, depending on elected leaders and the national climate for peace negotiations.[16]

Some might conclude from the impermanence of these initiatives that they failed. In fact, like armed conflict, such initiatives always rise and fall in response to changing contexts, conflicts and opportunities, and community and political organizing. Indeed, many of them were explicitly responsive to the armed conflict, to its worst excesses, or to particular local manifestations, which also rose and subsided over time. Others might observe that these communities were relatively small on the scale of a country with a population of more than forty million. Yet the armed conflict played out overwhelmingly in the countryside, so that rural initiatives by peasant, indigenous, and Afro-Colombian farmers with meager resources were both significant and impressive. They also faced powerful forces among landed elites, illegal armed groups, and the government seeking to control them and the territories where they live.

Collective Indigenous Resistance to War

Other rural nonviolent initiatives were not situational responses to armed conflict but grew out of millennial indigenous traditions and struggles for autonomy. The Nasa indigenous people, located in Cauca Department in Colombia's southwest, have their own territory and are organized in the Northern Cauca Indigenous Councils Association (Asociación de Cabildos Indígenas del Norte del Cauca, ACIN), affiliated with the Cauca Regional Indigenous Council and the National Indigenous Organization of Colombia (Organización Nacional Indígena de Colombia, ONIC). ACIN has developed what its members call "projects of life." Throughout the first decade of the twenty-first century, the Nasa led regional and national marches to oppose the Free Trade Agreement and Plan Colombia, to defend their territory, and to propose a different vision of the economics and power relationships in Colombia and the world. Forty percent of ACIN's membership is made up of Afro-Colombians, mestizo peasants, and other non-Nasa people—a diversity that ACIN embraces within a shared vision. Association assemblies are held in the Nasa language, with interpretation for non-Nasa speakers.[17]

In 1994 ACIN organized what is known as the Indigenous Guard, a sort of nonviolent defense force of eight thousand people armed only with their authority and hardwood staffs, which has had some success in saving those threatened by violence from the armed conflict. The indigenous guards are unpaid volunteers and coordinate with other area groups responsible for education, traditional medicine, earthquake and flood response, human rights training, and community development.[18]

The Indigenous Guard with support of the Nasa community has taken action to resist violence multiple times. These have included the rescue of a Swiss citizen and his assistant, kidnapped by FARC guerrillas in 2003, when two thousand indigenous guards surrounded the guerrillas with their captive; the rescue of a helicopter that was carrying public funds in 2009; deactivation of antipersonnel mines in El Carmen settlement; eradication of marijuana in 2008; and the rescue of others kidnapped in the area.[19]

One memorable incident occurred in November 2008. Members of the Indigenous Guard carry only staffs, but they are trained to defend the community nonviolently in case of any threat. On November 26, seven Nasa indigenous officials from a community called Jambaló were kidnapped on the road between Jambaló, Silvia, and the city of Popayán. They were riding in a minibus just before dark when it was intercepted by four hooded and armed men who said they were members of the FARC.

After intimidating them, the gunmen took the group toward the Pioyá Indigenous Territory with the purpose of taking them into the jungle. An hour later, the Jambaló community learned of events and immediately called indigenous authorities, who quickly began operations in the area to rescue those kidnapped. When the kidnappers realized they were being pursued by the community, they separated into two groups: three guerrillas took a couple and the other group took the rest in the vehicle, at about 9:00 p.m. The community continued in pursuit until they surrounded the armed men, who were forced to abandon the captives. "The Indians are here, the Council is here, better to leave them," the guerrillas said when they felt the community near, said Emilce Muñoz, one of those kidnapped.[20]

While this was happening, another group of men, women, youth, and children, guided by the community's radio station, followed the trail of the couple and caught up with them at midnight. The guerrillas tried to intimidate the community by firing shots in the air, but the civilian community's resistance prevailed, and the group of adults and children managed to rescue the last two captives. After the pursuit, the gunmen left behind a revolver that was seized by indigenous authorities.

In a public act the following morning, community leaders denounced what was happening, and the confiscated weapon was destroyed as a rejection of all the armed groups that provoke imbalance in their communities. They did this, they said, "because we don't agree with an army that victimizes the civilian population with 'false positives' nor with guerrillas that say they are of the people while they attack the people's rights."

Nasa communities continued to act boldly to demilitarize their territories, as in July 2012, when thousands of indigenous people peacefully disarmed seven soldiers who refused to leave a provisional army base. Nasa authorities had demanded the departure of both the army and FARC in the wake of combat that had been increasing costs to civilians in the area. President Juan Manuel Santos attempted to reseize the narrative (and the town) by claiming that indigenous people had been violent and by paying homage to a soldier who had been photographed crying as he was removed. But Nasa communities nevertheless asserted their constitutional right to autonomy and refuted the story espoused by Santos—and by the United States—that the army's presence provided security.[21]

Indigenous communities besides the Nasa also organized Indigenous Guards in other regions of Colombia, including the Emberá Chamí in Valle de Cauca and the Zenú and Dojura communities in Antioquia; the latter were mobilized to search for an assassin after a Dojura leader was killed in 2016.

Such nonviolent defense was not always safer than armed revolt: four indigenous guards were killed in May and June of the same year.[22]

The initiatives of Nasa and other communities and organizations to resist acts of war provided important narratives for activists in both Colombia and the United States, and in many cases they were partners with U.S. groups that sought to construct bilateral relations from below that were different from official policy.

A U.S. Policy from Below

When President Clinton signed Plan Colombia into law in July 2000, Saudi hijackers had not yet taken down the World Trade Center and thousands of lives, nor had the United States invaded Afghanistan as part of a new "global war on terrorism." Activists had only months before mobilized massive street protests to successfully stall the World Trade Organization in Seattle and against the World Bank in Washington, and the online activism and touch-screen isolation that would become dominant a decade later barely existed. Nonviolent protest against corporate globalization and U.S. militarism—including in Latin America—was still growing and yielding fruit. Yet analyses and histories of U.S. foreign policy and grassroots activism in 2001–2 often focus exclusively on responses to the September 11 attack and build-up to wars in Afghanistan and Iraq, bypassing the extensive actions around Colombia at the time.[23]

Organizations and activists, including veterans of the Central America solidarity and anti-intervention movements of the 1980s, and students learning about Latin America, drug policy, and racism, began in 2000 to co-alesce in response to Plan Colombia. Colombians living in the United States had already founded local human rights and solidarity organizations around the United States since the early 1980s, and hosted speaking tours by Colombian activists, published newsletters, and worked with Washington-based advocacy groups such as the Washington Office on Latin America. In 2001 sixty organizations came together in the Colombia Mobilization, a coalition formed to transform U.S. policy toward Colombia. The coalition called for ending U.S. military aid and aerial fumigation, expanding drug treatment in the United States, and increasing U.S. support for sustainable economic development, efforts for negotiated peace, and aid to Colombians displaced by the conflict. It was an agenda that pushed the envelope from what Washington groups were promoting by organizing protests outside the Beltway and by addressing domestic drug policy and the role of Plan Colombia's corporate beneficiaries. The coalition included peace and church organizations, environmental groups, drug policy reform groups, local Colombia human rights committees, campus organizations, as well as Central America–oriented organizations.[24]

Only two weeks after the September 11 attack, the Colombia Mobilization organized a national forum and lobby days in Washington. The coalition's groups organized speaking tours, protests, delegations, and advocacy throughout the rest of 2001 and 2002. One of the coalition's leading organizations was Witness for Peace, which established a team in Colombia in 2001 in order to organize U.S. delegations to regions impacted by the drug war and mobilize support for changing U.S. policy.

Annual protests against the U.S. Army School of the Americas (SOA) in Fort Benning, Georgia, continued to draw thousands of people from across the country and served as an important gateway for new activists to learn and become involved in work against U.S. military intervention in Latin America, and for building community among both veteran and newer participants. In 2001 the Senate joined the House in voting to nominally close the School of the Americas, in response to the persistent demonstrations against the school's history of teaching torture and graduates who became dictators. The new military training school established in the same legislation, Western Hemisphere Institute for Security Cooperation (WHINSEC), continued training Latin American officers by the same faculty, on the same site, with most of the same curriculum.[25] As the early twenty-first century progressed, the protest and movement to close WHINSEC increased its focus on Colombia, for example by including Luis Eduardo Guerra on the rally stage in November 2003.

In 2003 the Colombia Mobilization sponsored regional demonstrations in four cities where corporate beneficiaries of Plan Colombia had their headquarters: Atlanta (home of Coca-Cola, whose Colombian affiliate was implicated in paramilitary murders of trade unionists), St. Louis (home of Monsanto, whose glyphosate fumigant was sprayed on coca-growing areas in Colombia), Los Angeles (home of Occidental Petroleum, whose oil pipeline was protected by a $98 million military aid appropriation), and Hartford (home of Sikorsky, whose helicopters the United States was sending to the Colombian Army).[26]

These actions illustrated how Plan Colombia served U.S. corporate interests at a time when paramilitaries were responsible for three out of every four political murders in Colombia. They mobilized thousands of activists in cities around the country. But their timing was again unfortunate: they occurred just a week after the United States invaded Iraq. The Bush administration's multiple fronts for post-9/11 warfare were growing, as were the authorities Congress granted to the administration for engaging them. Journalists were being redeployed to the Middle East as well. Organizations still organized and advocated for the goals of the Colombia Mobilization, but opportunities for substantially changing U.S. policy toward Colombia appeared to have narrowed.

One particular episode illustrates the problem activists faced. In Washington, church, human rights, and solidarity organizations met regularly in a committee convened by the Latin America Working Group. The meetings served as a clearinghouse to share information about activities and coordinate legislative advocacy timed around the annual foreign aid bills. In 2006 some of these NGOs and Congressional opponents of Plan Colombia caucused on a legislative strategy. An amendment on the floor of the House had to attract Representatives for reasons beyond Colombia: champions of global AIDS initiatives, for example, or fiscal hawks who viewed coca eradication as a waste of funds. It also had to attract Republicans, who ruled the House. What activists came up with was an amendment to cut $30 million from the military aid package to Colombia. This represented approximately a 5 percent reduction in military aid, at best symbolic. But to rally grassroots support for the amendment, groups wrote appeals for grassroots action that celebrated the proposed cut as an important stride toward a decent policy.

In this context, many activists sought more direct ways to express their faith and values and to support human rights, peace, and justice in Colombia. While continuing to seek broader policy changes, U.S. communities and groups could at least develop their own bilateral relations with Colombians. These experiences typically occurred outside the dominant discourses about Colombia, below the radar of policy makers in Washington. Strategic solidarity and support for such nonviolent resistance came from the United States and other countries, in the form of sister community relationships, protest mobilizations, and physical accompaniment.

Sister Communities

Sister groupings brought together Colombian and U.S. cities and towns, churches, unions, and organizations in long-term relationships, exchanges, and solidarity. Many were initiated through the Colombia Support Network (CSN), which pioneered the practice in the 1990s through a relationship between Dane County, Wisconsin, and Apartadó, formally approved by their respective local governments. These relationships also gave rise to emergency responses from U.S. activists when their Colombian partners received threats or were attacked by armed groups, including letters to U.S. officials, calls to Colombia, visits, or material support. Both CSN and FOR, for example, organized emergency delegations to San José de Apartadó after the massacre in February 2005.

In a process of mutual learning, sister churches, communities, organizations, and labor unions visited each other and addressed barriers of language, culture, geography, and class to seek a common path for justice and peace. These processes were not born fully formed but were slow works in progress. "As peasants, we understand that, because the countryside has a slow process of production," said Pedro Acosta Fernández of the Colombian Evangelical Council, in Tierralta, Córdoba. Acosta's church was one of twenty-two peace sanctuary churches in Colombia, an initiative begun by Colombian Mennonites in 1999 that promotes peace and human rights from a perspective rooted in Christian gospel.[27]

Diverse communities on the Colombian Left, including Christians, had since the 1960s developed analyses of the United States related to its imperialism, the foreign debt and role of Washington in the International Monetary Fund and structural adjustment policies, and military intervention throughout the region. Other Colombians had images of the United States as a land of superheroes. Some groups, like the community of Cajibio, Cauca, previously had relationships with solidarity groups in Europe but not in the United States. Through direct contact with U.S. communities that occurred through sister group relationships, many Colombians came to know U.S. activists resisting empire and U.S. policy. When an upstate New York group approached Cajibio leaders about a partnership, the leaders agreed and then said, "You're going to give us a big problem." Why? the leaders were asked. "Because we've told the peasants that people from the United States are bad. And now we have to tell them that these [U.S. people] are good." This became a joke between the groups, said John Henry González of Cajibio, but it also complicated the community's analysis as they came to perceive that in the United States the government did not represent the citizenry any more than in Colombia. Colombians also saw that they could work with U.S. partners to lobby for reducing Washington's contributions to the war in Colombia.[28]

Christian church groups found important values and aspirations in common with their counterparts, as did farmers from rural U.S. and Colombian communities. When sister groups got to know activist counterparts, had moments together of witnessing the war's pain, it reminded Colombians that they were not alone, and it made it harder to generalize. "Personal contacts are key for discerning all that is behind a history," said Pedro Acosta. These relationships also helped activists from both countries to understand the importance of collaborating and working together for the changes they sought, not seeking them unilaterally. And they used the partnerships for learning in both directions, with the aim of transforming their realities, not tinkering at the edges. Colombians also frequently drew the U.S. communities into the challenges of protecting the security of civilians in communities located in war zones through action alerts to call Colombian authorities when community members were attacked or threatened.[29]

While material support for Colombian communities was typically also part of the relationships, many groups had learned from experiences in Central America to go beyond paternalistic aid relationships from earlier periods. At the same time, most economic assistance to Colombia came from European government aid programs, while U.S. tax monies went for military purposes. The military nature of U.S. aid and need for community-based assistance created a strong incentive for U.S. community groups to provide aid for agricultural projects, sponsor scholarships for students in sister communities, and organize fair trade purchases that more closely aligned with their values of nonviolence than did Plan Colombia. They also organized and financed visits by Colombian sister group representatives to the United States for speaking tours, advocacy, and building relationships.

Accompaniment and Policy Advocacy

While sister community relationships involved short-term visits by members of U.S. communities to Colombia, international accompaniment projects, such as those of PBI and FOR, brought individuals from Europe, the United States, and other countries to live full-time in Colombia for a year or longer to strengthen the security of threatened activists and communities. The United States supported Colombian government programs to protect human rights defenders and others threatened with political violence. Unlike such official programs, these projects assumed that responsibility from a pragmatic as well as ethical perspective: Pragmatic, because such accompaniment was often more effective than state protection agencies (Colombian or international) at safeguarding the lives and continued work of activists and community members at risk. Ethical, because the use of an unarmed presence did not seek to vanquish an enemy. Instead, it reinforced the values of nonviolence, truth, and reconciliation.

In addition to PBI and FOR, which began accompaniment in Colombia in 1994 and 2002, respectively, a range of international accompaniment projects began during this period, including the Red de Hermandad (a partnership of Colombian and mostly European organizations) in 1999; the U.S.-based Witness for Peace in 2000; Christian Peacemaker Teams (from the United States and Canada) in 2001; Projet Accompagnement Solidarité Colombie, from Quebec, in 2003; Swedish Fellowship of Reconciliation and the U.S. Presbyterian Peace Fellowship in 2004; International Peace Observatory in 2005; and the Italian Operation Dove in 2009.

These organizations and their Colombian partners successfully used the dissuasive influence of the international community to strengthen security for human rights defenders, communities, and others accompanied by international volunteers. The diversity of both international and Colombian groups and of the models they used enabled them to benefit a much broader set of Colombian activists than would have been possible with just one accompaniment organization or model. Groups without the resources to mount accompaniment throughout Colombia, for example, focused in one city or region. While PBI and some other groups conducted highly structured accompaniment, other accompaniment was ad hoc and permitted participation by international volunteers who could not commit to a full year in Colombia. The evidence from interviews with Colombians who were accompanied in diverse regions and from historical moments since the mid-1990s is overwhelming that such accompaniment benefited social movements and communities threatened by political violence. In one dramatic example, in 1997, paramilitaries went to assassinate Mario Humberto Calixto, the president of a local human rights committee. When two PBI members present in Calixto's house shouted that they were internationals, the assassins turned around and walked away.[30]

The security for human rights defenders was also fortified by advocacy that accompaniment organizations carried out with embassies in Colombia; Colombian civilian and military officials; United Nations agencies and other intergovernmental bodies; and legislators, foreign ministries, journalists, and grassroots communities in the groups' home countries. That advocacy, in turn, had greater credibility and impact as a result of the accompaniers' physical presence in Colombian communities and as witnesses to the daily work of threatened activists. Accompaniment served as a unique school in social movements, and many accompaniers went on to work for other human rights organizations, as public defenders, labor organizers, and in other committed activism.

In response to thousands of killings of Colombian trade unionists—Colombia accounted for 63 percent of the world's murdered trade unionists between 2000 and 2010[31]—U.S. labor activists also mobilized support. The American Federation of Labor and Congress of Industrial Organizations (AFL-CIO) became the largest organization in the United States to oppose U.S. military aid to Colombia in 2001. The AFL-CIO's Solidarity Center in 2001 established fellowships for hundreds of threatened unionists in Colombia to live in the United States for several months to a year. Especially after Washington and Bogotá signed the bilateral Free Trade Agreement in 2006, U.S. unions organized against the agreement's ratification (which did not occur until 2011).

Most of the advocacy conducted by these U.S. organizations and groups could only get traction for marginally changing U.S. policy, or for delaying ratification of policy initiatives such as the Free Trade Agreement. But starting in 2008, the Uribe government and Washington overreached in an attempt at regional militarization, and the advocacy in response by U.S. and Latin American activists was considerably more successful. When Bogotá and Washington undertook negotiations in 2008 for an agreement to institutionalize the presence of U.S. troops at seven Colombian military bases, human rights groups from both nations mobilized against the agreement, and they were joined by most South American governments. Leftist parties, human rights groups, and feminists organized against the agreement as a violation of sovereignty and perpetuation of internal war. The José Alvear Restrepo Lawyers Collective, which had been accompanied by PBI since the mid-1990s, filed a legal challenge shortly after the two governments signed an agreement in 2009. The Colombian Constitutional Court that heard the collective's case overturned the agreement in August 2010, on the basis that Uribe's government had not submitted it to the Colombian Congress for approval. The court ruling did not stop the U.S.-Colombian military cooperation that had been occurring throughout the decade, but it did put a brake on the regionalization and institutional entrenchment of that cooperation.[32]

In spite of the extensive networks developed by Colombian social movements, international accompaniment groups, and human rights organizations, achieving justice for a single egregious atrocity against Colombian civilians faced multiple levels of institutional inertia and resistance. The February 2005 massacre in San José and the cover-up that followed in its wake put the capacity of Colombian and U.S. human rights networks to the test.

CHAPTER 8
MASSACRE AFTERMATH AND COVER-UP

The massacre in San José de Apartadó and accusations that the military had participated in it made national and international news, and the military immediately launched a public relations offensive that served as an extension of the army's military operation. One week after the killings, on February 28, 2005, an international human rights worker was at the Bogotá airport and recognized the man in the line in front of her: Colonel Néstor Iván Duque, the Bejarano Battalion commander. Both were en route to Urabá, and she told him she was worried about the situation there. "Worried?" he asked. "Well, yes," she replied. "I imagine you have heard about the massacre this week." "Oh, of course. I'm also worried," Duque said. "We're all worried. But I have good information that it was the FARC." Looking at the woman straight in the eyes, Duque said that he was in Bogotá to file a lawsuit against NGOs that had made baseless accusations.

The next day, on March 1, the Defense Ministry issued a statement denying responsibility for the massacre, saying that troops had been far from the massacre site. It also stated that the Peace Community's February 24 statement asserting that the bodies had been cut up preceded the Fiscalía's February 25 disinterment of bodies. It said witnesses claimed that both Luis Eduardo and Alfonso Bolívar wanted to leave the community, and that Alejandro Pérez was a guerrilla with the alias "Cristo de Palo."[1]

The following day, Wednesday, March 2, a car carried Fiscalía investigators and police from Apartadó to San José de Apartadó. When the investigators arrived, community leaders refused to talk with them, saying the community would testify at the Inter-American Human Rights Commission two weeks later.[2] The investigators departed an hour before dark, and about a mile from the San José town center were attacked with rocket fire, wounding two men and killing a twenty-two-year-old policeman, Roger Jaraba Álvarez.[3] Police in Urabá attributed the attack to the FARC, which, if true, would add to suspicion that guerrillas were responsible for the massacre and did not want investigators poking around.

The next day, a Spanish television station broadcast an interview with a man who said he was a former guerrilla and knew Luis Eduardo Guerra as a fellow miliciano. The man recounted how, when the army killed a guerrilla in San José on February 20, the guerrilla's wife, son, and four-year-old daughter survived and were taken by army helicopter to the hospital. He said the military "could have killed them and they could have said it was in the cross-fire and they didn't want to. If they didn't do that, how can one think they would [kill] the others [massacre victims] when the others were defenseless, were civilians?"[4]

On Colombian radio, former interior minister Fernando Londoño interviewed the same guerrilla deserter, who accused Father Javier Giraldo—the community's most public supporter—of collaborating with the guerrillas. He said that the community at first had been neutral but changed after the 1999 massacre of its leaders.[5] He claimed that Luis Eduardo and Alfonso were both disillusioned with the community, wanted to leave the FARC, and had begun discussion about formally demobilizing from the guerrillas—a process that required collaboration with the army. This, the deserter said, could not be tolerated by the FARC, and so they had killed the two men and their families. He said he knew of other guerrillas who had discussed deserting and were killed. But he also said that he was not present in the area at the time of the massacre, and was not a witness.[6]

The deserter's narrative became the principal theory presented by the government and was adopted by judicial investigators. In one fell swoop, the military's version exonerated its own troops, charged the guerrillas with responsibility, and accused Peace Community leaders who had been murder victims of being guerrillas. It was audacious, if farfetched.

The Defense Ministry posted a transcription of the interview on its website as a PDF file, with information identifying its origin as coming from Liliana Parra in the Defense Ministry, but it showed an email address belonging to the Rendon Group (which has no relation to Renata Rendon of FOR). Parra worked for the Rendon Group in Bogotá from 2004 to 2009, designing communication strategies and training for crisis communication with the Defense Ministry, military high command, and Foreign Ministry.[7] The Rendon Group, in turn, was a Pentagon favorite for shaping public communications, with contracts amounting to more than $100 million in 2000–2012, and so was tapped for communications services in Colombia. U.S. Defense Department funding included $2.4 million in 2003 for devising and developing the Colombian military's communications strategy.[8] The Pentagon later suspended work with Rendon in Afghanistan because of Congressional objections to the company's exclusion of journalists who wrote critical stories, but it kept the company on contract for services in Colombia.[9]

Commander General Héctor Fandiño of the Seventeenth Brigade suggested in a press release as early as March 4 that the method of killing was typical of the guerrillas, and therefore that the military could not have done it.[10] Military officials also asked how the community's witnesses could have known that the Bolívar family had been dismembered before the Fiscalía exhumed the cadavers, implying that the community could have been party to the killing.[11]

Defense Minister Jorge Alberto Uribe Echavarría expanded the military's message on March 5, more directly accusing the Peace Community. He said that terrorists "have used [peace] communities as a refuge for their criminal activities, and the Peace Community of San José de Apartadó has been no exception." Uribe Echavarría concluded with an implicit assertion of the military's own mandate to operate in the community: "To confuse neutrality with 'dis-protection' and put at risk the lives of innocent civilians at the hands of terrorist organizations is a serious error."[12]

Both Colombian and international media reported on the massacre and the opposing claims about who was responsible.[13] In public statements, the U.S. State Department did not accept either the military's or the community's versions at face value. "We just don't know who did this," said a spokesman two weeks after the killings.[14]

The armed forces said that "no army troops were closer than two days' distance from the sites" of the massacre when it occurred.[15] This statement contradicted what international accompaniers knew about distances in the area from their own experience, as well as the military's own statements about army troop movements and operations. According to the Ministry of Defense, troops were present on February 20 in Los Naranjales, a sector of Las Nieves settlement. The daily newspaper *El Tiempo* verified with Apartadó hospital staff that a soldier and young girl were wounded in combat there on February 20.[16] But Los Naranjales is only an hour and a half by foot from

Mulatos, where Luis Eduardo and his family were killed. The military's public assertion that its troops were far from the massacre sites on February 21 was based on army documents called Troop Location Reports (Informe de Situación de Tropas, INSITOP), as well as dubious readings of the time required to transit the area on foot. The INSITOP reports later became critical evidence in the trials of soldiers.

In the meantime, the military's assertion that soldiers were far from the site of the killings permitted it to argue that the army's absence was a reason why the massacre could occur. On March 8, Defense Minister Jorge Alberto Uribe announced that the massacre could have been prevented if the military and police had had access in San José de Apartadó: "Our decision is to be present in the whole national territory. President Uribe has said that in Colombia there will be no *despeje*." (*Despeje* is an area without military presence, a reference to guerrilla areas where the state withdrew to facilitate the 1998–2002 negotiation process.) Echoing the insistence of President Uribe, when he was governor of Antioquia in 1997, that peace communities must exclude the presence only of illegal armed groups, the defense minister said that "there cannot be peace communities without the presence of the armed forces."[17] The regional police commander told journalists that others using the name "peace community" permitted the presence of armed forces, positing the idea of cooperative versus uncooperative communities.[18] In effect, the state was using the massacre to overrule the community's principles— as well as the community's proposal to create humanitarian zones that would be free of armed groups and combat—without even making reference to them.

The defense minister's statements also elided the community's rejection of the army's presence by equating that with a supposed rejection of *all* state agencies. "What we cannot permit is that there are some places in the country where the State cannot be present," he said. "What if, tomorrow, a community decides, for whatever reason, that there won't be a mayor, that they will govern as they like, that they won't accept the presence of the Education Ministry with the schools."[19]

Although army commander Reynaldo Castellanos was careful not to accuse peace communities of sheltering illegal armed groups, he did suggest that charges of human rights abuses could be the work of "our enemies." Asked by *El Tiempo* if these charges were a campaign to discredit the military, he said they "could be," because the military's "center of gravity is legitimacy. . . . What we have gained is what our enemies have tried to attack and discredit."[20]

In all the military's messages about the February 2005 massacre in the months that followed it, the paramilitaries were invisible. That June, more than four hundred paramilitaries of the Bloque Héroes de Tolová under the command of Don Berna demobilized in Córdoba state. Testimony of several paramilitaries would later show, however, that Don Berna held back some of the block's best weapons and men to provide security for coca fields and laboratories in Córdoba; they became the nucleus of a paramilitary successor group known as "Los Paisas."[21]

Government statements blaming the Peace Community culminated with one by President Álvaro Uribe himself on March 20. The president flew to Apartadó for a special security meeting that lasted five hours and included the defense minister, the army commander, other military leaders, and the governor of Antioquia, after which Uribe spoke to the media and local leaders. "There are good people in this community," the president read from a written statement. "But some of its leaders, sponsors and defenders are seriously accused by people residing there as supporting the FARC and of wanting to use the community to protect this terrorist organization." Uribe said that peace communities could not "obstruct justice, reject the armed forces, prohibit selling of legal goods, or restrict the freedom of citizens residing there."[22]

Uribe ordered the police to enter San José de Apartadó and set up a post there within twenty days.[23] Community leaders decided they would pack up and move out of the town center to a farm on the road to Apartadó, a decision that had been brewing since the fall, during negotiations Luis Eduardo had conducted over the placement of a police post. The leaders had learned of the police post two weeks before, and even knew where it would be installed. On March 9, they began construction of houses on land that was a ten-minute walk along the road from the town center. They also planned to inaugurate the humanitarian zones, in spite of the displacement of dozens of families from the same rural settlements.

Anger and Indignation

In the wake of the killings, the Peace Community on February 27 issued a strongly worded statement.

> We call for national and international solidarity to demand that the strategy of terror against the San José Peace Community and the civilian population in the district comes to an end. We ask that you demand respect

for the Peace Community's process and for the humanitarian zones developed in the region. This time it was eight deaths, innocent civilians, entire families, children who are victims of the terror. . . . But the words of Luis Eduardo, his ideas and arguments, will remain with us, and with more force than ever. He believed that the civilian population has the right to live in dignity. We also believe it and will continue defending this principle, even if it costs us our lives.[24]

The parents, sisters, brothers, and others close to those killed in the massacre struggled. The cruelty of the murders prolonged the grief of losing someone loved. Among those killed, Alfonso Bolívar had a previous spouse and children by her; Beyanira left several siblings; Luis Eduardo had three other children, several siblings, and his stepmother, Miryam; Alfonso's and Sandra's parents survived them. Nearly all of these family members lived in San José.[25]

"How can you blame children for the conflict? I think, what can an eighteen-month-old child know about what happens in the country?" asked Peace Community member Brígida González. "The children were cut to pieces. The eighteen-month-old child was chopped up like you'd do with a pig. The six-year-old girl's stomach was cut open. The son of Luis Eduardo, they cut his head off. The Seventeenth Brigade says they were killed because they were guerrillas. So that eighteen-month-old child was a guerrilla?"[26]

As news of the massacre spread through Colombian and international networks, many people responded viscerally, with action, especially those who had learned about or visited the Peace Community in the previous eight years. The murder of small children, the use of machetes and dismemberment of bodies, and the profile of the community's commitment to nonviolence mobilized strong emotions in those who had never been to San José as well as those who had. These emotions opened new spaces for the work of Colombian and U.S. advocates with policy makers and officials. As Winifred Tate has demonstrated, emotions often provide the framework used to justify and rationalize policy.[27]

Vigils for those killed in the massacre took place in Europe, the United States, and Colombia in the weeks following the massacre. In Medellín, the Peace Community's legal representatives and an active group of conscientious objectors, the Red Juvenil, organized a roving vigil in the city, while passersby showed solidarity with comments such as "This is exactly what they don't show on TV." Human rights and accompaniment organizations mobilized their networks to demand a prompt, complete investigation into the murders and guarantees of safety for the community.

FOR team member Renata Rendon was scheduled to return to the United States shortly after the massacre, and she eventually returned to New York on March 16. The following week, she spent three days in Washington, accompanied by staff from Amnesty International and PBI, visiting Congressional offices and telling the story of the massacre and the Peace Community.

Rendon knew little about Congress when she arrived. Accompanying Rendon in the Senate Hart Building, an Amnesty International staff person ran into Tim Rieser, Senator Patrick Leahy's senior staffer, in the hallway and told him he needed to hear her story. Rieser said he could not work on the issue because he was moving offices, Rendon remembered. "I've got books up to here," Rieser said, pointing to his neck. She said, "I just came from the jungle, where I had mud up to here," Rendon replied, pointing to her neck. They made an appointment for the following morning.

"Renata was one of the more courageous people I ever met," Rieser recalled later. "She not only spent time in a very dangerous environment, but she decided to do something about it. She was so angry, and so sad about what happened."[28] Rieser had already spoken publicly about the massacre, telling the Associated Press on March 4 that "if the army was involved, it would raise real concerns" about U.S. military aid.[29] By the end of the week, Rieser had gotten more involved in the case, speaking with the UN High Commissioner on Human Rights representative in Colombia, and began planning a trip to Colombia to discuss it with Vice President Francisco Santos. Rieser's response demonstrates what policy development can be like when someone cares, how it can be very personal in a policy world that is usually highly impersonal.

Others in Congress also spoke out. Working with Peace Brigades International and other groups and led by Congressman James McGovern, twenty-nine members of the House of Representatives wrote to President Uribe on March 9, citing witness charges that the army was "directly or indirectly responsible for these murders, along with members of local paramilitary organizations."[30]

The massacre had occurred just as the U.S. State Department was preparing to certify human rights conditions on military aid to Colombia, which would release a tranche of $35 million for the military. Until the State Department issued its certification, those funds could not by law be disbursed.[31] Before he was a senator, Leahy had been a criminal prosecutor, and the law that took his name emphasizes courtroom justice for state officials who commit crimes. Leahy's and Rieser's aim was justice for the San José Peace Community, using funding and policy as leverage. They subsequently would put a hold on some military assistance, in addition to funds that the State Department had not yet certified. Changing the policy itself would require a different kind of political calculus.

The Cover-Up Continues

The miliciano who had deserted the guerrillas and told a Spanish television program that Luis Eduardo was a guerrilla was in fact thirty-three-year-old Elkin Tuberquia, as later testimony revealed. In 2004, nearly a year before the massacre, the army had accused Tuberquia, together with young Apolinar Guerra, of a bombing attack by the FARC in Apartadó, but the two were released after telling a public defender that Colonel Duque had beaten and tortured them. (Apolinar Guerra was a cousin of Luis Eduardo Guerra.) When Guerra saw Duque again after his release, the colonel told him he had to become an informant or he would face consequences, Guerra later testified. Duque reportedly said Guerra 's statements would be used to sue the Peace Community's lawyers, and if all went well, the two could split a large financial settlement. Guerra was to say that he helped a leading Peace Community defender, Father Javier Giraldo, saddle a horse to meet up with guerrilla commanders in San José's mountains. Guerra and Tuberquia were brought to Bogotá, where they and other former guerrillas spoke at a meeting convened with the diplomatic corps and testified before the Colombian Congress on May 25.[32]

In June the Seventeenth Brigade interviewed another alleged former guerrilla about the massacre, twenty-year-old Luis Alberto Pino Rodriguez, captured by Duque's battalion. In his unsigned testimony, which was formatted by the brigade's intelligence section and which Duque later gave to me, Pino claims that "El Gurre," Luis Eduardo's half brother Dario, was hiding with Pino on February 21 at a farm a full day's hike away from the massacre site. Yet the Peace Community's account said that El Gurre was with Luis Eduardo when the group was ambushed where the massacre occurred. "How was El Gurre in two places at the same time?" Pino's testimony said. "Obviously the FARC committed the massacre in coordination with the Peace Community."[33] The testimony was an attempt to discredit Dario, who was one of the principal witnesses to the massacre and, according to files recovered from a FARC computer, had been a member of the guerrilla militia.[34] But, since testimony by paramilitary witnesses eventually confirmed Dario's account of events in Mulatos, the spurious claim in Pino's testimony shines more light on the brigade's construction of a false narrative than on Dario's credibility.

During the same period after the massacre, witnesses from the community were frightened and refused to speak on the record with government investigators. In meetings with human rights advocates throughout 2005, the Colombian government and the U.S. State Department insisted that the community's refusal to cooperate with the investigation into the massacre was impeding progress. Some witnesses did speak with a delegation from the United States, organized by the Colombia Support Network, that visited April 17–25. At the end of April, Colombian journalist Hollman Morris broadcast a two-part, one-hour documentary about the massacre in San José, in which he interviewed several community members, including a witness to the killings in La Resbalosa.[35] The discussion about the community members' refusal to give testimony neglected one important and salient point: among the key witnesses to what happened in the area of the massacre were dozens of Colombian Army troops. But for two years judicial investigators called in very few of them to give testimony about what happened.

Two U.S. Embassy officials—the human rights officer and assistant army attaché—visited Apartadó on May 12 and 13, but their itinerary focused on the military, business leaders, and community members critical of human rights groups. They did not meet with the Peace Community, accompaniment groups, or human rights organizations. The army officer misrepresented NGOs, saying they claimed there was no FARC in the region, an absurd contention to which the community members responded with laughter. Business leaders told the visiting officials that peace communities were "mini-Caguans," referring to the zone where FARC was concentrated during negotiations, and that Justicia y Paz and other NGOs were "doing the political work of the FARC." Police told the embassy staff that the number of families returning to the San José town center where police had a post had grown to forty-five. General Fandiño of the Seventeenth Brigade, for his part, told the group that guerrillas captured by the army on May 8 had information about the massacre.[36]

Pressure for progress on the case mounted both in Colombia and internationally. The Spanish Congress in mid-May demanded that the Uribe government investigate the massacre.[37] On June 15, Senator Barack Obama wrote to the State Department about the massacre in San José de Apartadó. On July 1, twenty-two senators urged Secretary of State Condoleezza Rice not to certify human rights progress in Colombia.[38] On July 13, prosecutors brought formal charges against Eighteenth Brigade soldiers for the killings of three unionists in Arauca a year before—another emblematic case on which the State Department had been pressing Colombia for judicial progress.[39]

On July 26, Undersecretary of State Nicholas Burns met President Uribe to prepare for a meeting between Presidents Bush and Uribe that would take place at Bush's ranch in Crawford, Texas, the following week, on August 4. Burns told Uribe that Bush would "deliver a message of strong continued support" at the summit meeting, according to an embassy officer, but then told the Colombian president that some in the U.S. Congress were skeptical of Uribe's human rights record, which "could affect ongoing U.S. support for the successor to Plan Colombia." He raised three specific human rights cases—the 1997 paramilitary massacre in Mapiripán, Meta; the army's 2003 killing of three trade unionists in Arauca; and the February massacre in San José de Apartadó—and said that without reporting further progress on these cases, the pending human rights certification, already delayed, would not be "credible," creating a "a danger that some members of Congress would attach additional restrictions to future aid to Colombia." In other words, visible impunity for crimes against the Peace Community had strengthened U.S. political forces that were opposed to or skeptical of Plan Colombia. Uribe replied that he had instructed Prosecutor General Mario Iguarán to release a statement about the San José massacre, and he was committed to calling Iguarán again to get out such a statement before the meeting between Presidents Bush and Uribe.[40]

On August 1, Secretary of State Condoleezza Rice formally certified Colombia's progress on human rights, thus triggering the release of about $60 million in military assistance that had been frozen since the massacre.[41] The certification document singled out the Colombian Army's Seventeenth Brigade for its poor human rights record, noting that the United States was giving no assistance to the brigade. It said that investigators had collected "18 types of ballistic evidence, biological evidence, personal effects, and a machete among other items." But it made clear that no Colombian government investigators had interviewed foot soldiers who were present in the area of the massacre in February. The document noted that the community was not cooperating with the investigation but did not mention the more than one hundred declarations its members had given in past investigations with no results, nor the killings of some of those who had given such declarations.[42]

The certification was closely timed in advance of the personal presidential meeting later that week in Crawford. Bush received Uribe, his wife, and members of his team, cementing their personal relationships and political alliance. Bush apparently spoke specifically about the San José case with Uribe, but human rights was just one of ten issues about which Bush was briefed for the meeting.[43]

Six months had passed since the massacre. But despite growing political and grassroots pressure for a serious investigation to identify those responsible, a strategy to blame the victims, the military's wide-ranging cover-up, and the misuse of Washington's influence appeared to ensure that the pattern of impunity for crimes against the Peace Community would prevail.

CHAPTER 9

WIDESPREAD AND SYSTEMATIC
THE DYNAMICS OF "LEGALIZED" MURDER

The killings in the 2005 massacre in San José de Apartadó received much attention, but they were the tip of the iceberg of allegations of army killings of civilians. Between 2000 and 2010, as the United States was administering its aid to the Colombian armed forces, those forces reportedly killed 5,763 persons extrajudicially—outside of combat—according to data from government investigations and human rights organizations.[1] Most of these deaths were of civilians whom the armed forces claimed were guerrillas killed in combat but were not.

The peak of these killings was in 2007, during the tenure as army commander of General Mario Montoya, who established incentives and applied pressures that accelerated the practice. One incident catalyzed the public conversation. In early 2008, sixteen young men in Soacha, a working-class suburb of Bogotá, disappeared after telling their families that they had gotten work and were leaving town. Civilian recruiters—later revealed to be in the army's pay—had promised them jobs. Their mothers went looking for them, and DNA tests that September identified their bodies, claimed by the military as guerrillas killed in combat—three hundred miles away and only a few days after their disappearance.

The growing awareness that the army was killing civilians and claiming they were guerrillas in combat boiled over into the ensuing Soacha scandal. In October 2008, President Uribe fired twenty-seven military officers, including three generals, and in early November, General Montoya resigned as army commander. Two dozen more officers were dismissed between November and January 2009.[2] The killings practically stopped cold.

The alleged executions spanned the country and the army as an institution. In 2007, the peak year of the problem, at least one execution each was directly attributed to 99 of the army's 219 combat battalions and mobile brigades, while 23 out of 33 army brigades were alleged to have committed executions. The pervasiveness of the practice led UN special rapporteur Philip Alston to conclude in 2010 that civilian killings by the army were "part of a pattern" and "widespread practice."[3]

The intentional killings of civilians whom the army fraudulently claimed to be members of illegal armed groups killed in combat came to be known as "false positives." The "positive" was the operational outcome asserted by the military, an enemy casualty; they were "false" because the dead person was in fact not a combatant. No one has calculated precisely how many of the extrajudicial killings reportedly carried out by the military and police in Colombia were "false positives." A 2016 study by the Fiscalía of 357 cases of homicides committed by the military found that 215 of them were planned "with the premeditated objective of presenting them as combat deaths."[4] Others were undoubtedly persons killed through excessive use of force or bad intelligence, in some cases covered up by a claim of combat when there was none. Ninety-two percent of killings denounced as executions had not gone to trial as of 2013, and a portion of these presumably were legal combat deaths.[5] An honest and thorough investigation could exonerate those soldiers who in fact followed international humanitarian law. But after the government of Juan Manuel Santos enacted peace accords in late 2016, even those convicted of committing those crimes would be set free, and the judicial investigations of army suspects were abandoned.

Córdoba: Cradle of Paramilitarism

Luis Esteban Montes served as an antiguerrilla soldier in the Antelope Company, Rifles Battalion, in Córdoba in April 2007. He was twenty-four years old. There was not much happening, he was bored, and he had malaria. As Mother's Day approached, pressure mounted from the unit's commanders to kill guerrillas; the soldiers had been promised fifteen days off as a reward for each killing. "Then we began to hear talk of 'legalizing' someone." Legalizing was when soldiers killed a civilian, then passed him off as a member of an illegal armed group. "This didn't surprise me at all since 'legalizations' are a daily affair," Montes later told the news magazine *Semana*.[6] The unit picked up a man from Guajira, the same province as Montes. It was a rainy moonless night, and as Montes stood near the tent of the condemned man, the man asked Montes for a cigarette. They began to talk. After a short while, Montes realized the man was his brother, Leonardo, whom he had not seen since he was nine years old, and they embraced.

Montes told Leonardo that the soldiers planned to kill him, and urged him to flee, but Leonardo had befriended the other soldiers and did not believe it. Montes then confronted his captain, saying that the man was his brother and they could not kill him. The captain and other soldiers did not believe him, and the captain said that if Montes tried to foil the plan, he would put Montes on a patrol where his legs could be blown up by a landmine. Nevertheless, Montes helped his brother escape that night.

Days later, after being transferred to a nearby post, he heard his unit had killed a man, and the body was already at the cemetery, being buried anonymously. Rushing there, he found that the dead man was Leonardo. Montes's family filed a lawsuit, but he remained in the army after that and was afraid that soldiers angered by his denunciation might poison his food.[7] A friend of mine who knew Luis Esteban said he was subsequently transferred to a site near Medellín. In 2011 five soldiers were convicted for killing Leonardo and sentenced to thirty years in prison.[8]

As Montes's account demonstrates, soldiers committed many civilian killings in response to pressures from commanders, but those commanders— many of them trained and aided by the United States—escaped prosecution. Montes's unit belonged to the Eleventh Brigade, with jurisdiction in Córdoba Department. In 2006 the brigade established a unit to combat kidnapping in forty-one counties in the northern department of Córdoba, but its members ended up kidnapping and killing civilians themselves, according to Captain Antonio Rozo Valbuena, a former army officer who was charged for several of the unit's civilian killings. In March 2006, then-president Álvaro Uribe was resting at his ranch in Córdoba when Major Óscar Acuña Arroyo, commander of the anti-kidnapping unit, reportedly ordered the killing of five civilians not far from the Uribe ranch, according to Rozo, in order to "stand out" for his performance. In another mission, a paid civilian recruited two of the youths with a false offer to work on a nearby farm, but on the way there they were detained by soldiers and shot at close range.[9]

"To do a false positive requires a logistical train, a very broad intellectual capacity to be able to set it up and plot the procedure well," said Rozo. "When a soldier gets hit with charges and says, 'I did it, I killed him, my colonel knew nothing,' it's a lie," he said. "They're sentencing the most idiotic ones. Don't look here, look higher."[10]

Rozo was convicted on seven counts of homicide in 2013.[11] In one of them, in 2007, nineteen-year-old Fabio Enrique Taboada was working as a bricklayer's assistant when he was contacted to work on a farm in the area, according to members of his family. He was then reported as a member of organized crime killed in combat, along with a man who was never identified, but Colombian prosecutors determined that there was no combat.[12] For his part, Major Acuña was sentenced in June 2009 to twenty-eight years in prison for the killings, but a second court in Córdoba overturned the conviction in 2010.[13]

In October 2011 Rozo publicly accused Eleventh Brigade commander General Javier Fernández Leal with collaborating in murders committed by his brigade's soldiers. Fernández Leal commanded the Eleventh Brigade from June 2005 to December 2006, during which time brigade units carried out more than fifty-three killings that the Fiscalía was investigating as of 2015.[14]

The Eleventh Brigade received U.S. assistance from 2005 to 2007, although the amount and kind of assistance is not known. In 2009 Fernández Leal sat on a military panel that stymied investigations into false positives, an army inspector general told U.S. Embassy officials.[15] He was promoted to chief of joint intelligence for the Colombian military in 2011, then to director of the Colombian Army's War School.[16]

Rozo received training from the United States in human rights and humanitarian law, topics in which he then became an instructor.[17] Acuña received training at the U.S. Army School of the Americas in 1992 and 1995, including a course in leadership and counterdrug operations.[18]

Patterns, Incentives, Causes

A closer examination of the dynamics of the military's practice of killing civilians—changes and differences over time, policy, army units, and leadership—helps us understand how and why these executions grew and then declined.

By 2007 credible reports of civilian killings had occurred in nearly every state and brigade operating jurisdiction. But the killings were not evenly distributed across Colombian Army units and regions. Rather, civilian killings followed some egregious commanders around from unit to unit.

In Antioquia, the country's most populous state, the army's powerful Fourth Brigade headquartered in Medellín developed the practice of "false positives" in the 1990s and subsequently launched it in other regions through command promotions and transfers. The Seventeenth Brigade, with jurisdiction in Apartadó, and the Fourteenth Brigade, which operates in the Middle Magdalena Valley, both in Antioquia, were under the same division command as the Fourth Brigade and also carried out many civilian killings. In 1991–93 the Fourth Brigade had participated in the army's war on the Medellín Cartel as well as counterinsurgency operations that targeted social movements. This combination of experiences strengthened commanders who fought the enemy by attacking its perceived collaborators or vulnerable links: business associates and family members, in the case of the Medellín Cartel; unarmed social activists and guerrilla militia members outside of combat, in the case of insurgents.

The Colombian Inspector General's Office, in a 2009 study, identified five principal modalities for "false positive" killings.[19]

1. The military detained a person alleged to have been a member or aided the guerrillas, and turned the person over to nearby paramilitaries to be executed by them.
2. Paramilitaries detained someone, similarly accused of having aided or been a member of the guerrillas, and turned him or her over to the military to be executed and then presented as a combat death. "The army collaborated a lot with us," one paramilitary commander told the anthropologist Aldo Civico. "We are like the military but illegal. . . . In operations against the guerrillas, if we killed, ten, fifteen, or twenty men, we gave them over to the military, who in turn presented them as their accomplishment." (The same paramilitary called killing a sport, a habit, and killed "so as not to lose the habit.")[20]
3. Working with a former guerrilla or "guide," the military arrested someone accused by the guide of having been a guerrilla collaborator or informer, often at night; the accused was then killed and the military claimed he (victims were nearly always men) had died in combat.
4. The military arrested a person in an urban area or on the edge of town on a pretext, and took him supposedly to verify his record. The victims typically were alone, poor, and not from the area. They were taken to a rural area where they were executed by soldiers, and sometimes dressed in uniform and photographed, a gun or other matériel placed by their side to reinforce the impression that they were criminals.

5. Private individuals recruited and delivered victims to the military to be executed. Typically victims fit a profile: unemployed and in need of money, living in poor areas; some of them also had worked with the recruiter on petty thefts, had criminal backgrounds, or had a history of drug use. A recruiter promised the victim work or criminal jobs, then brought him voluntarily by car or bus to other cities, where the victim believed the job would be. Often the victim's identification was taken from him, to prevent identification of his body. On the road, the military would stop and arrest the person to be killed, then put him in a military truck. The victim believed the recruiter was following by motorcycle, when in fact the recruiter had left the scene.

Some activists have also suggested that mass arrests in some areas were a prelude to subsequent murders. In Huila Department, the armed forces conducted mass arrests of hundreds of people who were accused of links with terrorist groups, especially between 2002 and 2004; the large majority was released for lack of evidence. The arrests were concentrated in municipalities, such as Algeciras, where there were eleven reported extrajudicial killings in 2004–6.[21]

Reasons for Rise in Civilian Killings

Analysts have identified several factors that contributed to the growth of extrajudicial killings in Colombia during 2002–7. These included the lack of consequences for these crimes, a system of incentives for killings, a risk-averse culture of "force protection," collusion with paramilitary forces, and the influence of specific leaders.[22]

No Punishment

An obvious factor was the lack of controls, including administrative and judicial mechanisms, to punish soldiers and officers implicated in extrajudicial killings—in other words, impunity. President Uribe's "Democratic Security Policy" included "carrots" for operational successes but no "sticks" to counter the production of fictional successes.[23] Many cases landed in military courts, where military judges—sometimes subordinate to officers commanding units on whose actions the judges ruled—reliably dismissed charges of human rights violations. Human Rights Watch in 2015 reported "compelling evidence that some military judges [even] actively helped troops cover-up false positive crimes."[24]

This lack of accountability meant that errors—when soldiers believed they were attacking insurgents in combat but were firing on civilians—were covered up and investigations suppressed. Until visibility of "false positives" led to tangible consequences for some officers and soldiers starting in 2008, the impunity for these crimes sent a message that no external force would stop the military from continuing to carry out intentional killings of civilians, whether for political reasons or to demonstrate operational results.

The pressure for a body count proceeded in phases, according to military historian Armando Barrero, beginning as early as the 1960s: "The first stage was to cover up errors: We kill a peasant, then dress him as a guerrilla, we put a weapon next to him, make him look like a guerrilla so we won't be punished. The next stage is we get kills, if there aren't any, in order to win points: to earn a privilege, a vacation, a trip, a change of unit, a better posting for promotion. And then comes something more perverse: criminal organizations that seek out and get victims in a systematic way."[25]

The Military Incentive System

The military created incentives for both officers and foot soldiers to measure success by the number of enemy kills—the so-called body count syndrome, which the U.S. military had promoted during the Vietnam War.[26] Under the dominant Colombian Army mindset from 2002 through 2007, presenting guerrillas killed in combat was an important measure of military success, reflected on multiple levels of hierarchy and reward. In November 2005, Defense Minister Camilo Ospina issued Directive 29, which established as policy monetary compensation to civilians for actions leading to the killing of members of illegal armed groups.

The Fiscalía's human rights director told U.S. officials in 2009 that she did not believe that Directive 29 played a role in extrajudicial killings. Instead, she pointed to local intelligence reserve funds of up to $1,500 monthly per unit that were controlled by battalion and brigade commanders and used to pay "recruiters" of civilian victims, as well as soldiers who participated in the killings.[27] Nevertheless, Directive 29 was associated with an increase of 65 percent to 150 percent in false positive killings in an analysis of 5,763 extrajudicial executions between 2000 and 2010 that tested correlation of the monthly rate of such killings with seventeen different political events.[28]

Incentives preceded the Uribe period as well. An army directive in 1996 set the number of enemy kills required for the commander of a company, battalion, brigade, and division to receive a military medal—a key measure of professional success. A brigade, for example, had to produce 150 enemy kills in a year for its commander to receive a medal for "distinguished service in public order." A battalion required 50 kills, a company 15, and a division 300 for the same recognition. Even greater numbers of enemy captured were required, but the incentive to kill remained strong.[29] A 2004 U.S. intelligence report characterizing the effect of incentives stated, "This mindset tends to fuel human rights abuses by well-meaning soldiers trying to get their quota to impress superiors."[30]

Officers with especially high body counts formed an "Army of the North," led by General Mario Montoya, that was responsible for a thousand deaths during Montoya's command, one fifth of them "false positives," Colonel Róbinson González del Río later testified.[31] Another officer told me that group was a "clan" whose members protected one another, and appointed each other to command positions in order to cover up executions.[32]

For example, Montoya's protégé was General Óscar González Peña, who followed him in positions commanding the Fourth Brigade in Medellín, the Caribbean Joint Command, and, after Montoya resigned in November 2008, the army as a whole. More than 140 killings by soldiers under González Peña's command in the Fourth Brigade from 2003 to 2005 were denounced as extrajudicial killings. When he became army commander in 2008, González Peña, in turn, appointed General Jorge Rodríguez Clavijo (whose daughter was married to González Peña's son) as head of the army's human rights directorate, where he could keep an eye on prosecutions.[33] Rodríguez Clavijo had commanded the Fourth Brigade, the Seventeenth Brigade in Urabá, and the Tenth Mobile Brigade, where under his command soldiers had reportedly committed sixty-one extrajudicial killings in 2005–8.[34] By 2018 Rodríguez Clavijo had retired from the army and was working as a consultant on corporate strategies and human rights for multinational security companies and extractive industries.[35]

Below the commanders, on the ground, soldiers who killed could also be chosen to receive vacation bonuses. The Colombian military deducted 10 percent from the salary of each officer and noncommissioned officer, directed to the Welfare and Recreation Fund that supported the construction and maintenance of military recreational facilities all around the country. In July 2005, the Defense Ministry issued a directive that sought to alleviate some of the hardships experienced by soldiers in the midst of war by establishing vacation discounts soldiers could use, specifically with their spouses, if married, or their mothers, if single.[36] The discounts included travel packages of five days and four nights to beautiful vacation hotspots such as San Andrés, Santa Marta, the coffee region, and Villa de Leyva.[37]

Several soldiers' narratives of "false positive" killings of civilians mention the imminence of Mother's Day, celebrated in the second week of May, and the desire for time off. In fact, in the sixteen months after Directive 29 was issued, the month with the largest number of reported executions (113) was April 2006—the month before Mother's Day. The next month with a higher number was December 2006 (124), coinciding with both the end of the calendar year (when a unit's kills would be measured for its commander's medal) and with ordinary soldiers' desire for time with their families.

Vacations were also canceled if units did not kill enough. Officers of the Voltigeros Battalion reportedly were denied Christmas vacations in 2004, six weeks before the unit was ambushed by the FARC in El Porroso. The Voltigeros officers "knew the only way out was by making combat deaths, [and] that is why they bit the FARC's bait," wrote Defense Ministry advisor Sergio Jaramillo in 2006.[38] The loss of soldiers in El Porroso then led the army to plot Operation Phoenix in San José de Apartadó in February 2005.

The pressures in some units became especially intense. In the Middle Magdalena River region in 2008, a battalion leader ordered every company commander to report one killing a month, and the intelligence section to produce three killings a month, according to a lieutenant in the unit. The battalion's operations center kept a message board showing how many days had passed since each company produced killings or entered combat. The commander told his troops, "now the war is measured in liters of blood, [and] the commander who does not have results of deaths each month, will be sanctioned."[39]

"Force Protection"
Once guerrillas effected a strategic retreat from many areas after 2004, engaging them in battle posed greater risks for the military, especially for non-elite units. As this occurred, performance measures "excessively valued—sometimes exclusively—the opponent's casualties, and disproportionately punished the [military's] own operational failures," security analyst Alfredo Rangel wrote in 2006. "Consequence: a tendency to achieve casualties without assuming risks, without exposing themselves much or, better, not at all."[40] This tendency was consolidated into a doctrine that all measures possible should be taken to protect the fighting force.

In the context of a traumatic hit to that force, this sometimes led to extreme responses. The army committed some of its most atrocious crimes against civilians in Urabá in response to guerrilla attacks on the military, including the kidnapping of ten Colombian Marines in February 1997, which was followed by the army-paramilitary Operation Genesis, in which paramilitaries beheaded a man and reportedly used his head as a soccer ball.[41] Another was the guerrilla ambush in El Porroso, followed by the massacre in San José de Apartadó.

The Role of Specific Leaders

The analysis of 5,763 killings from 2000 to 2010 also reviewed the incumbencies of Colombian presidents, armed forces commanders, army commanders, and U.S. ambassadors during the period. The results were strictly correlational but nevertheless offer insight. President Uribe's presidency from 2002 to 2010 was associated with an 84 percent to 101 percent increase in extrajudicial killings compared to other parts of the decade, a result that held when the analysis controlled for six other political events. Low-level soldiers perceived that Uribe offered them license for extrajudicial killings. "The guerrillas are cowards and like to mix with the people," said one soldier. "Sometimes you wonder, but they do intelligence on the case, and when [guerrillas] have been identified, sometimes they are 'returned' [killed] to the other side because if you arrest them, they will be free sooner than they go to jail. Those dogs deserve no consideration. I feel supported by the government because finally there is someone who understands us and encourages us to win this war."[42]

The tenure of General Mario Montoya, who commanded the Colombian Army from March 2006 to November 2008, was associated with the largest increase in executions, relative to the rest of the decade—144 percent—of any army commander. According to a high-ranking officer I spoke with, General Montoya told him, "Look, you've let up, you don't have kills. . . . What you have to do, if there's a kill, bring all the troops and give them fifteen days off and a million pesos for each soldier. Where to get the money? Take it from reserve expenses. Intelligence money."[43]

There were also particularly aggressive, ambitious, or unethical officers at the regional and local level, as the experiences in Urabá, Antioquia, and Córdoba demonstrate. The actions and omissions of these local commanders exacerbated other factors that contribute to civilian killings.

Paramilitary Influence

Some observers assert that the military outsourced its violence to paramilitaries after pressure from human rights conditions began to affect army operations.[44] But the close relationship of many military officers and units with paramilitary groups also lent itself to greater civilian killings by the military itself. In these units, officers had already crossed an ethical and legal threshold in their collaboration with paramilitaries, who murdered many civilians. Moreover, when pressure for killings by the military became more intense, army commanders could use paramilitaries to recruit or kill victims, then claim them as combat results. In some places, in any case, there was not much difference in practice between paramilitary gunmen and those they sometimes called their "cousins"—army soldiers.

Reasons for the Decline in Killings

The rate of executions allegedly committed by the military began to fall in late 2007, from a peak of 147 in August 2007 to 76 a month in the last quarter of the year. But in October 2008, the practice ceased almost completely, with 15 alleged civilian killings, and only 2 the following month.[45] The precipitous reduction in reported executions demonstrated that the military was able to control the practice, that ending it was an institutional decision. But what caused that decision? There were multiple factors and causes.

Human rights advocates worked on the principle that holding the material and intellectual authors of these crimes criminally responsible was key to stopping them. But in late 2008, although thousands of deaths were under investigation, Colombian prosecutors had tried and sentenced just fifty-nine soldiers and officers for only eleven killings committed since 2000.[46] The looming prospect of such prosecution may have contributed to the change, and as prosecutions increased in 2009–12, they may have consolidated the institutional reduction of the practice. But other causes must have been at play in 2008.

A key factor was the denunciations and persistent action by family members of those killed, for example, the mothers of young men from Soacha but also in many other parts of the country. The media conveyed their pain from losing sons and other loved ones, but it was also the false narrative of the victims as armed attackers that family members frequently cited as especially hurtful. An international mission organized by the Coordinación Colombia–Europa–Estados Unidos (CCEEU) in October 2007 that heard testimony by more than a hundred witnesses and family members reported at least 955 extrajudicial killings between 2002 and 2007, and the same month the Inter-American Human Rights Commission held a hearing on the issue in Washington.[47] The eruption in the media of the "false positives" scandal in September 2008 was strongly associated with a significant decrease in average monthly executions, between 149 percent and 160 percent.[48] Behind the scenes, the Office of the United Nations High Commissioner on Human Rights in Colombia pressed the Colombian military on the issue, focusing especially on army killings in eastern Antioquia.

The Colombian state took seriously its human rights image, and it consistently sent squads of officials to Inter-American and UN human rights hearings to present its case. This concern led the Uribe government to surveil and harass human rights defenders and journalists, to make its human rights record appear positive, but when the "false positives" crisis became undeniable, it also facilitated internal pressures to seek change in the military.[49]

Another important factor was the higher level of state control of territory by 2008–10, relative to previous years. Political scientist Stathis Kalyvas argues that zones in which one armed group in a civil war has hegemonic but incomplete control—as was the case in many Colombian regions in the late 1990s and the beginning of the following decade—the dynamics of defection and denunciation often make selective violence against civilians high. In contrast, "where levels of control are high, there is no defection, no denunciation, and . . . there will be little homicidal violence."[50] When, amid domestic and international political opprobrium, the "body count" approach did not serve the same political objectives, it was militarily easy to discard the practice, since the army and paramilitaries already controlled most territories where the civilian killings were taking place.

The demobilization of the paramilitaries organized in the AUC between 2003 and 2006 undoubtedly also played a part. Responsibility for killings of civilians that before the demobilization were carried out collaboratively between the army and paramilitaries could no longer be assigned to the AUC. While killings by paramilitaries did not end, the number of such killings dropped dramatically, reaching their lowest point in 2006. Paramilitary murders would increase again and spike in 2009, the first full year of the army's cessation of false positive killings. But even then—with more than 500 killings attributed to paramilitaries—it was not a return to 2001, when paramilitaries committed more than 1,600 extrajudicial killings.[51] Moreover, as the perceived risks from guerrilla insurgency to the state's direction and priorities diminished, the interests of neoparamilitary groups narrowed to more directly commercial ambitions, which—together with the arrests of paramilitary leaders—weakened the reach of army-paramilitary violence.

Finally, just as some military leaders stood out in their role in the growth of civilian killings, some officers took the lead in pushing to change the practice, even if their efforts occurred because many others were already pushing for change. One of these leaders was Brigadier General Carlos Arturo Suárez

Bustamante. As the army inspector general in 2008, he was tasked with leading a commission to investigate the killings of young men from Soacha who were buried in North Santander and Santander. His report in October 2008 found a lack of internal controls of intelligence, weapons, and operational reports, and led to the dismissal of twenty-seven officers and the resignation of Montoya.

Suárez appears to have been motivated more by his loyalty to the military than to human rights per se. "The institution of the army is sacred, and the [false positives scandal] was going to destroy the institution," he told me. Suárez believed war could be fought another way. As we walked out of his living room, he drew my attention to a painting. "What do you see?" he asked. It depicted soldiers resting on the ground in a vast plain, their rifles nearby, and other soldiers in the heavens above them. "The dream of the glory of victory," he said of the soldiers in heaven. To him, war was noble, still.[52]

CHAPTER 10
THE UNITED STATES EFFECT

IMPACTS ON "FALSE POSITIVE" KILLINGS

Media accounts of Colombia as early as 2003 cited statistics showing steep reductions in homicides, massacres, and kidnappings.[1] These crimes were committed in diverse circumstances, including common crime and paramilitary violence, but they were often conflated with the subsequent decline in army killings into a single human rights success story. U.S. supporters who promoted Plan Colombia as a model for U.S. foreign policy and for security policy in other nations seized on the overall reduced level of killings as evidence for the narrative that U.S. policy in Colombia was a success.

Measuring success by reductions in guerrilla violence is a way of answering the question, Did the government *win* the war? But what if, in the process of winning the war and so curtailing guerrilla violence, the state committed *more* killings of civilians and other human rights violations than before? Shouldn't a central measure of the human rights effects of U.S. assistance be the conduct of the institutions receiving that assistance, rather than the conduct of their opponents?

The Colombian military's insularity from civilian and international forces declined under pressures to counter the FARC's growing strength in the 1990s. Plan Colombia went hand-in-hand with increased involvement of Colombian political leaders, most notably President Uribe, who micromanaged the military and had a take-no-prisoners approach to the guerrillas, while accommodating paramilitary forces.

Increased U.S. support was accompanied by a human rights discourse, which Colombian military officers learned well. Those officers often emphasized to me that all units and officers receiving training and other assistance underwent a human rights review before receiving U.S. aid. But in the years that mattered most, when the army was committing thousands of civilian killings between 2002 and 2008, the U.S. State Department was unwilling to apply human rights conditions rigorously, with some exceptions. These exceptions included suspension of assistance to the Seventeenth Brigade and of the U.S. visas of officers like General Rito Alejo del Río.

But full implementation of human rights conditions and the Leahy Law would have required much more than suspension of aid to units when execution cases came to light. U.S. assistance was both institutional and highly fungible within the armed forces, as equipment, intelligence, and training passed from one unit to another. It also would have meant addressing the broader "body count" syndrome in the army, which was an institutional problem well before General Montoya took charge of the army in 2006. The United States would have had to require Colombia to analyze the reasons for the "false positives" disaster—something the Colombian executive branch and armed forces never did—and to show an interest in the effects of U.S. assistance on the practice of these killings.

Moreover, while complex variables often determine decisions by armed forces members to commit abuses, the material resources and time required to carry out human rights violations are dramatically less than what is required to achieve justice and to repair the damage of such violence. Similarly, in an environment of impunity, war, and habitual retaliation, outsiders are more capable of strengthening damage-inducing institutions and practices than they are able to help create healing and justice for the damage caused by violent conflict. The experience of U.S. support for the Colombian military and judiciary illustrates the problem.

Methodologies for Measuring Impact of U.S. Military Aid

Standards of evidence vary according to the purpose of the examination. Such standards may be determined by morality and ethics, journalistic criteria, judicial criminal processes, or an inquiry into statistical correlation and causation. For the purpose of evaluating and designing U.S. assistance, standards for determining criminal guilt are less relevant than is assessing the weight of evidence for the outcomes of policies. While failure to implement existing law may lead to individual or collective responsibility for an abuse, policy formation is not primarily an exercise in assigning judicial responsibility.

Finding ways to evaluate impacts of assistance is important for critics and believers alike. Human rights advocates and members of Congress increasingly called for such evaluation as military assistance programs proliferated after 2001, especially during President Obama's second term.[2] In 2016, for the first time, the U.S. Senate passed a requirement for monitoring and evaluation of the Pentagon's foreign assistance programs, while the House of Representatives approved a similar provision for evaluation of military aid, though nonbinding.[3] Two career policy makers in 2018 said the billions of dollars in military assistance do not provide the improved capacity, influence, or access in partner nations its supporters claim and that it is "money down a rat hole" until Congress and the executive branch assess the reasons for this.[4] Military proponents have their own objectives for evaluation, including the development of a database of foreign trainees to help U.S. military contractors find overseas customers.[5]

Studies of the relationship between U.S. foreign assistance and human rights violations illuminate the wide variation in clients' respect for human rights norms and describe mechanisms and processes through which foreign military assistance is allocated. But despite the well-recognized difficulties and uncertainties in making meaningful cross-national measurements of foreign military assistance or arms transfers, these are almost exclusively national-level studies.[6] Very few scholars have examined or analyzed how these important variables operate at the subnational level.

Martha Huggins theorized the cycles of human rights impacts of foreign police training, based on a case study of U.S. police assistance to Brazil in the 1960s.[7] A 2006 study by the RAND Corporation of popular perceptions of police after foreign aid was provided found that assistance was most likely to improve conduct in countries transitioning into democratic systems, but also that "assisting an increasingly competent but still highly repressive internal security force . . . may have the unintended consequence of improving the effectiveness of the repression."[8] A U.S. Army officer who later became military attaché in Bogotá, on the other hand, reviewed the relationship between the presence of U.S. advisors in diverse departments in El Salvador with atrocities reported in 1993 in the UN Truth Commission report and found a positive impact on human rights from the advisors.[9]

Most scholars who have addressed the human rights impacts of military aid and arms transfers have made cross-national comparisons.[10] One group commissioned by USAID found in 2008 that "democracy assistance is less powerful when the overall policy towards the recipient country is driven by security concerns."[11] However, the group measured military assistance in dollars, and the dollar value of military assistance resides disproportionately in equipment, especially aircraft and missile systems that are rarely used in the commission of the human rights violations, so the applicability of these studies to understanding the impacts of assistance on human rights abuses is limited. In Colombia, for example, the largest dollar value of U.S. assistance was in helicopters, whose operational deployments and potential use in human rights violations were difficult to track; most extrajudicial killings did not occur from the air. That is why I focus in the analysis that follows on unit assistance, officer training and cultivation, and higher-level policy messages as primary variables of assistance.

A 2011 study of military aid's influence on recipient states published in *Foreign Policy Analysis* concluded counterintuitively that, "with limited exceptions, increasing levels of US aid are linked to a significant reduction in cooperative foreign policy behavior with the United States." The study observed that some military aid recipients "exploit the fact that the United States relies on them to provide some specific good—and the availability of alternative arms suppliers—to defy the broader interests of the United States with impunity."[12] In this model, Colombia's capacity to obtain military equipment from suppliers other than the U.S. government and its perception that it would be costly for the United States to cut military aid increased Bogotá's leverage in defying State Department requests on human rights issues. Such an ability to ignore human rights concerns expressed by Washington might also reflect the lower priority assigned those concerns by the United States, compared to counterinsurgency and counterdrug programs.

Jerry Laurienti studied the U.S. military's human rights training programs in Latin America through 2005 and found that "Colombia represents the greatest success story for U.S. human rights promotion, as shown in the extensive implementation and cultivation of human rights awareness programs, policies, procedures, and institutions in the armed forces." But Laurienti conducted his research before the full scope of "false positive" killings carried out by the Colombian military was known. He also concluded that "the problem of impunity . . . represents a blatant failure to fulfill the civil-military criteria of judicial authority over the armed forces."[13]

Several case studies of U.S. assistance and military units' human rights records have adopted a narrow focus. Katherine McCoy examined the impacts of U.S. military training from a specific institution, the U.S. Army School of the Americas, on the number of gross violations committed by individual officers trained between 1960 and 2000, finding that more courses taken at the school correlated with increased probability of abuse.[14] In counterpoint to McCoy, Ruth Blakeley argued in 2006 that the most appropriate way "of establishing the relationships between the training and repression . . . involves assessing the nature of the training within the broader context of US foreign policy."[15] Several other writers adopted this approach to examine counterinsurgency and drug war doctrine in Latin America and Southeast Asia, the School of the Americas, and U.S. police assistance in Brazil. These scholars used qualitative and inductive methods, based on both document reviews and interviews of military trainers and trainees, to investigate specific Cold War programs and doctrines. These scholars found that the content of training and doctrine from the 1960s through the 1990s reinforced practices that denigrate civilian political opponents, in direct or subtle ways.[16] Such a qualitative analysis does not trace U.S. influence in facilitating or dissuading specific crimes, but it shows how U.S. policy placed human rights as a lower priority than other geostrategic aims.

An analysis in 2010 by Oeindrila Dube and Suresh Naidu of the effects of U.S. military assistance on combat, voting participation, and paramilitary attacks in Colombia found increased paramilitary attacks and reduced voter turnout in towns with military bases when military aid rose. However, the study did not distinguish between those units that received assistance and those that did not, nor did it measure violations committed specifically by assisted military units. It also measured assistance as a function of the location of Colombian bases, on the premise that the impacts of assistance would be greater near such bases, even though army operations typically occurred in the countryside, while most bases are located in cities.[17]

One of the most provocative theses is that U.S. human rights laws actually accelerated the growth of paramilitarism—and therefore of political violence in Colombia. Winifred Tate observes that the Colombian military outsourced counterinsurgent violence to paramilitaries, and she argues that these "Colombian paramilitary proxies were in part the product of human rights pressure on the security forces."[18] Much of the growth of paramilitarism, however, preceded U.S. human rights restrictions, and it responded to other pressures, including risks to elite interests generated by cycles of negotiation with insurgencies.[19]

The most direct way to disentangle opposing claims about the impacts of military assistance and intervention is to empirically examine human rights outcomes, specifically the conduct of those who were the greatest beneficiaries of U.S. aid, after they were trained or received equipment, political support, or intelligence. This is a more appropriate measure of impacts than macro, national conditions, which are influenced by an even larger set of causes. The outcomes for assisted units can be compared with those for the same entities before they received U.S. aid, or outcomes for other units or officers who did not receive aid. Another valid approach for understanding impacts on human rights is to identify patterns of serious violations or changes in human rights behavior, analyze the causes of those violations, and then examine what effects U.S. military assistance had on those causes, for good or ill. In addition, since the impact of foreign assistance may not be direct, and is never a sole cause of patterns or changes in human rights outcomes, this analysis particularly must weigh the role of foreign assistance with other factors causing the change.

Caveats on Measurement

Assessments of the impact on respect for human rights of foreign assistance to another nation's armed forces should consider diverse variables: the type, duration, intensity, and timing of training or other assistance; levels of human rights violations before assistance was given; the credibility of human rights reporting; levels of detail about who was responsible for reported violations; the arrival or departure of commanders; and other factors that might have impacted violations over time, such as the military balance in the area. The point of considering these factors is not to dismiss the effects of foreign assistance but to better understand when such assistance is more or less likely to have a positive or negative outcome for respect for human rights.

Quantitative measurement of these variables often presents uncertainty, even where apparently hard data is available. In the municipality of Vistahermosa, Meta, in southeastern Colombia, for example, there were seventy alleged extrajudicial killings occurring between 2000 and 2010 in which the victim was identified. Of the seventy deaths, military units responsible were identified for only thirty-one. Several U.S.-supported Task Force Omega units operated in Vistahermosa and were allegedly responsible for twenty of the thirty-one attributed killings, but so did other units not supported by the United States (allegedly responsible for the other eleven of those where a unit was identified). The Fiscalía was investigating an additional twenty-six killings of unidentified people in Vistahermosa by the armed forces during the same period. Moreover, the municipal cemetery had 155 bodies of persons killed during the conflict who were not identified as of 2013, some of whom may have been killed or disappeared by the armed forces, by the guerrillas, or by paramilitaries.[20]

Some Colombian officers obfuscate measurement of assistance by interpreting "support" or even "assistance" to mean only the permanent physical presence of U.S. soldiers. An assistant to then–army commander General Jaime Lasprilla Villamizar in 2014 insisted to me that U.S. assistance was not "assistance" unless U.S. soldiers were present.[21] This may result from the fact that most soldiers, and even commanders in the field, never saw the sixty U.S. military advisors who were stationed in divisions and brigades outside Bogotá after 2003.

Measurement of U.S. military and police assistance before 1996 is markedly fuzzy. The Defense Department's spending on international counternarcotics assistance, begun formally in 1992, was not disaggregated into country spending until 1997, so there are no public records of Pentagon assistance to Colombia for that period. Similarly, the State Department did not disclose costs of its aviation assistance to the Colombian National Police from 1990 to 1994.[22]

Beginning in the 1960s, the United States had a deep influence on Colombian military doctrine that did not distinguish armed insurgents from unarmed dissidents, but measurement of extrajudicial killings and forced disappearances in Colombia for periods before 2000—as well as the impact of U.S. doctrine and training on these—is problematic. The most complete database of extrajudicial killings, compiled by the Coordinación Colombia–Europa–Estados Unidos (CCEEU), begins in 1994. Another project, "Colombia Nunca Más," documented nearly ten thousand killings reportedly committed by the army, police, or paramilitary forces from 1966 to 1998, but only in some regions of the country.[23] Such fragmented national-level historical data on killings makes quantitative comparison of national outcomes before and after U.S. assistance difficult.

Two Officers in Contrast

While they should not be assessed in isolation, the career trajectories of individual officers offer important qualitative insights into the outcomes of U.S. training.

Colonel Hernán Mejía Gutiérrez had extensive U.S. training. Despite this, when he was arrested in 2007 for participation in the "false positive" killing of eighteen people in northern César, U.S. ambassador William Wood reported in a cable that neither Colonel Mejía nor his unit had ever received U.S. assistance.[24]

Mejía entered the army in 1981, beginning with a post in Argentina, still under military dictatorship. He met U.S. instructors at the Ranger School in Colombia; he later went to Fort Bragg, North Carolina, for ten months of training in psychological operations, and returned to Fort Bragg in 1992 for another ten months. He attended a course at the School of the Americas. He spent a year and a half in Washington in the Inter-American Defense Board, and he participated in the multinational operation in Haiti led by the United States. General Norman Schwarzkopf had agreed to write the introduction to his autobiography. He won a national prize for best soldier three times, he told me.[25] He was a rising star.

Mejía was assigned to command the "La Popa" Battalion in the northern city of Valledupar in late 2001. According to the court that sentenced him in 2013, Mejía entered into an agreement with the paramilitary capo known as "Jorge 40," in which "the military did not fight the paramilitaries and gave them weapons, munitions and supplies in exchange for individuals from guerrilla groups and punished paramilitaries in order for them to be extrajudicially executed and later presented as 'positives.'" An elite squad assembled and trained by Mejía began to produce many enemy kills.[26]

According to Mejía, on October 25, 2002, he received a call from President Uribe with information on an armed group on a farm in Bosconia, urging him to take action.[27] Eighteen people died in the resulting operation, all of them declared members of the ELN guerrillas killed in combat. But it turned out that they were paramilitaries; according to the Prosecutor General's Office, the battalion ambushed them as a favor to "Jorge 40." In September 2013, Mejia was sentenced to nineteen years in prison.[28] The human rights result of the U.S. investment in Colonel Mejía was roundly negative.

Carlos Alfonso Velásquez, on the other hand, also received extensive military training from the United States. He trained at the School of the Americas and returned to the school as an instructor for a year. He also attended the command and general staff course at Fort Leavenworth for a year. In the 1990s, he commanded the elite unit that pursued the Cali Cartel with U.S. support.[29] In 1996, when he served as chief of staff to the Seventeenth Brigade, he denounced brigade commander General Rito Alejo del Río in a letter to the armed forces commander for his permissive approach to paramilitaries, who were then murdering many civilians in an offensive in the region. He was thrown out of the army for his action.[30] As early as 1997, he reported to U.S. Embassy officers that there was "a body count syndrome" in the Colombian Army.[31]

The Case of WHINSEC

One of the most controversial institutions for U.S. training is the former U.S. Army School of the Americas (SOA), converted to the Western Hemisphere Institute for Security Cooperation (WHINSEC) in 2000. Under different names, the school trained more than sixteen thousand Colombians from 1966 through 2015.[32] The human rights movement led by the School of the Americas Watch documented the cases of hundreds of SOA students who later went on to commit atrocities and participate in coups in their home countries. For example, Colonel Bayron Carvajal attended SOA as a cadet for two weeks in 1985. He reportedly worked with paramilitaries in the Seventeenth Brigade that operated in San José de Apartadó in the early 1990s. Carvajal was later sentenced to fifty-four years in prison for leading an ambush in 2006 on behalf of the Cali-based drug mafia that killed ten Colombian policemen.[33]

WHINSEC has measured its effectiveness primarily by documenting how many of its graduates go on to become armed forces commanders, defense ministers, or even heads of state in their nations. The information available on Colombian military officers and army human rights violations provides an important test case for the statement made in 2012 by former WHINSEC commander Glenn Huber that he was not aware of any WHINSEC graduates who had been charged with human rights abuses.[34]

Some of the officers with the largest number of civilian killings committed under their command received significantly more U.S. training, on average, than other officers during this period. Officers with in-depth U.S. training are more likely to rise in rank, and similarly, those who are on the rise are more likely to have access to U.S. training opportunities. This does not mean that U.S. training caused or fomented civilian killings. But it suggests that measuring success of training by the ascendance of officers, as the Pentagon does, is a perverse way to measure human rights performance. With an institution with a poor human rights record, such measurements are likely to exacerbate an existing problem.

A review of WHINSEC graduates' records is limited by the Defense Department's refusal to release names of instructors or graduates since 2003. The large majority of 1,900 graduates in WHINSEC's first three years whose names have been disclosed were young cadets who took courses lasting only two or three weeks. While these experiences may have been formative in soldiers' subsequent careers, it is most meaningful to measure the performance of graduates who had longer experience at WHINSEC. These include Latin American instructors, who generally stay a year, and those taking the command and general staff course.

In WHINSEC's first three years (2001–3), twenty-one Colombians served as instructors, including an assistant commandant of the school, more than from any other nation, while eight Colombians took the command and general staff course. Of the twenty-five Colombian WHINSEC instructors and graduates for which any subsequent information was available, twelve of them—48 percent—were either charged with a serious crime or commanded units whose members had reportedly committed multiple extrajudicial killings after the officer's stint at WHINSEC.[35] To determine whether this percentage of Colombian officers implicated in violations or commanding units with multiple executions was disproportionate, I examined a random sample of twenty-five officers from approximately the same period, with the same combination of rank and military branch as the WHINSEC instructors and graduates. Of these twenty-five, four subsequently led units with multiple extrajudicial executions under their command. Another three officers led units with one execution under their command.

Why did this occur? Did the Leahy vetting process fail at the Embassy or State Department level, and allow violators to be admitted to WHINSEC training, which was then reflected in their subsequent records? Were the officers implicated in these crimes—as many Colombian military officers believe—the victims of "judicial warfare" by which guerrillas and their supposed agents in the judicial system fabricated stories about civilian killings? I believe it is more likely that these officers' experiences at Fort Benning gave them such added status and immunity within their own institutions to lead them to believe they could commit crimes with impunity. Another credible cause is that the selection of officers for WHINSEC instructors and command courses was based on operational results that prioritized kills, regardless of whether these people were killed in combat.

One U.S. Army officer associated with WHINSEC suggested to me that Colombia had a "systemic [human rights] problem across the country" that was reflected in the high percentage of WHINSEC instructors and graduates implicated in crimes. But if Colombia had such a systemic problem, how did the disproportionate representation of Colombian military instructors at

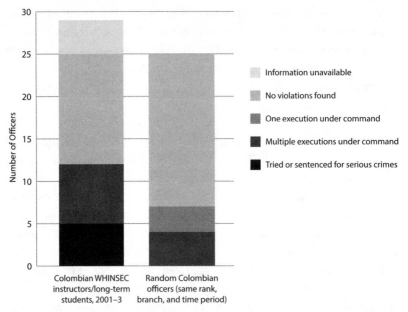

Fig. 10.1. Command responsibility and human rights outcomes of Colombian WHINSEC graduates versus random Colombian officers, 2001–3.

WHINSEC—42 percent of Latin American instructors in 2012—contribute to increased respect for human rights?[36]

In 2012 I met two of these Colombian instructors, who were teaching a course for analyzing operational information. They insisted that most military homicides under investigation by Colombian courts were legitimate combat kills. One told me that the San José Peace Community served as a resting place for FARC guerrillas. These were not attitudes that ensured WHINSEC instructors were promoting respect for human rights, but they were unlikely to be discovered through a Leahy Law review for criminal charges against officers nominated to be instructors.

An academic serving on the WHINSEC Board of Visitors who read the above analysis of Colombian WHINSEC graduates asked: "So if a student of mine leaves an ethics class and engages in criminal activity, does that make me or my university liable for her activity?" A more specific analogy would be this example:

1. a university professor taught a course on academic ethics, and of twenty-five students in his class, twelve were subsequently charged with plagiarism in other academic work, and

2. this occurred after a previous scandal in which it was found that some courses taught plagiarism and that the university's library carried a book on how to commit it, and
3. a number of previous students had committed plagiarism on a large scale.

In this case, the administration, students, and alumni might demand a serious examination of what happened and why it happened. The professor might be removed from the course, or even from the university. The accreditation gods might be awakened. There would presumably be a critical look at how students were recruited to the university. And there would be more follow-up evaluation for students of subsequent courses. Or, as at WHINSEC, the administration could try to hush it up, not even be curious about why so many students committed plagiarism, as if it never happened, as if it was just a problem of a student culture of plagiarism in the age of the Internet.

U.S. Support for Leaders and Institutions beyond WHINSEC

Given General Montoya's push for "body counts," widely perceived to be a central driver of extrajudicial killings both in brigades he commanded and subsequently as army chief in 2006–8, the United States' relationship with and responses to Montoya's conduct are important indicators of U.S. influence on respect for human rights. The counterdrug military task force Montoya commanded was a focus of U.S. assistance at the start of Plan Colombia in 2000–2001. When the United States promoted joint military commands, Montoya headed one of the first, the Caribbean Joint Command, in 2005–6.

A revealing moment came in March 2007, when the *Los Angeles Times* reported that a U.S. intelligence report found Montoya had "collaborated extensively with right-wing militias that Washington considers terrorist organizations, including a militia headed by one of the country's leading drug traffickers."[37] The day after its publication, the U.S. Army Mission chief and a U.S. Embassy official rushed to reassure Montoya and continue with business as usual, even as a U.S. officer suspected of responsibility for the leak had to be rushed back to the United States for his security.[38]

Colombian officers frequently assert two things that appear to be in tension with each other: that the help of the United States was important, even critical for Colombian military success, and also that there was not much support—especially when asked about specific units that the United States records as having assisted. These assertions may refer to different times and units, in which U.S. assistance arrived at diverse moments. But for some officers, the support that made the most difference was U.S. moral and political support, expressed publicly, at a high level, and at a time when the Colombian military was shunned by world opinion.

In light of Colombia's international isolation, a high-ranking military officer said, "US support was very important for morale, and not so much for military assistance."[39] General Mario Montoya affirmed to me that the most important support from the United States was moral and political support: "They have been our number-one ally. The United States is the only country that has supported us openly. They have been our unconditional allies."[40]

Colombia had a lot more U.S. government eyes on the ground than some large U.S. military aid programs that came later, such as in Syria. But the U.S. approach in Colombia was still mostly hands-off, allowing the Colombian military and President Uribe to drive the war. When Colombian units used U.S. assistance in ways that killed civilians, Washington might know little about the connection. The use of U.S. intelligence (described in chapter 5) provides an example. The intelligence cells established by the CIA to recruit informants were ultimately used not only by officers in the division headquarters where they were based, but by cohabiting units excluded from U.S. assistance because of their human rights records, such as combat battalions of the Fourth Brigade in Antioquia. Although the intelligence units were set up to pursue guerilla leaders—"high-value targets"—the capacities they provided were also used in operations against people accused of serving as civilian guerrilla collaborators, known as militias, especially in Eastern Antioquia, where the problem of extrajudicial executions was acute in 2004–6.

"There was a problem," said Colonel Juan Carlos Piza, who served on the Fourth Brigade's command staff from 2002 to 2007. "All of the [guerrilla] militias were totally secret, totally unknown to government officials. They gave me intelligence information that for Colombian authorities was no good. It's not judicial evidence." Militia members' names did not appear in the guerrillas' written combat plans. Piza told me that General Montoya developed military action against militia members, so that full-time combatants would be cut off from supplies, a strategy that was continued after Montoya left the Fourth Brigade in 2003. Piza had been commander of a battalion in Eastern Antioquia in 2004 and 2005—precisely when the battalion's soldiers reportedly killed at least a dozen civilians.[41] U.S. intelligence assistance to the intelligence cell in Medellín, though it may not have violated human rights by itself, supported units with strategies conducive to extrajudicial killing.

Would closer monitoring or supervision of the Colombian military intelligence center in Medellín by U.S. handlers have made a difference in the use of intelligence for committing executions? Possibly. The United States worked closely with the Colombian Special Operations Forces Command, which operated in areas away from populated centers, and there were no civilian killings alleged to have been committed by that command.[42]

But there are more plentiful examples that indicate negative human rights outcomes of U.S. aid. The brigades operating in Arauca Department received extensive U.S. training and equipment, for example, and a large spike in executions was reported for the period directly after Green Berets trained them. Only two executions were allegedly committed by Eighteenth Brigade troops in Arauca from 2000 through 2002. U.S. soldiers began training the "Revéiz Pizarro" Mechanized Group 18 in Saravena in December 2002. In the next three years (2003–5), as the brigade continued to be a focus of U.S. aid, soldiers in the brigade reportedly committed twenty extrajudicial killings. U.S. assistance to the Eighteenth Brigade continued at a high level through 2007, when it was cut entirely; the following year, the number of executions allegedly committed by Eighteenth Brigade troops dropped from nine to two.

The outcomes extended beyond killings by the Eighteenth Brigade itself. The "Revéiz Pizarro" commander in early 2003 working with the Green Berets was Colonel Santiago Herrera Fajardo. Herrera was rewarded for his results in Arauca with an invitation to serve as an instructor for a year at WHINSEC in 2004 (where Col. José Octavio Duque was deputy commander at the time).[43] Upon his return to Colombia, he commanded the Fifteenth Mobile Brigade in North Santander Department in 2006–7, where thirty-seven alleged executions occurred under his command, the most of any mobile brigade during the 2000–2010 period. These included several murders of the young men recruited from Soacha, on the outskirts of Bogotá, on false promises of work—the scandal that in late 2008 catalyzed the cessation of false positives as a widespread practice.[44] At the time he was dismissed for his role in these killings, he was army commander Montoya's assistant. He was jailed in 2010.[45]

There is also evidence that some U.S. trainers might look the other way or share callous attitudes about human rights with their protégés. One U.S. trainer working in Arauca told a reporter, for example, that "the paramilitaries are bad guys, but they're *good* bad guys."[46] Especially telling is that no U.S. or Colombian official whom I asked could name a single Colombian military unit whose human rights conduct improved after receiving U.S. assistance.

Some observers suggested that U.S. assistance would be directed to areas where the armed conflict was most acute, and that civilian killings might be more frequent in these areas. General Montoya responded to a U.S. Embassy official's concern about reported civilian killings by saying that military operations had tripled from 2002 to 2006.[47] "The number of combat deaths, the number of violent combat operations, all of those numbers there are much higher than in other parts of the country," a U.S. Embassy officer said in 2008, "and so the fact that we may have a high number of allegations of extrajudicial killings is actually consistent with this overall level, much higher levels of combat."[48] This argument supports the thesis that increased resources for an actor in combat will accelerate extrajudicial killings—essentially, that these killings are a product of war itself. This also would suggest that U.S. assistance contributed to greater violence overall.

If this is the case, then we would expect more atrocities at moments and places of intensive combat, but surveys of civil wars do not support this idea.[49] In the southern Colombian department of Huila, more than two out of every three alleged executions between 2000 and 2010 occurred more than thirty days after the most recent combat event reported in the same municipality, while only 13 percent of these killings occurred within eight days after a combat in the same municipality. These killings were not occurring in the context of combat or the "fog of war."[50]

Even after Directive 29—which offered cash incentives for killings of guerrillas—became public during the Soacha scandal, army commanders defended it by citing a historical example from the United States. Then–army commander General Óscar González Peña said in 2010 that it was just like the U.S. system, like the Wild West when the capture of outlaws was rewarded, "dead or alive."[51] (González Peña earlier served as an instructor at the School of the Americas and as military attaché in Washington.)[52]

Asked why "body count" measures of success became so pervasive in the 2004–8 period, former U.S. ambassador Myles Frechette (1994–97) responded:

Despite all of the money that had been spent in fighting the guerrillas, and the success against the guerrillas, the guerrillas were still there. . . . And they had a capacity to move all over the place. I frankly think that the Colombians by that time were understanding that the lack of more impressive results was affecting, or would affect, the amount of bilateral assistance. And that was a correct assessment. There was growing lack of appetite, or decreasing appetite for spending all that money when the results were not that impressive.[53]

U.S. assessments were concerned with body counts, typically aggregated in numbers of guerrillas captured and killed, as reflected in embassy reports on the U.S.-supported Task Force Omega.[54] In other words, Colombian officers correctly believed that many of their U.S. counterparts implicitly shared their criteria for success—body count. As one U.S. soldier working in Tolemaida said, "The State Department wants to eradicate coca. We want to kill the bad guys."[55]

The United States also set an example through "force protection" that prioritized their safety and prized "killing bad guys." U.S. military and contract personnel deployed to Colombia, for example, were protected through extensive infrastructure on Colombian bases, and were forbidden to engage in combat. Such measures likely reinforced Colombian Army commanders' reluctance to assume the substantial operational risks of venturing out to seek guerrilla combatants.

A high-ranking Colombian officer said that U.S. military personnel visited Colombian war rooms where tallies of killings by unit were posted on the wall. "The gringo doesn't ask me, 'Are they guerrillas? Are they militia members? Are they civilians?' The gringo doesn't know. He needs to know that what he is investing in is successful, to show Congress that it is getting results." But he also noted:

> I wouldn't consider so much the fact that the United States gave more support in year X, that they gave more equipment, more funding, more to increase troops, because it is a friendly government that is supporting a successful government. . . . And it turns out we are killing—guerrillas of course—but we are also killing innocent people to show you how effective your support is. I as a commander, if a gringo calls me, [asks] 'how is the war going?' 'Good, twenty casualties, three casualties.' I show him everything good because I am selling my results so you will give me more money.[56]

In this respect, U.S. intervention was not decisive for human rights practices but simply reinforced existing dynamics within Colombia.

What about U.S. personnel who were embedded in Colombian brigades and divisions? Did they know false positive killings were occurring? The operations officer for U.S. military advisory teams in 2004 said that the teams "are well connected in terms of the Colombian units. Our guys have great visibility over operations." In bimonthly meetings at the U.S. Embassy, he said, the advisor teams "painted a true picture of their units."[57] But if the advisors knew about the civilian killings, it has not come to light.

Fallacies of the Drug War

To the extent that U.S. involvement in Colombia responded to counterdrug objectives, the policy faced inherent tensions and contradictions. The dominant tendency in Washington to see problems and threats as external to white U.S. communities presents a dilemma when it comes to the problem of drug addiction, which is by nature a kind of internal enslavement to a substance or activity. That has not stopped policy makers from identifying the problem for more than a century as foreign in origin. Thus, promilitary advocates repeatedly refer to "taking the drug war to its source" in Latin America—identifying coca fields, rather than addiction (on the consuming end) or poverty (on the production side), as the source of the problem.

Because of high levels of hypocrisy regarding drug use and the enormous resources generated in an illegal market, it is increasingly difficult to distinguish between traffickers and law enforcement. The tactics and weapons used converge, and the logic of the market—expressed in the extreme by drug trafficking—leads traffickers to purchase special forces soldiers and police who have been trained by the state, and to purchase military weapons on the open U.S. gun market.

A similar logic applies to military training. In Colombia during the rise of paramilitaries, in Mexico during the creation of the Gulf and Zetas Cartels, and subsequently in Honduras, the most important recruiting pool for muscle for mafias and criminal organizations has been the military and police. While soldiers and police remain inside their organizations, they serve important operational functions. But ex-soldiers who have received military training are critical to setting up a paramilitary apparatus for illegal organizations that seek to control territory. In Colombia, at least a thousand soldiers joined the AUC paramilitaries[58]—a number of them in key leadership, founding, and training roles. One of them, known as JL, spent twenty years as an army sergeant before joining the AUC, where he trained thousands of gunmen.[59] Everardo Bolaños, the military commander of an AUC bloc in southern Caquetá, had been an army officer in a number of units, and had traveled to Fort Benning, Georgia, to receive training there in May 1993.[60]

The Decline of Civilian Killings

In early 2007 a Democratic majority took control of the U.S. Congress, led in the House of Representatives by Speaker Nancy Pelosi of San Francisco. Pelosi had been an outspoken opponent of the primarily military approach to U.S. policy in Colombia since the 1990s because of human rights concerns. The Democratic-controlled Congress cut military aid to Colombia for Fiscal Year 2008 by one-third. The amount of Pentagon-sponsored training of Colombians, although not controlled directly by Congress, also dropped significantly in 2008.[61]

These reductions, in turn, forced those who coordinated military aid in the U.S. Embassy to be more selective of the units that would be assisted. In 2008 the United States did not approve aid to a number of units that had received assistance in 2007—in most cases for multiple years—and had large numbers of extrajudicial killings attributed to them. These included the principal Colombian Army brigades in Arauca, Córdoba, North Santander, and Casanare Departments, as well as the Calibio Battalion in Santander and the Magdalena and Pigoanza Battalions in Huila. It is not clear whether the Leahy Law was invoked to suspend aid to these units, but the human rights issues leading to cutting the package probably highlighted human rights criteria for selecting a smaller number of units. The United States could no longer "sync" its assistance to the Colombian military's strategy as it did from 2004 to 2007. When the "false positives" scandal broke in 2008, pressure increased in U.S. media to sustain the aid cuts: "The U.S. should not be the financial backer of army-sponsored domestic terrorism," the Los Angeles Times editorialized.[62]

By 2016 four thousand Colombian soldiers were under investigation or had been tried for their participation in extrajudicial killings.[63] Compared to other nations with severe human rights records, this may be a triumph of the Colombian judicial system—although the number of convictions and sentences, especially of higher-ranking officers, is only a small fraction of that number.[64] But the prosecution in civilian courts of crimes reportedly committed by so many soldiers cannot be viewed as an achievement of the Colombian military itself, nor of U.S. assistance to that military.

U.S. assistance to the Colombian judicial system, however, is relevant for understanding impacts on military killings. The evidence for the U.S. influence on justice for killings by soldiers is mixed. On the one hand, Washington funded the Prosecutor General's Office's Human Rights Unit, which managed the overwhelming majority of execution cases brought to trial and conviction, compared to regional prosecutors.

On the other hand, the United States also promoted and funded Colombia's transition from the written inquisitive system of justice, known as Law 600, to the oral accusatory system used in the United States, called Law 906, whose implementation began in 2005. Eighty-eight percent of the

1,445 deaths investigated under the U.S.-supported oral system had not yet advanced beyond preliminary investigation in 2013, compared to only 25 percent of 2,691 deaths under investigation in the old written system; only 1 percent of oral system cases had reached sentencing, while written system cases had resulted in conviction for 8 percent of the deaths.[65]

The 2005 San José massacre would be investigated and tried under the old written system. The gravity of the crime, the public and diplomatic attention it received, and the narrative of army leaders made it a key test of whether any crime committed by the military could end in full justice.

CHAPTER 11
INVESTIGATION OF THE MASSACRE

> It's been eight or nine years of persecution and abuses.
> It's *rage* directed at us, even by the state. All because we
> don't want to let in anyone who carries weapons, since
> they all just want to use us.
>
> —San José Peace Community member, February 2005

The Peace Community's public denunciation of army participation in the February 2005 massacre, advocacy by Colombian human rights organizations and international accompaniment groups, and diplomatic communications created multiple and diverse pressures to bring those responsible to justice. But the depth and persistence of those pressures, which came from both above and below, together with the thin judicial results in this case, offer an important measure of how difficult it is to achieve justice when powerful military institutions enforce impunity for their members and leaders. As the judicial investigation unfolded during 2005 and 2006, army officers and their supporters deflected attention, practiced deception, blamed the victims, and protected each other. The United States made conflicting responses to these evasions of justice.

In April 2005, investigators of the San José massacre from the Prosecutor General's Office (in Colombia called the Fiscalía) returned to Resbalosa to collect evidence, and determined that Sandra Tuberquia, mother of the two small children, had been killed in her kitchen by a powerful detonation, possibly a mortar. The Fiscalía investigators also interviewed two officers and obtained operational orders at Seventeenth Brigade headquarters.[1]

In September 2005, investigators examined the TV documentary on the massacre, which had been produced in April by Hollman Morris, to identify witnesses who had been interviewed.[2] Around the same time, Guillermo

Mateus of the Inspector General's Office joined the team investigating the massacre; he would play a key role in uncovering responsibility.

On September 15, Faustino Martínez Córdoba, alias "Ferney," died in combat in the Mulatos settlement in San José. Ferney was reportedly the head of personnel for the FARC's Fifty-Eighth Front, which operated in the Abibe range, including in San José. The army recovered a laptop computer with Ferney's body, which was turned over to military investigators, and on September 21, civilian forensic specialists in Bogotá opened the chain of custody for the computer. In its files were profiles of alleged full-time combatants and part-time militia members of the FARC's Fifty-Eighth Front. The list of militia included both Dario Tuberquia ("El Gurre"), who was walking with Luis Eduardo Guerra's family when they were attacked and was the principal witness to the massacre, and Alejandro Pérez, who died at the Bolívar house. Although the military had the computer for several days before the chain of custody began, making it invalid as judicial evidence, Fiscalía investigators would soon cite this information, which undercut the Peace Community's credibility and its version of events.[3]

At the end of November judicial investigators questioned Colonel Néstor Iván Duque, the commander of the army operation when the massacre occurred. He told them that he learned of the massacre through a phone call from Carlos Franco, the human rights director in the presidency two days after the massacre, on the night of February 23. He claimed incorrectly that Luis Eduardo's stepmother, Miryam, was part of the Peace Community internal council, and reiterated testimony that El Gurre was hiding with other guerrillas some distance away on the day of the massacre.[4] Duque may have been especially anxious, because in May two previous commanders of the Bejarano Battalion that he commanded were indicted for not taking action against paramilitaries who robbed, threatened, and murdered Peace Community members between 2000 and 2002.[5] The charges were disciplinary, not criminal, and one of the battalion commanders was only eventually suspended for ninety days, but the sanctions were nevertheless unprecedented, and must have made Seventeenth Brigade officers worry.

There were more army killings of civilians in San José as 2005 went on, but the responses of some U.S. officials and Colombian military officers began to change. Increased awareness that had resulted from international responses to the massacre in February led to grassroots mobilizations after each killing—considerably greater than responses to killings in 1999–2001. For example, in October, FOR volunteers overheard a soldier who was patrolling with others in San José saying he would "like to cut off the head" of one of the FOR members. Fifty-six members of Congress referenced this threat four months later in a letter to Condoleezza Rice urging that she continue to withhold U.S. aid to the Seventeenth Brigade and withhold Colombia's human rights certification.[6] Concern about specific abuses in San José was translating into Congressional action seeking to affect the overall military aid package.

But the continued killings still required urgent attention. With community members having fled from settlements high in the mountains in the wake of the massacre, the military appeared to concentrate its attention on settlements that were not as far up. On the morning of November 17, Arlen Salas was tending a corn field in the San José settlement of Arenas Altas when soldiers opened fire, killing Salas and wounding another man, while other workers fled. When a Peace Community group hiked to the settlement to bring the wounded man to the hospital, soldiers shouted and shot at the ground in front of them but calmed down and became cooperative after learning that one member of the group was a Spaniard. An FOR team volunteer that night escorted Salas's body in a car to the Apartadó morgue, together with a woman whose ill baby died on the way. Several days later, the army's radio station said that guerrillas had killed Salas.[7] FOR gave the U.S. Embassy an account the same day as it received information, and U.S. political counselor Milton Drucker called and spoke directly with the Colombian vice president, Defense Minister Ospina, and the National Police chief to ask for details of what occurred. Ospina reportedly then asked that the case be given priority.[8]

The day after Christmas 2005, soldiers launched a surprise attack at 5:00 a.m. on a house in the Cristalina settlement in San José where three young men had been drinking with three local young women, killing all six of them as they slept. The army said those killed were guerrillas, and the young men may have been, though there is no evidence that the female youths were. Most of those killed were not older than seventeen; one of the girls was pregnant. According to Father Javier Giraldo, the youths had been invited to the party by a guerrilla deserter working with the army. The former guerrilla reportedly told his friends that the army had paid him 24 million pesos ($12,000) for the killings,[9] which was consistent with the army's use of paid informants in many other "false positive" killings in other parts of the country.

Less than three weeks later, on January 12, troops from the Thirty-Third Counter-Guerrilla Battalion killed fifty-three-year-old Edilberto Vásquez twenty minutes on foot from his house, again claiming afterward that he was a guerrilla. His twelve-year-old son identified Vásquez's body and saw that he had on boots that he only wore in the house.[10] Both Vásquez and Salas had been involved in the Peace Community's initiative to organize humanitarian zones, leading community leaders to believe that the military was specifically targeting the initiative. Any effects from changes in official responses to military abuses were not visible to community members on the ground.

In December 2005 Senator Patrick Leahy wrote to Colombian prosecutor general Mario Iguarán to ask about the status of investigations in both the February 2005 massacre and the killings of six Peace Community leaders in July 2000, which had led to the original request for FOR's accompaniment. One hundred people had provided evidence to the Fiscalía about the July 2000 massacre, but the investigation for that atrocity, too, had gone nowhere.[11] Leahy's key staffer, Tim Rieser, and ex-FOR team member Renata Rendon visited San José de Apartadó the same month.

A few months later, in April, Rieser went to Bogotá to meet with Colombian prosecutors, including the head of the Fiscalía's Human Rights Unit, Leonardo Cabana. Since the Senate subcommittee chaired by Senator Leahy funded the Human Rights Unit, the conversation also had a patron-client aspect, with Cabana saying he could "do more with more." But Rieser spent much of the two-and-a-half-hour meeting discussing cases from San José de Apartadó. Fiscalía investigator Nelson Casas told Rieser he had received threats because of his work, and trucks with tinted windows and no license plates had followed his wife.[12]

Another investigator, Luis Alejandro Guevara, told Rieser that army soldiers were "days away" from the judicial commission that was attacked on the road to San José on March 1—a clear falsehood. Casas had interviewed members of the military who reiterated that soldiers were a mile and a half from the massacre site on the day it occurred.[13] The army's report on soldiers' distance from the massacre had not been credible from the start. As early as March 11, 2005, the military had published annotated operational maps purporting to show how many days were required to get from one place to another.[14] But those who accompanied the community knew from experience that it took only an hour to hike between El Barro and the massacre site on the Mulatos River, a distance that the military said took three to four *days*.

The publication in July 2006 of an extensive report by Spanish jurists highlighted "the possible direct participation of army soldiers and paramilitary groups" in "the savage murder of eight people, including three small children," and emphasized the impunity for this and many other acts of violence against the Peace Community.[15] The annual U.S. process for human rights certification also continued to exert pressure on the Defense Ministry to address the Seventeenth Brigade's attacks on the Peace Community. That process required the State Department to certify the Colombian military's cooperation on human rights cases and to break military-paramilitary ties. In August 2006, General Montoya—now commander of the army—issued a directive to assign a human rights legal advisor to the Seventeenth Brigade commander, extend human rights training for brigade staff, and review the more than five hundred human rights charges by the Peace Community of army abuse.[16] These directives served to sustain scrutiny of the brigade's actions but did little to bring cases to justice. This persistent impunity was central to community members' decision not to give further testimony about the 2005 massacre.

Colombian investigators still worked from the thesis of the FARC's responsibility for the massacre, stating that army troops were "a considerable distance" from where the deaths occurred, and that intelligence reports showed that FARC members were in the area on those days. The thesis was linked to assertions that community leaders collaborated with the FARC. One investigator said that interviews with demobilized guerrillas showed "beyond doubt" that Peace Community leaders were supporting the FARC through supplies laden on horses and mules and by leaving homes temporarily vacant for guerrilla use. He referred to former community leader Arturo David, who had left the community to join the guerrillas. Judicial investigator Nelson Casas reported that in a Peace Community house he had seen seven teenage girls in olive-green T-shirts, an indicator of guerrilla presence.[17]

Casas wrote in August that "we have no testimony concretely incriminating anyone, and not a single statement by a witness present during the events." Fiscalía officers shared with U.S. officials their frustration with the Peace Community for refusing to give testimony, although the individuals from whom they sought testimony did not claim to have witnessed the massacre.[18] The State Department, in turn, publicly stated in May that the community's refusal to give testimony was making it difficult to advance the investigation.[19]

In September 2006 the capture and testimony of a twenty-six-year-old paramilitary named Adriano Cano Arteaga, who went by the alias "Melaza" (or "molasses"), provided what would become a break in the case. He had been a radio operator in the AUC's Banana Block, which operated in Apartadó when it demobilized in neighboring Turbo in November 2004. After that, he served as a guide in the army's Vélez Battalion. He was still with the Seventeenth Brigade's Vélez Battalion, he testified, when he was arrested, imprisoned in Medellín, and charged with participation in other paramilitary crimes; investigators believed he participated in a squad that killed former paramilitary chief Carlos Castaño in April 2004.[20] When Fiscalía and Inspector General investigators learned of Cano Arteaga's connection to Operation Phoenix, they set up an interview with him, though it would take several more months before he implicated other participants in the operation.

On February 20, 2007, prosecutor Nelson Casas issued a summons to sixty-nine soldiers from the Thirty-Third "Cacique Luitaima" Battalion—the Seventeenth Brigade unit that had been present at Miryam Tuberquia's home in Mulatos during Operation Phoenix—including two officers and nine noncommissioned officers. The summons to testify was not an arrest, suspension from duty, or indictment but signaled a stage immediately prior to detaining the soldiers for participation in the crime or dismissing the case against them. The soldiers "operated near the places where the bodies of the victims were found," according to Casas. He also said that the Fiscalía continued to investigate the possibility of FARC's participation in the massacre.[21]

The Peace Community viewed the summons as a confirmation of their initial claims of army responsibility for the massacre in spite of the Uribe government's denials of that responsibility. The community responded to the summons by stating: "Only when there is powerful international pressure are the crimes [against the community] barely recognized."[22] But the military had allies in the Fiscalía, which was experiencing considerable internal conflict over the case and other issues.[23] The agency's international relations director was an assertive young political scientist, María Fernanda Cabal, who had responsibility for dealing with the United States and other international donors to the agency, including its Human Rights Unit. Some U.S. officials thought very highly of her work.[24] But others believed she was not acting impartially; some pointed to the fact that her husband, José Félix Lafaurie, was president of the cattlemen's association (Federación Colombiana de Ganaderos, FEDEGAN), historically linked to support for paramilitaries.[25]

Cabal criticized the summons to the Cacique Luitaima soldiers in conversations with several officials inside and outside the Fiscalía. She said she thought the investigation pointed to the FARC as authors of the massacre, not the army, and asked the director of the Human Rights Unit, Leonardo

Cabana, for a written explanation. She expressed her discontent with the investigation's direction to other members of the government and to the Colombian media, and with her own and Cabana's letters in hand, went to armed forces commander General Freddy Padilla de León. Padilla suggested that she take them to Defense Minister Juan Manuel Santos, which she did, expressing to Santos her disagreement about the Fiscalía's summons.[26] Other officials suspected Cabal of leaking even more information about the case from its internal files—at a time when the Fiscalía was in the midst of a broader conflict over leaks of internal information.[27] Santos said publicly on February 27 that there was discord in the military about the summons, repeating the thesis that the guerrillas may have been responsible and saying he was meeting with Prosecutor General Mario Iguarán the following day.[28]

After Cabana learned of Cabal's maneuvering on the case, he submitted his resignation letter to Iguarán, followed by the resignation of the Fiscalía's investigator into the massacre, Nelson Casas, who in any case was also receiving threats.[29] Iguarán was thus forced to choose sides between Cabal, an official in good favor with the U.S. Embassy, and Cabana, the director of a unit funded by the United States, on a case of political importance to the United States. If Washington weighed in, that would have had significant influence on Iguarán's decision.

At least one account indicated that Iguarán still believed the FARC was responsible for the massacre, and he asked Cabana why he was summoning soldiers if evidence pointed to the guerrillas. He replied that evidence indicated soldiers were present in the area of the massacre at the time. Cabana submitted his resignation after this meeting with Iguarán.[30] When Colombian media on February 28 published word of Cabal's actions, U.S. human rights organizations responded, urging Senator Leahy to express concern about Cabal's interference with the investigation. Some NGOs even reportedly urged that she be fired.[31] U.S. Embassy officials met with Cabana on February 16—when they emphasized the importance of making progress on the case and offered security for Casas—and again on February 23. They also met with Iguarán on March 1 "to express our support for Cabana's and Casas' handling of the case and to urge continued progress."[32]

The same day, March 1, Iguarán publicly expressed his "unconditional support for Dr. Casas and Dr. Cabana" for their decision to issue the summons to the soldiers, while Cabal left the country for an indefinite vacation (she was not fired and eventually returned to her post).[33] "I don't think they expected such a strong response" from the international community, one human rights activist involved in the response told me at the time.

At the same time as the Fiscalía issued its summons for the sixty-nine soldiers, on February 20, the prominent Colombian news weekly *Semana* published a piece focused on a Peace Community leader, Brígida González, alleging that five of her children were members of the FARC. By that time, González had become a prominent spokesperson for the community, traveling to Europe and the United States and featuring in Hollman Morris's hour-long televised report on the massacre. Many visitors knew her because of her prolific paintings of the community and of violence against it. According to *Semana*, files reportedly captured by the army from the FARC showed that González's son Juan Carlos was also alias "Elkin," fighting with the Fifty-Eighth Front active in San José, and gave the names of six other children, four of them allegedly guerrillas, one disappeared, and one a farmer.[34] One of the children it accused of being a guerrilla was fifteen-year-old Elisenia, killed in her sleep during the army attack in La Cristalina settlement in December 2005.[35]

Semana also cited a twenty-two-year-old FARC deserter who left after mistreatment and a forced abortion, and claimed that her husband, a guerrilla known as "Richard," told her that the FARC had carried out the massacre because "they were in negotiations with the army to leave the San José de Apartadó area. He told me about a year later that they had done the execution because they were with the State. And the boys sometimes told how they would tie people up and later cut off their heads."[36]

While the narrative of the community's involvement with FARC continued during 2007, prosecutors' investigation of the army widened. The Fiscalía's summons focused on soldiers in the Thirty-Third Cacique Lutaima Battalion, but investigators also scrutinized other battalions. The order for Operation Phoenix that had resulted in the massacre named Bejarano Battalion commander Colonel Duque as operational commander, delegated by Seventeenth Brigade commander General Fandiño. In Washington, Rieser and Rendon continued to work together to urge the Fiscalía to investigate both Duque and Fandiño.

The Fiscalía began interviews in early May of soldiers from both the Thirty-Third Cacique Lutaima and Vélez Battalions.[37] None of the sixty-five soldiers interviewed admitted to participating in the massacre or knowing who did. Some of the soldiers stated that they carried machetes during the operation, and some also admitted to the presence of civilian "guides," who were in fact paramilitaries. All acknowledged that their unit had killed a guerrilla, alias "Machorusio," on February 20 in Las Nieves settlement in San José.[38]

In April 2007, investigators from the Inspector General's Office revealed that the paramilitary radio operator Adriano José Cano, "Melaza," gave testimony that confirmed the army's collaboration in the massacre. Although community leaders were not testifying to judicial investigators, Miryam Tuberquia's testimony and the community's public statements had referenced the presence of Melaza in her house during the week of the massacre. In his statement to the Fiscalía, Melaza mentioned that he had received a uniform and weapon from the army to participate in operations, in one of which he had helped kill a guerrilla known as "Cristo de Palo." Cristo de Palo was the nom de guerre of Alejandro Pérez, who was killed by gunfire just before the massacre of the Tuberquia family in Resbalosa.[39]

In his testimony, Melaza accused Captain Guillermo Gordillo Sánchez, commander of a company in the Vélez Battalion, of serving as commander of the paramilitaries who carried out the massacre. Gordillo later testified that General Fandiño called him in early November 2007, while he was in the field with a counterguerrilla unit in another region of Colombia. He went to Bogotá and met Fandiño in a private apartment, where the general showed him Melaza's testimony that named the captain. General Fandiño "told me that at no time should I say that there were armed civilian guides or any other personnel besides soldiers," Gordillo testified. Gordillo also said the general had spoken personally with a guide when Fandiño arrived in the area shortly after the massacre.[40]

Gordillo was arrested later that month and charged with homicide.[41] In his first testimony after arrest, however, Gordillo denied involvement in the massacre. It was only after investigators told him that paramilitary testimony was sufficient to convict him that he confessed to his participation, in July 2008. He was convicted three months later, just as the "false positives" scandal dominated Colombian news.[42]

In December 2007, Fiscalía investigators also interviewed a brigade intelligence officer, Didier Arley Correa Guisao, who monitored radio communications of guerrillas and paramilitaries and whose superior was Lieutenant Colonel Fernando Augusto Castro. Two of Correa's brothers had been in the Voltigeros Battalion and were killed in the Porroso guerrilla ambush that spurred Operation Phoenix. He revealed that the radio signals used by "Melaza" and "Cuatro Cuatro" could be received as far as the Seventeenth Brigade headquarters in Carepa municipality; he had heard them from there.[43] That could implicate the brigade's command staff in knowledge of collusion with paramilitaries in the operation.

Other testimony suggested an army cover-up of facts central to the massacre. Gordillo and others testified that fifty paramilitary gunmen patrolled with the army in Operation Phoenix—a presence that would require command authority and significant organization.

Early in the investigation, discrepancies appeared between multiple testimonies regarding the locations of army troops and the coordinates reported by army units, known as the INSITOP, during Operation Phoenix. Army statements had used the coordinates to insist that troops were far from the massacre sites, seriously exaggerating the amount of time required to walk between points in the area. The INSITOP reports showed troops had arrived at the home of Miryam Tuberquia in El Barro on February 25, contradicting Tuberquia and the paramilitary Melaza, who both testified that troops arrived at her house on February 21 and held her family captive.[44] The testimony in 2007 and 2008 of multiple military participants in Operation Phoenix also confirmed that Captain Gordillo arrived to lead the operation on February 17, but Lieutenant José Humberto Milanés testified in April 2008 that the Vélez Battalion altered the INSITOP records to show that the operation began two days earlier than it did.[45] And although officers in the field reported false coordinates to their commanders in brigade headquarters, the troops nevertheless received resupplies during the operation without difficulty, indicating that brigade officers knew of the falsified locations.[46]

As national and international attention increasingly focused on the army's extrajudicial killings nationally, the Seventeenth Brigade received an order—reportedly from army commander General Montoya—to destroy evidence of pressure for increased combat killings that led to "false positive" killings. In April 2008, the commander of the division that includes the Seventeenth Brigade ordered units to burn copies of a directive that rewarded soldiers for large body counts. Burning documents was not the usual way to abrogate a directive.[47] The military tried to appear as if it did not reward executions, which could be a step toward stopping the practice, or simply an act of covering its tracks, or both.

The demobilization of paramilitary commanders, initiated in 2003, began in 2006–7 to yield new revelations of army-paramilitary collaboration, including in Urabá. In May 2008, the former paramilitary commander of the "Banana Block" in the Urabá region, Hebert Veloza García, told investigators about his history of collaboration with military and police officers. According to Veloza, he met Bejarano Battalion commander Colonel Duque in

2005 in an assistance center for demobilized paramilitaries in Turbo, and in a closed office by themselves, Duque asked Veloza for 2 million pesos (about $1,000) to pay ex-FARC guerrillas to testify that the massacre had been committed by the FARC, and Veloza said he gave Duque the money. In testimony leaked to Colombian media in 2009, Veloza also stated that his second-in-command forwarded a request from Duque to kill "Melaza," the paramilitary who testified about the massacre, because he—Melaza—said while drunk that he knew who had killed the children in Resbalosa. Veloza testified that he turned down this request. "Duque was a collaborator of ours in Urabá with whom we coordinated and provided guides," Veloza explained. He also said that he and a paramilitary subordinate had met with Duque, to ensure the army did not deploy where the paramilitaries were operating, and that his paramilitaries had sent young men to the army to be killed and claimed as paramilitaries killed in combat.[48]

Other evidence also emerged that Duque acted to cover up military responsibility. In June 2009, the demobilized guerrilla militia member Apolinar Guerra testified that Duque had promised him money for testifying that the FARC had committed the massacre. Guerra was scared. Duque had obtained his phone number and financial information while Guerra was in prison for other crimes and called him in a furor.[49]

Veloza was not the commander of the Heroes of Tolová troops who carried out the massacre. That boss was Diego Murillo Bejarano, "Don Berna," who along with other paramilitary leaders was extradited to the United States in May 2008. Serving a thirty-one-year prison sentence in New York for drug trafficking, in June 2009 Murillo finally gave testimony about his crimes. He acknowledged that his troops were part of Operation Phoenix in San José de Apartadó and accused Lieutenant Colonel José Fernando Castaño, chief of staff of the Vélez Battalion, of giving the order to kill the children in Resbalosa.[50] In February 2010 Gordillo added to his testimony and charged Seventeenth Brigade commander General Fandiño with meeting two paramilitaries, "Jonas" and "Ratón," before the massacre.[51]

But these revelations did little to stem impunity for officers' participation in the massacre and subsequent cover-up. In August 2010 a judge acquitted ten soldiers of the Vélez Battalion who were accused of participating in the massacre, on the basis that it would have been too risky for the soldiers to confront the paramilitaries during Operation Phoenix.[52] The judge also concluded that there was no proof that officers had planned the massacre in advance and "did not know nor should have known the risks of their action" of patrolling with the illegal groups. The community's legal representative

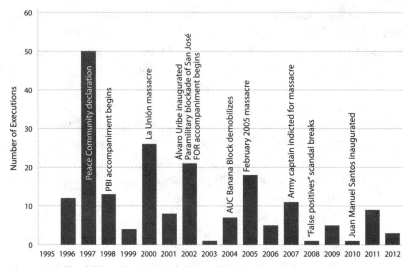

Fig. 11.1. Civilian killings in San José de Apartadó, 1995–2012.

SOURCE: COURTHEYN, "'MEMORY IS THE STRENGTH,'" 72.

in the case, Jorge Molano, contested the ruling's logic: "To consider that the prior meetings, use of paramilitary guides, joint patrols, and sleeping in the same place do not constitute a crime is an invitation to consolidate the criminal association between soldiers and paramilitaries."[53]

Even more important, the judge found that officers had no command responsibility for their subordinates' actions, even if they should have known about those actions. Molano said of the ruling that "the testimonies of Captain Gordillo and seven paramilitary men on military and paramilitary joint actions in the operation that led to the death of four children and four adults do not matter." He called the ruling "a major monument to impunity."[54]

By 2011 five paramilitary men from the Heroes of Tolová Block had been convicted of participating in the massacre and were sentenced to six to forty years each; another seven paramilitaries had been arrested.[55] But only one army soldier—Captain Gordillo—had been convicted for participating in the crime, based on his own confession, and sentenced to twenty years in prison. The cases against other army officers were not advancing.[56] In June 2012 a Medellín appeals court confirmed the acquittal of six soldiers, including Vélez Battalion commanders, while finding four low-ranking soldiers guilty.[57]

Parallel with efforts to achieve justice for the massacre, killings of San José Peace Community members declined steadily after 2005. Various factors probably contributed. In early 2009, General Hernán Giraldo assumed command of the Seventeenth Brigade and reportedly imposed a condition for assuming command: having carte blanche to purge the brigade of officers who collaborated with criminals or committed abuses. He ordered four hundred officers transferred out of the brigade (but not sanctioned), including most of the staff officers.[58] Persistent pressure by the Peace Community, accompaniment groups, and allies in Washington must have contributed to the commander's decision to purge "bad elements."

Colonel Néstor Iván Duque, then retired, agreed to meet me in September 2014 at the military club in Bogotá, at a table on the lawn apart from other officers, dressed in a black suit. He wanted to speak in private. For the next two and a half hours, we talked about his career, his antiguerrilla operations, the massacre in San José de Apartadó, and the work of human rights organizations. I told him I was writing about U.S.-Colombian military relations during 2000–2010. Though he said he knew I had a lot of information, he did not seem to be aware that I had worked for the Fellowship of Reconciliation.

Duque's style was scattershot. He told me that he had just come from a visit with General Rito Alejo del Río, in military detention for his role in paramilitary operations as Seventeenth Brigade commander in 1996. He said General Montoya had given orders for "false positive" killings and General Padilla was a "bandit." He said that everyone in the San José Peace Community was a guerrilla. He said he had been kicked out of the military because he had denounced administrative corruption in the leadership of the Twelfth Brigade in southern Caquetá, where he had been chief of staff in 2007–8, after his time in Urabá. He served briefly as a human rights officer and was dismissed from the army at the end of 2008.[59]

According to Duque, when he raided the house of a leading trafficker's wife in 1994, he found a room full of campaign literature for Ernesto Samper and took photos. But the unit's commander, Colonel Carlos Velásquez, deliberately damaged the photos, he said, and U.S. Embassy personnel knew this. (Velásquez was the officer who had denounced General Alejo del Río's permissiveness of paramilitaries in Urabá.) He also claimed that during the same period, he told his CIA counterparts about a drug traffic informant, who then informed the DEA, which killed the informant because the DEA was, at that time, very involved with drug trafficking and with the death squad organized to kill Pablo Escobar's associates. He said it made him so afraid that he asked his superiors for permission to go into hiding or to the United States, but instead he was sent abroad to another country in the 1990s.

By the time he was sent to Urabá in 2004, Duque "knew absolutely nothing of the situation" there, he said. "I liked going to war. I personally went on point [on patrols]." He trained a special forces group in the Bejarano Battalion, he said, and the battalion carried out ninety-seven combat operations in 2004 and 2005. The result: from one enemy killing in 2003 before he arrived in Bejarano, the battalion killed fifteen FARC guerrillas in 2004–5, according to Duque. It also captured sixty-two combatants during the same period, he said. According to him, this showed that he was not killing civilians. "I could have had many more killings with the system of 'false positives,'" he told me. He repeated what he told FOR in 2004: that he conducted many operations with the Thirty-Third Battalion. Unlike his own troops in Bejarano, who were conscripts, those in the Thirty-Third were professional soldiers, he said.

Duque took a pen and sketched out in my notebook how the operation in San José took place in February 2005. I asked what intelligence the army had used to plan the operation. "There was never any real intelligence," he said. "It was planning by intuition, we could say." The guerrillas who conducted the ambush in El Porroso could have retreated to several locations, he said— to Río Verde or Río Esmeralda, located in a corridor known as the Nudo de Paramillo, or to the Mulatos Canyon, in San José. The brigade officers chose to take the operation to Mulatos.

Duque insisted that he was not in command of Operation Phoenix, and that the tactical order listing him as operational commander was only signed after the massacre became known, on February 23, and backdated with Duque's signature to February 19.

He also said he was responsible for the feature story portraying Brígida González's children as guerrillas in the weekly newsmagazine *Semana* in 2007. "I did that story," Duque told me. He had given all the material for it to Gloria Congote, under whose byline the story ran, including the testimony by a young woman who had deserted the guerrillas and who claimed the FARC had committed the massacre.

I said I understood that paramilitary commander Hebert Veloza had claimed that Duque met with him. A few days later, Duque gave me a trove of digital files, including a folder of material about Veloza. Most of the files, however, were from what Duque said was a laptop computer recovered from a guerrilla killed in San José de Apartadó in September 2005. The files include hundreds of photos and videos of guerrillas posing in rural environments, as well as candid informal shots of FARC members, sometimes with girlfriends or children. Included was a database with detailed personal information on 44 militia members and 267 combatants from the FARC's Fifty-Eighth Front, which operated in and around San José de Apartadó.

Duque had produced a PowerPoint presentation in which he claimed, based in part on the FARC database files, that more than forty Peace Community members were guerrillas, guerrilla collaborators, or had immediate family in the FARC. Why did Duque give me this data, and was it authentic? Duque clearly wanted his name and legacy to appear better than they did, and he seemed to view the files as a way to cast doubt on the community's version of events and confer greater credibility to his innocence. The creation dates for the vast majority of hundreds of files—and all of the photos and videos—preceded September 2005, when the laptop was reportedly recovered. Creation dates can be altered, but even if some key files were altered, the sheer volume of detail in the personnel files would be difficult to fabricate and still appear authentic.

At the same time, Duque's analysis included fantastical claims, contradicted by the accumulated experience of international accompaniers, that Peace Community leaders had served as guerrilla commanders. Inhabiting a zone with historic presence and influence of the FARC, community members did not deny that San José residents had family members who joined the guerrillas. Some also joined the paramilitaries. Like several other army officers I interviewed, Duque used our two meetings to make his case that he had not violated human rights, but his defense was not credible. His M.O. was to take a piece of something true, such as familial relationships, and mix it with more stigmatizing false accusations and unfounded insinuations, going from defense to offense. His narrative continued the military's historical accusations that San José was a guerrilla community, as justification for continuing to make it a target of war. The facts that had emerged about the 2005 massacre, and the accounts from international accompaniers and those who visited the community, upended that military narrative.

CHAPTER 12
AN ENCOUNTER WITH POWER

In September 2014 army commander General Jaime Lasprilla Villamizar was a rising star in the Colombian military. The son of a sergeant killed by guerrillas and the brother of another army officer, he had been operations commander in Urabá in 2000 when the paramilitaries were killing at will. He was fluent in English and a favorite son of the U.S. military. As army commander in 2014 and 2015, he publicly defended other generals accused of ordering civilian killings, and his Tweets regularly praised his soldiers as heroic. But as he sat across the table from me in his office, General Lasprilla was angry and afraid. To understand why, we must examine Lasprilla's role in the false positives scandal.

Three months earlier, in June 2014, the Fellowship of Reconciliation (FOR) and Colombian human rights organizations, more than two hundred of which were grouped together in the Coordinación Colombia–Europa–Estados Unidos (CCEEU), had released a report titled "The Rise and Fall of 'False Positive' Killings in Colombia." The report found, among many other things, that General Lasprilla was the active duty officer with the largest number of alleged extrajudicial killings occurring under his command, when he led the Ninth Brigade in southwestern Huila Department from June 2006 to November 2007.[1] Lasprilla was also a U.S. protégé—an invited instructor for a year at Fort Benning, Georgia; a student for a year at National Defense University in Washington; and a commander of units that were a focus of U.S. assistance, including the twenty-thousand-man Task Force Omega and Colombia's Joint Special Operations Command.

Though the report's release received no media attention in Washington, it was amply covered by Colombian media, including by a TV news program called *Noticias Uno*. When *Noticias Uno* interviewed me, I mentioned our finding about General Lasprilla, and they then interviewed Lasprilla, who said that he "respected" our report but that all of the seventy-five deaths we had documented occurred in legitimate combat operations. It was a radical posture not to concede that even one killing may have occurred outside combat. But he also said that he had ordered forty-eight investigations of such deaths.[2]

Four days later, I was in the military command building in Bogotá, and my visit happened to coincide with a ceremony on the field just behind the building. As I was leaving, I could see many officers in their dress uniforms, milling about, leaving, or going to their offices. I did not know it at the time, but President Santos had just promoted Lasprilla to the rank of major general. As I descended the stairway, I saw coming up the stairs the clearly recognizable face of General Lasprilla. He had a large face and prominent ears, a straight-ahead gaze, his hair cut close to the skin. I looked at him, he looked at me, and we passed each other. Then, as he ascended the stairs, I looked up over my shoulder, and he looked back down over his own shoulder. "It's him," I thought, and surely he thought, "It's him." Though I could not read his look, it was a bit chilling.

A few weeks after returning to the United States, I got an email from another officer I had met who knew Lasprilla. He said Lasprilla was inviting me to meet with him in Bogotá so he could explain his operations, even offering to pay for my flight and hotel. I declined the payments but agreed to meet in September.

I had followed Lasprilla's career for some time, mostly because of the number of extrajudicial killings reported in Huila Department, which had received little attention, even in Colombia. In 2013 I had tried without success to obtain an interview with him, through one of his advisors whom I met. In February 2014, President Santos fired armed forces chief Leonardo Barrero for telling an officer who was detained and under investigation for extrajudicial killings to "get together and work up a mafia" that would go after human rights prosecutors. Barrero's comments to the detained officer were leaked to the newsweekly *Semana*, part of hundreds of recorded conversations that revealed extensive corruption among detained and active duty officers. The officers conspired to obtain army purchase contracts—such as for Blackhawk parts—and skim funds to benefit soldiers accused of civilian killings.[3] Barrero and four other generals were relieved of their posts. As a result of the shakeup, General Lasprilla was appointed commander of the Colombian Army.

The same month, I finally was able to add up the data on reported killings according to brigade and battalion commanders, and saw how prominent Lasprilla was. The army's commander was now an officer with a pattern of killings under his watch when he commanded the Ninth Brigade in Huila. This seemed to be an important test for the application of Leahy Law, which prohibits assistance to any military or police unit if the U.S. State Department has credible information that members of the unit have committed gross human rights violations, unless they have been brought to justice. And as it turned out, Defense Minister Juan Carlos Pinzón was scheduled to visit Washington in the last days of February. I contacted Senator Leahy's staff, anticipating that he might be meeting with Pinzón, and asked whether he could raise the issue of Lasprilla's record. From our perspective, the Leahy Law could be carried out in any of three ways: Colombia could prosecute the soldiers responsible for the killings under Lasprilla's command, Lasprilla could be removed as commander (which might not provide any justice for those crimes), or the United States could withhold assistance to the Colombian Army as long as Lasprilla was commander, until prosecutions for the Huila killings made significant advances. I sent Leahy's office a memo and a detailed list of seventy-five killings in Huila reportedly committed by soldiers under Lasprilla's command, including for each the names of victims, dates, locations, units, and information sources. Half of them were under investigation by the Fiscalía; NGOs had documented the other half. Leahy's staff did meet with Pinzón and raised the issue with him; he reportedly said he would look into it.

Before my meeting with Lasprilla in September, I asked his staff for any documentation the army had on the cases of reported killings under his command, since he had said he wanted the meeting to "explain operations" to me. The four-page response to Senator Leahy's inquiry to Pinzón was signed by the army's chief of operations, General Juan Bautista Yepes, and the army's human rights director, General Marcolino Tamayo Tamayo. Although Pinzón's Defense Ministry had its own human rights office that could have coordinated requests to other agencies for information that made up the bulk of the memo's substance, Pinzón tasked the inquiry to army officers who were subordinate to General Lasprilla. Any critical findings would have implications for them in the chain of command.

So it was not surprising that the memo showed little objectivity about Lasprilla, saying that "his subordinates and friends . . . give him unconditional subordination based on respect for the military vocation." It did not address any specific cases of executions under investigation by the Fiscalía or documented by human rights organizations. Instead, it offered statistics on the investigative status of cases of reported executions that occurred in Huila during 2006–7 and urged Leahy to "await the result of the respective investigations, so as not to stigmatize the individual actions of members of the institution." It did not offer any reason why Fiscalía investigations or documentation by independent human rights organizations should not be considered credible information, other than the existence of procedures for planning military operations under the rule of law. The memo's data on the investigative status of cases in the military, civilian courts, and disciplinary systems was inconsistent, but it did state that the military had transferred twenty-eight cases from Huila and Caquetá to civilian investigators—normally a result of a recognition that the criminal case has merit.[4]

When the appointed day came for the Lasprilla meeting, my colleague and I sat across from General Lasprilla, and four others with him, including General Tamayo, a civilian attorney, and two other officers. For the next four hours, without a break, we spoke about the armed conflict in Colombia, about deaths that occurred in Huila while Lasprilla was in command there, about legal definitions, about our report, and about human rights organizations, whom Lasprilla and others said were making money from taking legal cases of family members of people falsely claimed to be civilians killed by the army. The meeting was frequently contentious, with Lasprilla so mad that he was spitting at times, and with people talking over each other.

It was a meeting he had convened, but Lasprilla waited for me to begin. I said I understood he wished to explain military operations, and he talked first at some length about the context of the war in Colombia. After a while, I asked him to talk about his experience of U.S. assistance. He had gotten a master's degree during a year at the National Defense University in Washington, and before that, he was an instructor at the former School of the Americas (now called the Western Hemisphere Institute for Security Cooperation, WHINSEC) in 2002–3. He said the most important assistance the United States gave in Huila was in intelligence, and he denied that U.S. helicopters were available there (although the State Department stated that Plan Colombia helicopters were made available to the Ninth Brigade in 2006 when Lasprilla was there). He said that Huila was a place of many guerrilla fronts, and many kidnappings—although the U.S.-Colombian effort to rescue the three U.S. contractors was focused on Caquetá, where they were taken and held.

When we began talking about killings reported in Huila, he began to get angry. He said that NGOs in Huila were making money from denunciations of killings by the military by counting every combat death as an extrajudicial execution. General Tamayo asserted that some NGOs paid off witnesses. We pointed out that, although there were private attorneys in Huila that legally represent victims of alleged executions, there were no NGOs there who do. Lasprilla insisted there were but could not name them. There are human rights groups in Bogotá that represent victims, who have drawn on other groups' reporting of executions in Huila, including CINEP, which published a study of 951 cases of "false positive" killings from 1988 to 2011, called *Debt to Humanity*.[5] "Do you know who CINEP is?" Lasprilla asked us rhetorically. ("Yes," some friends said later, "it's the Catholic Church!") He said that NGOs make money from doing research and studies, and that our investigation was "vulgar."

Our report on army killings was "a strategy of the enemy to discredit the institution," General Tamayo said. This was an accusation that we as report authors were allied with the guerrillas. Tamayo, who was the most visibly aggressive participant, had a sister and brother in the Colombian Congress.[6] The power of his siblings was why he was appointed to that position in the army, a military officer told me. In October 2015, even as Tamayo was up for promotion to major general, the Fiscalía was investigating him for criminally obstructing investigations into false positive killings by the army in four regions of Colombia, including Urabá.[7]

Looking to ground the discussion, I raised a specific case: the killing of a family of three as they rode a motorcycle in Garzón, Huila, in November 2006. The shooting occurred on a rural road, as Daniel Alvarado and Alba Mejía were riding with their three-year-old daughter, Michel Dayana, who had Down syndrome, on their way to their farm in Florencia, Caquetá. As with the massacre in La Resbalosa in San José in 2005, a child was murdered, and no one could claim she was a combatant. Soldiers from the Pigoanza Battalion under Lasprilla's command were deployed on the side of the road when they shot at the couple. Soldiers later claimed that Alvarado was using a radio to communicate with guerrillas, giving him a military advantage in relation to the soldiers, and that they shot "in defensive operations." Both the Inspector General's Office and criminal prosecutors had investigated the case; a civilian court in Garzón found seven soldiers guilty of homicide and sentenced them in May 2013 to forty years in prison.[8]

"It's good that you mention that case, because I was there," Lasprilla exclaimed. It was a mistake, he said. He had gone to the scene after soldiers shot at the couple. The solders "shot involuntarily," he said, and had not seen the child behind the adults on the motorcycle. An execution is different, he said: it is when you deliberately kill someone who is defenseless—here he raised his arms as if holding a rifle and shooting downward—and this case lacked the element in law known as dolo, he said, which implies willful misconduct.

The Inspector General's Office had found that the nine soldiers who were involved not only fired indiscriminately, and thus violated the law with dolo, but they also lied about their reasons for shooting at the couple. The radio recovered at the scene had no antenna, and thus could not have been in use or even visible to the soldiers.[9] Human rights organizations have documented multiple accounts of soldiers placing a radio by the bodies of people they killed in "false positives."[10] The case exemplified soldiers' excessive use of force, followed by a false account that was supported by their unit commander.

General Lasprilla spoke of how controlled and supervised Colombia is, making it different, he said, from Rwanda—as if that were the human rights standard by which other countries should be measured. He was mad that so many soldiers—some 1,900—were in jail, many of whom, he said, were innocent, with 7,000 under investigation.[11] He mentioned 126 cases against soldiers in which he said there was manipulation by prosecutors. He acknowledged that the military had voluntarily transferred some investigations of killings to the civilian justice system. But the Fiscalía, he said, "has too much power."

I asked General Lasprilla if, in all the reports of killings in operations in Huila, he did not smell something bad, sense any irregularity, and he insisted he did not. Almost none of the killings by the military in Huila reported by human rights groups or investigated by prosecutors as extrajudicial executions had reached trial or conviction, but the army and human rights organizations read this fact in opposite ways. For human rights groups, it was a demonstration of the impunity and utter ineffectiveness of the justice system, while for military officers I spoke with it showed that these reports were false.

Lasprilla pointed to the list of Colombian organizations sponsoring our report and said it would be read all over the world. Although he was worried about the impact our report would have on the army as a whole, in our discussion he showed nearly exclusive concern for cases when and where he was commander and might be implicated. Then he said that our report was a violation of the right to presumption of innocence, even a criminal violation, and that he could take action, but he did not think he would. It was an oblique threat to sue us.

Our critique of the impacts of U.S. assistance especially angered him. He insisted that we were saying that the United States had trained Colombians on how to violate human rights, which we were not. He said he had lived in the United States as a child, when his father, a sergeant, was secretary to the Colombian defense attaché in Washington. "I know your country," he said, and he repeated that none of the U.S. courses he received ever suggested in the slightest that soldiers should violate human rights. He added that his father had been killed—presumably by guerrillas.

During our encounter, the officer who set up the meeting asked if we would print a correction if the army provided us with information showing that some cases were not executions: Lasprilla asked us to print a retraction. I replied that it was difficult to say without knowing what information they would provide, but I had no trouble publishing additional analysis if more information became available. General Lasprilla agreed to provide us with documentation from cases in the Military Justice System. As we spoke, the attorney sitting next to me had a large pile of files on the table, which appeared to be military investigation files. We thought perhaps they were preparing to share some of them with us, but they never did.

During the last hour or so of our encounter, Lasprilla was calmer, even cracking a smile. When we stood afterward, I said I was glad to see him smile. Lasprilla seemed to want to lighten things up, and he said to me, "Like you say in your country, 'It's nothing personal.'" He then offered to visit my Colombian colleague's hometown, which was not reassuring.

After we left the meeting, I felt as if my being were vibrating, as if I had absorbed a paroxysm of power in my eyes and hands.

Our meeting took place on September 16, from 5:00 to 9:00 p.m. The next day I tried to reach the coauthor of our report, Alberto Yepes, and another staff person at the CCEEU, but they were not answering their cell phones. In the afternoon, I called their office and learned they had been assaulted at 6:30 the evening before—at just the time my other colleague and I were meeting with General Lasprilla. Two men robbed Yepes at gunpoint of his computer and his cell phones—but not his wallet—on the street in a nice neighborhood of Bogotá.[12] It was an unmistakable message.

The robbery spooked Yepes. His name had appeared just the week before, for the first time, in a threat signed by the paramilitary group Aguilas Negras that listed more than ninety human rights defenders, saying they "will pay with their blood" and "should prepare to die" because the paramilitaries "will hunt them down."[13] That threat itself was one in a rash of threats that September. Because paramilitaries allied with the military killed so many people in recent history, activists take seriously their threats, even if there are fewer such killings than in the past. After the robbery, Yepes applied to the Inter-American Human Rights Commission to receive protective measures.

Why was there such concentrated aggression against human rights defenders, and why at this time? In early September, less than two weeks before my meeting with Lasprilla, Colombian newspapers had revealed that Colonel Róbinson González del Río, himself charged with selling munitions to paramilitaries and ordering six extrajudicial killings,[14] had spoken on tape for one hundred hours with prosecutors in June and July. He accused nine generals and two other officers of participating in more than fifty such killings between 2006 and 2008.[15] González and his family were receiving death threats, and he was being held in one of the Fiscalía's fortified cells.[16]

González's accusations were part of a string of army scandals that had led to Lasprilla's promotion in February to command the army after a shakeup of army leadership. The same month, the government dismissed three other generals in the wake of revelations that army intelligence had hacked into the communications of the government's peace negotiators in Havana.[17] "If they are spying on the negotiators, one could think that they are tapping all of us," Interior Minister Aurelio Iragorri said at the time.[18] Investigators would later learn that army intelligence operatives were selling classified information on the black market as well as the service of erasing the court records of criminal suspects.[19] Prosecutors in July revealed the existence of a developed plan to kill one of the principal hackers, Andrés Sepúlveda, after he testified from prison about the military's involvement in the intelligence operation.[20]

Although—or perhaps because—these high-level scandals reflected poorly on Colombian Army leaders, who were poster boys for "building partner capacity," U.S. officials said nothing about the scandals. But the revelations did have repercussions with other allies who mattered to the military.

In May, retired Colombian Army officers complained publicly that Canada was denying them visas because of alleged human rights abuses under their commands. General Lasprilla formally asked Colombian defense minister Pinzón to intervene on the issue.[21] Canada was relying on its Immigration and Refugee Protection Act, which requires rejection of a visa application if there are "reasonable grounds for suspecting" that the applicant violated human or international rights, similar to the standard of the Leahy Law for excluding units from receiving U.S. assistance.[22]

Moreover, one of the points of negotiation between the Colombian government and FARC guerrillas in 2014 was a transitional justice process, by which those on each side responsible for some of the worst crimes were to be held accountable. Most FARC leaders had already been indicted, tried, and sentenced, but no army officer above the rank of colonel had been tried for extrajudicial killings. And no one knew which officers would be prosecuted, if any, as a result of the peace talks until the process was completed. "The point that most worries [the military] about the negotiations in Havana is the victims, for the truths that could come out," someone who worked with the military for a decade told journalist Juanita León. "To confront those truths is hard," said León, who had interviewed many soldiers. "More than court investigations, what worries them is the historical truth. That pyramid that exists will not hold up when the truth starts to come out."[23]

Officers like Lasprilla also had complex relationships with the United States. The Colombian military "has an emotional dependence on U.S. support," according to a U.S. military mission chief in Bogotá quoted in 2007.[24] One Colombian officer asked me during an interview if I would intervene to help advance the promotion of a general to command the army. When a different general became army commander, he asked an army friend to help him improve his international image, to go to Washington and talk with the groups there that worked on U.S. policy in Colombia. The other officer's role was to offer human rights organizations the military's perspective. Human rights organizations "have to report on violations, that's their work," the envoy officer said to me. "But if they know how we see it, instead of saying it's *very, very bad*, maybe they'll just say, it's *bad*."

In conversations with army officers during 2013 and 2014, I perceived relentless surges of fear: fear of prosecutors, fear of the human rights NGOs, fear of peace, and above all, fear of each other. "Do you know what they think inside?" one officer said to me. "They see from your report that you are talking with people inside, and they think their enemies are using you, to get at them." In fact, I had used interviews with officers primarily to understand the role of U.S. assistance, how operations were financed, and attitudes toward human rights—not to document executions or investigations, which were reported by NGOs, the Fiscalía, and in the press. But the army's internal conflict, driven by the institutional uncertainty resulting from the peace process, was overheated.

Was the simultaneity of the assault on Alberto with my meeting with Lasprilla coincidental? Some people I talked with, including human rights defenders, Colombian journalists, and two high-ranking army officers, did not think so. They saw a coordinated effort to intimidate us and obtain what information we had—through both dialogue and force.

I was not so sure. It is certain that a number of army generals were preparing their legal defenses against possible prosecution for human rights crimes. But while Yepes's mugging was a professional job, we had no direct evidence that General Lasprilla or even active duty army officers had ordered it. Moreover, Yepes's work had focused more on an earlier generation of army leaders than did mine, a group that chafed more at U.S. oversight and human rights discourses than Lasprilla, whom one U.S. advisor who worked with him described to me as a "straight shooter."

It is also possible that those who robbed Yepes's computer planned to use the information for commercial purposes, or to blackmail the enemies of those who ordered the theft, or both. In the fall of 2012, army intelligence agencies established a cell, located in a Bogotá shopping mall and code-named "Andromeda," that specialized in the interception of email and data of political leaders, journalists, activists, and others, including negotiators in the peace process with the FARC, and even President Santos.[25] The operation used both intelligence agency personnel as well as privately contracted hackers. Santos said in a March 2014 interview, "The thing that worries me is I know the strategy of publishing true emails where they put in pieces of false emails. They put the pig in a poke to hurt you."[26] When Andromeda was exposed in early 2014, two generals, the army's chief of intelligence and chief of technical intelligence, were immediately sacked—an event that Lasprilla referenced in our meeting that September.[27] As a result of the proliferation of surveillance operations, a market for leaked classified information had grown in Bogotá, by which people could buy disks of intercepted data on the street.[28]

Since a wide array of retired and active army officers feared prosecution, a database of violations that might be used by prosecutors would be of interest to a large number of such officers, and anyone who owned the database could sell it, or use it as leverage in any conflict among them.

Moreover, it was not the first time that human rights groups had experienced computer thefts that did not look like common crime. The same directive from November 2005 that rewarded civilians for their assistance in killing subversives, Directive 29, also paid for digital information "of interest to State intelligence." Laptop computers or hard drives with such information were worth US$750 to those who turned them in.[29] This provided an incentive for both private and state-based operators to obtain such equipment from legal human rights organizations as well as from illegal armed groups.

In May 2011 and again in May 2012, teams of individuals orchestrated thefts of computers from Colombian human rights researchers, including members of the coalition that Yepes coordinated, at the outset of public events.[30] In June 2007, a rash of office break-ins in Bogotá targeted the computers and electronic data—but not other valuables—of the Fellowship of Reconciliation; the Christian Center for Justice, Peace and Nonviolent Action (Justapaz); and the human rights group Corporación Yira Castro.[31] The State Department noted the robberies in its human rights report for 2007, and thirty-five members of the U.S. Congress wrote to urge President Uribe to publicly condemn the attacks and conduct a thorough investigation of the robberies.[32] Neither occurred.

Two days after the robbery of Yepes, I wrote to General Lasprilla, relating the events of the theft and saying that they "lead to suspicion that the attackers may have been members or ex-members of the armed forces . . . or persons serving them" and urging him to "take appropriate measures to exercise influence on members or ex-members of the institution who may have acted in this way to help stop possible plans for further attacks." Lasprilla responded a few days later, saying that if he had any indication of military participation in the robbery, he would have initiated legal action and taken appropriate measures. He also objected to the statement that the events of the robbery led to suspicion of military involvement, until the courts established their participation through due process.

Yepes went to the Fiscalía the morning after the robbery to file a report, and he strongly urged investigators to obtain footage from public surveillance cameras mounted on the block where the robbery took place, on the block where the assailants approached him, and on the block by which they made their getaway. But the investigators did nothing for months, and never obtained the footage. Investigators were also informed about my simultaneous meeting with Lasprilla, but they did not investigate that coincidence.

It is easy to think that such events sink into obscurity, that forces of intimidation have triumphed. But just as activists remember and are impacted by the waves of paramilitary violence, powerful officials who have been frightened by a public association with war crimes in a time of accounting or have been scolded by foreign patrons do not forget it; nor often do their successors.

In June 2015, Defense Minister Pinzón was replaced by Luis Carlos Villegas, who had been serving as Colombia's ambassador to Washington. The same week, Human Rights Watch published a report focusing on Colombian commanders' responsibility for civilian killings, prominently naming Lasprilla and eighteen other generals. Lasprilla was the active duty officer in the report with the second largest number of alleged killings during his command under investigation by the Fiscalía.[33] The day before the report's release, the Fiscalía announced that it had summoned four generals, including Mario Montoya, to testify about false positive killings under their command.[34]

Senator Patrick Leahy stated he was troubled by the Human Rights Watch report, which he said "shows that as we provided billions of dollars in aid to the Colombian army over many years, its troops systematically executed civilians. Worse yet, the officers who were in charge have escaped justice, and some remain in senior positions of authority, without the United States or the Colombian government addressing the problem."[35] President Santos publicly defended Lasprilla and armed services commander Juan Pablo Rodríguez Barragán, also named in the report.[36]

Nevertheless, two weeks later Lasprilla was dismissed from his command.[37] The cumulative pressures generated by reports of so many killings under his command must have contributed to his dismissal. But prosecutions of the soldiers who carried out those killings still stagnated. Family members of civilians in Huila who had been killed by the army brigade under Lasprilla's command would have to continue waiting to clear the names of their husbands, brothers, sons, and daughters.

CHAPTER 13
JUDICIAL WARFARE

General Jaime Lasprilla was not unique in his visceral rejection of reports of civilian killings by the army. Get into a conversation with Colombian Army officers, and sooner or later you may get to the topic of the "false positives" scandal that so shook the institution and the Colombian populace. Reaction to the scandal led to the resignation in 2008 of army commander General Mario Montoya, just as he bathed in the glory of high-profile successful military operations. These included the rescue without violence in July 2008 of three U.S. military contractors, a presidential candidate, and ten police officers, all of whom had been held captive by the FARC for years in primitive jungle conditions. The scandal unfolded amid investigations of more than 1,500 members of the army, including more than 500 officers, and was referenced thousands of times in the Colombian media.[1]

I interviewed dozens of Colombian military officers between 2010 and 2014, and in most of these conversations, officers eventually articulated a thesis initially promulgated by the military's right-wing old guard but increasingly held by a majority, a thesis known as "judicial warfare."[2] In this narrative, the vast majority of killings investigated as "false positives" were legitimate killings in combat. The prosecution of these acts as crimes, officers say, is the result of a strategy by guerrillas to do through legal action what they could not accomplish on the battlefield—demobilize successful army units and delegitimize the armed forces by denouncing such combat operations as killings of innocent civilians.

Colonel José Octavio Duque, for example, was deputy commander of WHINSEC and the brother of Néstor Iván Duque, who played such an important role in the 2005 massacre in San José. José Octavio told me about Colonel Santiago Herrera, a fellow instructor at WHINSEC who was accused of involvement in civilian killings. "He is in jail now for the false positives question, but they haven't been able to prove it," he said. "All Colombian officers who have been in war have court cases. Because our enemy has a parallel war, which is judicial warfare."[3]

"For me, this is political warfare by the FARC," one active duty colonel said of "false positives." "It was a strategy by the FARC to discredit us."[4] The military's thesis reflects a widespread denial that army civilian killings occurred on anything near the scale reported by human rights groups and Colombian judicial investigators. Speaking of an officer who confessed to directing more than a dozen such killings and who accused former army commander Mario Montoya of involvement, the same colonel assured me, "I am absolutely certain that not even 1 percent of what he said is true." Another colonel spoke in 2013 of "more than two thousand soldiers arrested. Twelve thousand under judicial investigation. It's absurd. Absurd!"[5]

A Colombian Army major who was teaching an intelligence course at WHINSEC in 2012 told me he estimated that, of the three thousand killings investigated by the judiciary, "70 percent were casualties properly done and the [soldiers] are caught up, and 30 percent were planned, people they took from their houses and killed. But those people were bandits, they were not normal people, they were people with criminal records." Another officer present added, "What they do with political warfare is infiltrate people into high places—the Congress, the judiciary, the high courts," and then count all guerrilla casualties as "false positive" killings.[6]

"Among the documents [of the guerrillas] found, they say it is important to seek legal support and see how to attack the armed forces to discredit their results. So that is why all of [those killed] show up as this peasant or that peasant," said an army colonel who served in Antioquia under General Montoya.[7]

In 2010 I asked Brigadier General Jorge Rodríguez Clavijo, then the director of the army's human rights division, why reports of extrajudicial executions had been at such a high point in 2007. He said that the army's operations were high that year, and that the FARC, because it was losing, fought back by facilitating claims that many of those killed were civilians.[8] U.S. Embassy officers reported in a 2009 cable that Rodríguez, army commander General Óscar González Peña, and other high-ranking officers believed the Fiscalía's investigations of the military for extrajudicial killings were "judicial warfare."[9]

In part, the officers' incredulity is based on frustration that stems from the same problem described by human rights organizations: the inconclusiveness of judicial investigations. But the contention that claims of extrajudicial executions are a deliberate guerrilla strategy lacks any public documentation. One would expect, with thousands of such killings denounced and under judicial investigation, and the widespread promotion of the judicial warfare thesis, to find at least a few such cases corroborated by documents or intercepts of guerrilla communications. But the literature, court documents, and interviews with military officers have not surfaced a single such case. Guerrilla operatives sometimes attempted to exploit reports of human rights violations by the army for propaganda purposes. Yet the judicial warfare argument often conflates this unsurprising finding with the claim that the violations themselves were fabricated.

The Colombian military thesis about judicial warfare has a U.S. correlate that has become prominent in conflict literature, especially in the wake of U.S. wars in Kosovo and Afghanistan, known as *lawfare*. Defining lawfare in an influential 2001 paper published by Harvard College as "the use of law as a weapon in war," U.S. colonel Charles Dunlap Jr. asserted that, "in Colombia, insurgents use sensitivity to human rights abuses to attempt to decapitate the nation's military leadership."[10] Dunlap quoted a statement by Human Rights Watch leader José Miguel Vivanco that "we've come to the conclusion that [the guerrillas in Colombia are] using international humanitarian law as just part of a P.R. operation." Vivanco, however, was referring to guerrilla rhetoric, not to human rights claims filed in Colombian courts.[11] Dunlap also quoted Mary Anastasia O'Grady, a *Wall Street Journal* columnist who has made fantastically unreliable claims and been persistently hostile to human rights in Colombia, asserting that "rebels force peasants to use the 'courts to press false charges—anonymously—against the most capable military leaders.'"[12]

U.S. analysts and officers with a direct role in the Colombian conflict also promoted the thesis that legal actions are tools of warring parties, part of a broader category of "political warfare." "The use of the law as a form of tactical judo has long been part of insurgent or even terrorist repertoires," wrote Thomas Marks, a military analyst who served as an advisor to Colombian forces: "What became evident in the post–Cold War era, however, in theaters as diverse as Colombia, Israel, and Sri Lanka, was the convergence of the tactical and the strategic. The result is entire conflicts driven by the process of framing and narrative, with violence relegated to a supporting role in a virtual battle of images and contending plot-lines. The goal, as with traditional information warfare, is to have a tangible impact upon the conflict."[13] U.S. Southern Command chief General John Kelly went as far as to say in 2015 that Colombia "taught us that the battle for the narrative is perhaps the most important fight of all." Kelly showed his own commitment to narrative by casting the FARC as the sole actor denouncing army human rights violations while violating rights itself, and making paramilitary violence completely invisible.[14]

It is this concern with controlling the dominant narrative about "good" and "bad" actors in the armed conflict, about which has greater *legitimacy*, that appears to concern most Colombian Army officers I spoke with. In fact, some Colombian military officers have themselves resorted to forms of political warfare—at least in one case, as learned from U.S. mentors. Colonel Hernán Mejía told me that when he served under U.S. general Norman Schwarzkopf, Schwarzkopf told Mejía, "The best commander is the one who defeats the will of the enemy without armed combat."[15]

While some U.S. observers use the term "lawfare" to describe legitimate as well as illegitimate or unscrupulous uses of law in war, in the Colombian context, "judicial warfare" and "political warfare" refer entirely to illegitimate uses. A Colombian colonel, Juan Manuel Padilla, studying at the U.S. Army Command and General Staff College in Fort Leavenworth articulated the judicial warfare thesis in a fifty-three-page thesis in 2010 that examined the experience of San José de Apartadó (much of which he lifted directly from O'Grady's *Wall Street Journal* articles). "Terrorist groups have skillfully infiltrated the Colombian judicial system," Padilla wrote, "and are utilizing both the national legal institutions and the international law system against the government." Padilla made no distinction between legal political actions that participate in legitimate disputes of policy or litigation, and actions that are organic to and extensions of illegal armed insurgencies. He also claimed, falsely, that a guerrilla commander active around San José de Apartadó who deserted in 2008 had gotten twenty-four villages to break away from the peace communities.[16] Colonel Padilla was not a marginal figure. When he became director of the Colombian Army's cadet school in 2012, he was responsible for training the next generation of officers.[17]

Lawfare analysts in the United States and elsewhere frequently frame legal political action and litigation as less legitimate than military action— even illegal military action. Lawfare is a "strategy of using or misusing law as a substitute for traditional military means to achieve military objectives," according to Anne Herzberg, author of the 2008 monograph *NGO Lawfare*.[18] Officers often told me that lawfare is the guerillas' attempt to do what they could not accomplish on the battlefield—as if engaging in military conflict (even by illegal actors) were normative and adjudicating disputes in the courts were not.

Much of the published discussion by the U.S. military of lawfare emerged out of operations in Israel, Afghanistan, and Iraq, where civilians were harmed or killed in operations from 2003 through 2010. U.S. military concern about the impact of reports of violations on the legitimacy of its military actions does not appear to have preceded the Colombian Army's but, rather, paralleled it during the same period in a shared anxiety and development of public relations responses.

In 2010 the Lawfare Project—founded to combat "abuse of the law as a weapon of war against Israel, the Jews and the West," according to its website—convened a conference on the subject, airing multiple theses about insurgents' and terrorists' dishonest uses of domestic and international law in asymmetric warfare.[19] Some presentations focused on the use of defamation and libel lawsuits to silence critics of Islamist movements.[20] The project's concern was, as in my encounter with General Lasprilla, who controls the international narrative about conflicts and human rights.

The U.S. Special Operations Command showed greater concern about operations. Its journal *Special Warfare* in 2008 published an essay of "lessons learned" from Afghanistan about lawfare, whose author did not contemplate the possibility that allegations of rights violations by U.S. forces might have merit. Instead, the essay showed how, with sophisticated and rapid information operations, "a tactical-level unit can stop investigations [into reported abuses] before they start."[21]

While claiming that lawsuits burden officials with costs, distract their attention, or dissuade future counterterror actions, these discussions often are most concerned with questions of legitimacy and narrative. "A far greater concern to the United States Government should be countering the longer-term potential collective or compounded public perception impact that these [lawsuits] may create," wrote Colonel Mark Holzer of the U.S. Army's Judge Advocate General's office in 2012. "Unanswered or unopposed, these filings may present a much greater threat to national security than mere increased short-term monetary costs. The strategy of regularized complaints and allegations primarily supports the Islamist 'victimization' narrative." Holzer argues that the courts—both U.S. and European—have become a "battlespace" for counterinsurgency (COIN), and that "current COIN doctrine points out that eliminating all sanctuaries is a key ingredient for effective COIN operations." He writes: "The fundamental policy conversation should focus on acknowledging the expansion of the battlefield into this arena as a reality of 21st-century warfare and incorporating this battlespace into the national security strategy."[22] By arguing the primacy of maintaining advantage in the public narrative, the U.S. military subordinates the veracity of reported violations to military imperatives for dominance.

Though Holzer does not openly advocate it, he also implies that access to the courts should be denied to those whom military leaders believe to be part of the enemy, and who contest the claim that they are affiliated with a combatant group. The concept of "legal sanctuary" for terrorists conjures an image of captured combatants firing at their captors in the midst of battle, when in fact these are environments controlled by the state, in which civil litigants confront each other before a judge or detainees face criminal prosecution. More than the rights of detainees, however, the discussion casts doubt on claims of civilian deaths in war operations and on the legitimacy of the courts themselves.

In Colombia, the United States has so far escaped legal charges of responsibility for supporting Colombian forces that have committed crimes. In fact, remarkably few legal claims of any kind have been made against the United States, even for harms from direct U.S. military attacks, despite the number of civilians reportedly killed directly in such operations. "It is staggering that when faced with international wrongs, vulnerable third world states—precisely the ones that would most benefit from engaging in international legal argument—tend not to do so," wrote Pakistani legal scholar Dawood Ahmed in 2012.[23] Instead, most attention in Colombia focuses on the FARC's judicial accountability for abuses, and secondarily on civilian killings by the army.

Command Responsibility

Outside the limelight of drug war and counterinsurgency politics, other developments shaped the long-standing U.S.-Colombian military alliance. Beginning with the Korean War, the Colombian Army progressively incorporated U.S. doctrine, but changes were occurring in that doctrine. Although the U.S. military once stood out for its promotion of human rights standards, by the 1990s, it stood out for its exceptionalism to contemporary global human rights standards. One aspect of this shift concerns responsibility of commanders for crimes committed by their subordinates.

After World War II, as the victor judging the crimes of the vanquished, the United States promoted a demanding standard for military commanders. General Yamashita of Japan was convicted for atrocities committed by his subordinates in the Philippines because the court judged that he "knew or should have known" they were occurring, even though he apparently did not, and he did not act effectively to stop them. This "knew or should have known" standard for commander responsibility was applied in the 1990s by the international tribunals for war crimes in Rwanda and the former Yugoslavia, and incorporated into the Rome Statute, which established the International Criminal Court in 1998.[24]

Yet the United States no longer applies this standard to the behavior of its own commanders. The United States' exceptionalism and perceptions of its military imperatives during the Cold War substantially eroded this ethic. The shift occurred during the Vietnam War and was consolidated in 1971 in the judgments for the crimes of soldiers at My Lai into what became known as the "Medina standard."

Captain Ernest Medina was in charge of the company that carried out the My Lai massacre in March 1968, in which U.S. troops murdered between 175 and 400 Vietnamese civilians. Medina was in the physical area of his troops for four hours while they killed, and "should have known" what they were doing, according to military prosecutors, while Medina's defense was that he did not in fact know. The military judge's jury instructions during the trial, however, stated that the prosecution must establish that Medina had "actual knowledge" of the crime.[25] In the end, no officer above the rank of lieutenant was convicted of any wrongdoing in the massacre. In addition, apart from the verdicts, the judge's instructions retained the character of a precedent for future crimes by military personnel. In effect, it set a standard that permitted U.S. commanders to "look the other way" when their subordinates committed crimes and remain legally unscathed.

A principle similar to the Medina standard for commanders' lack of knowledge of crimes committed by subordinates was applied in the San José massacre case, when a judge dismissed charges against Vélez Battalion officers in 2012. Those officers *should have known* that joint army patrols with paramilitaries who were responsible for many atrocities against civilians in San José would lead to further crimes, and indeed, the joint patrols themselves were a crime.

When most Washington policy makers adopted the unquestioned premise that the United States' military justice system is better than any in Latin America, this had far-reaching implications. Although Colombian military officers were not bound by U.S. case law, the "Medina standard" would affect how U.S. officers—as well as high-ranking civilian officials—responded to crimes committed by Colombian officers' subordinates as U.S. involvement in the war in Colombia grew. Some of them would look the other way.

State Violence and the Uses of Legal Jurisdiction

Whether human rights crimes are tried by military or by civilian tribunals substantially affects both legal outcomes and the narrative about human rights. At least until 2009, the large majority of reported executions investigated by the Colombian Fiscalía's Human Rights Unit were previously adjudicated in the Military Justice System (Justicia Penal Militar, JPM), which had closed the cases. They landed in the Fiscalía because a victim's family member or family's attorney contested the decision, and a civilian prosecutor requested to "visit" the case file in JPM. The military usually contested jurisdiction, and jurisdiction was then decided by the Superior Judiciary Council, which passed a portion of these cases to the Fiscalía. The criterion for transfer was whether there was doubt about whether a death was in combat, based on testimony and other evidence. The JPM may voluntarily transfer cases to the Fiscalía as well. From 2007 to 2009, the director of JPM in charge of this determination, Luz Marina Gil, passed many cases to the Fiscalía. After Gil was dismissed in 2009, the number of extrajudicial killing cases voluntarily moved from military to civilian jurisdiction dropped dramatically.

In either case—voluntary transfer by JPM or a decision by the Superior Judiciary Council—an important factor that mitigated *against* transfer to the Fiscalia was that very little investigation had been done. Often the only testimony gathered was of members of the military who were involved in the incident. Many family members did not have resources to hire an investigator or to pay for lab results. That there was still sufficient doubt to transfer the case to the civilian justice system reinforced the credibility of claims that these cases were indeed not deaths in combat.

Colombian military officers frequently complain that civilian investigators and prosecutors do not understand military operations or combat, and therefore reach false conclusions about deaths at the hands of soldiers. But apart from how true this may be of some civilian officials, this is very different from the claim that the FARC is getting family members to fabricate human rights cases or that judicial agencies are infiltrated by guerrillas.

In response to the thousands of investigations of killings between 2000 and 2008 that the civilian Fiscalía was investigating in 2014, the Colombian military adopted a more fundamental and preemptive approach than contesting each case: reform the law in order to move jurisdiction for the cases back to the military. The army's civilian supporters in the legislative and executive branches, including ex-president Álvaro Uribe after 2014, when he became a senator, made repeated and multiple proposals between 2011 and 2015 to classify crimes committed by soldiers under international humanitarian law, and to place them under the jurisdiction of the JPM.[26]

One way this would be accomplished was to make exceptions to military jurisdiction for some serious crimes, including genocide, torture, and extrajudicial executions, which would be considered by civilian courts. That would have been consistent with international humanitarian law, except that "extrajudicial execution" does not exist as a crime in Colombian law. Soldiers being tried for civilian killings are accused of "homicide of a protected person" or "aggravated homicide," crimes that were not made exceptions from military jurisdiction in the proposed law. For this or other reasons, hundreds, perhaps thousands, of "false positive" killings were in the JPM, Colombian prosecutors told Human Rights Watch in late 2014.[27]

Many in the international community opposed these attempts at creating mechanisms for impunity. In 2012 eleven United Nations special rapporteurs and chairs of working groups made an unprecedented appeal to the Colombian Congress to reconsider the reform.[28] Legislative conditions for a portion of U.S. military assistance to Colombia the same year required that all cases of alleged human rights violations by members of the military "are made subject only to civilian jurisdiction for all stages of the investigation and prosecution, and the Colombian military is not opposing civilian jurisdiction in such cases."[29] The U.S. State Department certified several times, between 2012 and 2016, that Colombia was meeting this condition, even as the military criminal law reform advanced, thus throwing away U.S. leverage to stop the reform.

In April 2015, the Colombian Congress approved an amended reform that made international humanitarian law—the laws of war—the exclusive framework for trying crimes by members of both the military and police committed in relation to the armed conflict, moving adjudication of such crimes into military courts, ensuring more impunity. "False positive" killings were not committed as part of the armed conflict, and so would be tried in civilian courts—theoretically. But if the army successfully claimed that these killings were "military errors," it could retain jurisdiction.[30] The ambiguity in the reform led Colombian human rights organizations to challenge the reform's constitutionality in court.[31]

The government and the FARC were, meanwhile, negotiating a framework of postwar transitional justice for crimes committed during the war that would incorporate a similar ambiguity. The peace accords signed in September 2016 defined command responsibility narrowly, and could have shielded army commanders from prosecution for atrocities committed by troops under their effective control. That agreement was narrowly defeated by plebiscite shortly thereafter, in part because they lacked guarantees to punish crimes committed by FARC members. When the accords were amended, government and FARC negotiators agreed to use the definition of command responsibility in international law, which holds military officers responsible for their subordinates' actions if they have "effective control." Armed forces commander General Juan Pablo Rodríguez Barragán—himself under investigation for "false positive" killings—and retired military officers lobbied to remove the provision. Only hours before the new agreement was sent to Congress for ratification in November 2016, President Santos removed the international definition, while retaining it for FARC commanders.[32] Six months later in Washington, Congress removed from 2017 military aid legislation the provision that requires civilian court jurisdiction for human rights crimes before certifying a portion of the aid.[33]

By this time, international attention had shifted away from both Plan Colombia and civilian killings. Nevertheless, military responsibility for state violence against civilians will continue to be contested—by families and military officers, legislators, lawyers and judges, the government, human rights defenders, and international actors. U.S. government representatives have been mostly passive during this drama, in contrast to its human rights activism at other moments and places, and to its vocal support of the Colombian state's war against guerrillas. It was up to others from below—activists, organizations, and a few legislators—to fight impunity in Colombia.

CHAPTER 14
U.S. POLICY LESSONS

Between 2000 and 2010 the United States maintained a high-level and persistent commitment to military assistance to Colombia, while also explicitly promoting human rights. U.S. aid was channeled to hundreds of military and police units throughout Colombia. The same military also murdered thousands of civilians across the country, crimes for which judicial impunity remained at 98 percent during the decade. Yet Colombia also had a well-developed human rights community that documented the abuses and a sophisticated judicial apparatus that sought legitimacy by opening human rights investigations. And it had the distinction as the country where the U.S. State Department said it had its best human rights vetting operation. What conclusions did U.S. policy makers draw from these events, and what might we learn from a critical perspective on them?

Looking Back and Forward at Human Rights

In multiple meetings from 2008 onward, U.S. officials emphasized to me the application of Leahy Law vetting as a best practice to ensure the United States does not train or aid known violators. Since no one can be certain of a trainee's human rights conduct in the future, Leahy Law review looks backward, at the histories of prospective recipients of assistance. It is these recipients, not the United States or its personnel, whose behavior is judged in Leahy Law implementation. But U.S. officials, both civilian and military, have consistently resisted reviewing the human rights conduct of those military and police *after* they receive U.S. training or assistance. Such a review would imply evaluation and judgment of U.S. military policy, programs, and personnel.

In researching extrajudicial killings in Colombia during the first decade of the twenty-first century, you could scratch almost anywhere and find U.S. training or other assistance to a unit credibly alleged to have killed civilians. One reason was that U.S. support took what the Southern Command (SouthCom) called a "whole of government" approach that assisted leaders, units, and agencies across the country and spectrum of government functions. In the case of San José de Apartadó, the attacks on the Peace Community also took a "whole of government" approach, in which the military, judicial investigators, police, and civilian leaders from the mayor to the president collaborated in delegitimizing and, in many cases, attacking the community. The combination of U.S. institutional and political support with Colombia's institutionally pervasive human rights violations made it difficult to isolate and exclude "bad" units and agencies from assistance.

The links between alleged executions and U.S.-aided units and officers were not criminal indictments, but they were evidence that the United States had strengthened the hands of violators. At best, they showed that aid was ineffective against abuses. At worst, they were evidence of complicity, or even of a shared goal of using violence to make way for people and projects favored by capital. When the United States gave aid after these violations, as it frequently did, it was also evidence that other policy priorities, bureaucratic inertia, and institutional indifference overrode the intent of Leahy Law human rights vetting.

Despite the good intentions of some individual officials, the State Department's implementation of the Leahy Law and human rights certification in Colombia was not structured to stop serious state crimes or attain justice for them but to ensure delivery of assistance to foreign states in order to fulfill objectives that had a higher priority than respect for human rights. In Colombia as elsewhere, some of the assistance included training in human rights and international humanitarian law, but the vast majority of military and police aid (including almost all the equipment, which constituted the bulk of U.S. spending) focused on other tactical and strategic skills and objectives.

The starting point for U.S. policy makers was not understanding why state crimes occurred or preventing their reoccurrence. State Department officials applied human rights vetting and certification in a secondary stage, after setting objectives for aid and after the Colombian military had nominated trainees and units for assistance. U.S. ambassador William Wood said in 2010 that Leahy vetting, which his embassy was primarily responsible for implementing, "ended up becoming counterproductive."[1] As a result, even well-intentioned work to uphold human rights standards was not structured to address deeper human rights problems.

An account of how the State Department, on the one hand, and human rights groups, on the other, documented abuses is instructive in this respect. In 2007 the State Department began to disclose which Colombian units it had vetted to receive assistance. An Amnesty International examination of State Department reports on foreign military training showed that personnel from forty-eight military units that had not been vetted for human rights still received training in 2006. Some of the units receiving training had human rights records that were among the worst in Colombia.[2] The Human Rights Unit of the Colombian Prosecutor General's office, which the United States funded with millions of dollars annually in the first decade of the twenty-first century, took on most investigations into the growing number of extrajudicial killings, although many investigations remained in the military justice system. In 2009 the unit released to Colombian human rights organizations a list of investigations it had opened into 2,054 reported illegal homicides by armed forces, most of them committed since 2000. In addition, human rights groups and Colombian media had identified units responsible for nearly one thousand extrajudicial killings. By 2010, two years after these killings had become a public scandal, Colombia had still only successfully prosecuted soldiers for a few dozen executions. For 98 percent of the reported killings, no "effective measures"—the benchmark for cutting aid to units under Leahy Law—had been taken to bring those responsible to justice.[3]

From the perspective of human rights activists, who published extensive information on human rights violations and the units allegedly responsible, the State Department must have had sufficient credible information on the brigades implicated in these crimes to have applied Leahy Law restrictions, yet aid continued to flow to these units. The State Department and human rights activists appeared to have different interpretations of what was credible.

Yet the State Department either did not have this information or did not have it in a form that it could use. The U.S. Embassy's human rights officer told me in 2010 that it received from Colombia periodic lists of investigations into alleged executions, but not a complete list—it apparently had not requested such a list, and so comprehensive information it could have obtained from judicial investigators was not entered into the embassy's databases. For their part, Colombian activists and even soldiers often could not distinguish which units were receiving U.S. aid. They knew only that the United States was openly providing massive aid to the military.

In 2012 I assembled a database that brought together information from Colombian human rights organizations and public sources on six hundred extrajudicial executions for which a military unit had been identified, and I shared it with State Department officials. As a result, a State Department official told me at the time, ten Colombian military units named as responsible for extrajudicial killings that had been nominated for U.S. assistance were excluded later in 2012, and many additional units were not nominated for assistance because of this data.

But the United States also walled itself off from potential advocacy for applying human rights laws and norms. In 2011 the State Department made the list of Colombian units approved for U.S. assistance "classified to protect the operational capacity Colombian military units,"[4] although none of several officials I asked could point to a security concern arising from disclosure of what units received assistance. Criticism of the lack of implementation of the Leahy Law was politically inconvenient. From a human rights perspective, however, the public has a right to know which units of foreign military and police forces—who are authorized to take human life and may be in a situation of warfare—are receiving U.S. assistance.

The U.S. Government's Lessons

The conclusions reached by those in the U.S. military and police assistance apparatus were quite different from those of activists. The humanitarian and human rights disasters in Colombia that unfolded after Plan Colombia's implementation received little or no attention in the official U.S. narrative. A narrative of success, of a country "back from the brink" of collapse, served policy makers seeking to replicate the model of mentoring, "standing up" and assisting foreign military and police forces around the globe. It offered both an example to show that Washington's growing strategy of foreign military aid could be successful as well as a rationale for deploying Colombian forces to directly train soldiers and police of other U.S. client nations.

The Colombian military began to work with SouthCom and the State Department's counternarcotics bureau in 2004 to transfer its skills to other countries, and it sent police to train in Afghanistan the same year.[5] Such training of other countries under U.S. auspices had precedents in the use of Colombian instructors at WHINSEC in Fort Benning, Georgia, whose numbers grew to make up more than 40 percent of the school's foreign instructors by 2012.[6]

Beginning in 2007, and more intensively after 2011, the United States paid Colombia to train military and police forces in Central America, Mexico, and the Dominican Republic. U.S. support for training by Colombian military and police officers was founded on an interpretation of the Colombian army and police as "models" for other nations' armed forces. SouthCom chief General John Kelly testified in April 2014 that Colombian trainers were used to provide assistance to units and soldiers in other countries that have committed serious human rights abuses. "The beauty of having a Colombia—and they are such good partners, particularly in the military realm . . . —when we ask them to go somewhere else and train the Mexicans, the Hondurans, the Guatemalans, the Panamanians, they will do it almost without asking. . . . On the military side, I am restricted from working with so many of these countries because of limitations that are really based on past sins."[7]

In 2014, drawing on $15 million that the State Department's counternarcotics bureau designated for international assistance in its Bogotá Embassy,[8] Colombian police trained nearly six thousand Central American and Dominican counterparts—a majority of them Hondurans.[9] And U.S.-funded training by Colombians was still in expansion: the number of training activities more than quadrupled in 2014, and training was expected to expand to more Caribbean nations in 2015. The U.S. and Colombia projected to collaborate in training 1,500 police and soldiers from Guatemala, El Salvador, Honduras, and Panama in 2015.[10] Colombia also provided police training on its own to more than 21,000 police from other nations in 2009–13.[11]

After the false positives scandal of 2008–10, the Colombian Army used its work of training other nations' forces in an attempt to bolster its legitimacy within Colombia and internationally. Colombia's War College promoted international security programs as "part of a strategy at the War College to improve Colombia's image in the world," according to a colonel at the school.[12] Moreover, as the government negotiated an end to its fifty-year-old war with the FARC between 2012 and 2016, its military was seeking new missions. Exporting its skills, attitudes, and doctrine was part of that effort. Many courses took place in Colombia, but trainers also traveled to recipient countries for short-term instruction, or for extended periods to teach in war schools or policing academies.

The largest group receiving Colombian training in 2009–13 was of Mexican police, who had notorious records of corruption and human rights violations. For example, Pentagon support for Colombian training of Mexican personnel included $73.9 million in funding for the Regional Helicopter Training Center in Colombia from 2009 to 2013. The Defense Department did not track assignments of the center's graduates, and Mexico resisted disclosing to U.S. officials which units were receiving U.S. assistance and the subsequent assignments of such police.[13] U.S. Embassy personnel in Mexico told me in 2012 that they had no record of which units received U.S. military training or other assistance. Training activities with Mexico were left out of the formal action plan "because of political sensitivities," according to a former Colombian government official close to the issue.[14] And the State Department did not include police training in its annual military training reports.

Government disclosure of the details of foreign military and police training and other assistance is not a simple bureaucratic burden for the sake of pleasing Congressional appropriators. Its absence is an evasion of accountability and criticism, a sign of deep indifference toward the human outcomes of exporting the tools and skills of state violence, and a central element in the replication of war.

CONCLUSION

THE ARC OF IMPUNITY

When San José Peace Community leader Jesús Emilio Tuberquia visited California at the start of a speaking tour in 2011, he was asked, "What gives you hope?" Tuberquia works ceaselessly for the community, and he has endured an attempt on his life and false accusations by army intelligence, but he is known for his pessimistic outlook.

"We have no hope," he said. "We are working for the time when hope will be merited." He had no illusions that the Colombian state was working for the community's benefit. But he was determined to name the ongoing injustices and to participate in expressions of community solidarity. The Peace Community's radical rejection of the state, in both word and deed, inspires many people who are still caught in the web of the "aspirational" state—a state that serves all people—but who nevertheless understand that aspirations for a state that serves communities like San José are consistently betrayed.

After the 2005 massacre, the Peace Community made four demands of the Colombian state: establish a commission to address why investigations into all the previous crimes against the community had not advanced, remove the police post in San José's town center, recognize the community's humanitarian zones, and retract President Uribe's accusations that the community was a FARC front.[1] As of 2018, the first three demands have never been met; the police presence has actually grown dramatically.

In December 2013, though, during a speech on International Human Rights Day, President Juan Manuel Santos surprised his audience by addressing the San José Peace Community. "Some years ago, unjust accusations were made from the Presidency against a community, the Peace Community of San José de Apartadó," Santos said. "I recognize in the Peace Community a brave claim for the rights of Colombians who, notwithstanding having suffered the conflict in their own flesh, have persisted in their purpose to reach peace." He regretted "all those statements and attitudes that stigmatize those who seek peace and reject violence. For this we ask forgiveness. I ask forgiveness."[2] Unfortunately, community members were not present to hear Santos's apology in Bogotá, since they had not been advised of it in advance.[3]

Other actors also acknowledged their wrongs against the community. At a 2015 hearing, for example, after he had been sentenced to forty years in prison for the 2005 massacre, the commander of the Heroes of Tolová paramilitaries, Uber Darío Yáñez Cavadías, asked the surviving massacre victims to forgive him.[4]

Community leaders had long said that their lands were sought by international mining interests for the coal that is visible even at the surface in some parts of the district. In 2013 an Australian mining firm announced it had acquired a concession for five thousand hectares in Urabá, which straddled Peace Community lands in La Esperanza settlement in San José de Apartadó, though it later said it had decided not to seal the deal.[5] The 2016 peace accords generated conditions to advance such extractivist investment.[6]

Even as leaders of the Colombian Army and FARC sat together in negotiations in Havana through 2015, army soldiers and FARC members continued to patrol and engage in occasional combat in the mountains in San José. At the same time, armed and uniformed paramilitary gunmen of the Gaitanista Self-Defense Forces of Colombia often circulated freely and threatened residents of San José. The Peace Community reported in 2014 that paramilitary interests based in Nueva Antioquia (from which army and paramilitary forces launched their operation in February 2005) were building a road through the mountains to Mulatos and Resbalosa, which the Peace Community resisted by refusing to allow road construction through its property in Mulatos, which lay on the road's route.[7] In October 2016, Peace Community members organized a rescue for families confined by Gaitanista paramilitaries who had set up camp on community property in Arenas settlement, while army soldiers camped nearby.[8] In December 2017, amid a string of paramilitary threats, armed Gaitanistas attempted to kill community leader

Germán Graciano but were foiled by unarmed community members, who captured two of the attackers.[9]

The officers who planned Operation Phoenix, the paramilitary-army offensive that led to the 2005 massacre, escaped prosecution. Judicial agencies investigated General Mario Montoya for his involvement in planning the operation and for the pattern of "false positive" killings that occurred under his command from 2002 to 2008. In 2016 the prosecutor general indicted Montoya for acts of omission as army commander related to "false positives" in seven different units.[10] But prosecutors repeatedly postponed court dates on which Montoya would be detained. President Santos in June 2016 publicly promised military officers that soldiers would not get reduced sentences for giving testimony about the crimes of their superiors, that officers would not be prosecuted for crimes of negligence or permissiveness in their units, and that the sentences of officers already tried for human rights crimes in civilian courts would be reviewed. "Now they will be able to be tried in the framework of international humanitarian law [the laws of war] and will go free with no problem," Santos said.[11] In another measure of impunity, Colombia posted General Jaime Lasprilla, soon after his dismissal as army commander in 2015, to serve two years as defense attaché in Washington.[12]

Nor were any members of Chiquita Brands or other U.S. companies that directly supported paramilitary groups implicated in murdering San José residents and thousands of other Colombians ever held criminally accountable. In 2007 Chiquita pled guilty to violating antiterrorism laws for its payments to the AUC and agreed to pay $25 million to the U.S. government, but no victims of paramilitary violence ever received any of these funds.[13]

Policy Intentions and Indifference

Some critics believe that the human destruction that occurred during Plan Colombia's execution was deliberate on the part of those who propelled the policy, in order to pave the way for extractive industries and other international investment.[14] From this perspective, massive displacement from lands and from political spaces were intended results of civilian killings and other acts of state and paramilitary terror. This means that stopping such destruction requires more than just tinkering with policies, because they serve as deliberate state expressions of savage capitalism.

This book has told a more complex history of U.S. intentions, actions, and outcomes. Intentions of policy makers are often contradictory, both within and between agencies and individual officials, who sometimes dispute policy methods and even goals. While intentions shape goals, they are less relevant for evaluating policies than empirically evident results. U.S. actions and outcomes in Colombia were shaped by high-altitude perspectives and by varying degrees of indifference to outcomes for people who live far away, below the abstract and bunkered conversations of U.S. decision-makers.

Some analysts attribute human rights violations and political violence to a "lack of controls"—control by government of territory, of the military and its operations, or private companies that establish armed security apparatuses, of paramilitaries.[15] Their analysis is premised on the belief that the state wants to restrain military, corporate, and paramilitary behavior when such behavior attacks civilians or violates the law. Although state officials frequently say they oppose and will enforce the law against such forces, and some individual officials genuinely seek to do so, the United States and Colombia evidenced little political will, on balance, to stop those violations at the time they were occurring. Instead, most evidence points to the toxic logic of war and to deep institutional indifference: a low priority for addressing the vast majority of violations, an agenda in which some lives matter, and others do not, at least to high-level officials in the U.S. and Colombian governments. Such institutional priorities determine where resources go—what capacity and controls are developed or end up lacking.

When the lives of rural Colombians impacted by war mattered to U.S. citizens—grassroots activists or those officials who lent their ears to activists—the outcomes were sometimes quite different, especially for specific individuals, organizations, or cases. "If you guys did not show up every month we would have been dead a long time ago," one Colombian community activist told a member of a U.S. accompaniment team.[16] "Only because of international pressure did the truth come out" about the 2005 massacre in San José, Senator Leahy's staffer Tim Rieser told me in his office more than ten years later. "President Santos made an apology, which was unprecedented, although it was too little, too late. Soldiers were indicted and some were punished. That was more than had been achieved before for victims in the Peace Community."

Yet the enormous and sustained effort required to achieve partial justice in only a single case also indicates the deep structural obstacles to such justice. "We don't feel the judicial process is complete," Rieser continued. "Those responsible for ordering and covering up the crime have not been punished. It remains unresolved. But had Renata [Rendon] not made the effort to come here, and to insist that we do something, and had I not listened and gone there myself, I doubt that anything would have happened.

Senator Leahy and I had correspondence and meetings with the Colombian president, vice president, the attorney general, the defense minister, the prosecutors."[17]

Yet in the end, U.S. senators and Colombian presidents do not define a community's memory or dictate whether its members live with dignity. In San José, the Peace Community's living members remember those who died and continue to farm the land. They articulate their own narrative, from below, through relationships with accompaniers, speaking tours, and regular public statements about army and paramilitary activities and denunciations of impunity.

One of Luis Eduardo Guerra's sons stopped speaking for a long time after his father's murder. "Anything you said, he said no," Luis Eduardo's sister, who cared for the children after the massacre and the displacement from the town center, told me as she shelled cocoa bean husks. He finally changed after several years, she said, because he realized "one has to overcome all these losses."[18]

The Struggle to Define Success

Militarists have prevailed since the 1990s in the "battle for the narrative" about Colombia, a battle that SouthCom commander General John Kelly called "the most important fight of all." Narratives about conflicts and actors deeply shape U.S. policy in Colombia and far beyond it. A key expression of this narrative, in the case of Colombia, has been the State Department's certifications of human rights conditions, which Congress has required since 2000 in order to fully expend military assistance in Colombia. "The human rights certification of the armed forces by the U.S. Department of State is a recognition of the effort realized by the army in this matter," General Montoya said in April 2007.[19] Indeed, the State Department never failed or refused to certify Colombia's human rights records in order to deliver the assistance that had been reliably appropriated by Congress.

The narrative of success for U.S. policy in Colombia, despite evidence of human rights disaster, is all the more critical as the United States today is progressively less able to determine outcomes in places around the world where it exercises military force, especially in the Greater Middle East. Policy makers lean on the story of "where we got it right" in Colombia to maintain the rationale for continued military intervention, regardless of how catastrophic are the outcomes of that intervention. The use of U.S. involvement in Colombia as a model does not bode well for the outcomes of U.S. military assistance in other conflicts.

In 2010, when the Colombian Army's "false positive" killings were well documented and as drug war violence in Mexico was spiraling with blood, Secretary of State Hillary Clinton compared violence and U.S. policy in the two countries. In Plan Colombia, "there were problems and there were mistakes, but it worked," she said. "We need to figure out what are the equivalents for Central America [and] Mexico" where, she claimed, "these drug cartels are showing more and more indices of insurgency."[20] Indeed, Washington was already at that moment using Plan Colombia as a model in Mexico, and would do so in Central America in the years that followed. U.S. officials also promoted the narrative of Colombian success in Afghanistan, where they encouraged Afghan officials to copy the Colombian military's interagency counterdrug work.[21]

U.S. foreign policy is constructed through the interaction of multiple interests and subjective, sometimes emotional, responses to and interpretations of events. But debates and conflicts over policy are rarely winner-take-all affairs. When advocates for nonviolent approaches to conflict engage a militarized policy-making system with arguments and actions, they frequently affect the outcomes, though officials from above discourage recognizing such success. And when policy-making is so irrational or self-interested that it is impermeable, advocates may nevertheless lay groundwork for the moments when policy debates will be more evidence-based or humane. Advocates for drug policy reform made little headway in the 1990s, for example, but their research and work for local changes helped paved the way for broader reforms since 2010, as the evidence for the failures of prohibitionist and military drug policies became more difficult to deny.

The United States can take measures within the current framework of military assistance and Leahy vetting to better respect human rights, but the possibilities in that framework are limited. For example, if a military unit has a pattern of abuses under a given commander, then when that commander moves to a different unit, it should affect U.S. assistance to that unit. However, the diversity of military funding channels means that, if one channel is discredited, defunded, or decertified, other channels are available. The application of Leahy Law to suspend assistance to a unit, for example, does not affect the level of military aid to a country, which is fungible within the country. And Washington policy makers repeatedly frame conflicts or problems globally as requiring armed force for their resolution. As long as policy focuses on the immediate and acute symptoms of conflict more than on its causes, then the use of violent force will always be privileged over investment in social and economic programs, community participation, diplomacy, change in our own behavior that contributes to conflict, and other non-coercive approaches.

Plan Colombia will not be the last multibillion-dollar commitment by the United States to war through assistance to other nations' military forces. As U.S. policy makers support actors they dub the "good guys," many outcomes of that support have implicated the United States in crimes committed against civilians. But American exceptionalism leads most people in the United States, especially those who are "above," to overlook, to forget, or simply to never inquire about these implications.

The options from below are considerably broader—to construct, to connect, to accompany, to resist, to investigate, to tell our stories, to listen, to advocate, to heal, to create projects of life. Those working below may also attempt to access and leverage power located above, especially to affect conditions for specific local communities, groups, and individuals. The macro-policy outcomes may or may not be much different. But here, where we live, is the soil for our future, and the ground from which we construct healthy relationships among ourselves and between our peoples.

NOTES

PROLOGUE

1. Miryam Tuberquia, testimony, Fiscalía General de la Nación, Bogotá, Radicado 2138, December 9, 2005, Cuaderno 6, 258–61; December 20, 2007, Cuaderno 11, 180–86.
2. García, *Urabá*, 48.
3. World Wildlife Federation, "Northern South America: Northern Colombia," accessed February 11, 2018, http://www.worldwildlife.org/ecoregions/nt0137.
4. Jorge Molano, "Demanda de casación," unpublished manuscript, June 5, 2012, in author's possession, 11.
5. Molano, "Demanda de casación."
6. Translations from the Spanish are by the author, unless otherwise indicated.
7. Some of those killed were not formal Peace Community members, but they are listed in the community's database. CINEP, *San Josesito de Apartadó*, 119–32.

INTRODUCTION

1. Chairman, Joint Chiefs of Staff, "The National Military Strategy of the United States of America," June 2015, http://www.jcs.mil/Portals/36/Documents /Publications/2015_National_Military_Strategy.pdf.
2. "National Security Strategy of the United States of America," December 2017, 45, https://partner-mco-archive.s3.amazonaws.com/client_files/1513628003.pdf.
3. U.S. Department of Defense, *Sustaining U.S. Global Leadership*, 3.
4. Database available at Security Assistance Monitor, accessed August 5, 2016, https://securityassistance.org.
5. Emily Cadei, "Foreign Militaries, Domestic Tension," *CQ Weekly*, December 16, 2013, 2072.

6. Max Boot and Richard Bennet, "The Colombian Miracle," *Weekly Standard*, December 14, 2009, http://www.weeklystandard.com/Content/Public/Articles /000/000/017/301nyrut.asp; Spencer et al., *Colombia's Road to Recovery*; DeShazo, Primiani, and McLean, *Back from the Brink*.

7. General John F. Kelly, "Colombia's Resolve Merits Support," *Miami Herald*, May 3, 2015.

8. *Nomination of John F. Kerry to be Secretary of State: Hearing of the Senate Foreign Relations Committee*, 113th Congress (2013), 19; Michael E. O'Hanlon and General David Petraeus, "The Success Story in Colombia," *Brookings*, September 24, 2013, http:// www.brookings.edu/research/opinions/2013/09/24-colombia-success-ohanlon -petraeus.

9. Pentagon official, Washington, DC, February 18, 2010. Some interviews were conducted without attribution by mutual agreement.

10. School of the Americas students and faculty historical database, accessed March 2, 2008, http://www.soaw.org; "Joint, Interagency, Multinational Faculty and Staff," slide provided by WHINSEC, 2012.

11. White House, "On-the-Record Press Call to Preview the Visit of President Santos of Colombia," February 2, 2016, https://www.whitehouse.gov/the-press-office /2016/02/02/record-press-call-preview-visit-president-santos-colombia. As part of the expanded U.S. aid package, Foreign Military Financing for Colombia grew from $27 million in 2016 to $38.5 million in 2017. See data at https://securityassistance .org/data/program/military/Colombia.

12. Rajiv Chandrasekaran, "The Afghan Surge Is Over," *Foreign Policy*, September 25, 2012, http://foreignpolicy.com/2012/09/25/the-afghan-surge-is-over.

13. Linda J. Bilmes, "Current and Projected Future Costs of Caring for Veterans of the Iraq and Afghanistan Wars," June 2011, http://watson.brown.edu/costsofwar /papers/2011/current-and-projected-future-costs-caring-veterans-iraq-and -afghanistan-wars.

14. Belasco, "The Cost of Iraq," 45. Actual costs per soldier ended up ranging from $800,000 to $1 million, increasing to more than $2 million per soldier in 2014 as the number of U.S. soldiers in Afghanistan wound down.

15. Security Assistance Monitor, accessed May 20, 2015, https://securityassistanc emonitor.org.

16. Williams and Epstein, "Overseas Contingency Operations Funding," 17.

17. Matthew Cox, "Army Stands Up 6 Brigades to Advise Foreign Militaries," *Military .com*, February 16, 2017, http://www.military.com/daily-news/2017/02/16/army -stands-up-6-brigades-advise-foreign-militaries.html.

18. Peter Baker, "Trump Says NATO Allies Don't Pay Their Fair Share. Is That True?," *New York Times*, May 26, 2017.

19. Milton Drucker, "Clipped Wings: Colombia's Air Asset Limits," June 17, 2005, cable, https://wikileaks.org/plusd/cables/05BOGOTA5802_a.html.

20. Security Assistance Monitor, accessed October 14, 2017, https://www.security assistance.org.

21. Office of the Under Secretary of Defense (Comptroller), "Defense Budget Overview," May 2017, A-2; U.S. House of Representatives Committee on the Armed Services, "National Defense Authorization Act for Fiscal Year 2011, Report 111-491," 278.

22. Peyton M. Craighill, "Why Americans' Support for Bombing ISIS May Not Last," *Washington Post*, September 22, 2014.

23. Robert Pape, "It's the Occupation, Stupid," *Foreign Policy*, October 18, 2010.

24. Yochi Dreazen, "U.S. Troops Are Leaving Because Iraq Doesn't Want Them There," *The Atlantic*, October 21, 2011.

25. Guy Benson, "New Polls: Americans Strongly Oppose Syrian Intervention," *Townhall*, September 3, 2013, http://townhall.com/tipsheet/guybenson/2013/09 /03/syria-polls-n1690292; Andy Sullivan, "U.S. Public Opposes Syria Intervention as Obama Presses Congress," Reuters, September 3, 2013; Andrew Dugan, "U.S. Support for Action in Syria Is Low vs. Past Conflicts," *Gallup*, September 6, 2013, http://www.gallup.com/poll/164282/support-syria-action-lower-past-conflicts .aspx.

26. Pew Research Center, "Pakistani Public Opinion Ever More Critical of U.S.," June 27, 2012, http://www.pewglobal.org/2012/06/27/pakistani-public-opinion -ever-more-critical-of-u-s. Popular responses in recipient countries are also mixed. Four in ten Pakistanis, for example, believed U.S. military aid was having a negative effect in a 2012 poll; only 8 percent thought the impact was "mostly positive."

27. Adam Isacson, "Congress Doubles the Limit on U.S. Troops in Colombia," Center for International Policy, October 8, 2004, http://www.ciponline.org/research /entry/congress-doubles-the-limit-troops-in-colombia; Ingrid Vaicius, "The U.S. Military Presence in Colombia," Center for International Policy, February 26, 2003, http://www.ciponline.org/research/entry/us-military-presence-in-colombia. Before 2004, the troop cap was even lower, at four hundred. However, up to six hundred private contractor personnel also carry out U.S. military programs in Colombia, and the cap did not apply to personnel funded by the Defense Department aid or programs other than counternarcotics.

28. "Ciudadanos convocan a una marcha de unidad nacional contra Donald Trump," *Animal Político*, February 2, 2017, http://www.animalpolitico.com/2017/02/marcha -febrero-trump.

29. United States Embassy Bogotá booklet, "U.S. Support for Plan Colombia," February 2001.

30. Alan Philips, "President Juan Manuel Santos of Colombia," *Chatham House* 68, no. 4 (2012), https://www.chathamhouse.org/publications/twt/archive/view /185137.

31. Brian Winter, "U.S.-Led 'War on Drugs' Questioned at U.N.," Reuters, September 26, 2012.

32. Benjamin Bahney and Agnes Gereben Schaefer, "Assessing Mexico's Narco-Violence," *San Diego Union-Tribune*, May 14, 2009.

33. DeShazo, Primiani, and McLean, *Back from the Brink*, 51.

34. Kathryn Z. Guyton et al., "Carcinogenicity of Tetrachlorvinphos, Parathion, Malathion, Diazinon, and Glyphosate," *The Lancet* 16, no. 5 (2015): 490–91.

35. United Nations Office on Drugs and Crime, *Colombia Coca Cultivation Survey 2013* (Vienna: UNODC, 2014), 92.

36. Adam Isacson, "Even if Glyphosate Were Safe, Fumigation in Colombia Would Be a Bad Policy. Here's Why," April 29, 2015, http://www.wola.org/commentary /even_if_glyphosate_were_safe_fumigation_in_colombia_would_be_a_bad _policy_heres_why; Office of National Drug Control Policy, "Coca in the Andes," accessed October 14, 2017, https://obamawhitehouse.archives.gov/ondcp /targeting-cocaine-at-the-source.

37. Human Rights Watch, *The "Sixth Division."*

38. Human Rights Watch, "World Report 1999," https://www.hrw.org/legacy /worldreport99/americas/colombia.html.

39. Consultoría para los Derechos Humanos y el Desplazamiento, *Desplazamiento creciente y crisis humanitarian invisible* (Bogotá, 2012), 13.

40. Schoultz, *Human Rights*, 211.

41. Hylton, *Evil Hour in Colombia*; Richani, "Multinational Corporations."

42. Paley, *Drug War Capitalism*, 53–81; U.S. Office on Colombia, "Large-Scale Mining in Colombia: Human Rights Violations Past, Present and Future," Washington, DC, May 9, 2013, https://reliefweb.int/report/colombia/large-scale-mining-colombia -human-rights-violations-past-present-and-future; Stokes, *America's Other War.*

43. FOR and CCEEU, "The Rise and Fall of 'False Positive' Killings in Colombia."

44. Other military observers believe such disincentives, including the Leahy Law, have gone too far and punish innocent soldiers by denying assistance to units that are credibly alleged to have committed serious violations without judicial convictions. Moyar, Pagan, and Griego, *Persistent Engagement in Colombia*; see also Adam Isacson's review of the report, "This Report on Colombia's Lessons Learned Has a Lot of Problems," November 14, 2014, http://www.wola.org/commentary/this _report_on_colombiarsquos_lessons_has_a_lot_of_problems.

45. David Spencer, interview with author, Washington, DC, June 1, 2013.

46. Blakeley, "Still Training to Torture?," 1452.

47. General Mario Montoya Uribe, interview with author, Bogotá, June 2013.

48. Family members of Ayotzinapa students were especially upset by government versions stating that the students' bodies were burned, although the site of the alleged burning was entirely green and uncharred a short time later. Family members of Ayotzinapa students, conversations with author, Tixtla, Mexico, June 2016.

49. CCEEU, *Ejecuciones extrajudiciales en Colombia*, 116–17.

50. Ariel Fernando Ávila Martínez, "FARC: Dinámica reciente de la guerra," *Arcanos* 14 (2008): 4–23.

51. Referring to militaries trained by U.S. special forces in nations at war, Assistant Secretary of Defense Michael Sheehan told lawmakers in 2013 that "our relationship with them dramatically and steadily always moved in the direction of improving their respect for human rights and respect for rule of law." He offered no

evidence, and no member of Congress demanded any. Testimony before House Armed Services Committee, April 2013, quoted in Cadei, "Foreign Militaries, Domestic Tension," 2074.

52. Kate Doyle, "A Wretched Record of Military Cooperation," *New York Times*, April 7, 2013.

53. "Evo sugiere crear una Escuela de las FFAA Sudamericanas," *La Razón*, October 13, 2010, http://www.la-razon.com/index.php?_url=/nacional/Evo-sugiere-Escuela-FFAA-Sudamericanas_0_1266473356.html.

54. The term "disappeared" refers to the seizure by state agents of persons who are never acknowledged as being in state custody and never reappear. Though most of those disappeared are presumed to have been executed, family members remain in perpetual uncertainty.

55. McManus and Schlabach, *Relentless Persistence*.

56. Cardenas, *Conflict and Compliance*; Green, *We Cannot Remain Silent*.

1. THE LONGEST WAR

1. Rodríguez Hernández, *La Influencia de los Estados Unidos*, 49.
2. Brewer, "United States Security Assistance," 6-3.
3. Coleman, *Colombia and the United States*, 159–60.
4. Palacios *Between Legitimacy and Violence*, 148–51.
5. Coleman, *Colombia and the United States*, 162–64.
6. Coleman, *Colombia and the United States*, 163–65.
7. For a sense of what these funds could buy, consider that thirty-nine military aircraft were purchased with $3.6 million. Historical Division, Joint Secretariat, Joint Chiefs of Staff, "Latin America and United States Military Assistance," 1960, 121, http://www.dod.mil/pubs/foi/International_security_affairs/latinAmerica/613.pdf.
8. Rodríguez Hernández, *La Influencia de los Estados Unidos*, 100–101.
9. Leal Buitrago, "Una visión de la seguridad," 6.
10. Armando Barrero, interview with author, Bogotá, September 26, 2013.
11. Colombia Survey Team report, part III, Recommendations for US Action, RUS-1, Charles T. R. Bohannan Papers, Hoover Institution on War, Revolution and Peace, Stanford, CA.
12. Colby, *Thy Will Be Done*, 312; Colombia Survey Team report, part III, Recommendations for US Action.
13. Rempe, "Guerrillas, Bandits," 306–9.
14. Colby, *Thy Will Be Done*, 386–87.
15. Rempe, "Guerrillas, Bandits," 309.
16. United States Army Special Warfare Center, "Visit to Colombia, South America, by a Team from Special Warfare Center, Fort Bragg, North Carolina," February 26, 1962, 3–4.
17. Colby, *Thy Will Be Done*, 384.
18. McClintock, *Instruments of Statecraft*, 222.

19. McClintock, *Instruments of Statecraft*, 222.

20. Luis Eduardo Guerra, interview with author, San José de Apartadó, March 2000.

21. Rempe, "Guerrillas, Bandits," 312–14

22. CINEP, *Deuda con la humanidad*, 6.

23. Medina Gallego, *Autodefensas, paramilitares y narcotráfico*, 60–62.

24. "Colombian Army Officers Who Have Attended U.S. Service Schools," U.S. Army Missions, Record Group 334, box 3, National Archives and Records Administration, College Park, MD.

25. Medina Gallego, *Autodefensas, paramilitares y narcotráfico*, 60–62.

26. FOR and CCEEU, "'Falsos positivos' en Colombia," 24; Rempe, "Guerrillas, Bandits," 313–17.

27. Richani, *Systems of Violence*, 49.

28. David Spencer, interview with author, Washington, DC, June 1, 2013.

29. Dufort, "A Typology of Military Factions."

30. "FY 1976 and FY 1977 Military Assistance Programs," U.S. Embassy Bogota cable, November 7, 1975, https://wikileaks.org/plusd/cables/1975BOGOTA10780_b.html.

31. Database of School of the Americas students, based on disclosures from Freedom of Information Act requests, accessed March 2, 2008, http://soaw.org/about-the -soawhinsec/13-soawhinsec-graduates; Brewer, "United States Security Assistance," 5–7.

32. Porch and Muller, "'Imperial Grunts' Revisited," 169.

33. Human Rights Watch, *State of War*, 146–48; U.S. General Accounting Office, *The Drug War*, 46.

34. Washington Office on Latin America, *Clear and Present Dangers*, 53–55.

35. Stan Goff, "Inside U.S. Counterinsurgency: A Soldier Speaks," *Consortium News*, December 22, 1999, http://www.consortiumnews.com/1999/122299a.html.

36. Bowden, *Killing Pablo*, 140–54, 217.

37. "La historia del ex oficial de la Policía Danilo González: El 'Pepe' mayor," El *Espectador*, September 13, 2008.

38. Equipo Nizkor, "¿Cuál fue la relación de la DEA y la CIA con Los Pepes?," June 4, 2006, http://www.derechos.org/nizkor/corru/doc/pepes.html.

39. Bowden, *Killing Pablo*, 216–19.

40. Michael Evans, "Colombian Paramilitaries and the United States: 'Unraveling the Pepes Tangled Web,'" National Security Archives, February 17, 2008, http:// nsarchive.gwu.edu/NSAEBB/NSAEBB243/index.htm. Many more declassified documents relating to the PEPEs are accessible at http://www.pepes.exposed.

41. Néstor Iván Duque, interview with author, Bogotá, September 11, 2014; Duque, testimony, September 9, 2009, Fiscalía General de la Nación, Radicado 2138, Cuaderno 25, 4.

42. Ronderos, *Guerras recicladas*, 177–80; "Comandos Populares de Urabá, base de las ACCU," *Verdad Abierta*, November 17, 2011, http://www.verdadabierta.com/justicia -y-paz/versiones/394-el-viejo-rafael-garcia/3681-comandos-populares-de-uraba -base-de-las-accu.

43. "'Don Berna' y el arte de esquivar la verdad," *Verdad Abierta*, September 30, 2015, http://www.verdadabierta.com/justicia-y-paz/10-anos-de-justicia-y-paz/5999-don-berna-y-el-arte-de-esquivar-la-verdad.

44. Ronderos, *Guerras recicladas*, 218, 226.

45. U.S. General Accounting Office, "Drug Control: U.S. Counternarcotics Efforts in Columbia [*sic*] Face Continuing Challenges," report GAO/NSIAD-98-60, February 1998, 29; Priest, "U.S. Military Trains Foreign Troops."

46. *Oversight of United States Counternarcotics Assistance to Colombia: Hearing before the Subcommittee on National Security, International Affairs and Criminal Justice, House Committee on Government Reform and Oversight*, 105th Cong. 111 (1997) (testimony of Morris Busby, former ambassador to Colombia).

47. Robert Gelbard, Assistant Secretary of State, testimony, *Oversight of United States Counternarcotics Assistance*, 23.

48. Douglas Farah, "A Tutor to Every Army in Latin America," *Washington Post*, July 13, 1998, A1.

49. Priest, "U.S. Military Trains Foreign Troops."

50. Grimmett, "U.S. Arm Sales," 5.

51. Grimmett, "U.S. Arm Sales"; *Implementing Plan Colombia: The U.S. Role: Hearing before the Western Hemisphere Subcommittee, International Relations Committee, House of Representatives*, 106th Cong. 64 (2000).

52. Ramírez Lemus, Stanton, and Walsh, "Colombia: A Vicious Cycle of Drugs and War."

2. WAR ON THE FRONTIER

1. Uribe, *Urabá*, 53.

2. Uribe, *Urabá*, 103–8.

3. Botero, *Urabá, colonización, violencia*, 73–74.

4. García, *Urabá*, 38.

5. Uribe, *Urabá*; García, *Urabá*, 55–56.

6. Uribe, *Urabá*, 58.

7. García, *Urabá*, 41–44.

8. García, *Urabá*, 38.

9. Reiniciar, *Historia de un genocidio*, 48.

10. Uribe, *Urabá*, 115–17.

11. Aurora Guerra, interview with author, San José de Apartadó, January 13, 2015; Miryam Tuberquia, testimony, Fiscalía General de la Nación, Radicado 2138, December 20, 2007, Cuaderno 11, 181.

12. San José resident, interview with author, January 11, 2015.

13. Reiniciar, *Historia de un genocidio*, 47–49.

14. Gustavo Arenas, interview by Leah Carroll, November 30, 1992, notes provided to author; San José resident, interview with author, January 11, 2015; Reiniciar, *Historia de un genocidio*, 51.

15. Aparicio, *Rumores*, 223–24.

16. Reiniciar, *Historia de un genocidio*, 51.

17. Aparicio, *Rumores*, 225–26.

18. García, *Urabá*, 32–35.

19. Uribe, *Urabá*, 252.

20. Eduardo Castellanos Roso, Tribunal Superior de Bogotá, Sala de Justicia y Paz, sentence of Hebert Veloza García, October 30, 2013, 178.

21. Romero, *Paramilitares y autodefensas*, 173.

22. Uribe, *Urabá*, 252.

23. Carroll, *Violent Democratization*, 74.

24. Steele, "Electing Displacement," 430.

25. Steele, "Electing Displacement," 431.

26. Julin v. Chiquita Brands Int'l, Inc. (In re Chiquita Brands Int'l, Inc.), 6 NO. 08-01916-MD-MARRA (S.D. Fla. Jan 6, 2015).

27. Mario Agudelo, interview with author, Apartadó, January 14, 2015; Steele, "Electing Displacement," 423.

28. Romero, *Paramilitares y autodefensas*, 197.

29. Paul Wolf, Complaint against Chiquita Brands International, Inc., filed with U.S. District Court for the District of Columbia, March 17, 2011, 179–80.

30. CINEP, *Deuda con la humanidad*, 2.

31. Wolf, Complaint against Chiquita, 167. Fernando Londoño, who became Uribe's first interior minister, attributed the pacification of Urabá to Uribe and Army commanders of the time: "It was a young governor of Antioquia, Álvaro Uribe Vélez, [who] took on the task of reconquest, which was hard and bloody, but a glorious and liberating feat." Fernando Londoño, "San José de Apartadó," *El Tiempo*, March 14, 2005.

32. Paul Wolf, Case 1:10-cv-00404-RJL, document 3 (brief filed in U.S. District Court, District of Columbia, March 9, 2010), 75; International Human Rights Clinic, Harvard Law School, "The Contribution of Chiquita Corporate Officials to Crimes against Humanity in Colombia," May 18, 2017, http://www.refworld.org /docid/59242f6c4.html.

33. Wolf, Complaint against Chiquita, 247–48; Cárdenas Gómez, "Sentencia Primera Instancia, Bloque Héroes de Tolová," 125–29.

34. SINALTRAINAL, Complaint filed in United States District Court, Southern District of Florida, July 20, 2001, nos. 40–53, http://news.findlaw.com/cnn/docs /cocacola/clmbiacocacola72001.pdf.

35. Tovin Lapan, "Killer Cola?," *Berkeley Review of Latin American Studies* (winter/spring 2006): 35–39.

36. Pendergrast, *For God, Country*, 425.

37. Inter-American Commission of Human Rights, "Third Report on the Human Rights Situation in Colombia" (OEA/Ser.L/V/II.102, Doc. 9, rev. 1), February 26, 1999.

38. "Soldado que denunció al general r Rito Alejo del Río fue asesinado," *Noticias Uno*, June 28, 2012, https://www.youtube.com/watch?v=9h1F8DouR8w; Javier Giraldo,

"Ex soldado Oswaldo Giraldo Yepes: Otro testigo asesinado," http://www
.javiergiraldo.org/IMG/pdf/Oswaldo_Giraldo_Yepes.pdf.

39. Curtis Kamman, cable, August 13, 1998, http://nsarchive.gwu.edu/NSAEBB
/NSAEBB327/doc01_19980813.pdf.

40. "'Paramilitarismo en Urabá no habría sido posible sin Fuerza Pública': Fiscalía,"
Verdad Abierta, March 25, 2014, http://www.verdadabierta.com/justicia-y-paz
/imputaciones/5290-paramilitarismo-en-uraba-no-habria-sido-posible-sin-fuerza
-publica-fiscalia. Carvajal was sentenced in 2015 to fifty-four years in prison for
his role in a massacre of ten antidrug police agents, on top of prison time for
drug trafficking. "Byron Carvajal, el coronel de los 75 años de cárcel," *Las2Orillas*,
September 6, 2015, http://www.las2orillas.co/byron-carvajal-el-coronel-de-los-75
-anos-de-carcel.

41. CINEP, *San Josesito de Apartadó*, 36–37.

42. Reiniciar, *Historia de un genocidio*, 48–52; CINEP, *San Josesito de Apartadó*, 38.

43. Steele, "Electing Displacement," 437–38.

44. Romero, *Paramilitares y autodefensas*, 120–21.

45. "Recuerdan legado de reconciliación de Mons. Duarte en el Urabá," *Agencia
Católica de Información*, March 25, 2002, http://www.aciprensa.com/notic2002
/marzo/notic1512.htm.

46. Peace Community Internal Council, interview with author, San José de Apartadó,
January 2015.

47. Hernández Delgado and Salazar Posada, *Con la esperanza intacta*, 178–84.

48. Giraldo Moreno, "Imágenes interpelantes," 52–53.

49. Hernández Delgado, *Resistencia civil*, 381.

50. Steele, "Electing Displacement," 437–38.

51. Aparicio, *Rumores*, 239.

52. Giraldo Moreno, "Imágenes interpelantes," 55.

53. Hernández Delgado and Salazar Posada, *Con la esperanza intacta*, 75–76.

54. Hernández Delgado and Salazar Posada, *Con la esperanza intacta*, 79–82.

55. Giraldo Moreno, "Imágenes interpelantes," 54.

3. HOW PLAN COLOMBIA WAS SOLD

1. Hylton, *Evil Hour in Colombia*, 79–82.

2. Tate, *Drugs, Thugs, and Diplomats*, 20–21, 114.

3. See Teo Ballvé, "The Dark Side of Plan Colombia," *The Nation*, June 15, 2009, for
examples of how paramilitary forces benefited from U.S. economic assistance.
Determining U.S. intent regarding paramilitaries can be difficult, however.

4. Serafino et al., "'Leahy Law' Human Rights Provisions," 3.

5. Ramsey, *From El Billar*, 18.

6. Gregory Passic, DEA, "Debriefing of SZE-92-0053 re: Corruption in Colombia,"
memo to country attaché Joe Toft, July 30, 1993, in author's possession; Ronderos,
Guerras recicladas, 203–10.

7. Spencer et al., *Colombia's Road to Recovery*, xiii, 8; Ramsey, *From El Billar*, 17.

8. "Plan Colombia: Plan for Peace, Prosperity, and the Strengthening of the State," Peace Agreements Digital Collection, U.S. Institute of Peace, https://www .usip.org/sites/default/files/file/resources/collections/peace_agreements/plan _colombia_101999.pdf.

9. Vacius and Isacson, "'Plan Colombia.'"

10. Jeremy Bigwood, "DynCorp in Colombia: Outsourcing the Drug War," *Corpwatch*, May 23, 2001, http://www.corpwatch.org/article.php?id=672.

11. Jeremy Bigwood, "Toxic Drift: Monsanto and the Drug War in Colombia," *Corpwatch*, June 21, 2001, http://www.corpwatch.org/article.php?id=669.

12. Joseph Biden, *Aid to "Plan Colombia": The Time for Assistance Is Now: Report to Senate Foreign Relations Committee* (2000).

13. Serafino, "Colombia: Plan Colombia Legislation and Assistance," 21–22.

14. Tate, *Drugs, Thugs, and Diplomats*, 150–51.

15. William M. LeoGrande, "How the Pentagon Views Threats in Latin America," *Huffington Post*, April 21, 2014.

16. Tate, *Drugs, Thugs, and Diplomats*.

17. Michael Isikoff, "The Other Drug War," *Newsweek*, April 2, 2000.

18. Vacius and Isacson, "'Plan Colombia'"; International Consortium of Investigative Journalists, "The Helicopter War," July 12, 2001, http://www.icij.org/project/us-aid -latin-america/helicopter-war.

19. Jim Mann, "A Government by the People, for the Military-Industrial Complex," *Los Angeles Times*, September 27, 2000.

20. International Consortium of Investigative Journalists, "The Helicopter War."

21. Vacius and Isacson, "'Plan Colombia.'"

22. Arianna Huffington, "Colombia Chopper Wars," July 26, 2000, http://www.emperors -clothes.com/news/aria2.htm.

23. Vacius and Isacson, "'Plan Colombia.'"

24. Center for Responsive Politics, "Political Action Committees," accessed February 17, 2018, http://www.opensecrets.org/pacs; Fort Worth Chamber of Commerce, "Major Employers," accessed January 28, 2013, http://fortworthecodev .com/fort-worth-overview/facts-figures/major-employers/; Tarrant County, Texas, "Labor Force and Major Employers," accessed January 28, 2013, http://access .tarrantcounty.com/en/administration/staff/economic-development-coordinator /financial-status/labor-force-and-economic-base.html.

25. Center for Responsive Politics, "Political Action Committees," accessed February 17, 2018, http://www.opensecrets.org/pacs.

26. U.S. Congress, *Official Congressional Directory 109th Congress*, 394; U.S. Department of State, "Report to Congress on Certain Counternarcotics Activities in Colombia," accessed February 17, 2018, http://securityassistance.org/sites/default/files /0706cont.pdf; U.S. Congress, *Official Congressional Directory 110th Congress*, 392.

27. *Congressional Record*, September 23, 2008, H8641.

28. Colombian officers, interview with author, Bogotá, March 2013.

29. Contraloría General de la República, *Plan Colombia*, 28–30.

30. Thomas A. Marks, "A Model Counterinsurgency: Uribe's Colombia (2002–2006) vs. FARC," *Military Review*, March–April 2007, 41; Spencer et al., *Colombia's Road to Recovery*, 52–55; Ospina Ovalle, *Los años en que Colombia recuperó la esperanza*, 63.
31. Richani, *Systems of Violence*, 133.
32. Henry Holguín, "El primer bombardeo al Caguán," *El Espectador*, December 20, 2012.
33. Whittaker, Smith, and McKune, "The National Security Policy Process," 151.
34. See Consolidated Appropriations Act 2012, Pub. L., No. 112-74, Section 7045(a) (2012), maintained at least through 2017.
35. David Spencer, interview with author, Washington, DC, June 1, 2013.
36. Roselló, *East of the Orteguaza*, 179.
37. Medina Gallego, *Autodefensas, paramilitares*, 35–72.
38. Piccoli, *El sistema del pájaro*, 15–20.
39. Dunning and Wirpsa, "Oil and the Political Economy," 91.
40. DeShazo, Forman, and McLean, *Countering Threats to Security*, 14, 71, 77, 106, 134.
41. Sam Lowenberg, "Big Guns Back Aid to Colombia," Law News Network, February 23, 2000, http://colombiasupport.net/archive/200002/lnn-usaid-0223.html; Larry Luxner, "Business Bats for Colombia," *Multinational Monitor*, no. 18 (1997), http://www.multinationalmonitor.org/hyper/mm0597.04.html.
42. Dunning and Wirpsa, "Oil and the Political Economy," 93.
43. Martin Hodgson, "Oil Inflames Colombia's Civil War," *Christian Science Monitor*, March 5, 2002.
44. Tony Karon, "Gore's Big Oil Connection: An 'Occident' of Birth?," *Time*, September 25, 2000; Juan Forero, "New Role for U.S. in Colombia: Protecting a Vital Oil Pipeline," *New York Times*, October 4, 2002, A1.
45. Lawrence Meriage, statement, *The Crisis in Colombia: What Are We Facing? Hearing before House of Representatives Government Report Subcommittee on Criminal Justice, Drug Policy and Human Resources*, February 15, 2000, 168–74.
46. "El petrolero en Colombia," *Revista Cambio*, March 12–19, 2001.
47. "El petrolero en Colombia."
48. "'Miti' condenado y 'miti' absuelto," *El Espectador*, September 18, 2009.
49. "El petrolero en Colombia."
50. Washington Office on Latin America, "Protecting the Pipeline: The U.S. Military Mission Expands," *Colombia Monitor*, May 2003, 10. "The mounting security problems in Colombia . . . have made those operations, although proving to be productive, given [sic] very little value by the U.S. markets," a Harken Energy Corp. fact sheet stated in 2001. "Frequently Asked Questions," accessed March 2002, http://www.harkenenergy.com.
51. Ecopetrol eliminated any requirement for Colombian participation in 2004. Juan Forero, "Safeguarding Colombia's Oil," *New York Times*, October 22, 2004.
52. Dunning and Wirpsa, "Oil and the Political Economy," 95.
53. Clara Inés Rueda G., "E.U. cuidará sus intereses en Colombia," *El Tiempo*, February 10, 2002.

54. Dana Priest, "U.S. Instructed Latins on Executions, Torture," *Washington Post*, September 21, 1996.
55. "Fort Benning, GA: CPTers participate in vigil against SOA," November 24, 1998, http://www.cpt.org/node/989.
56. Vacius and Isacson, "'Plan Colombia.'"
57. U.S. Department of State, "Plan Colombia Certification Requirements," August 28, 2000, https://1997-2001.state.gov/briefings/statements/2000/ps000823.html.
58. Comisión Colombiana de Juristas, *Panorama de violaciones*, 16.
59. See, for example, Amnesty International, "Colombia Certification Consultation Briefing Paper," February 5, 2002, http://reliefweb.int/sites/reliefweb.int/files/resources/51636AED64749BE985256B58004FE398-hrw_col_05feb.pdf; FOR and USOC, "Military Assistance and Human Rights."
60. Tate, *Drugs, Thugs, and Diplomats*, 99–101.
61. I witnessed this support when NGOs in the Latin America Working Group's Colombia Steering Committee, in which I participated, annually developed recommendations on Colombia for Congressional appropriations committees.
62. James P. McGovern et al., letter to President Andrés Pastrana, March 30, 2001, in author's possession.
63. Vote on H.R. 3908, March 30, 2000, https://www.govtrack.us/congress/votes/106-2000/h95.
64. Vote on H.R. 3908; Sam Farr et al., letter to President Andrés Pastrana, May 24, 2002; Jan Schakowsky et al, letter to President Álvaro Uribe, June 25, 2004, in author's possession.

4. "WE WANT A WITNESS"

1. "Constancia histórica," email bulletin, Justicia y Paz, February 20, 2000, in author's possession.
2. Andrew Miller, "1999–2000: Hope and Bloodshed: My Year in Urabá," in Peace Brigades International, *15 Years of PBI*, October 2009, 19–20.
3. Miller, "1999–2000."
4. Roger Cohen, "U.S. Sergeant Gets Life in Murder of Kosovo Girl, 11," *New York Times*, August 2, 2000.
5. "Aseguran al alcalde de Apartadó," El Tiempo, February 25, 2000.
6. CINEP, *San Josesito de Apartadó*, 10.
7. Observatorio del Programa Presidencial de DH y DIH, Vicepresidencia de la República, "Dinámica reciente de la confrontación armada en el Urabá antioqueño," 2006, http://historico.derechoshumanos.gov.co/Observatorio/Publicaciones/documents/2010/Estu_Regionales/uraba.pdf; "Bloque Bananero," Verdad Abierta, February 3, 2009, http://www.verdadabierta.com/victimarios/832-bloque-bananero#7.
8. CINEP, *San Josesito de Apartadó*, 120–22.
9. Justicia y Paz, statement, April 5, 1999, in author's possession.

10. Corte Suprema de Justicia, ruling on appeal of Jorge Isabel Caicedo Valencia, 6. One of the gunmen, identified by a victim who survived the attack, was later sentenced to thirty-one years in prison.
11. Carlos Beristain, handwritten notes, February–March 1998, quoted with permission. Thanks to Francesc Riera for providing these notes.
12. Massacre is defined as the murder of four or more civilians. Suárez, *Identidades políticas y exterminio recíproco*, 51.
13. Steele, "Electing Displacement."
14. Corte Interamericana de Derechos Humanos, "Medidas Provisionales Solicitadas por la Comisión Interamericana de Derechos Humanos Respecto a Colombia," November 24, 2000, http://www.corteidh.or.cr/docs/medidas/apartado_se_02.pdf.
15. Coghlan, *The Saddest Country*, 74.
16. CINEP, *Noche y Niebla*, no. 15 (2000): 173.
17. CINEP, *San Josesito de Apartadó*, 48.
18. Corte Interamericana de Derechos Humanos, "Medidas Provisionales," November 24, 2000.
19. Decimoséptima Brigada, "Apreciación Sociopolítica de las Comunidades de Paz," n.d., Fiscalía General de la Nación, Unidad Delegada Corte Suprema, Expediente 12490-2.
20. Richard Chacón, "Colombia Neutrals Find No Peace," *Boston Globe*, February 21, 2001, A10.
21. James P. McGovern et al., letter to Andrés Pastrana, March 30, 2001, in author's possession.
22. United Nations Human Rights Commission, "Informe de la Alta Comisionada de las Naciones Unidas para los Derechos Humanos sobre la situación de los derechos humanos en Colombia," E/CN.4/2001/15 (March 20, 2001), 15–16, 32.
23. For literature on protective accompaniment, see Mahony and Eguren, *Unarmed Bodyguards*; Koopman, "Making Space for Peace"; Furnari, *Wielding Nonviolence*; PBI, "Protective Accompaniment," 2006, http://www.peacebrigades.org/en/about-pbi/what-we-do/protective-accompaniment; Mahony, *Proactive Presence*.
24. Lindsay-Poland and Weintraub, "To Be By Your Side," 34.
25. PBI's Medellín team closed in 2011. Lindsay-Poland and Weintraub, "To Be By Your Side," 30–32.
26. Peter Cousins, "Faith and Accompaniment: A Christian Response," *Fellowship* 77, nos. 7–12 (2013): 28.
27. For a theoretical discussion, see Mahony and Eguren, *Unarmed Bodyguards*.
28. Koopman, "Making Space for Peace," 255.
29. Koopman, "Making Space for Peace," 177–88.
30. Members of PBI, interviews with author, Bogotá and Apartadó, January 2015.
31. Lindsay-Poland and Weintraub, "To Be by Your Side," 50.
32. Colombian Presbyterian Church representative, interview with author, San José de Apartadó, January 2015.

33. Courtheyn, "'Memory Is the Strength,'" 72; Moreno, "Tasas de homicidio."
34. FOR, internal communication, April 17, 2002, in author's possession.
35. Corporación Jurídica Libertad, public statement, June 25, 2003.
36. Corte Interamericana de Derechos Humanos, "Caso de la Comunidad de Paz de San José de Apartadó," June 18, 2002, http://www.corteidh.or.cr/docs/medidas/apartado_se_03.pdf.
37. Rep. Sam Farr et al., letter to President Andrés Pastrana, May 24, 2002.
38. Corte Interamericana, "Caso de la Comunidad de Paz."
39. Chris Moore-Backman, email to author, February 14, 2016.
40. "Masacre de Apartadó 2002," *Rutas del Conflicto*, http://rutasdelconflicto.com/interna.php?masacre=713.
41. Grupo de Memoria Histórica, *Bojayá*, 26, 35–36.

5. MAPPING OUR WAR

1. "Gobernador de Florida Jeb Bush visita Colombia," February 18, 2005, https://web.archive.org/web/20050411014254/http://bogota.usembassy.gov:80/wwwsjb02.shtml.
2. Tate, *Drugs, Thugs, and Diplomats*, 137–41.
3. U.S. Department of State, lists of Colombian units supported by the United States, provided to Senator Patrick Leahy, 2008–9, in author's possession.
4. Amnesty International, "Assisting Units That Commit Extrajudicial Killings," 37–38.
5. Priest, "Covert Action in Colombia."
6. Leonardo Gómez Vergara, interview with author, Bogotá, July 5, 2013.
7. Vacius and Isacson, "'Plan Colombia.'"
8. Ramsey, *From El Billar*, 22–23, 50; Contraloría General de la República, *Plan Colombia*, 32–33.
9. Ramsey, *From El Billar*, 54.
10. Moyar, Pagan, and Griego, *Persistent Engagement in Colombia*, 19–20.
11. Linda Robinson and Ruth Morris, "Colombia's Messy, Complicated War," *U.S. News and World Report*, September 4, 2000.
12. Carlos Alberto Zambrano Barrera (consejero ponente), Consejo de Estado Sala de lo Contencioso Administrativo, Radicación 73001233100020020140201 (September 10, 2014), 24–27.
13. Interview with author, Bogotá, October 2013.
14. Jefatura Logística Conjunta, Comando General Fuerzas Militares, "FMS [Foreign Military Sales] Nacionalización," PowerPoint presentation, in author's possession, 2011.
15. Priest, "Covert Action in Colombia."
16. U.S. State Department, private communication, January 2011.
17. Juan Carlos Piza, interview with author, Medellín, September 25, 2013.
18. Priest, "Covert Action in Colombia."
19. Implementation agreements for Appendix 9 of the Annex to the General Agreement signed by the Governments of the United States and Colombia, September 27,

2000, disclosed by the Colombian Minister of Defense in 2011 and in the author's possession.

20. Anne Patterson, unclassified cable, May 17, 2002, obtained by the National Security Archives.

21. Milton Drucker, "SouthCom Deputy Commander Spears Visits Colmil Leaders," June 29, 2007, https://wikileaks.org/plusd/cables/07BOGOTA4722_a.html.

22. William Brownfield, "Embassy Supports SouthCom Recommendation of Palanquero for Cooperative Security Location," February 11, 2008, https://wikileaks.org/plusd/cables/08BOGOTA533_a.html.

23. "Full Spectrum Operations in Army Capstone Doctrine," 2008 *Army Posture Statement*, https://www.army.mil/aps/08/information_papers/transform/Full_Spectrum_Operations.html.

24. Sibylla Brodzinsky, "Possible US-Colombia Military Deal Raises Regional Tensions," *Christian Science Monitor*, July 29, 2009; "Venezuela Shops in Argentina after Colombia Spat," Reuters, August 11, 2009.

25. Department of the Air Force, "Military Construction Program, Fiscal Year 2010 Budget Estimates," May 2009, 215. The Air Force later amended the document to remove the reference to "full spectrum operations."

26. Fabio Valencia Cossio, memorandum to Senator Emilio Otero Dajud, July 28, 2009, in author's possession.

27. "Armed Forces Commander Padilla on FARC, Hostages, Palanquero, Regional Relations, and Human Rights," April 12, 2008, https://wikileaks.org/plusd/cables/08BOGOTA1391_a.html.

28. Fabrícia Peixoto, "Lula propone reunión UNASUR-EE.UU," *BBC*, August 10, 2009; Lindsay-Poland, "Obama's Choice."

29. Lindsay-Poland, "Obama's Choice."

30. Ewan Robertson, "Trade between Venezuela and Colombia Back on Track," *Venezuelanalysis.com*, February 11, 2013, https://venezuelanalysis.com/news/7727.

31. Colectivo de Abogados "José Alvear Restrepo," press statement, August 19, 2010.

32. William Brownfield, "Court Orders Further Investigation into Santo Domingo Bombings," November 3, 2009, https://wikileaks.org/plusd/cables/09BOGOTA3305_a.html.

33. John Lindsay-Poland, "Pentagon Building Bases in Central America and Colombia," FOR blog, January 27, 2011, http://archives.forusa.org/blogs/john-lindsay-poland/pentagon-building-bases-central-america-colombia/8445.

34. The cost for training in the United States was more than five times the cost in Colombia. Some of the difference can be attributed to the longer duration of some U.S.-based courses. Data in this paragraph is from https://securityassistance.org, which compiles it from annual official reports. See also U.S. Department of State, "Foreign Military Training and DoD Engagement Activities of Interest."

35. Data on military training is available through searches in Security Assistance Monitor, https://securityassistance.org.

36. Baca, "Colombia: 2003 Annual Terrorism Report," December 12, 2003, https://www.wikileaks.org/plusd/cables/03BOGOTA11615_a.html. The United States trained 176 army GAULA members in 2003–5, and continued to train GAULA units through 2007. U.S. Department of State, "Antiterrorism Assistance Program, Report to Congress for Fiscal Year 2005," https://www.state.gov/documents/organization/89959.pdf.

37. The locations were Apiay, Bogotá, Medellín, Buenaventura, Tolemaida, Cali, Palmira, Cartagena, Tres Esquinas, Marandúa, Macarena, Facatativá, Armenia, Coveñas, Santa Marta, San Andrés, Valledupar, Barranquilla, Riohacha, Ibagué, Corozal, Palanquero, Espinal, Bahía Málaga, and Puerto Salgar. Defense Minister Rodrigo Rivera Salazar, memo to Senator Jorge Enrique Robledo, February 21, 2011, in author's possession.

38. Porch and Muller, "'Imperial Grunts' Revisited," 175.

39. Finlayson, "OPATT to PATT," 92.

40. Curtis Marshall, "Colombian Chronicles," May 18, 2012, https://web.archive.org/web/20130515222648/http://crashleadership.com/2012/05/18/colombia-chronicles-part-4/.

41. John Haywood, "Challenges Associated with Long Term US Presence Advising Foreign Nations," January 14, 2008, http://ezinearticles.com/?Challenges-Associated-With-Long-Term-US-Presence-Advising-Foreign-Nations&id=927820.

42. Phone interview with author, February 21, 2016.

43. Porch and Muller, "'Imperial Grunts' Revisited," 175.

44. "U/S Burns Meets with President Uribe," August 4, 2005, https://wikileaks.org/plusd/cables/05BOGOTA7402_a.html.

45. Richani, *Systems of Violence*, 125.

46. FOR and USOC, "Military Assistance and Human Rights," 17.

47. Cepeda and Rojas, *A las puertas de El Ubérrimo*, 11–18.

48. Colonel Javier Fernandez Leal, "Costs of the War in Colombia," U.S. Army War College Strategy Research Project, March 18, 2005, http://handle.dtic.mil/100.2/ADA432728.

49. General Javier Fernández Leal, interview with author, Bogotá, September 17, 2014.

50. "Funcionario de EE.UU. dice que mejora el historial colombiano en derechos humanos," statement on U.S. Embassy website, https://web.archive.org/web/20040518235011/http://bogota.usembassy.gov:80/wwwsdhi4.shtml.

51. U.S. Department of State, "Memorandum of Justification Concerning Human Rights Conditions with Respect to Assistance for the Colombian Armed Forces," September 2009, in author's possession.

52. "Mindefensa se reunió con secretario de Defensa de EE. UU. en Bolivia," El Tiempo, November 22, 2010.

53. Rueda G., "E.U. cuidará sus intereses."

54. Ramsey, *From El Billar*, 100–101.

55. U.S. Department of State, "Foreign Military Training and DoD Engagement Activities of Interest," Fiscal Year 2003, IV, 259; David Adams, "Reclaiming Rural Colombia," *Saint Petersburg Times*, April 6, 2003.

56. Carvajal Martínez, *La seguridad dentro del estado de garantías*, 100–110; Carroll, *Violent Democratization*, 247.

57. U.S. Department of State, "Foreign Military Training and DoD Engagement Activities of Interest," Fiscal Year 2004, IV, 258; U.S. Department of State, "Foreign Military Training and DoD Engagement Activities of Interest," Fiscal Year 2005, IV, 207.

58. Ramsey, *From El Billar*, 100–101.

59. Ramsey, *From El Billar*, 110; U.S. State Department, lists of Colombian units supported by the United States, provided to Senator Patrick Leahy, 2008–9, in author's possession.

60. U.S. Embassy Bogota, statement, "Inauguración de instalaciones para protección del oleoducto Caño Limón-Coveñas," February 3, 2005; Colonel Jhon Norbey Zambrano, interview with author, Saravena, June 27, 2013.

61. Gran Tierra Energy, news release, April 3, 2006, accessed December 20, 2014, http://www.grantierra.com/news-archive.html?wnid=75.

62. Gran Tierra Energy, "2013 Annual Report," Calgary, 2014, 8–9.

63. Petrominerales, *Prospectus*, June 13, 2006, 3.

64. Petrominerales, news release, November 28, 2013, http://www.petrominerales .com/news-releases/view/472/petrominerales-announces-completion-of -acquisition-by-pacific-rubiales-and-launch-of-alvopetro-energy-ltd.

65. Ministerio de Minas y Energía, Dirección de Hidrocarburos, "Producción fiscalizada por empresa 2012," https://www.minminas.gov.co/documents /10180/478423/Produccion+de+Crudo+por+Empresa+%40%202012.pdf /e7e947a9-c111-4301-9b02-9ec20828ib01, and "Producción fiscalizada por departamento 2012," https://www.minminas.gov.co/documents/10180/478423 /Produccion+de+Crudo+por+Departamento+%40%202012.pdf/2802ce15-08ce -439c-9926-d9e117f9a84a.

66. Adam Isacson, "Consolidating 'Consolidation.'," Washington Office on Latin America, December 2012.

67. FOR and USOC, "Military Assistance and Human Rights," 20–21.

68. Colombian Army, Bejarano Battalion page, accessed October 7, 2012, http://www .ejercito.mil.co/wap/index.php?idcategoria=283486.

69. Amnesty International Urgent Action, 64/99, April 6, 1999, http:// colombiasupport.net/archive/amnestyua/ua6499.html.

70. Carlos Beristain, interview with author, May 28, 2016.

71. María Milena Vega Sarmiento, "Carta a nuestros heroes," November 5, 2011, http://cartaanuestroheroe.blogspot.com/2011/11/doctor-juan-manuel-santos -calderon.html. For his detention, see Observatorio del Programa Presidencial para los Derechos Humanos y DIH, August 24, 2010, http://historico .derechoshumanos.gov.co/Observatorio/Bitacoras/2010/Paginas/bitac_449.aspx.

72. FOR and CCEEU, "The Rise and Fall of 'False Positive' Killings in Colombia," 19. Mobile brigades and infantry battalions have close to the same number of troops, making them appropriate units of comparison.

73. "Condenado coronel (r) por falsos positivos en Ocaña," *Vanguardia*, March 31, 2014, http://www.vanguardia.com/actualidad/colombia/253471-condenado -coronel-r-por-falsos-positivos-en-ocana.

6. KILLING THE FUTURE

1. Peasant University participants, letter to media, August 27, 2004.
2. Courtheyn, "'Memory Is the Strength.'"
3. Héctor José Arenas, "La resistencia de las comunidades de paz en Colombia," *Minga/Mutirao Informativa*, August 3, 2006, http://movimientos.org/es/grito/show _text.php3%3Fkey%3D6561; Yolanda Villegas, "Testimony from San José de Apartadó," November 24, 2005, in author's possession.
4. Aparicio, *Rumores*, 270–71.
5. The other three communities signing the declaration were Consejo Comunitario de La Nupa, Asociación Campesina de Arauca, and Asociación Campesina del Valle del Río Cimitarra. "Declaran comunidades campesinas: Ruptura con la justicia colombiana," Agencia Prensa Rural, Bogotá, December 9, 2003, http://www .prensarural.org/recorre20031209.htm.
6. "Declaran comunidades campesinas."
7. Giraldo Moreno, *Fusil o toga*, 95.
8. Giraldo Moreno, *Fusil o toga*, 257–60.
9. Peace Community, statement, August 11, 2004, in author's possession; FOR, internal report, August 2004, in author's possession.
10. "EFE: Cronología de los incendios de discotecas en Latinoamérica y el mundo," *Noticias 24*, January 27, 2013, http://www.noticias24.com/internacionales/noticia /52858/reviva-las-tragedias-en-algunas-discotecas-de-latinoamerica-y-el-mundo/.
11. Equipo Nizkor, statement by seventy U.S. and Canadian religious and humanitarian leaders, June 17, 2004, http://www.derechos.org/nizkor/colombia/doc /cartacol2.html.
12. Gustavo Gualteros Barragán, DAS Seccional Antioquia, memorandum, July 30, 2004, in author's possession; "Extractos Bancarios," Fiscalía General de la Nación, Unidad Delegada Corte Suprema, Expediente 12490-2.
13. FOR, internal document, November 15, 2004, in author's possession.
14. "Informe de Inteligencia: Comunidades de Paz—San José de Apartadó," September 16, 2005, Fiscalía General, Expediente 12490-2.
15. Latin America Working Group, "Far Worse than Watergate," June 2010, http:// www.lawg.org/storage/colombia/farworsethanwatergatefinalfinal.pdf.
16. Peace Community Internal Council, interview with author, 2015; Miryam Tuberquia testimony, Fiscalía General, Radicado 2138, Cuaderno 6, 258.
17. Peace Community, statement, August 11, 2004; FOR report, August 2004.
18. Sarah Weintraub, "Luz Enit," unpublished manuscript, n.d., in author's possession, quoted with permission.
19. Weintraub, "Luz Enit."
20. Peace Community statement, August 11, 2004; FOR report, August 2004.

21. Peace Community statement, August 11, 2004; FOR report, August 2004; Javier Giraldo Moreno, "Derecho de Petición No. 8," September 20, 2004, http://www.javiergiraldo.org/spip.php?article111.

22. Apartadó Estéreo, broadcast, November 16, 2004, transcript provided by FOR.

23. Comisión Colombiana de Juristas, "Listado de víctimas de violencia sociopolítica en Colombia" (December 1, 2002–July 31, 2006), *Verdad Abierta*, http://www.verdadabierta.com/documentos/victimas-1/asesinatos-selectivos/814-listado-ccj-3004-asesinados-por-paramilitares/file.

24. "Las verdades inconclusas de 'H.H.,'" *Verdad Abierta*, October 28, 2015, http://www.verdadabierta.com/justicia-y-paz/10-anos-de-justicia-y-paz/6044-las-verdades-inconclusas-de-hh.

25. "'Paramilitarismo en Urabá no habría sido posible sin la Fuerza Pública': Fiscalía," *Verdad Abierta*, March 25, 2014, http://www.verdadabierta.com/justicia-y-paz/imputaciones/5290-paramilitarismo-en-uraba-no-habria-sido-posible-sin-fuerza-publica-fiscalia.

26. Uber Darío Yáñez Cavadías, testimony, October 2, 2009, Fiscalía General, Radicado 2138, Cuaderno 26; Cárdenas Gómez, "Sentencia Primera Instancia, Bloque Héroes de Tolová," 97.

27. "Instructor de los 'paras' no colaborará más con justicia," *Verdad Abierta*, October 31, 2013, http://www.verdadabierta.com/justicia-y-paz/versiones/5003-instructor-de-los-paras-no-colaborara-mas-con-la-justicia; Ronderos, *Guerras recicladas*, 185–89.

28. Cárdenas Gómez, "Sentencia Primera Instancia, Bloque Héroes de Tolová," 137.

29. Rubén Darío Pinilla Cogollo, Case of Uber Darío Yáñez Cavadías, Sala de Justicia y Paz, Tribunal Superior de Medellín, Acta No. 2, September 3, 2014, 100–101.

30. Peace Community, statement, November 19, 2004.

31. "Asesinan a otros tres líderes indígenas," *El Tiempo*, December 8, 2004, http://www.eltiempo.com/archivo/documento/MAM-1527044. A member of the FARC was sentenced to forty years in prison for the crime in 2008. "40 años de cárcel por crimen de líderes indígenas," *Semana*, October 14, 2008, http://www.semana.com/noticias/articulo/40-anos-carcel-crimen-lideres-indigenas/96216-3.

32. Rubio Maldonado, "Análisis del rol de las ONG como voceros en la escena internacional de las víctimas del conflicto armado en Colombia," 66.

33. FOR, internal document, December 17, 2004.

34. FOR, internal document, December 16, 2004.

35. FOR, internal document, December 16, 2004.

36. Witness #5, quoted in CSN, "A Massacre at Mulatos in Colombia, an Investigative Report" (hereafter CSN Report), June 26, 2005.

37. FOR, internal document, December 18, 2004.

38. Giraldo Moreno, "Imágenes interpelantes," 58.

39. DAS Seccional Antioquia and Banco Ganadero Sucursal Apartadó, correspondence, January 17, 2005, and February 2, 2005, Fiscalía General de la Nación, Expediente 12490-2.

40. Javier Moya, "Entrevista a Luis Eduardo Guerra (q.e.p.d.)," Agencia Prensa Rural, Cedsala, March 7, 2005, http://www.prensarural.org/moya20050307.htm.
41. Catalina Oquendo, "Más acciones de guerrilla en Urabá," El Tiempo, February 12, 2005; Equipo Nizkor, "Se producen combates entre el ejército y la farc en Antioquia," February 10, 2005, http://www.derechos.org/nizkor/colombia/doc/paz/farc14.html.
42. "Los guerrilleros nos encerraron," El Tiempo, February 11, 2005.
43. Elizabeth Yarce and Clara Isabel Vélez, "Cierran tramo en vía a Urabá por cuatro plagios," El Colombiano, February 12, 2005.
44. "Historia de una traición," Semana, March 6, 2005, http://www.semana.com /especiales/articulo/historia-traicion/71276-3.
45. Oquendo, "Más acciones de guerrilla."
46. General Héctor Jaime Fandiño, testimony, December 28, 2010, Fiscalía General Radicado 2138, Cuaderno 41, 133.
47. School of the Americas student database, http://soaw.org/about-the-soawhinsec /13-soawhinsec-graduates/4281-soa-grads-database-online-ur.
48. Nadja Drost, "A Massacre Explored: Murder in the Jungle," GlobalPost, March 16, 2010.
49. General Mario Montoya, interview with author, Bogotá, June 12, 2013.
50. "El martes de la semana pasada un fallo del Consejo de Estado les ordenó a las Fuerzas Militares y de Policía no enviar a zonas de conflicto soldados campesinos, bachilleres o auxiliares de policía debido a que no tienen la preparación necesaria para estar en 'zonas rojas.'" "Historia de una traición," Semana, March 6, 2005, http://www.semana.com/especiales/articulo/historia-traicion/71276-3.
51. Coronel Néstor Iván Duque, interview with author, Bogotá, September 11, 2014.
52. Guillermo Gordillo, testimony, May 12, 2008, Fiscalía General, Radicado 2138, Cuaderno 15, 210.
53. Peace Community, statement, "Una búsqueda de vida ante el terror y la muerte," February 18, 2005.
54. Federación Internacional de Derechos Humanos, statement, March 1, 2005, https://www.fidh.org/es/region/americas/colombia/Asesinato-de-Defensores-de.
55. csn Report, "csn Delegation Meeting with a Dozen Peace Community leaders."
56. Peace Community, statement, "Ante la muerte un camino de dignidad," April 27, 2005, http://ecuador.indymedia.org/es/2005/04/9269.shtml.
57. csn Report, "Notes Witness 3."
58. Fiscalía General, Radicado 2138, Cuaderno 11, 257; Giraldo Moreno, Fusil o toga, 102.
59. "Más de una contradicción en versiones sobre la matanza en San José de Apartadó," El Tiempo, March 12, 2005.
60. Valencia Caicedo, appeal.
61. Fiscalía General, Radicado 2138, Cuaderno 6, 260.
62. csn Report, "Notes Witness 2."
63. Abad Colorado, "Cuatro días en búsqueda."
64. csn Report, "Notes Witness 3."
65. Fiscalía General, Radicado 2138, Cuaderno 26, 268.

66. CSN Report, "Notes Witness 3."

67. Pinilla Cogollo, Acta No. 2, 97–100.

68. Cárdenas Gómez, "Sentencia Primera Instancia, Bloque Héroes de Tolová," 403.

69. In addition to other sources cited, the foregoing account is based on CSN Report, "Notes Witness 3"; Uber Darío Yáñez Cavadías, testimony, October 2, 2009, Fiscalía General, Radicado 2138, Cuaderno 26, 263–64.

70. CSN Report, "Notes Witness 3."

71. Jorge Luis Salgado David, testimony, February 8, 2008, Fiscalía General, Radicado 2138, Cuaderno 12, 33–35.

72. The following account is drawn from CSN Report; Fiscalía General, Radicado 2138, Cuaderno 6, 260; Cuaderno 11, 184; Abad Colorado, "Cuatro días en búsqueda."

73. Juan Guillermo Cárdenas Gómez, magistrado ponente, Sala de Justicia y Paz, Tribunal Superior de Medellín, Sentencia Héroes de Tolová y Uber Darío Yáñez Cavadías, July 7, 2015, 628.

74. Corporación Jurídica Libertad, statement in author's possession, March 1, 2005.

75. CINEP, San Josesito de Apartadó, 96.

76. CSN Report, "Interview with Witness #3."

77. CSN Report, "Interview with Witness #5"; FOR internal report, March 1, 2005, in author's possession.

78. Matthew A. Reynolds, Acting Assistant Secretary of State for Legislative Affairs, letter to Senator Barack Obama, July 6, 2005.

79. Patricia Abbott and Renata Rendon, written accounts, FOR internal documents; Abad Colorado, "Cuatro días en búsqueda."

80. Abad Colorado, "Cuatro días en búsqueda."

81. Abad Colorado, "Cuatro días en búsqueda."

82. Abad Colorado, "Cuatro días en búsqueda"; Romeo Laguna and Martínez Zapater, La comunidad de paz, 28.

83. Statements reported in FOR internal reports, March 2005, in author's possession.

84. Abad Colorado, "Cuatro días en búsqueda"; Contravía, "No podemos guardar silencio."

85. Roberto Elias Monroy and Luis Oraime Monroy, testimony, January 17, 2007, Fiscalía General, Radicado 2138, Cuaderno 8, 23–37.

86. Romeo Laguna and Martínez Zapater, La comunidad de paz, 28.

7. PROJECTS OF LIFE

1. Peace Community, statement, November 13, 2004.

2. CINEP, San Josesito de Apartadó.

3. Martha Ruiz, "La universidad de la resistencia," Semana, May 22, 2005, http://www.semana.com/on-line/articulo/la-universidad-resistencia/72716-3.

4. Tate, Counting the Dead.

5. Carlos Fernández, Mauricio García, and Fernando Sarmiento, "Movilización por la paz en Colombia, 1978–2002," Controversia, número extraordinario, February 2004, 18–23.

6. Ana Teresa Bernal, interview with author, Bogotá, August 2002.

7. American Friends Service Committee, *Building from the Inside Out*, 13.

8. Edwin Ortega, *Comunidades de Paz San Francisco—Natividad de María—Nuestra Señora de Carmen Riosucio: Chocó*, n.d.

9. Mons. Leonardo Gómez Serna, "Mogotes Municipal Constituent Assembly: Activating 'Popular Sovereignty' at a Local Level," *Accord* 13 (2002), 74–77; María Cristina Alvarado, "Cuando vibra un pueblo," *Revista de Ciencias Sociales* (Universidad de los Andes), no. 2 (1998): 105–6.

10. Hernández Delgado, *Resistencia civil artesana*, 405–51; Justin Podhur, "An Interview with Alirio Arroyave and Arquimedes Vitonás," A-Info News Service, September 22, 2002.

11. "Todos para Tarso," *Semana*, March 27, 2005, http://www.semana.com/especiales /articulo/todos-para-tarso/71565-3.

12. CINEP, *Sistematización y análisis*.

13. Oliver Kaplan, "Protecting Civilians in Civil War: The Institution of the ATCC in Colombia," *Journal of Peace Research*, 50 no. 3 (2013): 351–67.

14. Leonel Narváez, "Schools of Forgiveness and Reconciliation," *ReVista* 2, no. 3 (2003): 47–49.

15. "Constituyente divide a Mogotes," *El Tiempo*, July 13, 2004, http://www.eltiempo .com/archivo/documento/MAM-1555403.

16. Cécile Mouly, María Belén Garrido, and Annette Idler, "How Peace Takes Shape Locally: Experience of Civil Resistance in Samaniego, Colombia," *Peace and Change* 41, no. 2 (2016): 129–66.

17. Guillermo Padilla, "La Guardia Indígena y la ingobernabilidad en Colombia," *Pacarina del Sur* 5, no. 20 (2014), http://pacarinadelsur.com/dossier-12/978-la -guardia-indigena-y-la-ingobernabilidad-en-colombia.

18. Padilla, "La Guardia Indígena."

19. "Indígenas liberan a secuestrado," BBC, July 3, 2003; Javier Sule, "Guardia indígena, El poder de un bastón," February 7, 2013, https://javiersule.wordpress.com /2013/02/07/guardia-indigena-el-poder-de-un-baston/.

20. Tejido de Comunicación ACIN, "Crónica de una Liberación o de otro Secuestro Frustrado," December 23, 2008, http://mamaradio.blogspot.com/2008/12/story-of -heroic-liberation-or-another.html. The description and quotations in the following paragraphs are from this source.

21. Gina Spigarelli, "Indigenous Nasa Resist Militarization in Cauca," *FOR Colombia Update*, July 31, 2012, http://archives.forusa.org/blogs/for-colombia/indigenous -nasa-resist-militarization-cauca/10742.

22. Programa Somos Defensores, *¿Este es el fin?*, 27–32.

23. See, for example, "War, Terrorism and Our Classrooms," a *Rethinking Schools* special report, http://www.rethinkingschools.org/special_reports/sept11/index .shtml.

24. Colombia Mobilization, mission statement, August 2001, https://web.archive.org /web/20010815203405/http://www.colombiamobilization.org:80/mission.html.

25. *Congressional Record—Senate*, July 14, 2000, S6942.

26. "March 24: End Corporate Terror in Colombia," February 2003, https://web.archive .org/web/20030216173928/http://www.colombiamobilization.org.

27. Groundswell Productions, *Partnering for Peace*.

28. Groundswell Productions, *Partnering for Peace*.

29. Groundswell Productions, *Partnering for Peace*.

30. For more evidence and extensive examples, see Lindsay-Poland and Weintraub, "To Be By Your Side."

31. International Trade Union Confederation (ITUC), statement, June 10, 2010, http://www.ituc-csi.org/ituc-responds-to-the-press-release.

32. Susana Pimiento and John Lindsay-Poland, "U.S. Base Deal for Colombia: Back to the Status Quo," *Foreign Policy in Focus*, October 8, 2010, http://fpif.org/us_base _deal_for_colombia_back_to_the_status_quo/.

8. MASSACRE AFTERMATH AND COVER-UP

1. Comando General Fuerzas Militares, statement, March 1, 2005, https://www .mindefensa.gov.co/irj/go/km/docs/Mindefensa/Documentos/descargas /Apartado/Comunicado%20Comando%20General%20FFMM.pdf.

2. Interview with Luis González, national director of Prosecutor General's Office, *W Radio*, March 3, 2005, contemporaneous notes.

3. "Murió agente herido en emboscada," *El Colombiano*, March 4, 2005, http:// www.elcolombiano.com/BancoConocimiento/M/murio_agente_herido_en _emboscada/murio_agente_herido_en_emboscada.asp. The son of a cattle rancher in the neighboring state of Sucre, Jaraba himself and his father had been kidnapped by unidentified armed men less than four years earlier, and subsequently joined the police. "Secuestradas 16 personas en la Costa," *El Tiempo*, May 18, 2011.

4. "Entrevista a un miliciano desmovilizado," March 3, 2005, http://alpha .mindefensa.gov.co/index.php?page=407&id=1650.

5. Foreign NGO worker in San José, contemporaneous notes, March 3, 2005.

6. "Entrevista a un miliciano desmovilizado."

7. Liliana Parra, LinkedIn profile, accessed August 19, 2014, https://www.linkedin .com/in/liliana-parra-09a68238/.

8. Sergio Gómez Maseri, "Se destapan mercenarios," *El Tiempo*, June 19, 2003.

9. Tom Vanden Brook, "Pentagon Overseas Propaganda Plan Stirs Controversy," *USA Today*, November 20, 2012.

10. Romeo Laguna and Martínez Zapater, *La comunidad de paz*, 22.

11. Oficina de Información y Prensa, Comando General de la Fuerzas Militares, statement, March 1, 2005, in author's possession.

12. "Mensaje del Ministro de Defensa de Colombia Jorge Alberto Uribe Echavarría," email communication, March 5, 2005, in author's possession.

13. Pablo Bachelet and Steven Dudley, "Massacre Origin at Issue," *Miami Herald*, March 7, 2005; Andrew Selsky, "Colombia Massacre Raises Rights Issues," Associated

Press, March 5, 2005; Daniel Bland, "Killing Peace in Colombia," *Toronto Star*, March 7, 2005; Elizabeth Yarce, "Comunidad de paz pidió el apoyo internacional," *El Colombiano*, n.d.

14. Bachelet and Dudley, "Massacre Origin at Issue."

15. Ministry of Defense, statement, March 11, 2005, http://alpha.mindefensa.gov.co/index.php?page=407&id=1646.

16. "Más de una contradicción en versiones sobre la matanza en San José de Apartadó," *El Tiempo*, March 12, 2005.

17. "Comunidades de paz no podrán existir sin la Fuerza Publica, anuncia ministro de Defensa," *El Tiempo*, March 8, 2005.

18. Elizabeth Yarce, "Chocó: Comunidad de paz con Policía," *El Colombiano*, March 9, 2005.

19. "Toda Colombia debe ser una comunidad de paz: Mindefensa," *Caracol Radio*, March 10, 2005.

20. "'No somos unos criminales,' dice el general Reynaldo Castellanos, comandante del Ejército," *El Tiempo*, March 12, 2005.

21. "'Don Berna': De Inspector de las Auc a jefe de banda criminal," *Verdad Abierta*, September 9, 2014, http://www.verdadabierta.com/justicia-y-paz/juicios/601-bloque-heroes-de-tolova/5433-don-berna-de-inspector-de-las-auc-a-jefe-de-banda-criminal.

22. Catalina Oquendo, "El Presidente regresará a Urabá en abril," *El Tiempo*, March 20, 2005.

23. Oquendo, "El Presidente regresará."

24. Peace Community, statement, February 27, 2005, in author's possession.

25. Cárdenas Gómez, "Sentencia Primera Instancia, Bloque Héroes de Tolová."

26. Juan José Lozano, dir., *Hasta la última piedra* (Geneva: Earthling Productions, 2006).

27. Tate, *Drugs, Thugs, and Diplomats*, 8–9.

28. Tim Rieser, interview with author, Washington, DC, January 28, 2016.

29. Associated Press, "Colombia Killings Imperil U.S. Aid," *Washington Post*, March 5, 2005.

30. James P. McGovern et al., letter to Álvaro Uribe Vélez, March 9, 2005, in author's possession.

31. Associated Press, "Colombia Killings."

32. Giraldo Moreno, *Fusil o toga*, 268; Apolinar Guerra George, testimony, June 26, 2009, Fiscalía General, Radicado 2138, Cuaderno 23, 255–56; Colonel Duque, testimony, November 30, 2005, Fiscalía General, Radicado 2138, Cuaderno 6, 236. Apolinar Guerra was killed in October 2014. Peace Community, statement, November 10, 2014.

33. "Luis Alberto Pino Rodriguez (A. Jair)," Informe de Entrevista, unpublished manuscript, June 24, 2005, in author's possession.

34. Nelson Casas, letter to Tim Rieser, Fiscalía General de la Nación, August 1, 2006. Casas based his statement that Dario was a militia member on documents,

including photographs, taken from a computer recovered by Duque's Bejarano Battalion in combat with members of the FARC's Fifty-Eighth Front in September 2005. The author obtained copies of the documents, which dated information about Dario's alleged participation in the Fifty-Eighth Front to November 2002.

35. Contravía, "No podemos guardar silencio."

36. William Wood, "IDPs report NGO collaborating with the FARC," May 2005, https://archive.org/stream/05BOGOTA4961/05BOGOTA4961_djvu.txt.

37. "Congreso español pide que Uribe investigue la matanza de San José de Apartadó," Europa Press, May 18, 2005.

38. Matthew A. Reynolds, Acting Assistant Secretary of State, letter to Barack Obama, July 6, 2005; Hylton, *Evil Hour in Colombia*, 161.

39. U.S. Department of State, "Determination and Certification Related to Colombian Armed Forces under Section 563 of the Foreign Operations Appropriations Acts 2004 and 2005," August 1, 2005.

40. At other times, Uribe would insist that the prosecutor general was independent and the executive could not influence judicial investigations. "U/S Burns Meets with President Uribe," cable, August 4, 2005, https://wikileaks.org/plusd/cables/05BOGOTA7402_a.html.

41. Ambassador William Wood, "Scenesetter for President Uribe's Visit to Crawford," State Department cable, July 29, 2005, https://wikileaks.org/plusd/cables/05BOGOTA7191_a.html.

42. U.S. Department of State, "Determination and Certification Related to Colombian Armed Forces under Section 563 of the Foreign Operations Appropriations Acts 2004 and 2005," August 1, 2005, 4–5, 20.

43. White House Press Secretary, "President, President Uribe of Colombia Discuss Terrorism and Security," August 4, 2005, https://2001-2009.state.gov/p/wha/rls/rm/2005/50788.htm. The ten issues are outlined in Wood, "Scenesetter." The other issues were U.S. support, demobilization, Venezuela and the region, Plan Patriota, drug eradication, U.S. hostages, free trade, judicial reform, and reelection.

9. WIDESPREAD AND SYSTEMATIC

1. Numbers of reported extrajudicial killings by Colombian armed forces were compiled from data released by the Colombian Prosecutor General's Office (Fiscalía), principally its Human Rights Unit, and Colombian human rights organizations, organized in the CCEEU. See FOR and CCEEU, "'Falsos positivos' en Colombia."

2. William Brownfield, "Military's Human Rights Initiatives Meet Resistance," February 20, 2009, https://wikileaks.org/plusd/cables/09BOGOTA542_a.html.

3. Alston, "Report of the Special Rapporteur," 9.

4. Juan David Laverde Palma, "Las pruebas de la omisión del general Mario Montoya para evitar los falsos positivos," *El Espectador*, April 5, 2016.

5. Based on data on alleged extrajudicial killings disclosed by the Fiscalía and CCEEU.

6. Associated Press, "Mi hermano fue un falso positivo," *Semana*, October 25, 2008, http://www.semana.com/nacion/articulo/mi-hermano-falso-positivo /96639-3.

7. Associated Press, "Mi hermano fue un falso positivo"; Associated Press, "Revelan falso positivo de un militar en el que cayó su hermano," *El Espectador*, November 12, 2008.

8. Fiscalía General de la Nación, documents released to author in response to public records request, July 2015.

9. "Confesiones siniestras," *El Espectador*, October 8, 2011; "El peso de la ley," *Cambio*, October 2011, accessed October 23, 2011, http://www.cambio.com.co /informeespecialcambio/813/ARTICULO-WEB- NOTA_INTERIOR_CAMBIO-4780136.html.

10. "Confesiones siniestras," *El Espectador*.

11. Fiscalía General de la Nación, documents released to author in response to public records request, July 2015.

12. "Ex comandante del Gaula Córdoba a juicio por falsos positivos," *Radio Santa Fe*, October 28, 2010, http://www.radiosantafe.com/2010/10/28/ex-comandante-del -gaula-cordoba-a-juicio-por-falsos-positivos/.

13. "Por falso positivo en Montería condenados un mayor y un capitán del Ejército a 28 años de cárcel," *Semana*, June 3, 2009, http://www.semana.com/nacion /conflicto-armado/articulo/por-falso-positivo-monteria-condenados-mayor -capitan-del-ejercito-28-anos-carcel/103781-3; "Condenan militares por falsos positivos," *El Universal*, June 19, 2010.

14. "Confesiones siniestras"; Javier Fernández Leal, interview with author, Bogotá, September 17, 2014; Human Rights Watch, *On Their Watch*, 51.

15. William Brownfield, "Army Is Ordered to Stop 'False Positive' Investigations, Recommendations Dismissed," June 25, 2009, http://wikileaks.org/cable/2009/06 /09BOGOTA2050.html.

16. "Ejército se defiende de un dedo acusador," *El Espectador*, October 13, 2011; Fernández Leal, interview with author.

17. "Confesiones siniestras."

18. School of the Americas student database, http://soaw.org/about-the-soawhinsec /13-soawhinsec-graduates/4281-soa-grads-database-online-ur.

19. PGN, Ejecuciones Arbitrarias en Persona Protegida, Bogotá, 2009, in author's possession.

20. Civico, *The Para-State*, 73–74.

21. FOR and CCEEU, "'Falsos positivos' en Colombia," 109.

22. Alston, "Report of the Special Rapporteur"; FIDH and CCEEU, *Colombia: The War Is Measured*; CCEEU, *Ejecuciones extrajudiciales en Colombia*; FOR and USOC, "Military Assistance."

23. Cárdenas and Villa, "La política de seguridad democrática."

24. Human Rights Watch, *On Their Watch*, 80.

25. Armando Barrero, interview with author, Bogotá, June 21, 2013.

26. Even Colombian military officers speaking in Spanish about the false positive phenomenon commonly used the English phrase "body count."

27. William Brownfield, "GOC Discounts Directive 29 Link to Extrajudicial Murders," March 10, 2009, https://wikileaks.org/plusd/cables/09BOGOTA803_a.html. Fernández Leal told me that brigade intelligence officers and commanders could spend eight million pesos (about U.S. $4,000) monthly to pay informants. Fernández Leal, interview with author.

28. Tomas E. Monarrez, "Event Study: The Incidence of Extra Judicial Killings and the Political Environment in Colombia, 2000–2010," unpublished manuscript, 2014, in author's possession.

29. Sabogal Moreno et al., "Cómo prevenir las infracciones," 69.

30. Ramsey, *From El Billar*, 131.

31. "'Un 20 por ciento de las bajas eran falsos positivos': Del Río," *RCN Radio*, June 9, 2014, http://www.noticiasrcn.com/nacional-justicia/un-20-ciento-las-bajas-eran-falsos-positivos-del-rio.

32. Interview with author, Bogotá, June 2014.

33. Óscar González Peña and Jorge Rodríguez Clavijo, interview with author, Bogotá, June 18, 2010.

34. FOR and CCEEU, "'Falsos positivos' en Colombia," 75.

35. Rodga Soluciones Estratégicas, "Acerca de nosotros," accessed February 19, 2018, http://www.rodga.com.co/nosotros.html.

36. Ramsey, *From El Billar*, 66–67.

37. "El bienestar, una prioridad," *En Guardia* 121 (March–May 2011): 10.

38. Sergio Jaramillo, "La crisis subterránea del Ejército," *El Tiempo*, June 11, 2006.

39. FIDH and CCEEU, *Colombia: The War Is Measured*, 10; Human Rights Watch, *On Their Watch*, 28–29.

40. Alfredo Rangel, "¿Qué pasa en el Ejército?," *Revista Cambio*, no. 677 (June 19–25, 2006): 27.

41. "Rito Alejo del Río y el asesinato de Marino López," *Verdad Abierta*, October 5, 2011, http://www.verdadabierta.com/component/content/article/3586-rito-alejo-del-rio-y-el-asesinato-de-marino-lopez.

42. Alex Sierra Rodríguez, "Saturno sigue devorando a sus hijos" (thesis, Universidad Nacional, 2009), 24.

43. Retired Colombian officer, interview with author, Colombia, October 2, 2013.

44. Tate, *Drugs, Thugs, and Diplomats*, 108.

45. Data compiled by FOR and CCEEU, in author's possession.

46. Analysis by Janice Gallagher and the author of data provided by Unidad Nacional de Derechos Humanos de la Fiscalía General de la Nación, September 2013.

47. "Informe Final de la Misión Internacional de Observación sobre Ejecuciones Extrajudiciales e Impunidad," June 2008, http://www.lawg.org/storage/documents/informe_final_mission_ejecuciones_extrajudiciales_oct_08.pdf.

48. "It may not be straightforward to directly interpret a percent decrease that is larger than one hundred percent. However, this kind of large negative effects

are to be expected when the outcome variable is falling from a level that is much higher than its overall average during the time of the event." Tomas E. Monarrez, "Event Study: The Incidence of Extra Judicial Killings and the Political Environment in Colombia, 2000–2010," unpublished, 2014.

49. Salazar Volkmann, "Evaluating the Impact."
50. Kalyvas, *The Logic of Violence*, 203.
51. Compiled from data reported annually in *Noche y Niebla*, nos. 22 to no. 46, accessed August 16, 2016, http://www.nocheyniebla.org.
52. General Carlos Arturo Suárez Bustamante, interview with author, Bogotá, September 27, 2013.

10. THE UNITED STATES EFFECT

1. Steve Salisbury, "Crime Rate Down in Colombia," *Washington Times*, May 6, 2003; Juan Forero, "For Colombia's Ascetic Leader, Signs That Violence Is Easing," *New York Times*, November 10, 2003.
2. Eric Schmitt and Tim Arango, "Billions from U.S. Fail to Sustain Foreign Forces," *New York Times*, October 4, 2015, A1; Sarah Mulnick and Colby Goodman, "Unexamined Risks: The Pentagon's Military Aid Abroad," *Security Assistance Monitor*, May 17, 2016.
3. Diana Ohlbaum, "Three Rays of Sunshine on Pentagon Foreign Aid," *The Hill*, June 18, 2016.
4. Andrew Miller and Richard Sokolsky, "What Has $49 Billion in Foreign Military Aid Bought Us? Not Much," *The American Conservative*, February 27, 2018.
5. Joshua Kurlantzick, "Revamp the International Officer Training Program before Inviting Nations Like Myanmar," *Defense One*, June 8, 2016.
6. See Louscher and Salomone, *Marketing Security Assistance*.
7. Huggins, *Political Policing*.
8. Jones et al., *Securing Tyrants*, xviii–xix.
9. Chris L. Lukasevich, "U.S. Training and Advisory Assistance to the Armed Forces of El Salvador from 1981–1991 and the Resulting Decline in Human Rights Abuses: The Role of U.S. Army Special Forces," unpublished paper, May 2002, in author's possession.
10. Schoultz, *Human Rights*; Davenport, "The Weight of the Past."
11. Finkel, Pérez-Liñán, Seligson, and Tate, *Deepening Our Understanding*, 5.
12. Patricia L. Sullivan, Brock F. Tessman, and Xiaojun Li, "US Military Aid and Recipient State Cooperation," *Foreign Policy Analysis*, no. 7 (2011): 277, 287.
13. Laurienti, *The U.S. Military and Human Rights*, 90–92.
14. McCoy, "Trained to Torture?"
15. Blakeley, "Still Training to Torture?," 1441.
16. McClintock, *The American Connection*; McClintock, *Instruments of Statecraft*; Gill, *School of Americas*; Huggins, *Political Policing*.
17. Dube and Naidu, "Bases, Bullets and Ballots." Another academic argued that external military aid reduces political accountability in Colombia and therefore is

a contributor to human rights violations, but she did not use objective measures of accountability. See Fajardo-Heyward, "Understanding the Effect."

18. Tate, *Drugs, Thugs, and Diplomats*, 108. Tate does not provide evidence that paramilitary violence was caused by or correlated with human rights restrictions on U.S. assistance.

19. Romero, *Paramilitares y autodefensas*.

20. FOR and CCEEU, "'Falsos positivos' en Colombia," 115–16.

21. Interview with author, Bogotá, September 16, 2014.

22. Serafino, "Colombia: Summary and Tables," 6; U.S. General Accounting Office, *Drug Control*, 16.

23. Colombia Nunca Más, accessed February 24, 2008, http://www.movimientodevictimas.org/~nuncamas/.

24. William Wood, "Colmil Relieves Colonel of Command for Paramilitary Ties," January 31, 2007, https://wikileaks.org/plusd/cables/07BOGOTA696_a.html.

25. Colonel Hernán Mejía Gutiérrez, interview with author, Bogotá, March 9, 2013.

26. Juzgado Sexto Penal del Circuito Especializado de Bogotá, sentence of Hernán Publio Mejía Gutiérrez, September 6, 2013, 93.

27. Mejía Gutiérrez, interview with author.

28. Juzgado Sexto Penal, sentence of Publio Hernán Mejía Gutiérrez.

29. Colonel Carlos Alfonso Velásquez, interview with author, Bogotá, June 14, 2013.

30. Human Rights Watch, *War without Quarter*, 56–58.

31. U.S. Embassy cable, December 24, 1997, http://nsarchive.gwu.edu/NSAEBB/NSAEBB327/doc03_19971224.pdf.

32. Data compiled from http://www.soaw.org and http://www.securityassistance.org (accessed June 17, 2017).

33. Corte Suprema de Justicia, Acción de revisión, AP2332-2015, Radicación No. 43700, May 4, 2015.

34. Colonel Glenn Huber, interview with author, Fort Benning, GA, June 28, 2012.

35. The officers charged with crimes were Major Álvaro Quijano Becerra, Captain Wilmer Mora Daza (both accused of collaboration with paramilitary drug traffickers), Mauricio Ordoñez Galindo (convicted of killing four civilians), and Santiago Herrera Fajardo (who was imprisoned for involvement in extrajudicial killings). For a detailed accounting, see "What Happened? Evaluating the Records of Colombian WHINSEC Graduates," http://archives.forusa.org/sites/default/files/uploads/colombiawhinsecgrads.pdf.

36. WHINSEC, slide presentation, June 2012.

37. Paul Richter and Greg Miller, "Colombia Army Chief Linked to Outlaw Militias," *Los Angeles Times*, March 25, 2007.

38. Milton Drucker, "Intel Leak to L.A. Times," March 30, 2007, https://wikileaks.org/plusd/cables/07BOGOTA2117_a.html.

39. Ramsey, *From El Billar*, 54.

40. General Mario Montoya, interview with author, Bogotá, June 12, 2013.

41. Codehsel, Ejecuciones extrajudiciales: El caso, 53–107.

42. FOR and CCEEU, "'Falsos positivos' en Colombia," 72. This could have been a product of U.S.-supported discipline, though it is also possible that the command's follow-up operations after bombings of guerrilla camps led to unreported extrajudicial killings. Those bombing operations reportedly included "blast pressure [that] would kill anyone else close in" and "shooting the wounded trying to go for cover." Priest, "Covert Action in Colombia."

43. Colonel José Octavio Duque, interview with author, Bogotá, September 2014; María Milena Vega Sarmiento, "Carta a nuestros heroes," November 5, 2011, http://www .cartaanuestroheroe.blogspot.com/2011/11/doctor-juan-manuel-santos-calderon .html.

44. FOR and CCEEU, "'Falsos positivos' en Colombia," 114–15. Other soldiers implicated in the Soacha killings were in the Fifteenth Santander Infantry Battalion; the battalion was approved for assistance and one of its soldiers attended a course at WHINSEC for human rights instructors in October 2007, three months before the Soacha murders. U.S. Department of State, "Foreign Military Training Reports."

45. "'Nos daban cinco días de descanso por cada muerto,'" Semana, January 26, 2008, http://www.semana.com/nacion/articulo/nos-daban-cinco-dias-descanso -cada-muerto/90680-3; Vega Sarmiento, "Carta a nuestros heroes."

46. Kaplan, Imperial Grunts, 64.

47. Milton Drucker, "Chargé Raised Human Rights Concerns with Army Commander Montoya," February 26, 2007, https://wikileaks.org/plusd/cables/07BOGOTA1322 _a.html.

48. FOR and USOC, "Military Assistance," 13.

49. Kalyvas, The Logic of Violence.

50. FOR and CCEEU, "'Falsos positivos' en Colombia," 112.

51. General Óscar González Peña, interview with author, Bogotá, June 18, 2010.

52. Curriculum vitae of Major General Óscar González Peña, in author's possession.

53. Myles Frechette, interview with author, Washington, DC, October 31, 2013.

54. William Wood, "Colombia Security Update—Q1'06," May 1, 2006, https:// wikileaks.org/plusd/cables/06BOGOTA3814_a.html.

55. Porch and Muller, "'Imperial Grunts' Revisited," 175.

56. Interview with author, October 2, 2013.

57. Finlayson, "OPATT to PATT," 94.

58. "'Paramilitarismo en Urabá no habría sido posible sin Fuerza Pública': Fiscalía," Verdad Abierta, March 25, 2014, http://www.verdadabierta.com/justicia-y-paz/82 -justicia-y-paz/imputaciones/5290-paramilitarismo-en-uraba-no-habria-sido -posible-sin-fuerza-publica-fiscalia.

59. Ronderos, Guerras recicladas, 186.

60. Centro Nacional de la Memoria Histórica, Textos corporales, 143; SOA graduate database, accessed February 19, 2018, http://soaw.org/about-the-soawhinsec/13 -soawhinsec-graduates/4281-soa-grads-database-online-ur.

61. U.S. Department of State, "Foreign Military Training Reports."

62. "Bogota's Bad Apples," *Los Angeles Times*, September 6, 2008.

63. Juan David Laverde Palma, "Las pruebas de la omisión del general Mario Montoya para evitar los falsos positivos," *El Espectador*, April 5, 2016.

64. Of 2,100 cases of homicide by security forces, representing 3,964 victims, investigated by the Fiscalía in 2014, 62 (3 percent) had reached sentencing. Only three colonels had been sentenced, and no generals. Fiscalía General de la Nación, response to Proposition 007 initiated by Senator Alirio Uribe Muñoz, September 22, 2014.

65. FOR and CCEEU, "'Falsos positivos' en Colombia," 135–37.

11. INVESTIGATION OF THE MASSACRE

Epigraph: Community member quoted in Abad Colorado, "Cuatro días en búsqueda."

1. U.S. Department of State, "Determination and Certification Related to Colombian Armed Forces under Section 563 of the Foreign Operations Appropriations Acts 2004 and 2005," August 3, 2005, 20.

2. Fiscalía General, Radicado 2138, Cuaderno 6, 74–85.

3. Giraldo Moreno, *Fusil o toga*, 294–95; Néstor Iván Duque López, interview with author, Bogotá, September 16, 2014; Nelson Hernando Casas Puentes, letter, August 1, 2006, in author's possession.

4. Néstor Iván Duque López, testimony, November 30, 2005, Fiscalía General, Radicado 2138, Cuaderno 6, 235–37.

5. PGN, "Pliego de cargos contra cuatro altos oficiales del Ejército por incursión de AUC en Apartadó," *Boletín* 151 (May 23, 2005); PGN, "PGN sancionó a dos oficiales del Ejército por omisión en caso de comunidad de paz de Apartadó," *Boletín* 118 (April 2, 2006).

6. Sam Farr et al., letter to Condoleezza Rice, March 1, 2006, in author's possession.

7. FOR, internal reports; Giraldo Moreno, *Fusil o toga*, 79.

8. Milton Drucker, "Armed Confrontation in Vicinity of San José de Apartadó," November 23, 2005, http://wikileaks.wikimee.org/cable/2005/11/05BOGOTA10949.html.

9. Javier Giraldo Moreno, S.J., "Derecho de Petición No. 13 al Presidente Uribe," March 16, 2006, http://www.javiergiraldo.org/spip.php?article137.

10. FOR, internal reports; Giraldo Moreno, *Fusil o toga*, 80–81; Casas, letter, August 1, 2006.

11. Romero Laguna and Martínez Zapater, *La comunidad de paz*, 58.

12. William Wood, "Senate Staffer Rieser Discusses Human Rights, San José de Apartadó Cases with Prosecutor General Officials," April 26, 2006, http://wikileaks.wikimee.org/cable/2006/04/06BOGOTA3617.html.

13. Wood, "Senate Staffer Rieser."

14. Colombian Ministry of Defense, statement, March 11, 2005, http://alpha.mindefensa.gov.co/index.php?page=407&id=1646.

15. Romero Laguna and Martínez Zapater, *La comunidad de paz*, 87–90.

16. U.S. Department of State, "Determination and Certification Related to Colombian Armed Forces under Section 556 of the Foreign Operations, Export Financing, and Related Programs Appropriations Act, 2006," April 4, 2007, 15–16.

17. Casas, letter, August 1, 2006.

18. Casas, letter, August 1, 2006.

19. U.S. Department of State, "Determination and Certification Related to Colombian Armed Forces under Section 556 of the Foreign Operations, Export Financing and Related Programs Appropriations Act, 2005," May 26, 2006, 19.

20. Adriano Cano Arteaga, testimony, September 20, 2006, Fiscalía General de la Nación, Radicado 64.968.

21. Nelson H. Casas Puentes, letter to María Fernanda Cabal, February 23, 2007, issued by Defense Ministry as press release, in author's possession; Milton Drucker, "Prosecutor General to Interrogate 69 Soldiers over 2005 San Jose de Apartado Massacre," March 2, 2007, http://wikileaks.org/cable/2007/03 /07BOGOTA1455.html.

22. Peace Community, statement, March 2, 2007.

23. Wilson Baquero, "División en la Fiscalía por el caso de San José de Apartadó," W Radio, February 27, 2007, http://www.wradio.com.co/nota.asp?id=396099; "Las dos caras del Fiscal," Semana, March 3, 2007, http://m.semana.com/nacion /articulo/las-dos-caras-del-fiscal/83786-3.

24. "Las dos caras del Fiscal."

25. In 2014 Cabal won a Congressional seat on a campaign with former president Uribe's party. Cabal regularly visited Colonel Hernán Mejía and many other soldiers imprisoned for civilian killings, who she said were "unjustly jailed for confronting terror." Juan Sebastián Rojas, "Coronel sentenciado por aliarse con paramilitares fue felicitado por Uribe," Noticias Uno, May 1, 2016, https:// canal1.com.co/noticias/coronel-sentenciado-por-aliarse-con-paramilitares-fue -felicitado-por-uribe/.

26. Nestor Julio Gonzalez, "'No he vacilado en tomar decisiones': Fiscal Mario Iguarán," W Radio, March 9, 2007, http://www.wradio.com.co/noticias/actualidad /no-he-vacilado-en-tomar-decisiones-fiscal-mario-iguaran/20070309/nota /400248.aspx.

27. "'Zar antimafia' se va de la Fiscalía, señalado de haber falsificado un acta de grado," El Tiempo, March 1, 2007.

28. Baquero, "División en la Fiscalía."

29. "Las dos caras del Fiscal."

30. "Fiscalía enfrenta crisis en tres de sus dependencias más importantes," Radiosucesos RCN, March 1, 2007, in author's possession.

31. "Las dos caras del Fiscal."

32. Drucker, "Prosecutor General to Interrogate."

33. Nestor Julio Gonzalez, "'No he vacilado en tomar decisiones': Fiscal Mario Iguarán," Caracol, March 9, 2007, accessed March 15, 2007, http://www.caracol .com.co/noticias/actualidad/no-he-vacilado-en-tomar-decisiones-fiscal-mario -iguaran/20070309/nota/400248.aspx.

34. Gloria Congote, "La 'diplomática' de la paz," Semana, February 20, 2007, http:// www.semana.com/on-line/articulo/la-diplomatica-paz/83613-3.

35. Peace Community, statement, February 21, 2007.
36. Congote, "La 'diplomática' de la paz."
37. U.S. Department of State, "Determination and Certification Related to Colombian Armed Forces under Section 556 of the Foreign Operations, Export Financing, and Related Programs Appropriations Act, 2006," July 28, 2008, in author's possession, 27.
38. Fiscalía General, Radicado 2138, Cuaderno 23, 72–73.
39. "'Para' que reconoció ser guía del Ejército sería clave para aclarar masacre de San José de Apartadó," El Tiempo, April 26, 2007.
40. Guillermo Gordillo Sánchez, testimony, July 29, 2008, Fiscalía General, Radicado 2138.
41. "Detienen a capitán Guillermo Armando Gordillo Sánchez por masacre de San José de Apartadó," El Tiempo, November 23, 2007.
42. Juzgado Primero Penal del Circuito Especializado de Antioquia, sentence of Guillermo Gordillo Sánchez, February 26, 2010, 15.
43. Fiscalía General, Radicado 2138, Cuaderno 11, 172–77.
44. "Esquema Maniobras," Batallón Contraguerrilla 33, February 15–25, 2005, Radicado 2138, Cuaderno 4, 241; Adriano José Cano Arteaga, November 6, 2007, Radicado 2138, Cuaderno 10, 126; Miryam Tuberquia, December 5, 2005, Radicado 2138, Cuaderno 6, 260.
45. José Humberto Milanés, April 28, 2008, Radicado 2138, Cuaderno 18, 139.
46. Jorge Eliécer Molano Rodríguez, "La Masacre de San José de Apartadó," in author's possession, 33.
47. Human Rights Watch, "Colombia: New Evidence against Ex-Army Chief," December 20, 2016, https://www.hrw.org/print/297908.
48. Hever Veloza García [sic], testimony, May 22, 2008, Radicado 2138, Cuaderno 23, 233–41; "'HH' pagó para acusar a las Farc de masacre de San José de Apartado en 2005," August 4, 2009, http://www.verdadabierta.com/victimas-seccion/desaparecidos/1485-hh-pago-para-acusar-a-las-farc-de-masacre-de-san-jose-de-apartado-en-2005.
49. Apolinar Guerra George, testimony, June 26, 2009, Radicado 2138, Cuaderno 23, 254–60.
50. Gordillo Sánchez sentence; Project Counselling Service, "Diego Fernando Murillo Bejarano, alias 'Don Berna,'" in author's possession.
51. "Piden vincular a Mario Montoya a masacre de San José de Apartadó," El Espectador, February 23, 2010. Duque confirmed to me in 2014 that Fandiño met with "guides" before the operation.
52. Molano, "La Masacre de San José de Apartadó"; "Absueltos diez militares por masacre," El Tiempo, August 7, 2010.
53. "La perversidad de la justicia," Folios de Impunidad Caso No. 1 (Bogotá, Colombia, n.d.).
54. Susana Pimiento, "Monument to Impunity: Medellin Judge Acquits Officers Involved in Massacre," Colombia Update, August 2010, http://archives.forusa.org

/blogs/susana-pimiento/monument-impunity-medellin-judge-acquits-officers
-involved-massacre/8158.

55. "Medida a siete exparamilitares por masacre de San José de Apartadó," *Verdad Abierta*, July 12, 2011, http://www.verdadabierta.com/victimarios/3384-medida-a
-siete-exparamilitares-por-masacre-de-san-jose-de-apartado.

56. Gordillo Sánchez sentence, 17.

57. Jorge Molano Rodríguez, brief for appeal to Corte Suprema de Justicia, Radicado 2010–2473, n.d.

58. William Brownfield, "Uraba Security Update," June 26, 2009, https://wikileaks
.org/plusd/cables/09BOGOTA2062_a.html.

59. Duque, testimony, September 9, 2009, Radicado 2138, Cuaderno 6.

12. AN ENCOUNTER WITH POWER

1. FOR and CCEEU, "'Falsos positivos' en Colombia," 18.

2. Juan Sebastián Rojas, "Gral. Jaime Alonso Lasprilla asegura que no es responsable de falsos positivos," *Noticias Uno*, June 21, 2014, https://canal1.com.co
/noticias/gral-jaime-alonso-lasprilla-asegura-que-no-es-responsable-de-falsos
-positivos/.

3. "Los negocios en el Ejército," *Semana*, February 16, 2014, http://www.semana.com
/nacion/articulo/red-de-corrupcion-entre-los-militares/377311-3.

4. MG Juan Bautista Yepes Bedoya and BG Marcolino Tamayo Tamayo, letter to Defense Minister Juan Carlos Pinzón Bueno, March 5, 2014.

5. CINEP, *Deuda con la humanidad 2*.

6. Fernando Tamayo Tamayo was elected to the Senate in 2010 (see http://www
.fernandotamayotamayo.blogspot.com/). Soledad Tamayo was elected to the House of Representatives in 2011 after many years as a Bogotá city councilor (see http://lasillavacia.com/quienesquien/perfilquien/soledad-tamayo).

7. Noticias Caracol, "General es investigado por presunta obstrucción en casos de 'falsos positivos,'" *El Espectador*, November 25, 2015; Las2orillas, "Los fantasmas de los falsos positivos que amenazan el ascenso del general Marco Lino Tamayo," December 1, 2015, http://www.las2orillas.co/los-fantasmas-de-los-falsos
-positivos-amenazan-el-ascenso-del-general-marco-lino-tamayo/.

8. "Cuarenta años de prisión para soldados comprometidos en falsos positivos en el Huila," *Caracol Radio*, May 15, 2013, http://www.caracol.com.co/noticias/judiciales
/cuarenta-anos-de-prision-para-soldados-comprometidos-en-falsos-positivos-en
-el-huila/20130515/nota/1898859.aspx.

9. PGN, Fallo Sancionatorio, Radicado no. 161-4920.

10. See the cases of Juan de Jesús Rendón Alzate (Sonsón, April 23, 2004), unidentified peasant Cocorná (June 3, 2004), and Luis Arturo Naranjo (Granada, September 21, 2004), in Codehsel, *Ejecuciones extrajudiciales: El caso*. In another case of three deaths in Mulatos in San José de Apartadó in February 2004, soldiers reported recovering a radio after combat, but the radio never appeared during the judicial process. CINEP, *Deuda con la humanidad 2*, 286.

11. The prosecutor general reported approximately 5,749 members of the armed forces under investigation for homicide, forced disappearance, sexual violence, illegal intercepts, and links with paramilitary groups. Fiscalía General de la Nación, response to Representative Alirio Uribé Muñoz, September 22, 2014, in author's possession.

12. CCEEU, statement, September 17, 2014, http://www.derechos.org/nizkor /colombia/doc/cceeu1.html.

13. CCEEU, statement, September 9, 2014, http://www.coljuristas.org/documentos /comunicados_de_prensa/com_2014-09-09.pdf.

14. Santiago Martínez Hernández, "El 'reclutador' del coronel (r) González del Río," *El Espectador*, April 22, 2014. González del Río (unrelated to General Rito Alejo del Río) subsequently confessed to involvement in more civilian killings.

15. "Once militares en la mira de la Fiscalía por falsos positivos y corrupción," *El País*, September 3, 2014; "Coronel González del Río salpica a generales por 'falsos positivos,'" *El Tiempo*, September 4, 2014.

16. "Lista la primera condena contra coronel (r) Róbinson González del Río," *El Tiempo*, July 27, 2014.

17. "Esta es la cúpula de inteligencia relevada por escándalo de chuzadas," *El Tiempo*, February 4, 2014; "Supuesta red de corrupción en el Ejército tumbó al general Javier Rey," *El Universal*, February 17, 2014.

18. "Califican de inaceptables chuzadas a los negociadores de paz," *El Universal*, February 4, 2014.

19. "Dos generales tendrán que dar explicaciones por caso 'Andrómeda,'" *El Tiempo*, October 6, 2014.

20. "¿Quién quiere matar al 'hacker'?," *Semana*, August 2, 2014, http://www.semana .com/nacion/articulo/quien-quiere-matar-al-hacker/397734-3.

21. Stefanie Matiz Cortés, "Sin visa para Canadá," *El Espectador*, May 30, 2014.

22. See Ezokola v. Canada (Citizenship and Immigration), 2013 SCC 40, [2013] 2 S.C.R. 678.

23. Juanita León, "Los cuatro temores de los militares frente al proceso de paz," *La Silla Vacía*, October 29, 2014, http://lasillavacia.com/historia/historia-militares -juanita-49005?page=1.

24. Porch and Muller, "'Imperial Grunts' Revisited," 175.

25. "Alguien espió a los negociadores de La Habana?," *Semana*, February 3, 2014, http://www.semana.com/nacion/articulo/alguien-espio-los-negociadores-de-la -habana/376076-3.

26. María Isabel Rueda, "'Ultraderecha obtuvo menos del 40% que dijo que iba a sacar': Santos," *El Tiempo*, March 14, 2014.

27. "Relevan a dos altos generales del Ejército por 'chuzadas,'" *Semana*, February 4, 2014, http://www.semana.com/nacion/articulo/chuzadas-relevan-jefe-de -inteligencia-del-ejercito/376155-3.

28. See "Los primeros cuatro capturas por 'chuzadas,'" *Semana*, October 1, 2014, http://www.semana.com/nacion/articulo/la-fiscalia-anuncia-las-primeras-cuatro

-capturas-por-chuzadas/404670-3; "Caso 'Hacker': Fiscalía acusa a militares y policías detenidos," *Semana*, February 4, 2015, http://www.semana.com/nacion/articulo/caso-hacker-fiscalia-acusa-policias-militares-detenidos/416810-3.

29. Directiva Ministerial 29, Ministerio de Defensa, November 17, 2005.

30. "Robo de información a organización de derechos humanos CCEEU," June 7, 2012, http://justiciaypazcolombia.com/Robo-de-informacion-a-organizacion.

31. The FOR robbery was also notable because of FOR's close identification with accompaniment of the San José Peace Community, as well as its international status.

32. U.S. Department of State, *Country Reports*, 2:2500; Rep. James Langevin et al., letter to President Álvaro Uribe Vélez, July 17, 2007, in author's possession.

33. The active duty officer with the largest number of executions under investigation by the Fiscalía reportedly committed under his command was General Henry William Torres Escalante, who was also under investigation for his personal role in the killings. Human Rights Watch, *On Their Watch*, 54–55.

34. "General Mario Montoya, a declarar el 16 de julio," *Semana*, June 23, 2015, http://www.semana.com/nacion/articulo/general-mario-montoya-declarar-el-16-de-julio/432300-3.

35. "Reaction of Senator Patrick Leahy . . . ," June 24, 2015, http://www.leahy.senate.gov/press/reaction-of-senator-patrick-leahy-d-vt-author-of-the-human-rights-conditions-in-us-law-on-military-aid-for-colombia-to-human-rights-watchs-report-today-implicating-top-colombian-army-officers-in-atrocities.

36. Associated Press, "Report: Colombia Generals Go Unpunished in Civilian Killings," June 24, 2015.

37. Rodríguez Barragán remained as armed forces chief. "Cambios en cúpula militar," *El Espectador*, July 6, 2015.

13. JUDICIAL WARFARE

1. Agence France Presse, "Investigan a 22 generales por ejecuciones extrajudiciales," April 13, 2015, http://www.elheraldo.hn/mundo/830373-217/investigan-a-22-generales-por-ejecuciones-extrajudiciales.

2. The thesis was common among Colombian officers in the 1990s as well. See Tate, *Counting the Dead*, 266–70.

3. Colonel José Octavio Duque, interview with author, Bogotá, September 11, 2014.

4. Interview with author, Bogotá, June 26, 2014.

5. Interview with author, Bogotá, October 19, 2013.

6. Interview with author, Columbus, GA, June 28, 2012.

7. Interview with author, Medellín, September 25, 2013.

8. Jorge Rodríguez Clavijo, interview with author, Bogotá, June 18, 2010.

9. William Brownfield, "Military Human Rights Advances Face Growing Resistance," June 9, 2009, http://wikileaks.org/cable/2009/06/09BOGOTA1845.html.

10. Colonel Charles J. Dunlap Jr., "Law and Military Interventions: Preserving Humanitarian Values in 21st Century Conflicts" (paper presented at the Humanitarian Challenges in Military Intervention conference, Carr Center for Human Rights Policy, Kennedy School of Government, Harvard University, November 29, 2001), 5, 36.
11. Juan Forero, "Rights Group Lists Abuses by Guerrillas in Colombia," *New York Times*, July 10, 2001.
12. Dunlap, "Law and Military Interventions," 36, citing Mary Anastasia O'Grady, "What about Colombia's Terrorists?," *Wall Street Journal*, October 5, 2001. On O'Grady, see Joel Gillin, "Why Is the *Wall Street Journal* Dismissing Colombia's War Crimes?," *New Republic*, February 24, 2015.
13. Thomas A. Marks, "Lawfare's Role in Irregular Conflict," *inFocus* 4, no. 2 (2010), http://www.jewishpolicycenter.org/1740/lawfare-irregular-conflict.
14. Kelly, "Colombia's Resolve Merits Support."
15. Colonel Hernán Mejía Gutiérrez, interview with author, Bogotá, March 10, 2013.
16. Though referencing multiple "peace communities," Padilla names only the San José de Apartadó community. Padilla, "Lawfare: The Colombian Case."
17. Escuela Militar de Cadetes, https://web.archive.org/web/20130630112003 /http://www.esmic.edu.co/esmic/index.php/vicerrectoria/egresados/prensa.
18. Herzberg, *NGO Lawfare*, 2.
19. The Lawfare Project, "Lawfare: The Use of Law as a Weapon of War" (conference material, New York County Lawyers Association, March 11, 2010), http://www .thelawfareproject.org/conferencebook.pdf.
20. See Brooke Goldstein and Aaron Eitan Meyer, "'Legal Jihad': How Islamist Lawfare Tactics Are Targeting Free Speech," *ILSA Journal of International and Comparative Law* 15, no. 2 (2009): 139–54.
21. Dungan, "Fighting Lawfare at the Special Operations Task Force Level," 15.
22. Colonel Mark W. Holzer, "Offensive Lawfare and the Current Conflict," *Harvard Law School National Security Journal*, April 10, 2012, http://harvardnsj.org/2012/04 /offensive-lawfare-and-the-current-conflict.
23. Dawood Ahmed, "Turning the Doctrine of 'Lawfare' against Aggressors," *The Guardian*, April 25, 2012, www.theguardian.com/commentisfree/cifamerica/2012 /apr/25/turning-doctrine-lawfare-against-aggressors.
24. For this section, I am indebted to Rockwood's *Walking Away from Nuremburg*.
25. Rockwood, *Walking Away from Nuremburg*, 122–24.
26. "De nuevo sobre la reforma al Fuero Penal Militar," *Observando*, no. 18 (May–June 2015).
27. Human Rights Watch, *On Their Watch*, 78.
28. "Open letter by Special Procedures Mandate Holders," October 22, 2012, http:// www.oidhaco.org/uploaded/content/article/830162173.pdf.
29. U.S. Senate Report 112-172, May 24, 2012, 71.
30. "De nuevo sobre la reforma al Fuero Penal Militar."

31. "Demandan ante la Corte Constitucional modificación del fuero penal militar," El *Espectador*, July 15, 2015, https://www.elespectador.com/noticias/judicial/demandan-corte-constitucional-modificacion-del-fuero-pe-articulo-572776.

32. Daniel Wilkinson, "How Santos Tarnished His Peace Prize," *Financial Times*, December 15, 2016, https://www.ft.com/content/e2e7986e-c575-302f-a7ff-1e23c4573ca4.

33. "Explanatory Statement for Division J of P.L. 115-31, Consolidated Appropriations Act, 2017," May 5, 2017, https://defenseoversight.wola.org/primarydocs/2017_state_foreign_ops_approps_narrative.pdf.

14. U.S. POLICY LESSONS

1. FOR and USOC, "Military Assistance," 16.

2. Amnesty International, "Assisting Units," 6–7.

3. FOR and USOC, "Military Assistance," 8.

4. Alfredo Valenzuela, letter, January 26, 2011 (recipient name redacted), in author's possession. This classification may have responded to the FOR and USOC report in 2010, which generated much attention within the State Department and the U.S. Embassy.

5. Former Colombian government official close to issue, interview with author, Washington, DC, July 28, 2014.

6. WHINSEC, "WHINSEC Board of Visitors Commandant's Update," slide presentation, June 2012.

7. General John F. Kelly, testimony before House Foreign Affairs Committee Subcommittee on the Western Hemisphere, "Confronting Transnational Drug Smuggling: An Assessment of Regional Partnerships," April 29, 2014, http://foreignaffairs.house.gov/hearing/joint-subcommittee-hearing-confronting-transnational-drug-smuggling-assessment-regional.

8. Tickner, "Colombia," 5; "U.S.-Colombia Action Plan on Regional Security Cooperation," 2013, released to author in response to Freedom of Information Act request.

9. U.S. Department of State, responses to inquiry from Rep. Hank Johnson, May 19, 2005, in author's possession.

10. "Mindefensa anunció más apoyo y trabajo conjunto para enfrentar el narcotráfico en Centroamérica y el Caribe," August 2, 2014, http://www.cgfm.mil.co/CGFMPortal/faces/index.jsp?id=25881.

11. Tickner, "Colombia," 3.

12. Interview with author, Bogotá, June 26, 2014.

13. U.S. Government Accountability Office, "Building Partner Capacity: DOD Is Meeting Most Targets for Colombia's Regional Helicopter Training Center but Should Track Graduates," GAO-13-674, July 2013, 4.

14. Former Colombian government official close to issue, interview with author, Washington, DC, July 28, 2014.

CONCLUSION

1. Courtheyn, "'Memory Is the Strength,'" 463.

2. "Palabras del Presidente Juan Manuel Santos, en la entrega del documento 'De la violencia a la sociedad de los derechos,'" December 10, 2013, http://wsp .presidencia.gov.co/Prensa/2013/Diciembre/Paginas/20130913-05-Palabras-del -Presidente-Santos-en-la-entrega-del-documento-De-la-violencia-a-la-sociedad -de-los-derechos.aspx.

3. Peace Community, statement, December 16, 2016.

4. Cárdenas Gómez, "Sentencia Primera Instancia, Bloque Héroes de Tolová," 660–61.

5. "Ascot Signs Heads of Agreement to Acquire Urabá Coal Mining Concession in Colombia," Ascot Resources, July 22, 2013, http://www.ascotresources .com/images/news/Heads_of_Agreement_to_acquire_Uraba_coal_mining _concession_-_22_July_2013_1.pdf; personal communication to author, February 2, 2015.

6. Forrest Hylton and Aaron Tauss, "Peace in Colombia: A New Growth Strategy," *NACLA Report on the Americas* 48, no. 3 (2016): 253–59.

7. Peace Community, statement, December 11, 2014; Peace Community members, interviews with author, San José de Apartadó, January 2015.

8. Peace Community, statement, October 12, 2016.

9. "Comunidad de paz de San José de Apartadó ha denunciado amenaza paramilitar todo el año," El Espectador, January 1, 2018.

10. "Las sombras que persiguen al general Montoya," *Semana*, March 28, 2016, http:// www.semana.com/nacion/articulo/falsos-positivos-antecedentes-del-general -mario-montoya/467060.

11. "El fin del conflicto es la victoria de ustedes, dijo el Presidente Santos a los integrantes de las Fuerzas Militares y la Policía," June 27, 2016, http://es .presidencia.gov.co/noticia/160625-El-fin-del-conflicto-es-la-victoria-de-ustedes, -dijo-el-Presidente-Santos-a-los-integrantes-de-las-Fuerzas-Militares-y-la -Polic%C3%ADa.

12. Kevin Hall and Brittany Peterson, "Why Was This Colombian General Posted to His Country's Washington Embassy?," McClatchy, April 11, 2017, http://www .mcclatchydc.com/news/politics-government/article144011929.html.

13. Matt Apuzzo, "Chiquita to Pay $25M Fine in Terror Case," *Washington Post*, March 15, 2007.

14. Paley, *Drug War Capitalism*, 53–81.

15. See Cárdenas and Villa, "La política de seguridad"; Fajardo-Heyward, "Understanding the Effect"; Salazar Volkmann, "Evaluating the Impact."

16. Lindsay-Poland and Weintraub, "To Be By Your Side."

17. Tim Rieser, interview with author, Washington, DC, January 28, 2016.

18. Aurora Guerra, interview with author, San José de Apartadó, January 13, 2015.

19. "Con satisfacción recibe Comandante del Ejército certificación de Estados Unidos," April 11, 2007, cited in FOR and USOC, "Military Assistance," 15.

20. "A Conversation with U.S. Secretary of State Hillary Rodham Clinton," September 8, 2010, Council on Foreign Relations, http://www.cfr.org/world/conversation -us-secretary-state-hillary-rodham-clinton/p34808.

21. "Afghan Ministers Discuss Counter-Narcotics with DASD Wechsler," August 13, 2009, https://wikileaks.org/plusd/cables/09KABUL2347_a.html.

BIBLIOGRAPHY

Abad Colorado, Jesús. "Cuatro días en búsqueda." *El Tiempo*, March 25, 2005.

Alston, Philip. "Report of the Special Rapporteur on Extrajudicial, Summary or Arbitrary Executions: Mission to Colombia." March 31, 2010. A/HRC/14/24/Add.2.

American Friends Service Committee. *Building from the Inside Out: Peace Initiatives in War-Torn Colombia*. Philadelphia: Fellowship of Reconciliation, 2004.

Amnesty International. "Assisting Units That Commit Extrajudicial Killings: A Call to Investigate U.S. Military Policy toward Colombia." April 9, 2008. AMR 23/016/2008.

Aparicio, Juan Ricardo. *Rumores, residuos y Estado en "la mejor esquina de Sudamérica": Una cartografía de lo "humanitario" en Colombia*. Bogotá: Universidad de los Andes, 2012.

Baldwin, James. *No Name in the Street*. New York: Vintage, 1972.

Belasco, Amy. "The Cost of Iraq, Afghanistan, and Other Global War on Terror Operations since 9/11." Congressional Research Service, December 8, 2014.

Blakeley, Ruth. "Still Training to Torture? US Training of Military Forces from Latin America." *Third World Quarterly* 27, no. 8 (2006): 1439–61.

Botero, Fernando. *Urabá, colonización, violencia y crisis del Estado*. Medellín: Universidad de Antioquia, 1990.

Bowden, Mark. *Killing Pablo: The Hunt for the World's Greatest Outlaw*. New York: Penguin, 2002.

Brewer, Capt. Barry L. "United States Security Assistance Training of Latin American Militaries: Intentions and Results." Master's thesis, Air Force Institute of Technology, 1995.

Cárdenas, Ernesto, and Edgar Villa. "La política de seguridad democrática y las ejecuciones extrajudiciales." *Ensayos sobre Política Económica* 31, no. 71 (2013): 64–72.

Cardenas, Sonia. *Conflict and Compliance: State Responses to International Human Rights Pressure*. Philadelphia: University of Pennsylvania Press, 2007.

Cárdenas Gómez, Juan Guillermo. "Sentencia Primera Instancia, Bloque Héroes de Tolová." Sala de Justicia y Paz, Tribunal Superior de Medellín, July 7, 2015.

Carroll, Leah Anne. *Violent Democratization: Social Movements, Elites, and Politics in Colombia's Rural War Zones, 1984–2008*. South Bend, IN: University of Notre Dame Press, 2011.

Carvajal Martínez, Jorge Enrique. *La seguridad dentro del estado de garantías*. Bogotá: Instituto Latinoamericano de Servicios Legales Alternativos, 2008.

Centro de Investigación y Educación Popular (CINEP). *Deuda con la humanidad: Paramilitarismo de estado en Colombia, 1988–2003*. Bogotá: CINEP, 2004.

——. *Deuda con la humanidad 2: 23 años de Falsos Positivos (1988–2011)*. Bogotá: CINEP, 2011.

——. *San Josesito de Apartadó: La otra versión*. Noche y Niebla. Bogotá: CINEP, 2005.

——. *Sistematización y análisis de las Asambleas Constituyentes en Colombia*. Bogotá: CINEP, 2007.

Centro Nacional de la Memoria Histórica. *Textos corporales de la crueldad: Memoria histórica y antropología forense*. Bogotá: Centro Nacional de la Memoria Histórica, 2014.

Cepeda, Iván, and Jorge Rojas. *A las puertas de El Ubérrimo*. Bogotá: Random House, 2008.

Civico, Aldo. *The Para-State: An Ethnography of Colombia's Death Squads*. Oakland: University of California Press, 2016.

Coghlan, Nicholas. 2004. *The Saddest Country: On Assignment in Colombia*. Montreal: McGill-Queen's University Press, 2004.

Colby, Gerard. *Thy Will Be Done: The Conquest of the Amazon; Nelson Rockefeller and Evangelism in the Age of Oil*. With Charlotte Dennett. New York: HarperCollins. 1996.

Colectivo de Derechos Humanos Semillas de Libertad (Codehsel). *Ejecuciones extrajudiciales: El caso del Oriente Antioqueño*. Bogotá: Coordinación Colombia–Europa–Estados Unidos, 2007.

Coleman, Bradley Lynn. *Colombia and the United States: The Making of an Inter-American Alliance, 1939–1960*. Kent, OH: Kent State University Press, 2008.

Colombia Support Network (CSN). "A Massacre at Mulatos in Colombia, an Investigative Report." June 26, 2005. Accessed July 22, 2005. http://www.colombiasupport.net.

Comisión Colombiana de Juristas. *Panorama de violaciones a los derechos humanos y al derecho humanitario en Colombia*. Bogotá: Comisión Colombiana de Juristas, 2000.

Contraloría General de la República. *Plan Colombia: Cuarto informe de evaluación*. Bogotá: Contraloría General de la República, 2004.

Contravía. "No podemos guardar silencio." Documentary, 2005. YouTube, May 13, 2011. https://www.youtube.com/watch?v=VDXh_yPRcuo.

Coordinación Colombia–Europa–Estados Unidos (CCEEU). *Ejecuciones extrajudiciales en Colombia, 2002–2010*. Bogotá: CCEEU, 2013.

Corte Suprema de Justicia (Colombia), Sala de Casación Penal, Proceso 23099, ruling on appeal of Jorge Isabel Caicedo Valencia, April 11, 2008, Bogotá.

Courtheyn, Chris. "'Memory Is the Strength of Our Resistance': A Critical Performance Geography of Peace, Memory, Territory, and Politics in the San José Peace Community, Colombia." PhD diss., University of North Carolina, Chapel Hill, 2016.

Davenport, Christian. "The Weight of the Past: Exploring Lagged Determinants of Political Repression." *Political Research Quarterly* 49, no. 2 (1996): 377–403.

DeShazo, Peter, Johanna Mendelson Forman, and Phillip McLean. *Countering Threats to Security and Stability in a Failing State: Lessons from Colombia.* Washington, DC: Center for Strategic and International Studies, 2009.

DeShazo, Peter, Tanya Primiani, and Phillip McLean. *Back from the Brink: Evaluating Progress in Colombia, 1999–2007.* Washington, DC: Center for Strategic and International Studies, 2007.

Drost, Nadja. "A Massacre Explored: Murder in the Jungle." *GlobalPost*, March 16, 2010.

Dube, Oeindrila, and Suresh Naidu. "Bases, Bullets and Ballots: The Effect of U.S. Military Aid on Political Conflict in Colombia." Center for Global Development, Working paper no. 197, January 2010.

Dudley, Steven S. *Walking Ghosts: Murder and Guerrilla Politics in Colombia.* New York: Routledge, 2003.

Dufort, Philippe. "A Typology of Military Factions within the Colombian Corps: Origins and Evolutions of Colombian Counter-insurgency." Paper presented at the Latin American Studies Association Congress, New York, May 2016.

Dungan, Capt. C. Peter. "Fighting Lawfare at the Special Operations Task Force Level." *Special Warfare* 21, no. 2 (2008): 10–15.

Dunlap, Col. Charles J., Jr. "Law and Military Interventions: Preserving Humanitarian Values in 21st Century Conflicts." Paper presented at the Humanitarian Challenges in Military Intervention conference, Carr Center for Human Rights Policy, Kennedy School of Government, Harvard University, November 29, 2001.

Dunning, Thad, and Leslie Wirpsa. "Oil and the Political Economy of Conflict in Colombia and Beyond: A Linkages Approach." *Geopolitics* 9, no. 1 (2004): 81–108.

Fajardo-Heyward, Paola. "Understanding the Effect of Security Assistance on Human Rights: The Case of Plan Colombia." *Latin Americanist* 59, no. 2 (2015): 3–27.

Federación Internacional de Derechos Humanos (FIDH) and Coordinación Colombia–Europa–Estados Unidos (CCEEU). *Colombia: The War Is Measured in Litres of Blood.* Bogotá: Editorial Códice, 2012.

Fellowship of Reconciliation (FOR) and Coordinación Colombia–Europa–Estados Unidos (CCEEU). "'Falsos positivos' en Colombia y el papel de la asistencia militar de Estados Unidos, 2000–2010." Bogotá, 2014.

———. "The Rise and Fall of 'False Positive' Killings in Colombia: The Role of U.S. Military Assistance, 2000–2010." Nyack, NY, May 2014. http://archives.forusa.org /sites/default/files/uploads/false-positives-2014-colombia-report.pdf.

Fellowship of Reconciliation (FOR) and U.S. Office on Colombia (USOC). "Military Assistance and Human Rights: Colombia, U.S. Accountability, and Global Implications." Washington, DC, 2010.

Finkel, Steven E., Aníbal Pérez-Liñán, Mitchell A. Seligson, and C. Neal Tate. *Deepening Our Understanding of the Effects of US Foreign Assistance on Democracy Building.* Washington, DC: USAID, 2008.

Finlayson, Kenneth. "OPATT to PATT: El Salvador to Colombia and the Formation of the Planning and Assistance Training Teams." *Veritas* 2, no. 4 (2007): 91–94.

Fiscalía General de la Nación (Colombia), Unidad Nacional de Derechos Humanos y Derecho Internacional Humanitario. Court testimony in Case (Radicado) 2138, Bogotá.

Furnari, Ellen, ed. *Wielding Nonviolence in the Midst of Violence*. Wahlenau, Germany: Institute for Peace Work and Nonviolence Conflict Transformation, 2016.

García, Clara Inés. *Urabá: Región, actores y conflicto, 1960–1990*. Bogotá: Cerec, 1996.

Gill, Lesley. *School of Americas: Military Training and Political Violence in the Americas*. Durham, NC: Duke University Press, 2004.

Giraldo Moreno, Javier. *Fusil o toga, toga y fusil: El Estado contra la Comunidad de Paz de San José de Apartadó*. Bogotá: n.p., 2010.

———. "Imágenes interpelantes de un espejo retrovisor." In *Sembrando vida y dignidad: Quaderni Satyagraha*, 52–59. Pisa: Gandhi edizioni, 2007.

Green, James N. *We Cannot Remain Silent: Opposition to the Brazilian Military Dictatorship in the United States*. Durham, NC: Duke University Press, 2010.

Grimmett, Richard F. "U.S. Arm Sales: Agreements with and Deliveries to Major Clients, 1996–2003." Congressional Research Service, December 8, 2004.

Groundswell Productions. *Partnering for Peace: Colombian and North American Communities in Solidarity*. Oakland, 2005. DVD.

Grupo de Memoria Histórica. *Bojayá: La guerra sin límites*. Bogotá: Comisión Nacional de Reparación y Reconciliación, 2010.

Hernández Delgado, Esperanza. *Resistencia civil artesana de paz*. Bogotá: Pontificia Universidad Javeriana, 2004.

Hernández Delgado, Esperanza, and Marcela Salazar Posada. *Con la esperanza intacta: Experiencias comunitarias de resistencia civil no violenta*. Bogotá: Oxfam, 1999.

Herzberg, Anne. *NGO Lawfare: Exploitation of Courts in the Arab-Israeli Conflict*. Jerusalem: NGO Monitor, 2008.

Huggins, Martha K. *Political Policing: The United States and Latin America*. Durham, NC: Duke University Press, 1998.

Human Rights Watch. *On Their Watch: Evidence of Senior Officers' Responsibility for False Positive Killings in Colombia*. New York: Human Rights Watch, 2005.

———. *The "Sixth Division": Military-Paramilitary Ties and U.S. Policy in Colombia*. New York: Human Rights Watch, 2001.

———. *State of War: Political Violence and Counterinsurgency in Colombia*. New York: Human Rights Watch, 1993.

———. *War without Quarter: Colombia and International Humanitarian Law*. New York: Human Rights Watch, 1998.

Hylton, Forrest. *Evil Hour in Colombia*. New York: Verso, 2006.

Jones, Seth G., Olga Oliker, Peter Chalk, C. Christine Fair, Rollie Lal, and James Dobbins. *Securing Tyrants or Fostering Reform? U.S. Internal Assistance to Repressive and Transitioning Regimes*. Santa Monica, CA: RAND, National Security Research Division, 2006.

Kalyvas, Stathis. *The Logic of Violence in Civil War.* Cambridge: Cambridge University Press, 2006.

Kaplan, Robert D. *Imperial Grunts: The American Military on the Ground.* New York: Vintage, 2006.

Kelly, General John F. "Colombia's Resolve Merits Support." *Miami Herald,* May 3, 2015.

Koopman, Sara. "Making Space for Peace: International Accompaniment in Colombia, 2007–2009." Ph.D. diss., University of British Columbia, 2012.

Laurienti, Jerry. *The U.S. Military and Human Rights Promotion: Lessons from Latin America.* Westport, CT: Praeger, 2007.

Leal Buitrago, Francisco. "Una visión de la seguridad en Colombia." *análisis político* 24, no. 73 (2011): 3–36.

Lindsay-Poland, John. "Obama's Choice: New Documents Show United States Seeks Colombian Bases for Training and Operations." *Americas Program,* August 13, 2009.

Lindsay-Poland, John, and Michael Weintraub. "To Be By Your Side: Unarmed Protection and Accompaniment in Colombia." In *Wielding Nonviolence in the Midst of Violence,* edited by Ellen Furnari, 25–67. Wahlenau, Germany: Institute for Peace Work and Nonviolent Conflict Transformation, 2016.

López Hernández, Claudia, ed. *Y refundaron la patria: De como mafiosos y políticos reconfiguraron el Estado colombiano.* Bogotá: Random House, 2010.

Louscher, David J., and Michael D. Salomone. *Marketing Security Assistance: New Perspectives on Arms Sales.* Lexington, MA: Lexington Books, 1987.

Mahony, Liam. *Proactive Presence: Field Strategies for Civilian Protection.* Geneva, Switzerland: Centre for Humanitarian Dialogue, 2006.

Mahony, Liam, and Luis Enrique Eguren. *Unarmed Bodyguards: International Accompaniment for the Protection of Human Rights.* West Hartford, CT: Kumarian, 1997.

McClintock, Michael. *The American Connection.* London: Zed Books, 1985.

———. *Instruments of Statecraft: U.S. Guerrilla Warfare, Counter-insurgency, Counter-terrorism, 1940–1990.* New York: Pantheon, 1992.

McCoy, Katherine E. "Trained to Torture? The Human Rights Effects of Military Training at the School of the Americas." *Latin American Perspectives* 32, no. 6 (2005): 47–64.

McManus, Philip, and Gerald Schlabach. *Relentless Persistence: Nonviolent Action in Latin America.* Philadelphia: New Society, 1991.

McNerney, Michael, et al. *Assessing Security Cooperation as a Preventive Tool.* Santa Monica, CA: RAND, 2014.

Medina Gallego, Carlos. *Autodefensas, paramilitares y narcotráfico en Colombia.* Bogotá: Documentos Periodísticos, 1990.

———. *FARC-EP: Notas para una historia política, 1958–2006.* Bogotá: Universidad Nacional de Colombia, 2009.

Moreno, Javier. 2014. "Tasas de homicidio en Colombia, 1990–2013." Accessed February 18, 2018. http://finiterank.github.io/homicidios.

Moyar, Mark, Hector Pagan, and Wil R. Griego. *Persistent Engagement in Colombia.* JSOU Report 14-3. MacDill AFB, FL: Joint Special Operations University Press, 2014.

Ospina Ovalle, Carlos. *Los años en que Colombia recuperó la esperanza*. Bogotá: Universidad Pontífica Boliviarana, 2014.

Padilla, Col. Juan Manuel. "Lawfare: The Colombian Case." United States Army Command and General Staff College, May 20, 2010. http://www.dtic.mil/get-tr-doc/pdf?AD=ADA523182&Location=U2&doc=GetTRDoc.pdf.

Palacios, Marco. *Between Legitimacy and Violence: A History of Colombia, 1875–2002*. Durham, NC: Duke University Press, 2006.

Paley, Dawn. *Drug War Capitalism*. Oakland, CA: AK Press, 2014.

Pendergrast, Mark. *For God, Country, and Coca-Cola: The Definitive History of the Great American Soft Drink and the Company That Makes It*. New York: Basic Books, 2013.

Piccoli, Guido. *El sistema del pájaro: Colombia, laboratorio de barbarie*. Bogotá: Instituto Latinoamericano de Servicios Legales Alternativos, 2005.

Pinilla Cogollo, Rubén Darío. Case of Uber Darío Yáñez Cavadías. Sala de Justicia y Paz, Tribunal Superior de Medellín, Acta No. 2, September 3, 2014.

Porch, Douglas, and Christopher Muller. "'Imperial Grunts' Revisited: The US Advisory Effort in Colombia." In *Military Advising and Assistance: From Mercenaries to Privatization, 1815–2007*, edited by Donald Stoker, 168–91. London: Routledge, 2008.

Priest, Dana. "Covert Action in Colombia." *Washington Post*, December 21, 2013.

———. "U.S. Military Trains Foreign Troops." *Washington Post*, July 12, 1998.

Programa Somos Defensores. *¿Este es el fin?* Bogotá, 2016.

Ramírez Lemus, María Clemencia, Kimberly Stanton, and John Walsh. "Colombia: A Vicious Cycle of Drugs and War." In *Drugs and Democracy in Latin America: The Impact of U.S. Policy*, edited by Coletta Youngers and Eileen Rosin, 99–142. New York: Lynne Rienner, 2005.

Ramsey, Robert D., III. *From El Billar to Operations Fenix and Jaque: The Colombian Security Force Experience, 1998–2008*. Fort Leavenworth, KS: Combat Studies Institute Press, 2009.

Reiniciar. *Historia de un genocidio: El exterminio de la Unión Patriótica en Urabá; El plan retorno*. Bogotá: Gente Nueva Editorial, 2006.

Rempe, Dennis. "Guerrillas, Bandits, and Independent Republics: US Counterinsurgency Efforts in Colombia 1959–1965." *Small Wars and Insurgencies* 6, no. 3 (1995): 304–27.

———. "The Origin of Internal Security in Colombia: Part I—A CIA Special Team Surveys La Violencia, 1959–60." *Small Wars and Insurgencies* 10, no. 3 (1999): 24–61.

Richani, Nazih. "Multinational Corporations, Rentier Capitalism, and the War System in Colombia." *Latin American Politics and Society* 47, no. 3 (2005): 117–44.

———. *Systems of Violence: The Political Economy of War and Peace in Colombia*. Albany: State University of New York Press, 2002.

Rivera Salazar, Rodrigo. Colombian Minister of Defense. Unpublished memo to Colombian Senator Jorge Enrique Robledo, in author's possession, February 21, 2011.

Rockwood, Lawrence P. *Walking Away from Nuremburg: Just War and the Doctrine of Command Responsibility*. Amherst: University of Massachusetts Press, 2007.

Rodríguez Hernández, Saúl Mauricio. *La influencia de los Estados Unidos en el ejército colombiano, 1951–1959*. Medellín: Universidad Nacional de Colombia, 2006.

Romeo Laguna, Juan José, and Luis Fernando Martínez Zapater. *La comunidad de paz de San José de Apartadó: Alrededor de los hechos de febrero de 2005*. Bogotá: Magistrats européens pour la démocratie et les libertés (MEDEL), 2006.

Romero, Mauricio. *Paramilitares y autodefensas, 1982–2003*. Bogotá: Instituto de Estudios Políticos y Relaciones Internacionales, 2003.

————, ed. *Parapolítica: La ruta de la expansión paramilitar y los acuerdos políticos*. Bogotá: Intermedio, 2007.

Ronderos, María Teresa. *Guerras recicladas: Una historia periodística del paramilitarismo en Colombia*. Bogotá: Random House, 2014.

Roselló, Victor M. *East of the Orteguaza: The Story of an American Military Advisor and the Colombian Drug War*. Williamsburg, VA: Victor M. Roselló, 2010.

Rubio Maldonado, María Carolina. "Análisis del rol de las ONG como voceros en la escena internacional de las víctimas del conflicto armado en Colombia." Master's thesis, Universidad del Rosario, 2012.

Sabogal Moreno, Maj. José Freddy, et al. "Cómo prevenir las infracciones al derecho internacional de los conflictos armados, por militares." Thesis, Escuela Superior de Guerra de Colombia, 2006.

Salazar Volkmann, Christian. "Evaluating the Impact of Human Rights Work: The Office of the United Nations High Commissioner for Human Rights and the Reduction of Extrajudicial Executions in Colombia." *Journal of Human Rights Practice* 4, no. 3 (2012): 396–460.

Schoultz, Lars. *Human Rights and United States Policy toward Latin America*. Princeton, NJ: Princeton University Press, 1981.

Serafino, Nina M. "Colombia: Plan Colombia Legislation and Assistance (FY2000–FY2001)." Congressional Research Service, July 5, 2001.

————. "Colombia: Summary and Tables on U.S. Assistance, FY1989–FY2004." Congressional Research Service, May 19, 2003.

Serafino, Nina M., et al. "'Leahy Law' Human Rights Provisions and Security Assistance: Issue Overview." Congressional Research Service, January, 29, 2014.

Spencer, David E., et al. *Colombia's Road to Recovery: Security and Governance, 1982–2010*. Washington, DC: Center for Hemispheric Defense Studies, 2011.

Steele, Abbey. "Electing Displacement: Political Cleansing in Apartadó, Colombia." *Journal of Conflict Resolution* 55, no. 3 (2011): 423–45.

Stokes, Doug. *America's Other War: Terrorizing Colombia*. London: Zed, 2004.

Suárez, Andrés Fernando. *Identidades políticas y exterminio recíproco: Masacres y guerra en Urabá, 1991–2001*. Medellín: Universidad Nacional de Colombia, 2007.

Tate, Winifred. *Counting the Dead: The Culture and Politics of Human Rights Activism in Colombia*. Berkeley: University of California Press, 2007.

———. *Drugs, Thugs, and Diplomats: U.S. Policymaking in Colombia*. Stanford, CA: Stanford University Press, 2015.

Tickner, Arlene B. "Colombia, the United States, and Security Cooperation by Proxy." Washington Office on Latin America, March 18, 2014.

Uribe, María Teresa. *Urabá: ¿region o territorio?* Medellín: Instituto de Estudios Regionales, Universidad de Antioquia, 1992.

U.S. Agency for International Development (USAID). *U.S. Overseas Loans and Grants (Greenbook)*. Washington, DC, 2018. https://www.usaid.gov/developer/greenbookapi.

U.S. Congress. *Official Congressional Directory 109th Congress*. Washington, DC: Government Printing Office, 2005.

———. *Official Congressional Directory 110th Congress*. Washington, DC: Government Printing Office, 2007.

U.S. Department of Defense. *Sustaining U.S. Global Leadership: Priorities for 21st Century Defense*. Washington, DC: Department of Defense, 2012.

U.S. Department of State. *Country Reports on Human Rights Practices for 2007*. Vol. 2. Washington, DC: Government Printing Office, 2008.

———. "Foreign Military Training and DoD Engagement Activities of Interest." Accessed February 17, 2018. http://www.state.gov/t/pm/rls/rpt/fmtrpt/index.htm.

U.S. General Accounting Office. *Drug Control: U.S. Counternarcotics Efforts in Colombia Face Continuing Challenges*. GAO/NSIAD-98-60. Washington, DC: General Accounting Office, 1998.

———. *The Drug War: Colombia Is Undertaking Antidrug Programs, but Impact Is Uncertain*. Washington: Human Rights Watch, 1993.

Vacius, Ingrid, and Adam Isacson. "'Plan Colombia': The Debate in Congress, 2000." Center for International Policy Brief, December 4, 2000. https://www.ciponline.org/research/html/plan-colombia-the-debate-in-congress-2000.

Valencia Caicedo, Jorge Isabel. 2007. Appeal filed before Colombian Supreme Court in Radicado 23099. May 30, 2007.

Washington Office on Latin America. *Clear and Present Dangers: The U.S. Military and the War on Drugs in the Andes*. Washington, DC: Washington Office on Latin America, 1991.

Whittaker, Alan G., Frederick C. Smith, and Elizabeth McKune. "The National Security Policy Process." In *Affairs of State: The Interagency and National Security*, edited by Gabriel Marcella, 97–170. Carlisle, PA: Strategic Studies Institute, 2008.

Williams, Lynn M., and Susan B. Epstein. "Overseas Contingency Operations Funding: Background and Status." Congressional Research Service, February 7, 2017.

Wolf, Paul. Case 1:10-CV-00404-RJL. Document 3. Brief filed in U.S. District Court, District of Columbia. March 9, 2010.

———. Case 11-cv-00582. Complaint against Chiquita Brands International, Inc., filed with U.S. District Court for the District of Columbia. March 17, 2011.

INDEX

Guerra, Diener, 1–2, 4, 104–5, 112–13, 116, 119–21

Guerra, Luis Eduardo, 1–4, 66–68, 73, 184; aftermath of 2005 massacre and, 140–41, 145, 147; early life of, 40; international travel of, 101; interrogations of, 104–5, 107, 113; murder of, 2–4, 34, 113–14, 116, 120–22, 143, 230; Peace Community deaths witnessed by, 68, 99, 112

Guerra, Moisés, 40

guerrilla organizations: Colombian military and, 57, 78, 83, 86–88, 109–10, 159–60, 196, 227, 256n34; demobilization of, 4, 9, 51, 53, 129; human rights violations and, 62; indigenous communities and, 131–32; "judicial warfare" and, 210–13, 217; killings by, 4, 68, 81, 107, 109, 128–29; oil production and, 97; Peace Community accused of collaboration with, 65, 82, 104–6, 141–44, 147–48, 174, 187, 190, 195, 197; protective accompaniment and, 77; reductions in guerrilla violence, 164; resistance to U.S. imperialism, 24. *See also* Revolutionary Armed Forces of Colombia (Fuerzas Armadas Revolucionarias de Colombia, FARC)

Guevara, Luis Alejandro, 186

Guzmán, Alexander, 78

Harken Energy Corporation, 59, 98, 243n50

Helio Couriers, 29

Herrera Fajardo, Santiago, 100, 177, 211, 261n35

Holzer, Mark, 214–15

Honduras, 180, 224

Huber, Glenn, 172

Huggins, Martha, 166

Huila Department, 156, 178, 181, 198, 199–203, 209

humanitarian zones, 111–12, 128, 143–45, 186, 226

human rights: abuses in Arauca Department, 149, 177, 181; in Colombia, 17–19, 96, 125; drug war and, 53; extra-

judicial executions and, 23; harassment of human rights organizations, 199–200, 204–8; international human rights advocacy, 23–25, 52; international human rights organizations, 69, 72, 146, 208–9; Leahy Law, 52, 61–62, 84, 165, 181, 200, 205, 220–23, 231; paramilitary organizations and, 168; Plan Colombia and, 9, 14, 17, 61–63, 149, 223; reduction in violence and, 164; SOA trainees and, 167–68; trials for human rights crimes, 216–17, 220; U.S.-Colombia relationship and, 36, 61–63, 80, 82, 96, 146–49, 164–65, 185, 187, 218, 220–22, 230; U.S. foreign policy and, 17–19, 52, 61–63, 146–47, 166–69, 215–16, 231; U.S. military aid to Colombia and, 61–63, 146–47, 164–65, 167–69, 177–79, 181, 185, 187, 204, 218–19, 220–23, 230, 231, 260n17; U.S. training of foreign soldiers and, 172; Vietnam War and, 216

Human Rights Watch, 16, 156, 208–9, 212, 218

Hundred Municipalities for Peace project, 129

Iguarán, Mario, 149, 186, 189

indigenous communities, 107, 124–25, 131–33; active neutrality and, 48

Indigenous Guard, 125, 131–33

Infrastructure Security Strategy (ISS), 60, 97

Inter-American Human Rights Commission, 68–69, 141, 161, 205

Inter-American Human Rights Court, 68, 72, 80

international accompaniment. *See* protective accompaniment

International Peace Observatory, 138

Iragorri, Aurelio, 205

Iraq: arms sales to, 11; sanctions against, 70; U.S. war in, 8, 10, 13, 133, 135, 214, 234n14

Islamist "victimization" narrative, 214

Israel, 212, 214

Italian Operation Dove, 138

trained at SOA, 9; 2004 demobilization and, 106; U.S.-Colombia relations and, 16, 62–63, 95–96, 149, 168, 261n18; U.S. human rights laws and, 168; violence against unions and, 45–46; Voltígeros Battalion, 43–44, 109, 159

paramilitary organizations, killings by, 16, 62, 170; in Afro-Colombian communities, 128; of banana workers, 44; commemoration of, 70; cooperation with army, 4, 9, 21, 46–47, 52, 66, 73, 80, 95–96, 99–100, 155, 160–61; drug trafficking and, 58; legal convictions for, 194; "legalization" of, 46–47, 152–53; by Los Pepes, 33, 35; of Peace Community members, 4, 67–68, 70–71, 99; perpetrated by minors, 106–7; San José massacre of 1996, 47–48, 66; San José massacre of Feb. 2000, 65; San José massacre of 2005, 2–3, 34, 83, 107, 113–17, 186–87, 191; following 2004 demobilization, 106–7, 162; of union leaders, 46, 134, 139. See also Colombian Army, killings by

Parra, Liliana, 141–42

Pastrana Arango, Andrés, 59, 62, 73, 78, 80

Patriotic Union (Unión Patriótica, UP), 35, 43–44, 49, 51

Patterson, Anne, 60, 81–82, 89, 96

PBI. See Peace Brigades International (PBI)

Peace Brigades International (PBI), 65, 71, 101; conflict with Colombian government, 103–4; investigation of 2005 San José massacre and, 117, 119–20; protective accompaniment and, 74–75, 77, 137–38

Peace Community of San José de Apartadó, 2, 5, 42, 48–50, 226–27; accused of collaboration with guerrillas, 65, 82, 104–6, 141–44, 147–48, 174, 187, 190, 195, 197; accused of collaboration with paramilitaries, 129; accused of obstructing justice, 103, 144; active neutrality of, 49, 66, 72; Afro-Colombian Peace Communities, 48, 72, 78, 125, 128; award won by, 64; blamed for 2005 massacre, 141–44, 147, 187–88; blockade

of, 80; Catholic Church and, 4, 128; collective walk organized by, 66, 69–70; conflict with Colombian government, 103–4, 108, 141–44, 221; conflict with paramilitaries, 184, 227–28; establishment of "humanitarian zones" by, 111–12, 143, 145, 186, 226; international human rights organizations and, 69, 72, 80, 268n31; investigation of 2005 San José massacre and, 117–20, 140, 144–45, 147, 183–84, 187–88; legal impunity for violence against, 73, 149–50, 187; members traveling abroad, 101, 226; "peasant university" and, 124–25; post-2005 decline in violence against, 194–95; principles of, 66; public acknowledgment of wrongs against, 227, 229; statements following 2005 San José massacre, 144–45, 183, 226; U.S.-Colombia relations and, 73, 80, 149, 187; violence directed against members, 4, 22, 67–68, 70–73, 79–80, 99, 116, 184, 186–87, 227–28, 233n7

Peasant Self-Defense Forces of Córdoba and Urabá (Autodefensas Campesinas de Córdoba y Urabá, ACCU), 35, 44–45

Peasant Workers Association of Carare River (Asociación de Trabajadores Campesinos del Carare, ATCC), 129–30

Pelosi, Nancy, 180–81

Peña Nieto, Enrique, 14

People Persecuted by Pablo Escobar (Los Pepes), 33–35

Pérez Castaño, Alejandro, 2, 114, 140, 184, 191

Pérez Molina, Otto, 14

Peru, 52, 91

Petraeus, David, 9

Petrobank Energy and Resources, 98

Pino, Daniel, 99

Pino Rodriguez, Luis Alberto, 147–48

Pinzón, Juan Carlos, 200, 205, 208

Piza, Juan Carlos, 88, 176

Plan Colombia, 5, 7–12, 231–32; aid contrasted with arms sales, 11–12; construction aid, 88–89; as counterinsurgency operation, 8, 14, 26, 56–57, 84; as

suicide attacks, 13
Swedish Fellowship of Reconciliation, 138
Syria, 13, 176

Taboada, Enrique Fabio, 154
Tamayo, Soledad, 266n6
Tamayo Tamayo, Fernando, 266n6
Tamayo Tamayo, Marcolino, 200–202
Tarso, Antioquia, 129
Task Force Omega, 95, 169, 179, 199
Tate, Winifred, 84, 145, 168, 261n18
Texaco corporation, 57–58
Tolliver, Mari, 79
Torres, Luz Helena, 104–5
Torres Escalante, Henry William, 268n33
transitional justice, 206, 219
Trump, Donald, 7, 10–14
Tuberquia, Elkin, 102–3, 147
Tuberquia, Gildaro, 4, 64
Tuberquia, Jesús Emilio, 226
Tuberquia, Miryam, 145, 184, 191; San Jose
    massacre of 2005 and, 1–2, 113, 115–16,
    120–21, 192
Tuberquia, Sandra, 2, 114, 145, 183
Tuberquia, Wilmar Dario "El Gurre," 1–2,
    68, 99, 112–14, 117, 147, 184, 256n34
Tuttle, Stewart, 60

United Fruit, 38–39; Chiquita Brands,
    44–46, 66, 228
United Self-Defense Forces of Colombia.
    See Autodefensas Unidas de Colombia
    (United Self-Defense Forces of Colom-
    bia, AUC)
United States, foreign policy of: *above* and
    below perspectives on, 20–22; American
    exceptionalism and, 18; arms sales
    and, 11–12; Central America and, 23–25,
    61, 133; costs of, 10; Cuban Revolution
    and, 28–29; drug war and, 13–15, 52, 84;
    emphasis on security, 16; grassroots
    opposition to, 23–25, 133–35; guerrilla
    resistance to, 24; human rights and,
    17–19, 52, 61–63, 166–69, 215–16, 231;
    intentions of policy makers, 228–29;
    Japan and, 11; *lawfare* and, 212–14;
    military and police aid, 7–8, 10–12, 20,

36, 84, 165–68, 236n51; monitoring of
    military assistance, 166; operational
    outcomes of, 19–20; political costs of,
    12–14; post–Cold War military strategy
    of, 7–8; security goals of, 16; Syria and,
    13; U.S. exceptionalism, 18, 216–17;
    Vietnam War, 18, 157, 216. *See also* Plan
    Colombia; United States–Colombia
    relationship; United States military aid
    to Colombia
United States–Colombia relationship, 100;
    during Cold War, 27–32; Colombian ju-
    dicial system and, 181–82; construction
    aid, 88–89; drug war and, 13–15, 32–37,
    52–54, 180; Escobar and, 32–34; "false
    positive" killings and, 165; Free Trade
    Agreement, 139; General Lasprilla and,
    206; human rights and, 36, 80, 82, 146,
    149, 164–65, 220–22, 230; human rights
    certification and, 61–63, 96, 146–49,
    185, 187, 218, 221, 230; intentions of pol-
    icy makers, 228–29; investigation into
    2005 San José massacre and, 188–89;
    Korean war and, 27; military aid (*see*
    United States military aid to Colombia);
    nonmilitary aid, 137; oil industry and,
    57–60, 96–98; paramilitaries and, 37,
    95–96, 241n3; Peace Community and,
    80; prior to Cold War, 26–27; protective
    accompaniment and, 79–82, 137–39;
    reaction to 2005 San José massacre, 146,
    148–49; sister community movement
    and, 135–37; U.S. capital investments
    in Colombia, 39; U.S. decertification
    of Samper's government, 36, 58; U.S.
    grassroots activism and, 133–39; U.S.
    labor movement and, 139; U.S. trade
    with Colombia, 16, 83. *See also* Plan
    Colombia; United States military aid to
    Colombia
United States military aid to Colombia,
    83–85, 100, 137, 146; during 1950s,
    27–29; Colombian soldiers as trainers,
    12, 225; counterinsurgency operations,
    29–31, 35–37, 81, 87–88; counterterrorist
    objectives of, 57, 93–94; drug war and,
    32, 34–37, 52–54, 180; economic costs